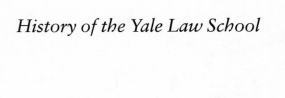

History of the Yale Law School

EDITED BY
ANTHONY T. KRONMAN

History of the Yale Law School

THE TERCENTENNIAL LECTURES

Yale University Press
New Haven &
London

Published with assistance from Elizabeth Stauderman, Director of Public Affairs,
Sachi Sugimoto, Special Projects Coordinator, Yale Law School, and the
foundation established in memory of Amasa Stone Mather of the Class of 1907,
Yale College.

Printed in the United States of America by R. R. Donnelley, Harrisonburg,
Virginia.

Library of Congress Cataloging-in-Publication Data
History of the Yale Law School : the tercentennial lectures / edited by Anthony T.
Kronman.
    p.   cm.
Includes bibliographical references and index.
ISBN 0-300-09564-3 (cloth : alk. paper)
1. Yale Law School — History. 2. Law — Study and teaching — Connecticut —
History. I. Kronman, Anthony T.
KF292.Y314Z657 2004
340'.07468 — dc22   2003070399

A catalogue record for this book is available from the British Library.

The paper in this book meets the guidelines for permanence and durability of the
Committee on Production Guidelines for Book Longevity of the Council on
Library Resources.

10 9 8 7 6 5 4 3 2 1

The publication of this volume for alumni, students, and friends of the Yale Law School was made possible by a grant from the Anchorage Charitable Fund made upon the recommendation of Elizabeth R. Varet and Michael A. Varet '65 J.D.

Contents

Introduction

ANTHONY T. KRONMAN

The Yale Law School is today an institution of national renown. It plays a conspicuous role in the legal profession, and its influence reaches beyond the law into the realms of politics, business, and culture. But how the Yale Law School came to be the place it now is — how it grew from its roots in the New Haven law office of Seth Staples, survived the fiscal crises of the nineteenth century, developed a distinctive style of teaching and research, became a center of iconoclastic scholarship and reformism in the 1930s, and adjusted to the upheavals of the 1960s — all this remains, at best, incompletely understood. The history of the Yale Law School has yet to be written.

Of course, there are some bright spots in the dark. Frederick Hicks, the Law School's librarian from 1928 to 1945, produced a brilliant series of pamphlets on its early history, bringing to life the personalities of its founders but leaving unanswered many questions regarding the school's organization and early development. Laura Kalman, the distinguished legal historian whose chapter concludes this volume, has written an insightful book about legal realism at Yale. Other authors have touched on particular aspects of the Law School's history with varying degrees of thoroughness and detail. But no one has yet attempted to write a comprehensive history of the school, to survey the evolution of its main features from their beginnings and to explain how they came to assume their current form.

This book does not attempt to do this either. It is a collection of six chapters written by five authors, each addressed to a particular period or theme, limited in focus and (with the exception of John Langbein's two contributions) making little or no attempt at connection with the others. What the reader finds here is a series of expeditionary forays into a territory largely unexplored, written in the hope that they will provide spots of light and be an inspiration to others to fill in the many dark spaces that remain.

These chapters originated as public talks in a lecture series on the history of the Yale Law School, sponsored by the school in the spring of 2001 as part of Yale University's tercentennial celebrations. I had originally intended to commission a legal historian to write a comprehensive history of the Law School for Yale's tercentennial, but after consulting with a group of historians (on and off the Yale faculty), I concluded that such an enterprise could not be undertaken without much preliminary work of a more detailed kind. The decision was made instead to invite each of a small group of historians to address an aspect of the Law School's history of particular interest to him or her, giving some — but only some — attention to chronological coverage. The goal was not completeness — and it certainly was not the unattractive species of self-congratulation that one often finds in commissioned histories of schools and other institutions. The goal instead was provocation: the illumination of a few specific episodes in the history of the Yale Law School in a manner that would sharpen our curiosity about the rest and remind us of how little we really know about the school's career and the evolution of its modern personality. The six provocative essays gathered in this volume may serve as a tantalizing prelude to the comprehensive history of the Yale Law School that remains to be constructed.

Robert Stevens's opening essay sketches the social, economic, and political environment of colonial Connecticut, out of which Yale College and eventually the Yale Law School emerged, and with broad panoramic strokes outlines the school's history over the more than two hundred years from its establishment to the beginning of Gene Rostow's deanship in 1955.

The next two chapters, by John Langbein, explore the origins of the Litchfield Law School — the first proprietary law school in America — and its New Haven offshoot, the successful teaching program run by Seth Staples and his partners. Langbein traces the migration of Staples's program into the Yale curriculum (a process that took place by fits and starts over a period of twenty years), the fiscal and administrative crises that beset the Law School at regular intervals until the last third of the nineteenth century, and its turn toward a more academic and interdisciplinary conception of law teaching in the 1870s, during the Yale presidency of Theodore Woolsey.

Robert Gordon picks the story up in the late 1920s, with a chapter that describes the increasing involvement of Yale Law School faculty in the outside world of law and politics, in the exciting milieu of the early New Deal. He links the growing activism of the faculty to the school's emphasis on public law, already evident a half century earlier, and to a distinctively practical conception of legal education, which, even before the legal realists made it an article of faith, appears to have been embraced, rhetorically at least, by Deans Rogers and Swan.

Gaddis Smith's chapter explores the sometimes rocky relationship between the Law School and Yale University during the middle years of the twentieth century, a relationship that was troubled by continuing anxieties about the place of professional education in a university devoted to pure research, and by worries (in the Yale Corporation and President's Office, at least) that the association of certain faculty with left-liberal causes might jeopardize the reputation — and support — of the University among its more conservative graduates.

Laura Kalman's closing chapter brings us almost to the present hour. Her main subject is the 1960s, the most tumultuous decade on American campuses in the history of the country. The struggle of deans and faculty to maintain order in the face of rising student demands for curricular and grading reform; the sharpening of racial tensions and the debate over affirmative action; the emergence of new and more critical forms of legal scholarship and their implications for faculty hiring: these are Kalman's themes, and even today, thirty-five years later, one feels their urgency and importance in a history we are still making.

Many questions remain. What exactly were the motives that caused Yale (and other colleges) to incorporate the proprietary law schools that sprang up in the early part of the nineteenth century, and by doing so to bring law teaching within the walls of the academy — perhaps the most fateful step in the history of American legal education? What role did philanthropy play in saving Yale's financially pressed Law School, which might easily have disappeared on several occasions, and what effect did philanthropic support have on the evolving shape of the institution (on its low student-faculty ratio, for example)? How did the emphasis on public law — which appears to have been especially strong at Yale in the latter part of the nineteenth century — originate and grow? When did the idea that the Law School would be an interdisciplinary enterprise linked to the humanities and social sciences, an idea forcefully articulated by President Woolsey in 1874, first become an active organizing principle in the school's curriculum and hiring policies? And what, more generally, was happening at the Yale Law School in the forty-some years between Woolsey's address and Thomas Swan's appointment as dean in 1916?

Clearly, this was a formative period at the Yale Law School, when many of its modern features first took shape. But just as clearly, it is the period we know the least about. John Langbein's researches have helped us better understand the school's origins, and the period that begins with the realist explosion of the 1930s is also relatively well understood (though still subject, of course, to interpretative debate). But the period between—the period that opens with Woolsey's address and closes with Swan's deanship—remains obscure. We do not know much about what was happening at the Yale Law School in these years, let alone how to interpret it. Here, in particular, more work needs to be done. Ideally, this volume will provide the inspiration and spur to do it.

History of the Yale Law School: Provenance and Perspective

ROBERT STEVENS

Historians irritate lawyers. Whenever I talk, as a historian, to a group of lawyers, I am asked, "So what is your solution?" Historians, however, do not normally offer normative solutions; they seek to encourage intelligent normative and political debate. What historians are engaged in is the telling of a story. We no longer believe, as did the German historians of the second part of the nineteenth century, that if we assemble all the facts, history will write itself and be in some mysterious way objective. History is an art. It flourishes with a strong element of the subjective. Responsible historians, faced with largely similar facts, will interpret them in surprisingly different ways. In this and the chapters that follow, you will experience this very process as different writers look at different aspects of the Yale Law School.

The Setting: Connecticut before 1701

Early Connecticut[1] was the embodiment of Matthew Arnold's view of "the Protestantism of the Protestant Religion and the Dissidence of Dissent." The Reformation on the Continent in the sixteenth century had not been entirely attractive to the Tudors, who had produced in England, by the late fifteenth century, a nation-state. Henry VIII, whom the pope had rewarded with the title of "Defender of the Faith," eventually nationalized the Catholic

Church, attracted by the prospect of the wealth of the monastic lands and the opportunity for easier divorce. In creating what was to become the Episcopal Church, however, he was not attracted by the intellectual excesses of the Reformation.

Henry's daughter Elizabeth continued the policy of the *via media* — making the break with Rome clear, but eschewing the increasingly radical brand of Puritanism emanating from the Continent. It was not easy, however. Religious refugees from Philip II's colonies in the Low Countries flooded into East Anglia. Continental theologians of a radical disposition found a warm welcome in the dour flatlands that harbored the University of Cambridge. When Elizabeth died, to be replaced by James VI of Scotland (James I of England), the Puritans expected a change of heart. They were sadly disappointed. James had seen enough of Presbyterians to know that he disliked Puritans in general — and Congregationalists in particular.

It was at the University of Cambridge that the future leaders of New England learned their trade. After Cambridge, Thomas Hooker found Charles I's Personal Rule (1629–1640) even less attractive than the reign of James I, and as Archbishop Laud's Court of High Commission attempted to control religious thought, he and other Protestant divines moved to Holland. Although Calvinist, Holland did not appeal to them, so Massachusetts beckoned as the basis of a Congregational state. Hooker's people were given land in Newtown (Cambridge), where it was assumed that Hooker would provide religious leadership with that other leading Cambridge divine, John Cotton. An observer noted, however, that "a couple of great men might be more serviceable asunder than together." While Hooker denounced Roger Williams for apostasy, it was not long before he and his adherents were leaving Cambridge for the new colony, based in Weathersfield, Hartford, and Windsor — the Connecticut Colony. By 1635 the race to settle in the Connecticut Valley was on. Winthrop was made governor based on the royal grants, and Winthrop confirmed those given to Hooker.

There was, however, another colony established within the present geographical boundaries of Connecticut. In 1638 a group of settlers, led by John Davenport, a preacher, and Theophilus Eaton, reflecting the merchant element and consisting mainly of immigrants from the City of London, established Quinnipiac, later to be known as New Haven. The settlers in this colony brought with them a vigorous and extreme Puritanism — coupled with something of the leveler philosophy. When the inhabitants of the new colony started taking this latter sentiment seriously, however, Davenport was driven to establish a council, arguing that this was the basis of governance in the City Livery companies. Soon New Haven was known for its prosperity — and its discrepancies in wealth.

Both Connecticut and New Haven, as they expanded, adapted Massachusetts' system of government, which in turn was based on English local government. The scheme left the magistrates responsible for administration and justice. Magistrates provided for the militia and for the regulation of roads and the price of bread. They sought to control relations with the indigenous population, and they imposed a theocratic form of government and criminal law, based on the Old Testament and adapted from the *Body of Laws of Massachusetts* in 1641 (although Connecticut had produced a primitive outline of government in 1639). Murder and treason were, of course, capital offenses, but so were denying the existence and omnipotence of God and disobedience to one's parents.

Virginia may have welcomed the return of Charles II in 1660, but it was not an enthusiasm shared in New England. New England had been strongly pro-Parliament. Between the leaders of Massachusetts and the Parliamentarians, there were philosophical and political bonds; the English Civil War not only gave power to the Roundheads, but the Protectorate also left New England alone. David Yale and others in Connecticut were so pleased with Puritan rule in England that they returned home. The Restoration of the Stuarts in 1660 seemed to herald no good. The return of Charles II and the abolition of all moral crimes in England were greeted with distrust or worse in New England. In England during the Protectorate, just as in New Haven Colony, adultery had been a capital offense. Charles II turned adultery into a national sport. A man on the throne with a stable of mistresses and a brood of illegitimate children was bad enough; but for New England the Restoration also brought the return of the Anglican interest and an interest in tightening control over the colonies.

This interest was manifested early in New Haven. Three of the regicides (those who had signed Charles I's death warrant in 1649), Edward Whalley, William Goffe, and, later, John Dixwell, fled to New Haven, where they were pursued by British troops. They were hidden by the citizens of New Haven in a cave on West Rock — the judge's cave — and the redcoats could not find them.[2] This put the colony at a disadvantage when the Crown was in the business of reissuing charters. Other colonies lobbied hard in London; New Haven did not. Indeed, unlike Connecticut, which had assumed the Warwick Charter, New Haven never had had a charter, and Charles II was not about to issue one. The inhabitants' loyalty to the regicides ensured the demise of New Haven Colony.

By 1665, New Haven had been merged with Connecticut. The more faithful in New Haven were horrified. They believed the citizens of Hartford were neither as puritanical nor as pure nor as devout as they. Whereas the laws of Connecticut were almost as draconian as New Haven's, they did not, for instance, provide the death penalty for having intercourse with a woman during her period. This was evidence to some in New Haven that God and state were not synonymous in the Connecticut Colony. Rather than be merged with the less than pure, eighty-six families fled from New Haven in search of the New Ark of the Covenant, eventually founding Newark, New Jersey.

The new colony of Connecticut obtained a new charter after a visit to London by Governor John Winthrop Jr., son of the original governor, armed with a resolution of the legislature, emphasizing "our loyalty and allegiance to His Majesty." The 1662 charter was a generous document allowing a wide range of self-government. With the reluctant merger of New Haven and Connecticut, there were to be joint capitals, Hartford and New Haven, an arrangement that survived until 1876. Otherwise the 1662 Charter was a conventional one of the earlier period, based on town and county government and with little functional separation.

The Colony of Connecticut and the Founding of Yale

The arrival of modernized constitutions in New York (1685) and Massachusetts (1691) heralded a different way of life. If we take Bernard Bailyn's view of the eighteenth century, these constitutions marked the beginning of the "re-Anglicization" of the American colonies. New York, taking over from New Amsterdam in the 1670s, already had the core trappings of a modern colony, including a legal profession. After 1691, Massachusetts had royal courts staffed by British judges, who brought with them their English ways. The courts were soon serviced by local lawyers, educated at Harvard, but tempted into the wicked ways of being lawyers rather than ministers and, as the eighteenth century progressed, increasingly becoming Episcopalians and royalists.

Connecticut in 1700 was basically built on subsistence agriculture. Only in New London, New Haven, and Hartford, where there were ports, were there merchants and trade. The Connecticut Colony was almost unanimous in its loyalty to the established church — Congregationalism — a group to which all citizens, whatever their beliefs, paid tithes. It looked to Harvard College to produce its ministers and teachers. Without superior courts, it scarcely needed lawyers. As the eighteenth century dawned, however, the leaders of the Congregational Church in Connecticut, who coincided closely with the leaders of

Connecticut, began to have doubts about Harvard. In England, "the Glorious Revolution" of 1688 had produced the Bill of Rights and the Toleration Act of 1689, the end of press censorship in 1694, triennial Parliaments, and, by 1701, the Act of Settlement.

The era, however, was more than a political revolution; it was an intellectual and social one. No longer would Gwyneth Paltrow have to pose as a boy in order to act; by the 1670s Nell Gwyn was both a successful actress and mistress of the king, a tradition her profession continued for some considerable period thereafter. The writings of Locke in political theory and Hale in law presaged a new era. England, and much of Europe, moved rapidly into that period we know as the Enlightenment. In England the architecture of Christopher Wren was paralleled by the scientific advances of Isaac Newton. The work of Samuel Johnson was matched in law by the work of his fellow Pembrokian, William Blackstone. The Enlightenment affected other countries; witness David Hume and Adam Smith in Scotland and Montesquieu and Voltaire in France. For the educated, God and monarch were slowly losing their centrality. The Enlightenment, however, was not an approach that appealed to those Englishmen who had become settlers in Connecticut. They preferred to cleave to God and the Bible; but they worried that in Boston the new notions of the dawning Enlightenment were not rejected out of hand.

After the Treaty of Ryswick in 1697 ended King William's War, a group of Congregational ministers, interested in maintaining the tradition of a pure, but educated, ministry and magistracy, began lobbying for a college in the Connecticut Colony. In October 1701, the General Assembly, meeting in New Haven, passed the enabling legislation, and, noting that their fathers had come to the American colonies to plan and propagate "the blessed Reformed, Protestant Religion," they recorded their need to provide a "Liberal and Religious Education of Suitable Youth." In November 1701, the new college began at Saybrook — perhaps appropriately, since it was a town established for upscale colonists by Lord Saye and Sele and Lord Brooke (hence its name). Abraham Pierson was chosen as the college's first president, or rector. Pierson was rector (minister) of Killingworth (Clinton), while his father, inevitably a minister, had been one of those who felt that there was too great a divide between the teachings of church and state in the Connecticut Colony, leading him to move his family from New Haven colony to Newark, New Jersey, in the fateful year of 1665. As Ronald Bainton observed: "Yale was conservative before she was born." She was also a state institution. The legislature voted the new College £120 per annum.

As the eighteenth century progressed, the leading colonies developed their institutions. In Massachusetts the legal profession developed so that, by the time of the Revolution, there were close to a hundred lawyers and the hint of a divided profession — attorneys and barristers.[3] New York had an extensive bar, and appeals to the Judicial Committee of the Privy Council were becoming common. South Carolina boasted a division between barristers and solicitors, and both Virginia and North Carolina produced a regular supply of appeals to the Privy Council in London, as well as sending aspiring advocates back to be trained — or at least immersed — as barristers at the Inns of Court. The Anglicization of the leading colonies, with their royal courts, brought an increasingly modern-looking legal profession. It also brought contact with the Enlightenment. The colonial law students in London read Blackstone and met Johnson's set. The medical students, who favored Edinburgh, fell under the spell of David Hume and Adam Smith. Madison, Hamilton, and Jefferson were part of that European Enlightenment.

The Enlightenment was far from the minds of the ministers and magistrates of Connecticut. The colony basically lacked a modern legal or medical profession. The Anglican pretensions of Kings College (Columbia) and the College of William and Mary were despised. Moreover, British colonial policy played into the parochialism of Connecticut. Insofar as there was a coherent policy, it was that Connecticut and Rhode Island should not be interfered with in the hope of detaching them from tiresome Massachusetts; thus Connecticut and Rhode Island never had modernized Charters. The charter of 1662, establishing the Congregational model, had no provision for a High Court on the English model. It was to remain the Constitution of Connecticut until 1818. There were appeals from the Connecticut courts that did exist to the Judicial Committee of the Privy Council, but only four were taken before the Revolution, the most famous of which, *Winthrop v. Lechmere* in 1728, appeared to strike down Connecticut's intestacy law.

In addition to taking judicial appeals to the Privy Council in London, there was another inherent royal power, the power of vetoing colonial legislation. Ironically, in the end, again in the hope of isolating Massachusetts, the British did not enforce this power against Connecticut. That decision, however, was made after the Privy Council had retained counsel to review Connecticut's legislation. It had not proved physically easy to obtain the Connecticut legislation to have it reviewed; indeed, the request of 1697 was not complied with until 1715, or perhaps 1731, and then only after the British had instructed the governor in Albany to intervene. In 1732, Francis Fane began reviewing the legislation to see "whether some or any of them are repugnant to the Laws of this kingdom." Statutes are not necessarily a fair way of evaluating how a society actually works, inasmuch as we have no idea how actively enforced the laws were; but Fane's review of the laws of Connecticut gives us some sense of how the society in which the new "Collegiate School" (which in 1716 moved to New Haven and in 1718 was named after Elihu — son of David — Yale) was expected to operate. It was a society very different from Fane's — he an urbane, intellectual bachelor barrister MP with illegitimate children.

It took nine years for Fane to plough through the statutes.[4] In general, they were the laws of an agricultural community, with a strong element of theocracy, but he was dismayed by their authoritarian tone and abuse of civil rights. It was a crime to live separately from your spouse; and it was a crime to entertain a Quaker or have a Quaker book in your house. Adultery attracted not only a severe whipping for both parties, but also branding and the permanent wearing of a halter. Fane recommended repeal, as he did for branding for theft ("liable to great objections as it makes a man so notorious that he can never after become a useful member of society"). The capital penalty statutes, based on Leviticus, Deuteronomy, and Exodus, appalled him. ("The foregoing Act requires great consideration, and tho' it be chiefly taken from the Scriptures, will want much alteration.") The idea of putting to death anyone who worshiped "any other God, but the Lord God" or who committed blasphemy or cursed seemed "very extraordinary." As to some aspects of the death penalty, one can almost see him holding his intellectual nose: "The next clause is against witchcraft, which is humbly submitted would be much better left out, especially considering the great abuse that has been made in New England of the laws against witches and that many innocent people have thereby lost their lives." So he went through all the criminal statutes, expressing degrees of horror about such things as the crimes of lying and night walking,[5] lascivious carriage[6] or insulting a judge, for which a person might be banished. Fane's reports leave us in little doubt that he viewed with distaste the parochial Puritanism, anathema to one basking in the Enlightenment.

While Yale College had by this time come to teach a four-year course based on the curriculum of the Scottish universities, the atmosphere of Connecticut meant that such broader education was taught in the context of the revealed truth of the Bible. Yale was training ministers, and while not all its graduates became ministers — except during periods such as the New Lights and the Great Awakening, the first manifestation of which appeared in Connecticut in the 1730s — the atmosphere of strict biblical interpretation prevailed. Across the colony, the absence of courts of general jurisdiction made it difficult for the legal profession to grow. Law jobs were performed by magistrates and tradesmen. There were, by the Revolution, some one hundred persons describing themselves as lawyers, but only isolated persons one might describe as professional lawyers. Oliver Ellsworth, signer of the Declaration of Independence, was one, but his elegant dress in the portrait on the main stairs of the Law

School suggests his intellectual approach — and his tailor — were not in Connecticut. Perhaps they were a relic of his Princeton education.

Revolution and Change

Connecticut behaved much as one would have expected during the Revolutionary War. Governor Trumbull, to the irritation of Massachusetts, made conciliatory noises to the British even after Lexington. Although Connecticut's four delegates to the Continental Congress — Samuel Huntingdon, Roger Sherman, William Williams, and Oliver Walcott — voted for the Declaration of Independence, and although British stores were seized, most notably in New Haven, and Connecticut provided troops to the Continental Army and suffered some incursions from Royal troops, Connecticut's war was a passive and conservative one. Loyalists were harassed — especially if they were Anglican priests — but the Whig leadership was conservative. Connecticut became known as "the Provisions State" and while legitimate trade was hampered by the British blockade, fortunes were made by importing contraband British goods and by supplying the Continental Army. A serious radical element in the Revolution was notably absent in Connecticut.

Nor did the postwar Federalist period change the bourgeois ethos. The Federalist period confirmed the legal apprenticeship system in Massachusetts counties, which gave Yale College graduates the same benefit as Harvard ones, namely a lesser period of legal apprenticeship. Connecticut was developing a similar system. Yale was still, however, under the guise of a prescribed four-year liberal arts degree, primarily a training ground for ministers, although some concessions to law were made. The four-year B.A. allowed lectures on a range of subjects in the fourth year, and Ezra Stiles, president of Yale from 1777 to 1795, was sympathetic to an element of law: "It is scarcely possible to enslave a Republic where the body of the People are civilians well instructed in their Laws, Rights and Liberties," he wrote early in the war, in 1777. His resolve was no doubt further enhanced by the British attack on New Haven on July 4, 1779. New Haven was not burned, it is said, because the British General's secretary was a Yale man (he was later given an honorary degree), but still Stiles complained that British troops plundered, raped, and were indelicate to the opposite sex. It was enough for Stiles. Just as he felt Yale needed a professor of Physic because the Connecticut Colony needed physicians, he called for the establishment of a Chair of Law to provide political leaders.

While Elizur Goodrich was appointed Professor of Law at Yale in 1801, the burdens laid on him were not onerous. He lectured to the fourth-year undergraduates, the only year in which electives were allowed, but after a while he gave up even that responsibility. With the links to London severed, however, a new possibility for legal training had emerged. By 1783, most of the thirteen colonies had a developed system of apprenticeship for attorneys, based on the English system of training solicitors. Yet the nature of the common law was changing. Perhaps the medieval system of law, with substantive law lurking behind procedure, never really survived the interregnum and the return of Charles II. The Restoration of 1660 provided only a limited return to law Latin and law French; the writings of Hale in the 1690s and, most important, Blackstone in the eighteenth century, together with the beginning of the end of the writ system, meant that it was possible to look at substantive doctrine increasingly unencumbered by the forms of action. Apprenticeship had many admirable aspects, but Blackstone made it logical for that apprenticeship to have a structured didactic base.

It was in this context that the Litchfield law school emerged. Tapping Reeve's School was founded in 1784, in the town that had, despite (or perhaps because of) its Tory sympathies, become prosperous during the Revolutionary War. It was this school that heralded the beginning of the American law school. Moreover, it was the merging of Litchfield and Yale's Law Department in the 1820s that sowed the seeds of the modern Yale Law School. As the century progressed, the Law School began to take on its peculiar character-istics — the broad curriculum, an especial concern with public law, favorable faculty-student ratios, and the beginning of an endowment. John Langbein will examine these events in his chapters in this volume.

Over these years, the economy of the state was changing. In the decades after 1800, manufacturing began competing with agriculture. By 1818, there were sixty-seven cotton mills in the state; Danbury boasted fifty-six hat opera-tions. Eli Whitney, having developed the cotton gin, had established a gun factory in New Haven, emphasizing Yankee ingenuity by making parts inter-changeable. The industrial revolution called for a more modern legal profes-sion; and within the state Yale College increasingly provided candidates for that, although for the first half of the century the requirements for practice, as in most other states, became less strict. Congregationalism remained the es-tablished religion, but the opposition to the Federalist-Congregationalist ma-chine (which embraced Yale) grew. The Republicans made an unlikely alliance with the Episcopalians and, at the Constitutional Convention of 1818, the Congregational Church was disestablished; and there was at last an effort to introduce the separation of powers and a reform of the courts.

There was not, however, a redrawing of legislative constituencies; that had to wait one hundred and fifty years until after *Baker v. Carr*. It was an in-creasingly unsatisfactory arrangement, as the state became progressively more urban, with the emergence of large factories in New Haven, the Saugatuck Valley, and the Connecticut Valley. The New York, New Haven and Hartford Railway became a powerful economic force, and by the Civil War the state was a hub of industry. Increasingly the inhabitants of the rapidly growing urban areas were not the Anglo-Saxon Yankees who still ran the State, but immigrants from Ireland and, later in the century, from continental Europe. As a home to groups of abolitionists, Connecticut towns had attracted freed slaves, but after the state abolished the last vestiges of slavery in 1848, towns with large African American communities began to emerge.

Yale College, however, continued to be run by the Congregational Old Guard. With the collapse of the Federalists and the emergence of what for convenience we call Jacksonian Democracy, flexibility (or the skeptical would say lower standards) descended on the American college, but not on Yale. The Day Report of 1828 restated the classical curriculum, ultimately derived from the medieval *trivium* and *quadrivium*. The broadening of the curriculum, achieved at Harvard by the arrival of professors like Tichenor, the modern linguist, was unknown at Yale. As the century progressed, Dwight, Day, and Woolsey slowly moved Yale College toward becoming a university, but it was indeed a slow process. The Corporation did intervene by providing encouragement and modest financial help when, in 1837 and 1869, it looked as if the Law School — still a proprietary school loosely attached to the University — would collapse entirely. Science through the Sheffield Scientific School ultimately appeared, but on the margins of Yale College. For the University as a whole, gifts and fees slowly began to replace grants from the state as the basis of funding, but the legislature continued to help in capital matters. When Senator Morrill's land grant colleges began in the 1860s, the funds went to "Sheff" until 1893, when the state began an institution that became the University of Connecticut. While the senators on the Yale Corporation were replaced by alumni in 1873, the governor and lieutenant governor remained members, and Yale still presents its accounts annually to the legislature. By 1900, however, Yale, founded as an integral part of the State of Connecticut, may be said to have been privatized.

The Yale Law School: Squaring the Circle

The last three chapters of this book, by Robert Gordon, Gaddis Smith, and Laura Kalman, bring us to the twentieth century. Certainly my task is not to compete with the insights of the three distinguished scholars, but I will make two comments.

First, I should like to explore the conundrum of when Yale became a serious player in legal education nationally. Second, I should like to do that most unscholarly thing — to end with some of my personal observations; for in 1957, I was, as a graduate student here, attempting to understand where American legal education had come from and where it might be going.

On the issue of when Yale became a serious player, I suspect that we may find John Langbein, in the third chapter, arguing the case for ex-President Woolsey's 1871 *Discourse*, when he pontificated — if that is not too cruel — about the future of the law school. It was a vision that saw jurisprudence, international law, legal history, comparative and public law emphasized over local law — and it is understandably seen by many as the beginning of the modern Yale Law School. Woolsey's was indeed a noble aim, and one that was increasingly supported by the beginning of an endowment, a full-time dean, and, by the early 1890s, a building constructed specifically to house it. (Until that time the law school had existed in a loft of a building adjoining the courthouse.) By 1900, there was indeed a large range of courses and graduate programs offered, and there were also some overseas students present from the newly emerging American empire — Cuba, Hawaii, and the Philippines. If one looks at the returns of the number of students taking these courses, however, the Carnegie Endowment reports them as few in number. No doubt there is a link between our current school and those days, as there is between Alfred the Great and Elizabeth II, but it was a school, despite its pretensions, of little moment outside Connecticut, either in terms of its graduates or its scholarship. Harvard and Columbia, in contrast, had already moved to three-year courses and were central to their universities, populated by those with undergraduate degrees, and staffed with full-time professors.

At the turn of the century, law at Yale was still often an undergraduate activity. The law degree could still be completed in two years. In 1903 the quarterback of the Yale football team and another player were undergraduate students in the Law School. Yale Law School existed at the margins of the University, essentially a proprietary institution, with professors remunerated directly out of the fees paid by students. The University's interest felt almost like a survival of its obligation to continue its role of producing lawyers for the state. The Law School still competed with the College for undergraduates, but it lacked Yale College's cachet. Moreover, in 1900, apart from the dean there was no full-time member of the faculty. That is not strictly true: Theodore Dwight Woolsey, son of the former president, had no other job, and had the title of Instructor, and later Professor, for which he was not paid. As the librarian of the 1930s, the author of the only history of the Law School, put it, however: "He was a modest, scholarly gentleman, who loved his work, but did not become excited about it. He would have been an ideal Oxford don."[7] I am still puzzling about what is meant by that.

As the twentieth century arrived, there were certainly some effective teachers among the group of practitioners; but it was still a school that struggled for students—most of them still local—and even for the budget to advertise for them. Change was of course coming. In 1903 Arthur Linton Corbin was appointed as the first full-time faculty member (he was still an active presence when I became an assistant professor), and teaching by the case method was allowed in the third year. Basically, however, Yale was only slowly moving to become a three-year school. Ten years later most courses were taught by the case method, and, as the younger Woolsey observed, "the old way bred great lawyers, but like the caste mark of the Brahmin, the case system is the cachet of the crack law school today." The change, and the preeminent place of the Harvard Law School, was recognized by the appointment of Thomas Swan, a Harvard man, as dean in 1916. The advocates of the "broad" Yale approach were reported to be horrified. The barbarians were at the gate.

As so often at Yale, things were not what they seemed. Yale was still basically a local school with pretensions. Most of the teaching was done by local practitioners, although many of them were highly cultivated, with interests beyond the borders of the state and mere substantive law. The only serious way, however, that Yale could compete with Harvard was by claiming a different intellectual philosophy. Such calls appeared on a regular cycle. In the style of the Woolsey manifesto of 1871, in 1917 the Law School issued a call for the establishment of a School of Law and Jurisprudence. (The purpose of the Law School should be "the study of law and its evolution, historically, comparatively, analytically and critically, with the purpose of directing its development in the future, improving its administration and on perfecting its methods of legislation.") By this time the school had some endowment, and so the claims were not hollow. Yale still had difficulty attracting good students, and the best students from Yale College, together with those from other leading colleges, still went to law school either at Harvard or Columbia.

Yale began to make strides when it limited its enrollment to one hundred in 1926—Thurman Arnold alleges in order to make certain it had a hundred applicants. Be that as it may, Yale did become more selective and received considerable publicity, a process accelerated by the appointment of Robert Hutchins, barely more than a student, as dean the following year. Hutchins was a firebrand who put more faith in the social sciences than he should have (and he lost his faith after leaving Yale). He left Yale within two years because the Corporation refused to move the Law School to the new building at the

Medical School being built to house the Institute of Human Relations. "I asked for a place to work and got a goddamn Gothic Bowling Alley." The Yale Law School was forced to live its life in the Gothic splendor of that building, built at the height of the Depression and recently restored with such opulent elegance.

By this time, however, Charles Clark was the dean, and Yale was to enter what some — although I do not know whether Robert Gordon shares this view — have regarded as its greatest period: the 1930s. Certainly there was important empirical work, mainly by Charles Clark and Underhill Moore — although Dean Clark also lost his faith in the social sciences and made his greatest contribution by developing the Federal Rules. The great names of the period were of course the realists — but if I may digress for a moment, the mystique surrounding them is difficult to unpack. After all, Harvard had its share of those who were skeptical of formalism, including Frankfurter and Powell, and indeed the much criticized Dean Pound. The cult of realism has canonized only some of the functionalists — perhaps the noisiest polemicists. At Yale they included William Douglas, Hessel Yntema, Karl Llewellyn, Thurman Arnold, Abe Fortas, Walton Hamilton, and Jerome Frank. Of course they were important (and possessed of obscene energy, as Robert Gordon will attest), but these seven cumulatively taught at Yale for only some dozen years as full-time teachers.[8] Here I also differ from the Kalman thesis.[9] Those canonized as realists were as much a phenomenon of Columbia and Johns Hopkins as of Yale. Yale was an interesting school, one attracting increasingly better and more national students, but not necessarily the intellectual center of ferment some have claimed. Its faculty was more a collection of iconoclasts with a flair for publicity — little affected by the demise of interest in realism, which coincided with the rise of Nazism. It is with these turbulent years that Robert Gordon will deal, seeking to probe how the New Deal transformed the professorate.

It was this congeries of characters who composed Yale Law School as it survived World War II and the arrival of veterans more interested in learning law than flirting with the social sciences. The school was by then led by Dean Gulliver, a mild-mannered man and one of the few people in the common-law world who understood every aspect of future interests and the rule against perpetuities. It was a faculty made up of well-known exponents of various substantive fields, such as J. W. Moore in procedure and Jimmy James in torts. There was a bright new generation of law teachers moving out from doctrine, such as Grant Gilmore in commercial law and Boris Bittker in tax law. Myres McDougal and Harold Laswell represented an attempt to link law with the then-accepted assumptions in the social sciences, but history may well come to regard these efforts as superformalism rather than the manifestation of postrealism.

The student body was more national and better, but by the early 1950s the national hysteria known as McCarthyism was sweeping the country and anxious alumni—especially of Yale College—were demanding that something be done about the "communists" at the Law School—particularly "Fred the Red" (Fred Rodell) and "Tommy the Commie" (Thomas Emerson). While to European eyes they seemed wobbly and woolly liberals, the atmosphere, even in a university town like New Haven, was unattractive. While President A. Whitney Griswold deserved credit as something of a civil libertarian, the Yale Corporation was less reliable.

Moreover, Yale was a conservative institution. Griswold referred to the freshmen of Yale College as a "Thousand Christian Gentlemen," and he meant it. Even Kingman Brewster, in his early years, talked of Yale's obligation to produce a "thousand male leaders," although it was Brewster who ultimately made Yale a cosmopolitan university and brought the institution through the student troubles, even if he stayed too long and adopted unwise financial policies. When Brewster arrived, Yale College still tried to avoid admitting or appointing Jews—or Catholics for that matter—as students and faculty. The odd black was admitted; women were forbidden. Harvard, Columbia, and Brown had coordinate colleges; Pennsylvania and Cornell both admitted women. In the Ivy League, Yale stood with Dartmouth and Princeton as a male bastion. Yale found it difficult to compete with Harvard, which benefited from far more diversity in faculty and student body.[10]

Although the Yale Law School was open to Jews and even had a trickle of women and blacks, its atmosphere was less cosmopolitan than Cambridge, Massachusetts, or Cambridge, England. Yet Yale Law School's reputation was considerable, significantly because it was associated with a highly prestigious college at a time when, nationally, colleges appeared as more significant than graduate and professional schools. It is possible to argue, however, that had the Yale Law School been attached to a state institution in the early 1950s, its reputation would have been far more modest. It still had difficulty attracting its fair share of the best faculty and students. Indeed, by the late 1950s, it was still finding difficulty filling its classes with well-qualified students.

I argue, then, for a relatively recent date for the arrival of the modern Yale Law School. I would choose the appointment of Eugene V. Rostow as dean in 1956. Clearly Gene built on existing strengths, but out of the combination of friendship with Whit Griswold and a casual and creative approach to accounting and fundraising, he effectively doubled the size of the faculty while keeping the student body stable. It was this move that made Yale Law School unique, with its small groups and diversified program. Rostow fought the entrenched interests in Yale College so that all in the core Law School faculty might become tenured full professors. Harry Wellington, Alexander Bickel, Leon Lipson, Arthur Leff, and Ronald Dworkin came from Harvard — to the horror of Gene's opponents — but they were among the stars of the new institution; Guido Calabresi, Louis Pollak, John Simon, Ellen Peters (the first woman faculty member), Abraham and Joseph Goldstein, Ralph Winter, Charlie Reich, and Charles Black — among others — were recent Yale graduates; Robert Bork and Ward Bowman were from Chicago; and there were many others. There was no single approach, but a critical mass of energetic, talented, and wonderfully creative — albeit iconoclastic and sometimes impossible — people.

Those of us who survived these years, one must admit, were arrogant, and we suffered a fall when the students, who were supposed to admire us, rebelled, emphasizing the inherent conflicts in the modern university, which Gaddis Smith will be examining. By the 1970s, however, Yale had become a much more research-oriented and cosmopolitan university, committed to a far more diverse existence. There was a serious university to which a serious law school might be attached. It was in this sense that, for all its failings, it is Gene Rostow's law school that you have today — retrenched and reformed by Louis Pollak and Abraham Goldstein, financially enhanced — and the Rostow academic scheme emphasizing a generous faculty-student ratio, small classes, philosophy, and public law — carried to its logical conclusion by Harry Wellington and Guido Calabresi. The fiscal independence that Dean Calabresi negotiated with the university, coupled with the American economy in the 1990s, has gone hand in hand with academic and intellectual flowering.

With this introduction I have, I hope, in the broadest outline set the stages: from Puritan colonial college to international university that has seen the flowering of a unique law school in its midst. With respect to the many wrong — or iconoclastic — interpretations, those who follow in this book will no doubt set me — and us — right.

Notes

I would like to thank Alison Booth, Robert Gordon, Adrian Gregory, Laura Kalman, John Langbein, and Katherine Booth Stevens for their comments. Errors and interpretations are, however, mine alone. Gene Coakley, as always, was a superb aide to research.

1. The standard layman's history of Connecticut remains Albert E. Van Dusen, *Connecticut* (New York, 1961). I have relied primarily on this work, but readers desiring to probe further should consult Christopher Collier and Bonnie Collier, *The Literature of Connecticut History* (Hartford, 1983). The best history of the University is Brooks M. Kelley, *Yale: A History* (New Haven, 1974).

2. Some sixty persons signed Charles I's death warrant in 1649. The Declaration of Breda, covering the return of Charles II and providing for a general amnesty, excluded the regicides. By 1660, some twenty were dead, and in the early 1660s some twenty were executed with maximum cruelty, as was the wont with those guilty of treason. Another twenty or so survived. When the redcoats arrived in 1661 in New Haven, the population was uncooperative, and two regicides, Colonels William Goffe and Edward Whalley, were hidden in the judges' cave until the royal troops left to search for them in New Amsterdam (New York). They then lived in Milford until a second royal search party arrived to search for them. After another brief stay in the cave, they fled to Hadley, Massachusetts, where Goffe continued to live in hiding in an attic. He emerged briefly in 1675 to lead the inhabitants against a raiding party of Indians. David H. Fischer, *Albion's Seed: Four British Folkways in America* (New York, 1989), 168. The third regicide, Colonel John Dixwell, later moved to New Haven, lived (and married twice) under the name of John Davids, died in 1688 and is buried in the cemetery of the Center Church on the Green.

3. The best study of this remains Gerald W Gawalt, *The Promise of Power: The Emergence of the Legal Profession in Massachusetts, 1760–1840* (Westport, 1979).

4. *Reports on the Laws of Connecticut by Francis Fane K.C., Standing Counsel to the Board of Trade and Plantations*, Acorn Club, Hartford, 1915.

5. That Connecticut—the land of steady habits—does not change rapidly is illustrated by the fact that Professor Charles Reich, not the most conventional of dressers, was arrested for night walking in the 1960s. He wrote about his experiences: Charles Reich, "Police Questioning of Law Abiding Citizens," 75 *Yale L. J.* 1161 (1966).

6. Another survival. When I was a student in the 1950s, the SSS (Special Sex Squad) of the New Haven police, then composed mainly of Irish cops, took some pleasure in enforcing this against WASP Yalies by raiding hotels on dance weekends.

7. Frederick C. Hicks, *Yale Law School: 1895–1915 — Twenty Years of Hendrie Hall* (New Haven, 1938), 47.

8. In some ways, the most interesting of the realists was J. Howard Marshall II, the assistant dean from 1931 to 1933. His work in law and economics ultimately had a major impact on the New Deal, while he was working for the Secretary of the Interior, Harold Ickes. Leaving government in 1944, he went on to make a fortune in the oil industry. See *Done in Oil: An Autobiography of J. Howard Marshall II* (College Station, 1944). Howard Marshall achieved considerable public notice when, at eighty-nine, he married the twenty-five-year-old Vicki Smith. (See the *National Enquirer.*) Litigation out of the union is currently helping to subsidize the legal profession. See, for example, "Honky-Tonk Love Gets Its Day in Probate Court," *New York Times*, Feb. 2, 2001.

9. Kalman would, of course, define the realists more broadly: Laura Kalman, *Legal Realism at Yale 1927–1960* (Chapel Hill, 1986). My approach would be closer to John Henry Schlegel, *American Legal Realism and Empirical Social Science* (Chapel Hill, 1995).

10. See, for example, A. Whitney Griswold, *Essays on Education* (New Haven, 1954); Brooks M. Kelley, "The Brewster Years: A Question of Survival," *The New Journal*, Dec. 12, 1974.

Blackstone, Litchfield, and Yale: The Founding of the Yale Law School

JOHN H. LANGBEIN

The origins of the Yale Law School trace to the earliest days of the nineteenth century, when there was as yet no university legal education. Law was learned mostly by clerking as an apprentice in a lawyer's office. The first law schools, including the New Haven school that became Yale, developed from the apprenticeship system. The Yale Law School originated as a proprietary school in the law office of a practicing lawyer. This New Haven school was inspired by a forerunner, located in upstate Litchfield, Connecticut. The Litchfield Law School was an astonishingly successful venture, which shaped the development of early university legal education in the United States in ways that I shall discuss.

The New Haven Law School became associated with Yale in the 1820s, although its graduates did not receive Yale degrees until 1843. Yale was so hesitant about its attachment that in 1845 and again in 1869 Yale seriously considered dissolving the School.[1] It may strike us as unthinkable that so prominent a university could wash its hands of its Law School, but a variety of university-linked law schools were in fact shut down in the nineteenth century. For example, Princeton's law school, begun in 1846, was shuttered in 1852. Lafayette College had a law school from 1841 to 1852 and again from 1875 to 1884. The University of Indiana Law School, begun in 1842, lapsed in 1877; it was refounded in 1889. A variety of others populate the graveyard of nineteenth-century law schools.[2]

Yale's commitment to its law school was not firm until the 1870s, the period that I will emphasize in my second lecture in this series. As late as the 1870s the Yale Law School was located in rented quarters over a storefront[3] on a downtown business street.[4] In these premises a single "dingy"[5] room served as library, classroom, and lounge. The School acquired a home on the Yale campus only in the 1890s, when Hendrie Hall (facing the New Haven Green) was built for it. Into the dawning years of the twentieth century, the so-called professors at the Yale Law School were in fact practicing lawyers from the New Haven bar, who taught law more or less as a sideline. Not until the early twentieth century did the professors become salaried instead of drawing shares of the school's net income.[6]

I. The Novelty of Academic Legal Education

What explains Yale's long hesitance about sustaining a law school? And how could a place as important as Princeton let its law school simply die out? These events underscore that the very idea of a university law school was novel in the nineteenth century. The leaders of Yale and Princeton knew what a college was supposed to be, but they were not at all certain that a law school was within their mission. The reason they were so ambivalent about law is that the American colleges patterned themselves on the English universities, and the English universities did not have law schools.

Neither Oxford nor Cambridge taught English law until well into the nineteenth century,[7] and when they finally did institute university legal education in the common law, they would act under the influence of the American example. Like the Continental universities of the day, Oxford[8] and Cambridge[9] taught some Roman law, which was useful for the courts of the English church and in a few so-called civilian jurisdictions such as the court of admiralty. In 1846, a committee of the House of Commons reported candidly that "[n]o legal education worthy of the name . . . is at this moment to be had in . . . England."[10] As late as the 1880s, Dicey was still echoing this tradition. In his inaugural lecture as Vinerian Professor at Oxford, he observed, "English law must be learned and cannot be taught . . . . [T]he only places where it can be learned are the law courts or [in barristers'] chambers."[11]

University legal education in the common law was an American innovation, which is noteworthy, because the American legal system was in most respects quite derivative. Both the doctrinal side of American law (that is, the substantive law) and the institutional life (bench and bar, the jury system, civil and criminal procedure, law and equity) were English transplants, albeit with local variances. Moreover, the Americans produced virtually no indigenous legal literature for the first quarter century after independence,[12] which left them dependent on English reports and treatises. In this setting, it is striking to see the Americans veer off from English models and pioneer the university law school. The founding of the Yale Law School was one of the first chapters in that experiment.

II. Apprenticeship

How were young lawyers trained in a world without law schools? In England, from the late Middle Ages into the early seventeenth century, the professional bodies called the inns of court conducted training programs for law students.[13] The quality of legal education at the inns appears to have declined in the early decades of the seventeenth century, perhaps earlier. The training role of the inns lapsed entirely during the turmoil of the English civil war and Interregnum in the 1640s and 1650s.[14] The inns "ceased to be educational institutions."[15] Thereafter, beginners were left to learn the law by a combination of private study and formal apprenticeship.[16]

The would-be lawyer started by reading elementary primers, then he plunged into the primitive treatise literature,[17] practice manuals, yearbooks, and law reports.[18] The student would typically buy an alphabetized blank volume called a commonplace book,[19] into which he would enter topically organized notes on his reading. The idea was not only to learn the law but also to create a reference work, a personalized encyclopedia, to which the compiler might refer across his career. Commonplace books of this sort survive in vast numbers in the legal manuscript collections in England and in the United States.

After reading and commonplacing for a time, the student typically advanced to a period of apprenticeship. In eighteenth-century England an intending barrister would commonly clerk for a solicitor, despite the social distance between the two branches of the profession.[20] In the American colonies, where the lawyer population was too thin to sustain the divided profession, intending lawyers routinely trained as apprentices with practicing attorneys.[21] Apprenticeship involved learning law the way we expect someone today to learn plumbing: in the workplace, as a practical trade. You do not go to university to study the theory of plumbing. You learn plumbing by working with, observing, and imitating an experienced master.

Apprenticeship entailed a bargain[22] between the lawyer-master and the student-apprentice. The lawyer pocketed a substantial fee from the apprentice's family, typically £100 a year. Moreover, the apprentice was required to assist the lawyer, especially by copying documents, which was an important part of the work of a law office in a pre-Xerox age. The apprentice, for his part, obtained access to the lawyer's library of practice books and law reports, which was a considerable privilege at a time when law books were scarce and costly.[23] The lawyer was meant to guide the student in a course of reading, and to show the student the ropes while the student assisted with the business of the office.

In the American version, apprenticeship was often connected to bar admissions. After the apprentice had served his time, the lawyer would certify him for admission.[24] This linkage of education and licensure is a deep theme in the history of legal education. It was characteristic of the inns of court in their heyday (call to the bar of the inn followed years of participation in the learning exercises of the inn), and it has played a significant role in the life of American law schools to this day. I tell no secrets when I mention that modern American law schools are obliged to be part of an accreditation cartel, operated by the American Bar Association[25] and the Association of American Law Schools, in conspiracy with the state bars. The central mission of this cartel, conducted under the cover of enforcing supposed educational standards, is to increase lawyers' profits by driving up the price of entry into the profession, which restricts the supply of lawyers.

Apprenticeship training in the eighteenth century had serious drawbacks. Few apprentices had good words for it. William Livingston, who clerked for a New York lawyer in the 1740s, complained of receiving no instruction in his studies and of being overworked in "servile Drudgery."[26] Thomas Jefferson counseled a young relative against apprenticeship on the ground that "I have ever seen that the services expected in return have been more than the instructions have been worth."[27] Similar grievances were voiced in England. Apprenticeship was, therefore, a risky business, in which the student was frequently exploited. Nevertheless, students continued to apprentice themselves, because they had no practical alternative.

III. Blackstone

Among the many critics of apprenticeship was the eighteenth-century English jurist William Blackstone. Blackstone focused not on the danger of exploitation, but rather on the underlying premise of apprenticeship training. He contended that apprenticeship was an ill-conceived way to learn law even when the lawyer-master behaved responsibly. Apprenticeship training begins "at the wrong end" by plunging the student into the fine points of legal practice while he is still "uninstructed in the . . . *principles* upon which the rule of practice is founded." Because a student trained in this way learns to imitate rather than to reason, Blackstone feared that "the least variation from established precedents will totally distract and bewilder him . . . ."[28]

Blackstone's emphasis on redirecting the initial phase of legal study away from practice and toward the study of principles was the theme that pointed toward university legal education. This concern with principles reflected (and reinforced) changes then underway in how English law was organized and conceptualized. The English law of Blackstone's day was undertheorized. The writ system that had been inherited from the Middle Ages treated substantive law as an incident to pleading, inspiring Henry Maine's celebrated aphorism that in primitive legal systems substantive law is "secreted in the interstices of procedure."[29] By Blackstone's day, the writ system had become archaic. A single writ, trespass, had been manipulated to cover most of the law.[30] What Blackstone did in his four-volume *Commentaries on the Law of England,* published from 1765 to 1769, was largely to abandon the writs as organizing categories, in favor of concepts of substantive law.[31] (This development also permitted civil procedure to be disentangled from particular writs and generalized into a trans-substantive field.)

Blackstone's book resulted from a failed effort to initiate university legal education. Beginning in 1753, Blackstone began offering a course of lectures on English law at Oxford.[32] A bequest from Charles Viner gave Oxford a chair in English law, to which Blackstone was elected in 1758.[33] Blackstone aimed his lectures mainly at the young gentlemen who would go off to manage their estates and serve as local officeholders and members of Parliament, but he also meant the lectures (and the book version that he published as the *Commentaries* in the 1760s) to serve intending lawyers. He hoped to make "academical education a previous step to the profession of the common law," as well as to make "the rudiments of the law a part of academical education."[34] Despite Blackstone's later renown, this experiment with university legal education did not succeed. Blackstone attracted some following at Oxford,[35] but he wanted a career in London. In 1759, a year after being elected to the Vinerian chair, he reestablished chambers at the bar. He entered Parliament in 1761, resigned the chair in 1766, and in 1770 became a royal judge.[36] In the hands of his successors, the Vinerian chair became a sinecure until the university reforms of the later nineteenth century.[37]

I must say something about the structure and contents of the *Commentaries,* because Blackstone's book became the template for Litchfield,[38] and thereafter, for the curricula of early Harvard[39] and Yale.[40] Blackstone had studied Roman law before turning to the common law, and his familiarity with European legal literature suffuses his book.[41] Borrowing from the European tradition of institutional writing that traces back to Gaius and Justinian,[42] Blackstone divided his work into the law of persons, things, and actions. Volume One, on persons, contains an account of English constitutional and administrative structure. Blackstone bundled these public law chapters with his account of what we might call the law of status — that is, master and servant, domestic relations, and guardianship. Volume Two, on things, covers property law, including estates in land, inheritance and donative transfers, personal property, and bankruptcy. For his Volumes Three and Four, Blackstone departed from the Roman convention and spoke of wrongs rather than actions. Volume Three, on private wrongs, discusses tort law, as the title suggests, but eighteenth-century tort law was primitive,[43] and most of what the volume is really about is civil procedure, including the jury system and the law/equity division. Volume Four, on public wrongs, is devoted to criminal law and procedure.

Blackstone's presentation of legal rules as a body of reasoned principles drew on the European natural law tradition. Blackstone's reasons do not always impress us as the right ones. He was famously apologetic for the law of his day. For example, he defended the subordination of the wife's property interests to the husband by reasoning that since the "husband and wife are one person in law," the wife does not need any rights.[44] Most of us can think of some objections to Blackstone's reasoning on this issue, but that is a different point. His legacy was to establish the primacy of theory in the common law. Rules have reasons. Because the reasons limit the rule, a good lawyer learns to think about the reasons as well as to master the rules.

Blackstone's *Commentaries* was an instant publishing success, both in England and in the colonies.[45] The first American edition (the famous Bell edition published in Philadelphia in 1771) had what was for the time and place an immense press run of 1,587 copies, subscribed in advance.[46] Thereafter, the *Commentaries* went through innumerable editions and abridgments. (The Yale Law Library has one of the world's great collections of these various editions.[47])

The *Commentaries* appeared on the eve of the American Revolution. For the Americans, Blackstone was even more important than he was on his home turf. The successful outcome of the Revolution raised the question of why Americans should continue to adhere to rules laid down in ages past by judges serving a distant sovereign, whom the Americans had just defeated in the Revolutionary War. Blackstone's book, by conflating common law and natural law, supplied the answer that the Americans needed. English common law would apply in the new nation not because the king's judges commanded it, but because the common law embodied enduring principles of justice. Blackstone gave the common law a seeming universality that allowed the Americans to retain it despite its English taint.

By making law a field of principle, Blackstone made it resemble the fields that were already at home in the university — philosophy, theology, mathematics, the natural sciences. In this way Blackstone facilitated the movement to university legal education in the United States. Oddly, however, the place where Blackstone's vision of legal education was first realized was not in an English university, but in a proprietary law school located toward the edge of the then-known world, in the town of Litchfield in northwestern Connecticut.

IV. Litchfield

In the United States, the shift from the apprenticeship system to university legal education did not happen in one clean step. Rather, there was an intervening phase, of proprietary law schools, including the one in New Haven that would become Yale. Systematic legal education first appeared in close association with apprenticeship. Law offices sprang classrooms. Only after these law-office schools demonstrated the appeal of systematic legal education did the universities step in and capture the field.

The New Haven law school that became Yale was one of several such proprietorships.[48] Harvard and Columbia had similar but less prominent connections. The Harvard Law School, although begun in 1817, had dwindled by 1829 to a single student.[49] It was effectively refounded in 1829 when Harvard teamed U.S. Supreme Court Justice Joseph Story as a part-timer with John Hooker Ashmun, whose proprietary law school, originally located in Northampton, Massachusetts, was then merged into Harvard.[50] The modern Columbia Law School was founded in 1858, when the Columbia trustees succeeded in mounting what was in effect a takeover bid for a proprietary law school operated by Theodore Dwight at upstate Hamilton College.[51]

The earliest, the largest, and by far the most influential of these proprietary schools was the Litchfield Law School. Across the half century of its operation, from the 1780s to the 1830s, Litchfield trained about a thousand lawyers,[52] drawn from every state of the then-Union. This number is all the more astonishing if we bear in mind how small the bar then was. Around the year 1800 in all of Connecticut there were perhaps 120 practicing lawyers,[53] and how much actual practice many of them had is a matter of doubt. Litchfield alumni included two vice presidents of the United States (Aaron Burr and the antebellum political leader John C. Calhoun), three U.S. Supreme Court justices, and thirty-four state supreme court justices. More than a hundred Litchfield alumni, roughly one in ten, served in the U.S. Congress, including twenty-eight in the Senate. Fourteen became state governors.[54]

By establishing the market for systematic classroom instruction as the entryway to the legal profession, Litchfield originated the American law school. The Litchfield model spread to other proprietary schools[55] (some, such as the Northampton school, founded by Litchfield alumni[56]), and then to the university-affiliated schools, especially Harvard and Yale, which ultimately drove Litchfield out of business.

A. REEVE AND GOULD

The founder of the Litchfield Law School was one Tapping Reeve, the son of a Long Island parson. Reeve graduated Princeton in 1763, remaining there for a time as a tutor before apprenticing with the prominent Hartford lawyer, Jesse Root.[57] Reeve settled in Litchfield and opened a law office in 1773.[58]

The town of Litchfield was at that time the fourth largest in Connecticut. It was an agricultural center and county town, as well as a coaching station on major north–south and east–west roads. Litchfield was a cultural center for its day, with an unusually large number of college-educated men.[59] Three courts (superior, county, probate) sat there, and the bar, although small, was distinguished for the day.[60]

Reeve married Sally Burr,[61] the sister of Aaron Burr, the future vice president. Like other lawyers of the day, Reeve took in apprentices. His first apprentice was Aaron Burr, who came to study with him in 1774,[62] the year after he graduated from Princeton. Perhaps on account of Reeve's connections to the Burr family, which was intertwined with the equally prominent Edwards family,[63] he had a stream of notable young men as his early clerks.[64]

Reeve developed a reputation for devotion to the training of his apprentices, and as his renown spread, he found himself taking apprentices in larger numbers. As the numbers of his students grew, Reeve found that it made sense to organize instruction by means of formal lectures.[65] In the early 1780s Reeve wound down his law practice to concentrate on teaching. In this way, Reeve's law office metamorphosed into a law school. When Reeve's school outgrew the physical limits of his office, he arranged in 1784 for the construction of a tiny one-room schoolhouse to serve as the classroom and library.[66] This building, not much larger than a modern garden shed, has been restored and is now maintained in the loving care of the Litchfield Historical Society. I sometimes take a group of legal history students to visit the Litchfield Law School. We begin these expeditions from our base in the halls of the Yale Law School, now refurbished to Versailles-like splendor. I never cease to marvel at the contrast with the tiny, unheated wooden shack on South Street in Litchfield, where American legal education effectively began.

In 1798 Reeve took on an associate, James Gould, to help him with the school. Gould was a former student, and in 1820, after more than two decades of collaboration, Gould succeeded Reeve as the sole proprietor. He operated the school until it closed in 1833. Both Reeve and Gould became part-time judges[67] and were addressed by that title.

B. THE STUDENTS

When Gould joined Reeve in 1798, the school had twenty students. Enrollment increased to a peak of fifty-five in 1813.[68] A few of the students lodged with Reeve and his wife, but most lived with families scattered around Litchfield. The students were, of course, all male.

A striking attribute of the Litchfield student body is that this first American law school was a national school. Biographical records[69] have been compiled for 903[70] of the students who are believed to have attended the school from the 1770s until it closed in 1833. About a third came from Connecticut, a quarter from New York and Massachusetts, and a fifth from the South.[71] Seventy students came from what was then the most distant state, Georgia.[72] Bearing in mind the difficulty and expense of travel in those days, it is astonishing that this tiny proprietorship could draw students from such distances and in such numbers.

What attracted these young men to study in Litchfield was not only law but also ladies. If you played your cards right, you could leave Litchfield with a bride as well as a career. From 1792,[73] the town was home to a hugely successful school for women, Sarah Pierce's Female Academy.[74] Like Tapping Reeve's law school, Pierce's school attracted young women of good family from great distances. Some, indeed, were the siblings of law students, the young women being allowed to go to Litchfield to study under the erstwhile protection of a brother. Litchfield law students married women from the female academy by the dozens.[75] It is reported that "[a]t the beginning of every semester, Pierce and Reeve exchanged lists of the 'eligible' students under their respective tutelage."[76] One young man wrote home in the year 1830 that he planned to concentrate on his studies in the near term, because Mrs. Reeve had told him "that all the marriageable young ladies have been married off, and that there is at present nothing but young fry in town .... The young ladies, she tells me, all marry law students, but ... it will take two or three years for the young crop to become fit for the harvest ...."[77]

Americans who became lawyers tended to obtain a liberal education in one of the colleges before beginning apprenticeship, which was also the pattern in England for intending barristers. Recent scholarship has established that over half the barristers admitted to the inns of court during the years from 1688 to 1754 had studied (something other than English law) at one of the three universities — Cambridge, Oxford, or Trinity College, Dublin.[78] Because the Litchfield Law School was an outgrowth of apprenticeship training, it is not surprising that patterns inherited from apprenticeship persisted, and that Litchfield law students continued to come from the universities. The Litchfield Law School student body was composed prevailingly (nearly two-thirds) of men who had already attended college.[79] Litchfield had a particularly heavy draw from Yale College, which provided a quarter of the students.[80] Brown, Columbia, Dartmouth, Harvard, Princeton, Union, and Williams were also strongly represented in the Litchfield student body.[81] We see, therefore, that from its earliest apprenticeship phase, American legal education has exhibited a trait that has ever since distinguished it from legal education on the Continent: In the United States, legal education is graduate education. Law students already hold a first university degree in something else.[82]

Although the Litchfield Law School drew a student body composed prevailingly of college graduates, Litchfield did not award its students a further degree for the course of postgraduate study in law.[83] Rather, Litchfield retained the rubric of apprenticeship. John Doe, the Litchfield student, received a letter from Reeve or Gould saying that Mr. Doe has read law in my office and attended my lectures there from such-a-date to such-a-later-date.[84] The student would present this letter to his local bar authorities, in order to satisfy at least part of the requirement that students clerk in a law office for a prescribed period before being admitted to the bar.[85]

Not only was there no Litchfield degree, there were no examinations either.[86] You passed your time, and you got your letter. This happy state of affairs carried over to the early university law schools, both Yale and Harvard, which awarded their degrees, like parole, for time served. Joseph Choate, who entered Harvard Law School in 1852, recalled that "there were absolutely no examinations to get in, or to proceed, or to get out." [87] The introduction of annual examinations was one of Langdell's principal innovations at Harvard in the 1870s.[88]

C. THE CURRICULUM

What did the Litchfield instructors actually teach? This is a matter of some importance, because decades after the Litchfield Law School had been shuttered, American university law schools were teaching a curriculum whose contours had been shaped at Litchfield. Happily, this is also a subject about which much is known, because detailed student notebooks from Litchfield survive literally by the dozen in various manuscript collections. The Yale Law Library and the Litchfield Historical Society have the most extensive holdings. There are also important holdings of Litchfield notes in Hartford, in Washington, and at the Columbia and Harvard law libraries.[89]

How did Tapping Reeve decide what to teach? The answer is quite clear: He followed Blackstone. Reeve's law school of the 1780s, perched on the edge of the North American wilderness, would have been unthinkable had not Blackstone's *Commentaries* already sketched out the curriculum in the 1760s. Part of what disposed Reeve[90] and other early law teachers[91] to a national curriculum rather than one focused on the laws of the home state was the cosmopolitanism of Blackstone, although as Zephaniah Swift showed in his *System of the Laws of the State of Connecticut,*[92] the first American law treatise, it was possible to mold an account of one state's practice around the organizational scheme and the topics that Blackstone identified.

Reeve and Gould presented lectures that they updated across the years as the law developed. One or the other teacher lectured for an hour and a half each morning, reading slowly enough for the students to transcribe the lecture word for word. Gould published a proud account of his dictation style of instruction in a law journal in 1822. The students took down in full "[a]ll the principal rules and distinctions, given out in the lectures, together with the references intended to support them . . . ."[93]

Gould positively discouraged his students from reading reported cases. He thought that case study was too challenging for novices.[94] The contrast with later developments in American legal education is striking. Harvard under Langdell in the 1870s was a direct descendant of Litchfield's emphasis on the importance of teaching legal doctrine in a principled way,[95] but Langdell would insist on having the students derive the principles from the study of appellate cases. He disparaged secondary material such as the textbooks employed in the text-and-recitation system of legal education, which had become prevalent by Langdell's day.[96] Litchfield's system of dictated lectures was a primitive forerunner of the textbook.

To the modern observer, the most striking feature of a Litchfield legal education was this emphasis on having students transcribe, embellish, and preserve a set of lecture notes. The premise was that the teacher had acquired a storehouse of valuable knowledge[97] about the rules and their rationale, and the classroom was the place for him to transfer this information orally to the student. Each morning the student would scribble down raw notes in class. That afternoon, after comparing the treatment of the same topic in practice books and law reports found in the school's library, the student would prepare a fine copy of the lecture notes, which he entered into a bound blank volume.[98] Producing an encyclopedic notebook of this sort served something of the function of the old-time commonplace book. A course of lectures at Litchfield lasted about fourteen months,[99] and by the 1820s the student would routinely fill up five volumes of these fine-hand notes.[100] As late as 1828, the Litchfield Law School was boasting that such student notes "constitute books of reference, the great advantages of which must be apparent to every one [who has] the slightest acquaintance with the comprehensive and abstruse science of the law."[101] The Litchfield instructors also ran a moot court program "[t]o assist the students in investigating, for themselves, and in forensic exercises . . . ."[102]

The fourteen-month elapsed time for the Litchfield course seems odd to the modern observer, because it would not have fit the pattern of annualized course offerings that we now expect. Litchfield did not have an academic year as such. Rather, students could start when they wanted and finish fourteen months later, much like going to the cinema in the good old days of the mid-twentieth century, when you could enter at your pleasure and leave when that part came around again. The early university law schools also operated in this way.[103] The so-called phased curriculum, in which certain subjects are identi-fied as fundamental, and have to be mastered before the student advances, was part of the package of reforms that Langdell devised at Harvard in the 1870s. The package also included annual or course-level examinations and a partially elective upper-level curriculum.[104] These reforms ultimately became the indus-try standard, but long after Litchfield had been shuttered.

Litchfield students learned the law in an almost literal sense. They came to Litchfield to capture the law, to write it down and take it back with them, often to places where law books were rare. This conception of the purpose of legal education would not, of course, endure. It presupposed a relatively static body of law and extreme scarcity of legal literature, conditions that would change markedly across the nineteenth century.

Because the Litchfield instructors updated their lectures to take account of the latest developments in the law, Litchfield student notes would lend them-selves to a project that has been suggested[105] but never carried out. The early notes, from the 1780s and 1790s, stem from a time when there was almost no American legal literature. By the last years of Litchfield (in the 1830s), how-ever, American law reports and statutory compilations had so burgeoned[106] that contemporaries were becoming uneasy about coping with the quantity. By comparing Litchfield notebooks across the decades, it should be possible to form a fairly detailed view of the Americanization of the common law. The Litchfield notebooks remain in manuscript, however. Until modern scholarly editions of selected sets become available, the genre will not be widely usable for historical study.[107]

What subjects did Litchfield teach? Reeve and Gould followed Blackstone's *Commentaries* but with revealing changes. They deleted the coverage of the En-glish constitution from Blackstone's Volume One — understandably, since the Americans had just got finished overthrowing this regime. The Litchfield instructors basically ignored public law.[108] Another possibility, realized by Chancellor Kent in his Blackstone-inspired *Commentaries on American Law*,[109] would have been to substitute American constitutional law for English.[110]

The Litchfield course tracked and amplified Blackstone's Volumes Two and Three, dealing with property, succession, tort, and civil procedure. Blackstone's handling of contract was primitive, even though he worked in the age of Lord Mansfield, when English contract and commercial law flowered.[111] "Blackstone grouped contracts not in terms of what elements made an enforceable contract, but in terms of the effects of various types of contracts on property rights."[112] The Litchfield lecturers added considerable coverage of the emerging law — their topics included bills of exchange, promissory notes, insurance contracts, and charter parties.[113]

The most striking departure from Blackstone's plan is that the Litchfield course dropped crime, to which Blackstone had devoted essentially the entire fourth volume of his *Commentaries*. Litchfield's coverage was so brief that in 1822 Gould was teaching it in what he called "supernumerary" evening lectures.[114] This dismissive attitude toward criminal law as well as the disinterest in constitutional law underscore how totally the Litchfield curriculum was devoted to private law. We see in this respect the influence of the law-office culture from which the Litchfield Law School emerged. Crime was relatively rare in provincial Litchfield, and it was not a market the upper crust of the legal profession expected to serve. Likewise, constitutional law was as yet scarcely a field of law office practice. The curricular traditions of American legal education would long bear the influence of the law offices from which the first law schools grew.

D. THE DECLINE

The Litchfield Law School withered in the later 1820s and died in 1833.[115] The main reason Litchfield closed is that it could not effectively compete with the newly founded university law schools, especially its near neighbor, Yale. Enrollments from Massachusetts declined after the founding of Harvard in 1817,[116] and total enrollment declined steeply in the later 1820s, as the New Haven Law School became Yale.[117] Yale College graduates, who had supplied a quarter of the Litchfield student body, were ever less likely to trek up to remote Litchfield for law school.[118] When ill health forced Gould to retire, no successor wanted the business.

We know in the light of hindsight that Litchfield and the other proprietary law schools of the day constituted a transitional phenomenon, way stations on the path to university legal education.[119] Why was Litchfield unable in the end to hold its own against the university-linked schools? Not only did Litchfield lack the cachet of the universities, Litchfield had four fatal weaknesses when pitted against the university law schools.

1. *Proprietorship*. The proprietorship format was a loser. The Litchfield Law School resembled any other proprietorship, for example, Sammy's Delicatessen. We do not expect Sammy's Delicatessen to endure across the ages. Sometimes when Sammy retires or dies, he arranges for a child or a buyer or a partner or an employee to take over the deli, but often enough there is nobody suitable. In that case, Sammy just closes shop, or his executor does it for him. The salami slicer gets sold off, and the deli is wound up.

My point is that in a proprietorship, succession frequently poses difficult or insurmountable problems (as was the case at Litchfield, where there had been friction between Reeve and Gould in the 1820s when Reeve became unable to continue,[120] and when in the 1830s Gould was unable to attract a successor). Universities, by contrast, are long-lived; they are designed as institutions of perpetual succession. They have an administrative capacity to manage succession problems, and they have an institutional interest in doing so. We see this contrast in the differing fates of Litchfield and Yale. Whereas Gould's law school died a proprietor's death in 1833, Yale's leaders would intervene in 1845 and again in 1869 to manage succession crises that occurred at the proprietary law school that was attached to Yale.[121]

2. *Pedagogy*. Litchfield's increasingly archaic pedagogy was not sustainable.[122] The system of lecturing, which had been such an advance over apprenticeship in the 1780s, became retrograde by the 1830s. Litchfield's most effective competitors, the new university law schools at Yale[123] and Harvard,[124] were supplementing, and increasingly replacing, set-piece lectures with a different and superior technique, the so-called text-and-recitation system, about which I shall say more in my next lecture in this series.[125] (Yale clung to text-and-recitation instruction[126] — the "Yale Method"[127] — for a generation after Harvard began abandoning it for the case method and related reforms in the 1870s.[128])

The oral tradition put Litchfield at a disadvantage not only in competing with other schools and methods of pedagogy, but also against the advance of the printed law book. Having students construct a handwritten legal encyclopedia became a fool's errand in the changed circumstances of the revolution in legal publishing that got underway in the last decades of Litchfield. In the language of today's financial pages, the Litchfield proprietors failed to adapt to technological changes that made their business model obsolete. They were hostile to publishing at a time when the cost of publishing was plummeting.[129] They tried to sustain an archaic tradition of imparting knowledge by lecture just when the age of the textbook and the treatise was bursting upon them. Litchfield's demise may stand in this regard as a cautionary tale for law schools and universities in our own times, as we grapple with the implications of the new electronic technologies for instruction, research, and the dissemination of knowledge.

3. *Philanthropy.* A further disadvantage under which Litchfield and the other proprietary law schools suffered vis-à-vis their university-based competitors was their inability to attract philanthropy. Even if you have enjoyed your visits to Sammy's Delicatessen, you tend not to include Sammy in your annual giving nor to remember him in your will. The personal proprietorship as a mode of organization tends to restrict the amount of capital that can be brought into an enterprise. The Litchfield proprietors were limited to the investment that they could obtain in their personal capacities. Across time as the need for facilities, library, and faculty grew, personal capital would not be enough to sustain a law school. The law school as an extension of the small-town law office was an inherently transitional and unsustainable form.

Access to philanthropy gave a decisive advantage to Harvard and Yale, Litchfield's two most formidable competitors. Harvard used the Royall devise to launch its law school in 1817;[130] donations from Nathan Dane permitted the refounding of the school under Joseph Story in 1829.[131] I explain in my next lecture in this series[132] how Yale's ability to be an object of philanthropy was crucial to the survival of Yale Law School in its first succession crisis in 1845, and to its flowering in later decades.

4. *Isolation.* The deepest flaw that would inevitably have doomed the Litchfield Law School in the long term was, I believe, its isolation, by which I mean not only its location in a remote town, but also its isolation from the other intellectual currents of a university. Litchfield exemplified the view that law was an autonomous discipline, so autonomous that a single lecturer could master it and then impart it by dictation in a fourteen-month course. We learned across the twentieth century what the Litchfield proprietors had no particular reason to know in their day, that law schools thrive in association with the study of cognate fields of knowledge. Nowhere more than at Yale would this insight be taken to heart. Beginning in the 1870s in circumstances discussed in my next lecture,[133] the Yale Law School began that remarkable lurch toward association with the academic disciplines that came to distinguish it.

E. LITCHFIELD'S LEGACY

I am now going to depart the Litchfield hills for the trip down to New Haven. As I do so, let me remind you why this failed enterprise, the Litchfield

Law School, was so important. It impressed a triple legacy on the history of American legal education. First, Litchfield established that pedagogy dominates apprenticeship for introducing students to the law. For the future, the question was not whether law would be studied in the classroom, but where and how. It was the where and the how that Litchfield got wrong. The universities would suppress proprietorship legal education, and they would teach in ways more congenial to the exploration of knowledge. Second, Litchfield established the conventions of the national law school. Legal education would not center on the law of an individual state, and accordingly, the students could be drawn from throughout the country. Third, the law office origins of Litchfield and the other proprietary law schools that Litchfield inspired imparted a pronounced private-law bias to the curricular traditions of American legal education. As I shall discuss in my next lecture, disquiet about the narrowness of this private-law orientation would begin to surface at Yale in the 1870s, just when the private-law tradition had been powerfully reinforced (in rather different ways) at Dwight's Columbia and at Langdell's Harvard.

V. Yale

I said at the outset of this lecture that the Yale Law School had a prehistory of sorts, because the School was the outgrowth of a proprietary law school that began operating from a New Haven law office sometime in the early years of the nineteenth century, before the School affiliated with Yale.

A. THE FOUNDERS: STAPLES, HITCHCOCK, AND DAGGETT

The original proprietor, Seth Staples, was born in 1776 and graduated Yale College in 1797. He studied law in the New Haven office of David Daggett (about whom more below) and was admitted to the bar in 1799.[134] Staples must have been a person of some wealth, because the next year, in 1800, he was able to import from England what was for its day an exceptionally good law library,[135] to which he added all his life.[136] This library made his office an attractive place for would-be apprentices to read law. Staples probably began, like Reeve at Litchfield, by taking apprentices in the older way. We do not know when his operation turned into a school. Staples kept a list of his students only from the year 1819;[137] for earlier years we have only incidental and incomplete information about who may have studied with him. Looking back a half-century later, Simeon E. Baldwin reported that it was remembered of Staples that he "undertook the charge of a class of half a dozen law students, who recited to him in the intervals of business, generally before breakfast, every morning."[138]

The Litchfield Law School had been operating for perhaps twenty years when Staples opened his New Haven law office, and Staples was acutely aware of what went on at Litchfield. Staples did not attend the Litchfield Law School,[139] but in 1798, while still a student in Daggett's office, Staples copied by hand a set of Litchfield notes. (This notebook, which survives in the Yale Law Library,[140] gave the mistaken impression[141] that Staples studied at Litchfield.)

Unlike Tapping Reeve, Staples remained active at the bar. In 1820 Staples took on a former student, Samuel Hitchcock, as a partner in his combined law office and law school.[142] Hitchcock would come to personify the Yale Law School from the mid-1820s until his death in 1845. He was born in 1786 and graduated Yale College in 1809. He remained at Yale as a tutor, read law in Staples' office, and was admitted to the bar in 1815.[143] In 1824, four years after Hitchcock joined him, Staples withdrew from the office and from the school. He relocated his practice to New York City, where he built his career in a field that has become hot again in the computer age — intellectual property law. Staples became the patent lawyer for Charles Goodyear. In a string of lawsuits Staples vindicated Goodyear's patent on the vulcanizing process for rubber manufacture.[144] In 1839 Staples took on a case of a different sort: He served as one of the lawyers who represented[145] the captured Africans whom the U.S. Supreme Court freed in the now celebrated *Amistad* case.[146]

When Staples withdrew from the school in 1824, Hitchcock became the sole proprietor. Hitchcock bought some of Staples' library and added to it across the years. Hitchcock continued to practice law, and he also served as a judge in the county and city courts. He was mayor of New Haven from 1839 to 1841.[147]

The oldest of the three men who are reckoned as the founders of the Yale Law School was David Daggett, the last to become associated with the school. He was the lawyer with whom Staples had apprenticed in the later 1790s. Daggett was born in 1764, graduated Yale College in 1781, studied with a New Haven lawyer, and was admitted to the bar in 1786.[148] He became a prominent Federalist politician, held a variety of state offices, and from 1813 to 1819 served as U.S. Senator from Connecticut. In 1824 when Staples left for New York, Daggett joined Hitchcock in teaching law at the school. Daggett remained active at the bar and in politics.[149] From 1826 to 1832 he was a superior court judge, from 1828 to 1830 he was the mayor of New Haven, and in 1833–34 he was chief justice of the Connecticut Supreme Court.

B. AFFILIATION WITH YALE

In 1826, the year Daggett became a judge, and two years after he began teaching at the law school, Daggett was named to yet another job, as professor of law in Yale College. There was one precedent for this appointment. Back in 1801, Yale College had appointed a local politician and alumnus, Elizur Goodrich, as the first professor of law in the College.[150] Goodrich seems to have had some time on his hands, having just been sacked by the incoming president, Thomas Jefferson, from the post of customs collector for the port of New Haven.[151] Yale engaged Goodrich to present a course of lectures on jurisprudence and the American constitution. Goodrich soon acquired local and state political office. It appears that Goodrich ceased giving his Yale course in 1806; he resigned the appointment in 1810.[152] The professorship lapsed until 1826, when Yale renewed it for Daggett. Thereafter for many years Daggett gave some lectures in the College on what we would today call public law and government. This professorship in the College became the Chancellor Kent chair in 1832, when funds were raised to name it in honor of the New York jurist, James Kent (Daggett's classmate in the College class of 1781), as part of Yale's first fundraising campaign, the Centum Millia Fund.[153] (The chair was last held in the College by William Howard Taft,[154] in the interval (1913–21) between his presidency and his chief justiceship of the Supreme Court. The chair migrated from the College to the Law School in the second half of the twentieth century, when Alexander Bickel was named to it.)

There are two longstanding puzzles about Yale's affiliation with the Hitchcock/Daggett proprietary law school: When did it happen and why?

The Yale Corporation did not take a formal vote to affiliate with the Law School. On the evidence available, I incline to treat Yale's appointment in 1826 of the New Haven law school professor Daggett to be the law professor in the College as marking the date of the affiliation. From that year the College catalogue began to identify "The Law School" and to describe its instructors and course of study[155] in the same pages as Yale's other two graduate schools, the "Theological Department" (today's Divinity School, founded in 1822[156]), and the "Medical Institution"[157] (today's Medical School, established in 1813[158]). A further milestone in the affiliation occurred in 1830, when Yale conferred a courtesy title of professor on Hitchcock.[159] Not until 1843 did Yale begin awarding its degree to the Law School's graduates — prompted by competitive pressure from Harvard.[160]

The official version[161] of the story of the Law School's affiliation with Yale fixes the event in 1824, when the Yale College catalogue begins to have a separate listing for "Law Students,"[162] but this evidence is weak. The student listings in the otherwise skimpy College catalogue of this period served as a kind of directory or address book, showing (under the column heading of "Rooms") where the students were living (for example, "Mr. Smith's," "Hon. Mr. Edwards").[163] The catalogue listed not only current students in the College, but also some resident alumni and some graduates of other colleges who were doing postgraduate study in town. The listing of graduates studying law in New Haven may have been little more than a courtesy. In any event, 1824 is *not* when the practice of listing law students began. Michael Sansbury has examined the early catalogues and found law students listed as early as 1814.[164] Furthermore, there is little correspondence between the list that Staples and Hitchcock kept of their students, which shows six students for 1824,[165] and the 1824 Yale catalogue, which lists fourteen "Law Students," of whom only four were studying with Staples and Hitchcock.

For two decades after Staples' departure in 1824, Hitchcock and Daggett were the Yale Law School's only faculty members. Daggett was the headliner whose reputation in public affairs helped attract students, Hitchcock was the insider who did most of the teaching. Hitchcock owned the library, and he held the lease for the school's premises.[166] This pattern of a headliner whose other business prevented him from wholly regular teaching and an insider who bore the brunt of the teaching had been developed in the previous decade at Harvard. Harvard founded its law school in 1817 with Isaac Parker, the Chief Justice of Massachusetts, as the headliner and Asahel Stearns as the insider.[167] After some troubles in the later 1820s, Harvard sacked both of them and brought in a new pair, U.S. Supreme Court Justice Joseph Story as the headliner[168] and John Hooker Ashmun, the successor proprietor of the Northampton law school,[169] as the insider.

The deeper puzzle about Yale's affiliation with Hitchcock and Daggett's proprietary New Haven law school is not when it occurred but why. Why did Yale College want to have anything to do with this place? Obviously, the cachet and perhaps some of the library resources of Yale were attractive to the proprietors. But what was in it for Yale? Why should Yale lend its name to this local trade school, owned and operated for profit by a couple of local practicing lawyers? It is as though today's Yale University were to announce a merger with the New Haven School of Pipefitting or the New Haven Auto Driving School.

In order to understand Yale's disposition to do something about law, one has to recall the brief experiment in 1801 with the appointment of Elizur Goodrich as Professor of Law in Yale College. The aspiration to extend the mission of the American colleges to law had been widely voiced in the last decades of the eighteenth century, as an outgrowth of the American Revolution. There was a sense that it was important to educate the elite about the theory and character of the new republican institutions.[170] At Yale, President Ezra Stiles proposed the creation of a chair in law as early as 1777.[171] Both the University of Pennsylvania (as it was later known) and Columbia experimented with such courses in the 1790s, appointing respectively U.S. Supreme Court Justice James Wilson and the future New York Chancellor James Kent to teach law to college students.[172] Yale's appointment of Goodrich in 1801 was in the same vein. For various reasons, these experiments did not succeed, but they evidence how broad the inclination was among the American colleges to extend their mission to law.

By affiliating with the Hitchcock/Daggett law school, Yale was able to enlarge its sphere of activity to include law without having to commit itself financially or otherwise. Yale was pitifully endowed in this period,[173] which made the proprietary structure of the Law School especially attractive. Yale was determined to quarantine itself from financial responsibility for the Law School. Into the 1870s, the Corporation was reiterating that the Law School's professors operated the school at their own risk.[174] Thus, it was the Yale Corporation, not the law faculty, that insisted upon retaining the proprietorship form. The attraction to having the Law School in independent hands was that, in the event that this experiment with university legal education failed, it would be easier to pull the plug on outside venturers.

And fail it almost did. In 1845 and again in 1869, the Yale Law School neared extinction. In my next lecture, I shall recount the saga of Yale's two rescue operations. The second, in 1869, led to a profound rethinking of Yale's relations with the Law School. Yale began to make the commitment to have a law school worthy of the University. From the 1870s we begin to discern traits that subsequently came to define the Yale Law School — the linkage of law to other disciplines within the University; the pursuit of public law in defiance of the Litchfield-derived, private-law canon of the times; and the ability to stay small and humane in student relations as Yale's most prominent competitors grew ever larger. Intertwined with these developments would be the recognition that such a law school could not be financed from tuition. The Yale Law School would begin to develop the philanthropic basis that would be needed to support a place of the character it was about to become.

Notes

I wish to record my gratitude to Nancy Lyon, Yale University, Sterling Library, Department of Manuscripts and Archives, for help with the Yale archives; to Catherine Fields, director of the Litchfield Historical Society, for guidance on the Litchfield sources; and for the diligent research assistance of Stuart Chinn (YLS '03) and Robert James (YC '05).

1. I discuss these events at some length in my second lecture in this series, John H. Langbein, "Law School in a University: Yale's Distinctive Path in the Later Nineteenth Century," infra this volume (hereafter Lecture II), text at notes 23–63.

2. These and other lapsed law schools are listed in Alfred Z. Reed, *Training for the Public Profession of Law*, 421–33 (Carnegie Foundation) (1921). This work, commissioned by the Carnegie Foundation, is hereafter cited as Reed, *Carnegie*. Stevens discusses Reed and his mission. See Robert Stevens, *Law School: Legal Education in America from the 1850s to the 1980s*, at 112–13, 120–21 & nn. 4, 6 (1983) (hereafter Stevens, *Law School*). Three Virginia schools are discussed in W. Hamilton Bryson & E. Lee Shepard, The Winchester Law School, 1824–1931, 21 *Law & History Rev.* 393, 399 (2003). Reed lists two of the three. I have been told that Wesleyan University (not on Reed's list) had a law school for a time in the mid-nineteenth century, but I have been unable to trace the claim.

3. Frederick C. Hicks, *Yale Law School: From the Founders to Dutton: 1845–1869*, at 25–27 (1936) (describing the premises into which the School moved in 1850 from its former location next door) (hereafter Hicks II). The cited work is the second of four pamphlets written by the Yale Law Librarian of the period. The others, in sequence, are *Yale Law School: The Founders and the Founders' Collection* (1935) (hereafter Hicks I); *Yale Law School: 1869–1894: Including the County Court House Period* (1937) (hereafter Hicks III); and *Yale Law School: 1895–1915: Twenty Years of Hendrie Hall* (1938) (hereafter Hicks IV). The four pamphlets were recently reissued in a one-volume photographic reprint edition as Frederick C. Hicks, *History of the Yale Law School to 1915* (2001) (hereafter 2001 ed.). That volume preserves the page numbering of each pamphlet but also assigns continuous page numbers to the four pamphlets; thus, the material in Hicks II:25–27, cited supra, appears as 2001 ed. at 75–77. When citing the Hicks pamphlets, I cite the original pamphlet, and I supply a parallel citation to the additional page number assigned to it in the reprint edition for Hicks II, III, or IV (the numbers are the same for Hicks I). Hicks' four pamphlets constitute the only comprehensive account of the history of the first century of the Yale Law School. Although they do not compare well with such works as Goebel and Howard on Columbia (see infra note 51) or Warren on Harvard (see infra note 21), we are lucky to have them. The grievous shortcoming of Hicks' history is that he seldom disclosed his sources. He did not use footnotes, although he sometimes mentioned the sources in his narrative. When relying upon Hicks, I have attempted where possible to locate and supply citations to Hicks' likely sources. I have found no evidence of any fabrication in Hicks, and accordingly, I sometimes rely on information found in Hicks even when I have not been able to confirm the sources.

4. Hicks reproduces a photograph of the building, located just off Church Street. Hicks I, following 16. He explains, Hicks II:26, 2001 ed. at 76, that the photograph dates from after 1873. The site is further discussed at Hicks I:10.

5. Brooks Mather Kelley, *Yale: A History* 256 (1974). In addition, "[a]djoining the lecture room was a small office for the use of the instructors." Hicks II:27, 2001 ed. at 77.

6. I discuss these mid- and late-nineteenth-century developments in Lecture II, text at notes 64–115.

7. See [J. H. Baker], *750 Years of Law at Cambridge: A Brief History of the Faculty of Law* (1996); F. H. Lawson, *The Oxford Law School* (1968). Regarding the failure of the effort to institute legal study at the new London University, founded in 1826, see Christopher W. Brooks & Michael Lobban, "Apprenticeship or Academy? The Idea of a Law

University, 1830–1860," in *Learning the Law: Teaching and the Transmission of Law in England, 1150–1900*, at 353, 359–60 (Jonathan A. Bush & Alain Wijffels eds., 1999) (hereafter Bush & Wijffels).

8. Oxford was teaching Roman-canon law as early as the 1190s. See Peter Stein, *Roman Law in European Legal History* 56 (1999).

9. I have discussed the teaching of Roman Law at Cambridge in John H. Langbein, Trinity Hall and the Relations of European and English Law from the Fourteenth to the Twenty-First Centuries, in *The Milestones Lectures* 75 (Trinity Hall, 2001).

10. Report from the Select Committee on Legal Education (1846), quoted in William Twining, *Blackstone's Tower: The English Law School* 25 (1994). The Committee's work and report are discussed in Peter Stein, "Legal Theory and the Reform of Legal Education in Mid-Nineteenth Century England," in id., *The Character and Influence of Roman Civil Law*, 231, 234–38 (1988). He reprints the Committee's "concluding resolutions," id. at 248–50, which begin by noticing the "unsatisfactory" contrast with legal education in Europe and America.

11. Albert Venn Dicey, *Can English Law Be Taught at the Universities? An Inaugural Lecture* 1 (London, 1883).

12. Systematic law reporting in the United States began only in 1804, in Massachusetts and New York. I have discussed the circumstances in John H. Langbein, Chancellor Kent and the History of Legal Literature, 93 *Columbia L. Rev.* 547, 574–75 (1993) (hereafter Langbein, *Kent*).

13. On the glory days of the inns, see John H. Baker, *The Third University of England: The Inns of Court and the Common-Law Tradition* (Selden Soc., 1990); see also id., *An Introduction to English Legal History* 159–62 (4th ed. 2002); Wilfred R. Prest, *The Inns of Court under Elizabeth I and the Early Stuarts, 1590–1640* (1972).

14. On the decline of the inns, see 6 William Holdsworth, *A History of English Law* 48–193 (1922–66) (16 vols.) (hereafter Holdsworth, HEL).

15. 12 Holdsworth, HEL, supra note 14, at 16.

16. David Lemmings, *Gentlemen and Barristers: The Inns of Court and the English Bar, 1680–1730*, at 95–97 (1990); 12 Holdsworth, HEL, supra note 14, at 85–89.

17. The textbook and treatise tradition in England was slender until the end of the eighteenth century. See A. W. B. Simpson, The Rise and Fall of the Legal Treatise: Legal Principles and the Forms of Legal Literature, 48 *U. Chicago L. Rev.* 632 (1981).

18. Lemmings, supra note 16, at 101–3.

19. The practice of commonplacing was by no means limited to law. See Earle Havens, *Commonplace Books: A History of Manuscripts and Printed Books from Antiquity to the Twentieth Century* (2001), drawing on examples from the collections of Yale's Beinecke Library.

20. Lemmings, supra note 16, at 95–97.

21. See generally Paul M. Hamlin, *Legal Education in Colonial New York* (1939). Apprenticeship education thrived throughout the nineteenth century, especially away from urban centers, and it survived well into the twentieth century. On the patterns of self-study and apprenticeship in colonial times, see 1 Charles Warren, *History of the Harvard Law School and of Early Legal Conditions in America* 126–50 (1908) (3 vols.) (hereafter Warren, *Harvard*).

22. For the text of an indenture of apprenticeship from 1723, see Hamlin, supra note 21, at 165–66.

23. On the scarcity of law books in colonial America, see Charles Warren, *A History of the American Bar* 157–64 (1911).

24. See Reed, *Carnegie,* supra note 2, at 82–84; Charles R. McKirdy, The Lawyer as Apprentice: Legal Education in Eighteenth Century Massachusetts, 28 *J. Legal Ed.* 124, 125 & n. 10 (1976).

25. See George B. Shepherd & William G. Shepherd, Scholarly Restraints? ABA Accreditation and Legal Education, 19 *Cardozo L. Rev.* 2091 (1998), showing how ABA cartelization suppresses new schools that would offer cheaper and more efficient legal education, raising entry barriers that disadvantage the poor.

26. See the document captioned "William Livingston's Criticism of the Treatment of Apprenticed Law Clerks," reprinted in Hamlin, supra note 21, at 167. The indenture of apprenticeship between Livingston's father and the lawyer-master, James Alexander, appears id. at 41–42.

27. Thomas Jefferson to John G. Jefferson, June 11, 1790, in *The Writings of Thomas Jefferson* 180 (1892), quoted in Marian McKenna, *Tapping Reeve and the Litchfield Law School* 14 n. 38 (1986) (hereafter McKenna, *Litchfield*). Further on Jefferson's views, see Morris L. Cohen, Thomas Jefferson Recommends a Course of Law Study, 119 *U. Pennsylvania L. Rev.* 823, 827–28 (1971).

28. William Blackstone, *Commentaries on the Laws of England* 32 (Oxford 1765–69) (4 vols.) (emphasis supplied) (hereafter Blackstone, *Commentaries*). Joseph Story tracked these themes in his critique of apprenticeship, written in part to tout the opening of the Harvard Law School in 1817. He disparaged "the common delusion, that the law may be thoroughly acquired in the immethodical, interrupted, and desultory studies of the office of a practicing counsellor," unless "the student shall have laid the foundation in elementary principles, under the guidance of a learned and discreet lecturer. . . . [W]ithout such elementary instruction, [the student] will . . . become a patient drudge, versed in the forms of conveyancing and pleading, but incapable of ascending the principles that govern them . . . ." Joseph Story, "Course of Legal Study," reprinted in *The Miscellaneous Writings of Joseph Story* 66, 92 (William W. Story ed., Boston, 1852), cited in Daniel R. Coquillette, "Mourning Venice and Genoa": Joseph Story, Legal Education, and the Lex Mercatoria, forthcoming, October 2002 draft, at 11.

29. Henry Sumner Maine, *Dissertations on Early Law and Custom* 389 (New York ed., 1883).

30. "By the end of the seventeenth century . . . the great bulk of the litigation of the Kingdom was conducted through the various forms of action which had developed from trespass . . . ." T. F. T. Plucknett, *A Concise History of the Common Law* 375 (5th ed., 1956).

31. Plucknett wrote of Blackstone that "in his pages we find the first comprehensive attempt to state (as far as was then possible) the whole of English law in the form of substantive rules." Id. at 382.

32. 12 Holdsworth, HEL, supra note 14, at 91–92; Lucy Sutherland, William Blackstone and the Legal Chairs at Oxford, in *Evidence in Literary Scholarship* 229 (R. Wellek & A. Riberio eds., 1970).

33. On the university politics surrounding the naming of Blackstone to the Vinerian chair, see David J. Ibbetson, "Charles Viner and His Chair: Legal Education in Eighteenth-Century Oxford," in Bush & Wijffels, supra note 7, at 315, 321–28.

34. 1 Blackstone, *Commentaries* 33. Holdsworth reprints the text of an advertisement in which Blackstone expressed similar aspirations for his first lectures on English law in 1753. 12 Holdsworth, HEL, supra note 14, at 745–46.

35. "Even the hypercritical Bentham admitted that [Blackstone's lectures] were well attended by the standards of the other professors, in so far as [Bentham] was one of thirty to fifty auditors in Michaelmas 1763." David Lemmings, Blackstone and Law Reform by Education: Preparation for the Bar and Lawyerly Culture in Eighteenth-Century England, 16 *Law & History Rev.* 211, 226 (1998), citing 10 *The Works of Jeremy Bentham* 45 (J. Bowring ed., Edinburgh, 1838–43).

36. Blackstone sat briefly on the court of King's Bench, then for a decade on Common Pleas. His career is succinctly recounted in Gareth H. Jones, "Introduction," *The Sovereignty of the Law: Selections from Blackstone's Commentaries on the Laws of England* xvii–xxi (1973). On Blackstone's judicial service, see Edward Foss, *Biographia Juridica: A Biographical Dictionary of the Judges of England* 99 (1870). Blackstone's sources and influence have been much discussed, but a careful scholarly biography remains to be written. There is a pair of adulatory accounts by American writers: Lewis C. Warden, *The Life of Blackstone* (1938), and David A. Lockmiller, *Sir William Blackstone* (1938). A shorter sketch, privately published, appeared recently: Ian Doolittle, *William Blackstone: A Biography* (2001).

37. On the "period of eclipse" during the years 1793–1880, see Harold G. Hansbury, *The Vinerian Chair and Legal Education* 79–97 (1958). On the parallels between the Vinerian chair and the chairs of national law founded in European and American universities in the eighteenth century, see M. D. Gordon, "The Vinerian Chair: An Atlantic Perspective," in *The Life of the Law* 195 (P. Birks ed., 1993). The American chairs for the teaching of law to undergraduates in the colleges are noticed infra, note 82, and text at notes 150–54, 170–72.

38. Infra, text at notes 90–92.

39. The course of study at Harvard in 1825, according to Asahel Stearns, entailed "[i]n the first place a reading of Blackstone, more or less particular, of the whole work. This practice has been found by experience to be highly useful." 1 Warren, *Harvard*, supra note 21, at 333 (quoting Stearns' report to the Harvard overseers, spelling modernized).

40. Speaking of the course he was teaching at Yale, David Daggett wrote that "Blackstone's Com[mentaries] are the outlines, and I endeavor to fill up certain of his topics such as mortgages, evidence, pleadings, contracts, equity, etc., etc." Daggett to James Dana, Dec. 9, 1831, David Daggett Papers, MS 162, series I, box 3, folder 88, at 1, Yale Univ. Sterling Libr., Dept. of Manuscripts and Archives (hereafter Sterling M&A), reproduced in Hicks II:51, 2001 ed. at 101 (spelling and punctuation modernized) (document hereafter cited as Daggett, Letter).

41. In addition to the works by Alan Watson, cited infra note 42, see Michael Lobban, *The Common Law and English Jurisprudence: 1760–1850*, at 19–26 (1991); John W. Cairns, Blackstone, An English Institutist: Legal Literature and the Rise of the Nation

State, 4 *Oxford J. Leg. Studies* 318 (1984); John W. Cairns, Institutional Writings in Scotland Reconsidered, 4 *J. Leg. History* 76 (1983).

42. See Alan Watson, *Roman Law and Comparative Law* 147–81 (1991), which expands on id., The Structure of Blackstone's *Commentaries*, 97 *Yale L.J.* 795 (1988). On the European-wide phenomenon of institutionalist legal literature, see Klaus Luig, The Institutes of National Law in the Seventeenth and Eighteenth Centuries, 17 *Juridical Rev.* (N.S.) 193 (1972) translating id., Institutionenlehrbücher des nationalen Rechts im 17. und 18. Jahrhundert, 3 *Ius Commune* 64 (1970).

43. I have elsewhere explained why. John H. Langbein, Historical Foundations of the Law of Evidence: A View from the Ryder Sources, 96 *Columbia L. Rev.* 1168, 1178–79 (1996).

44. 1 Blackstone, *Commentaries* 430.

45. 12 Holdsworth, HEL, supra note 14, 712, 714–15.

46. William Blackstone, *Commentaries on the Laws of England* (Philadelphia 1771–72) (4 vols.), discussed in Catherine S. Eller, *The William Blackstone Collection in the Yale Law Library: A Bibliographical Catalogue* 37 (1938). As a result of aggressive marketing and pricing (facilitated by not having to pay Blackstone any royalties on a pirate edition), Bell was able to get 840 subscribers to buy 1,587 copies. The list of subscribers appears in the front papers to Volume Four. Most were individuals, but some were booksellers ordering bulk lots. See Whitney S. Bagnall, Robert Bell and the Selling of Blackstone's *Commentaries* (unpublished paper, Jul. 19, 2000; Bagnall is curator of rare books and manuscripts at Columbia Law School).

47. Catalogued in Eller, supra note 46.

48. See the compilation of "early private law schools," in Reed, *Carnegie,* supra note 2, at 431–33; see also Craig E. Klafter, *Reason over Precedents: Origins of American Legal Thought* 133–77 (1993) (discussing the proprietary law schools founded before 1830).

49. 1 Warren, *Harvard,* supra note 21, at 364.

50. At Northampton Ashmun had been the colleague of and then the successor to Judge Samuel Howe, a Litchfield alumnus who died in 1828. See Samuel H. Fisher, *Litchfield Law School: 1774–1833: Biographical Catalogue of Students* 65 (1946) (hereafter Fisher, *Catalogue*) (entry for Howe). The Northampton school, opened in 1823, was operated from Howe's law office. It advertised that students would have access to his "extensive" library. Elizabeth Forgeus, The Northampton Law School, 41 *Law Libr. J.* 11, 11–12 (1948). When Harvard hired Ashmun to the Royall chair in 1829, "the Northampton school came to an end — although it might almost be said to have merged into the Harvard Law School, since a group of the students decided to follow Ashmun to Harvard." Id. at 13.

The method of instruction in Northampton was advertised to be "by means of lectures, recitations, and discussions" of texts. Id. at 12. This recitation method characterized the early university law schools and is discussed in Lecture II, text at notes 8–22. A four-volume set of student notes from the Northampton School, noticed by Forgeus, supra, at 11, survives in the Yale collection. "Manuscript Notes of Lectures by Samuel Howe and John Hooker Ashmun at the Northampton Law School, taken down by Nathaniel J. Lord" (1825–27) (Yale Law Libr. RB shelfmark MssB +L88).

Unlike the early Yale Law School, the early Harvard Law School enjoyed significant financial support from the university. Using the Royall devise, Harvard took the active hand in founding its law school in 1817 under Isaac Parker and Asahel Stearns, and the university provided its law school with rooms and books. But the main instructor, Stearns, received no salary; he pocketed whatever tuition income his efforts could generate. Reed, *Carnegie,* supra note 2, at 138. Reed complained that Harvard thereby "lent the prestige of her name to the doctrine that calling a practitioner a university professor is equivalent to making his proprietary law class a university school . . . ." Id. at 140. Although Stearns was "[t]he working member of the Faculty," he prudently remained in practice and "never relinquished the office of County Attorney . . . ." *The Centennial History of the Harvard Law School: 1817–1917,* at 6–7 (1918). Stearns has surfaced lately in Fisher's study of Massachusetts prosecutorial practice, serving as county prosecutor for Middlesex in the 1820s and early 1830s. See George Fisher, Plea Bargaining's Triumph, 109 *Yale L.J.* 857, 869 n. 19, 877–79 (2000). From 1829, Harvard used the funds contributed by Nathan Dane to provide the salary for Joseph Story. See R. Kent Newmyer, *Supreme Court Justice Joseph Story: Statesman of the Old Republic* 240 (1985).

51. Dwight was already on the staff of Hamilton College as an undergraduate teacher of history, political science, and law. He proposed founding a graduate law school, which began under Hamilton's auspices in 1853. Tuition was $20 per term, of which Dwight kept $15; the classes met at his home. The year before Dwight left for Columbia, his law school had fifteen students. Walter Pilkington, *Hamilton College: 1812–1962,* at 116–17 (1962). The Columbia trustees moved Dwight to Yale by guaranteeing him a $2,000 minimum income in the event his fee income from tuition fell short of that. Julius Goebel Jr. [& Samuel F. Howard], *A History of the School of Law: Columbia University* 29 (1955) (hereafter Goebel & Howard). Dwight's success at Columbia turned his professorship into a gusher. In 1878 Columbia effectively bought in Dwight's proprietorship by giving him "the then tremendous salary of $15,000 a year, twice that of any other Columbia professor." Id. at 83.

Columbia's short-lived effort to launch legal education under Chancellor Kent in the 1820s may have prevented Kent from founding a proprietary law school of his own. Forced to retire from the bench at age sixty, Kent wrote his long-time associate, the New York law reporter William Johnson, that he was considering "opening a Law School in Albany upon the plan of the Litchfield Law School." James Kent to William Johnson, Sept. 27, 1823, Library of Congress, Kent Papers. He changed his mind a few weeks later when the Columbia trustees offered him the professorship in law that he had held there in the 1790s, and which had been dormant in the interval. See Trustees of Columbia College to Kent, Nov. 3, 1823, Kent Papers, Library of Congress, discussed in Langbein, *Kent,* supra note 12, at 564; see also infra, note 109.

52. Fisher, *Catalogue,* supra note 50, at 2.

53. McKenna, *Litchfield,* supra note 27, at 107, n. 1; see also id. at 40.

54. Fisher, *Catalogue,* supra note 50, at 3–4.

55. Discussing "imitators of the Litchfield School," Reed points to "[m]ore than a dozen such competing ventures . . . known to have been started during the life of the Litchfield school, in seven states, ranging from Massachusetts to North Carolina." Reed, *Carnegie,* supra note 2, at 132. Including schools that started after Litchfield's demise,

Reed counts "over twenty such experiments prior to 1850. The actual number was probably much greater." Id.; see also his compilation of these schools, id. at 431–33.

56. Supra note 50.

57. Root later served as Chief Justice of Connecticut from 1796 to 1807. He is now remembered as the compiler of one of the earliest American law reports, Reports of Cases Adjudged in the Superior Court and Supreme Court of Errors . . . 1789 to . . . 1793 (1798). See 16 *Dictionary of American Biography* 148 (D. Malone et al. eds., 1928–37) (hereafter DAB).

58. McKenna, *Litchfield,* supra note 27, at 35.

59. Lynne Templeton Brickley, "Sarah Pierce's Litchfield Female Academy," in *To Ornament Their Minds: Sarah Pierce's Litchfield Female Academy 1792–1833,* at 20 (Catherine Fields & Lisa Knightlinger eds., 1993) (Litchfield Historical Society).

60. Including Ephraim Kirby, who in 1789 would publish the first American law reports, *Reports of Cases Adjudged in the Superior Court of the State of Connecticut, from the Year 1785, to May 1788; with Some Determinations of the Supreme Court of Errors* (Litchfield, 1789). See 10 DAB 424.

61. Reeve had tutored her in her youth. On the courtship, see McKenna, *Litchfield,* supra note 27 at 27–34.

62. Id. at 41–42; Fisher, *Catalogue,* supra note 50, at 28. Reeve had previously tutored Aaron Burr in Burr's youth. McKenna, *Litchfield,* supra note 27, at 26–27.

63. Id., at 22–29.

64. For example, Stephen R. Bradley of the Yale College class of 1775 became one of Vermont's first U.S. senators. Oliver Wolcott Jr. and Uriah Tracy were classmates in the Yale College class of 1778. Tracy served for a decade as U.S. Senator from Connecticut. Wolcott was the son and grandson of Connecticut governors. He later held that job himself, then succeeded Alexander Hamilton as Secretary of the Treasury. See Fisher, *Catalogue,* supra note 50, at 25, 127, 138; McKenna, *Litchfield,* supra note 27, at 55–57.

65. Recent research has shown that similar developments were occurring in London. "[B]y the turn of the century, there were a number of experienced pleaders who took large numbers of pupils." Christopher W. Brooks & Michael Lobban, "Apprenticeship or Academy? The Idea of a Law University, 1830–1860," in Bush & Wijffels, supra note 7, at 353, 356. "The elder Joseph Chitty, for instance, often had more than twenty pupils at one time, whom he provided with lectures, and the students formed their own mooting society to discuss what they learned. Chitty also became one of the most prolific legal writers of his age by converting his lectures into texts for a wider public." Id. at 358. By the 1820s, several law lecturers were offering proprietary courses. Id. at 358 n.23.

66. See McKenna, *Litchfield,* supra note 27, at 177–78 (republishing the rules that Reeve promulgated to govern the circulation of library books).

67. Reeve was a judge of the superior court from 1798 to 1814 and chief justice of the supreme court of errors from 1814 to 1816. For Reeve, see 15 DAB 465; for Gould, see 7 DAB 453, and Fisher, *Catalogue,* supra note 50, at 55.

68. McKenna, *Litchfield,* supra note 27, at 151, counting enrollments of persons catalogued in Fisher, *Catalogue,* supra note 50.

69. Reeve did not keep good records in the early years of the school. Reliable enrollment records begin when Gould joins him in 1798.

70. The number of persons for whom Fisher was able to supply biographical details. Fisher, *Catalogue*, supra note 50. There are some ghosts on Fisher's list, people whom Fisher mistakenly reckoned as Litchfield students in the early years for which Reeve kept no records. One such entry is No. 757, for Seth Staples, founder of the New Haven law school that became Yale. The mistaken attribution is discussed infra, notes 140–41.

71. Brooke Harlow, "Litchfield's Legacy in Law: A Study of the Litchfield Law School's Influence on Legal Training in America: 1784–1833," Appendix 3 (unpaginated) (unpublished student paper) (Apr. 17, 1996) (hereafter Harlow, *Legacy*). Harlow's count is based upon the entries in Fisher, *Catalogue*, supra note 50. McKenna reports totals that are smaller than Harlow's. McKenna, *Litchfield*, supra 27 at 145, apparently taking her numbers from 1 Warren, *Harvard*, supra note 21, at 181–82. Warren's figures came from an earlier catalogue that has been superseded by Fisher's work.

72. Brooke Harlow, "The Litchfield Law School: An Examination of Its Influence and Impact in the South" 3 (Mar. 29, 1996) (unpublished student paper) (hereafter Harlow, *South*), tabulating entries in Fisher, *Catalogue*, supra note 50. What accounted for the disproportionate number of Georgians at Litchfield I cannot say. Regarding cultural and commercial links between Connecticut and Georgia, see O. Burton Adams, Yale Influence on the Formation of the University of Georgia, 51 *Georgia Hist. Q.* 175 (1967); Constance Green, *Eli Whitney and the Birth of American Technology*, 40–96 (Whitney's cotton gin, manufactured in New Haven, was developed for the Georgia market, but led to hostility over his patent). (I owe these references to Joyce Chaplin.)

73. Until 1833, when both schools closed.

74. See the valuable modern account by Brickley, supra note 59. See also Emily Noyes Vanderpoel, *Chronicles of a Pioneer School from 1792 to 1833: Being the History of Miss Sarah Pierce and Her School* (1903).

75. In research that continues, Brickley has been able to document eighty-four marriages between law students and women attending the female academy. See Litchfield Female Academy Collection, Brickley Research File, LHS Archives. Regarding the patterns of courtship in Litchfield, see E. D. Mansfield, *Personal Memories: 1803–1843*, at 128–30 (Cincinnati, 1879).

76. Andrew M. Siegel, "To Learn and Make Respectable Hereafter": The Litchfield Law School in Cultural Context, 73 *N.Y.U. L. Rev.* 1978, 2011 (1998).

77. Anon., reprinted in Dwight C. Kilbourn, *The Bench and Bar of Litchfield County, Connecticut: 1709–1909*, at 188, 189 (1909). (The Mrs. Reeve being quoted was Tapping Reeve's second wife and former housekeeper, whom he married in 1798, a year after the death of his first wife, Sally Burr Reeve, who has been mentioned above in text. See McKenna, *Litchfield*, supra note 27 at 87, 92.

78. Lemmings, supra note 16, at 93–95 & table 4.2a.

79. McKenna supplies a count of Litchfield students by undergraduate college attended. McKenna, *Litchfield*, supra note 27, at 146. Harlow reports larger numbers, tabulated from Fisher, *Catalogue*, supra note 50. Harlow, *Legacy*, supra note 71, Appendix 3 (unpaginated). Fisher was able to locate biographical information on 908 of the known 1,016 Litchfield students. Harlow reports that 588 of these 908, or nearly two thirds, are shown as having attended college.

80. Harlow reports that 225 students, or 25 percent of the 908 for whom Fisher was

able to compile biographical accounts, attended Yale College. Harlow, *Legacy*, supra note 71, Appendix. McKenna counted 185, or 20 percent. McKenna, *Litchfield*, supra note 27, at 146.

81. Harlow counts fifty-seven from Princeton, forty-two each from Harvard and nearby Union, thirty-four each from Brown and Columbia, twenty-eight from Williams, and twenty-six from Dartmouth. Harlow, *Legacy,* supra note 71, Appendix. Harlow also noticed, in an earlier draft, that the Princeton enrollment correlated with the high enrollment from the South; twenty-five of the fifty-seven Princeton graduates who attended Litchfield came from southern states. Harlow, *South*, supra note 72, at 4.

82. There was also interest in the early national period in teaching law, mostly public and constitutional law, to undergraduates within the liberal arts curriculum. See Paul D. Carrington, The Revolutionary Idea of University Legal Education, 31 *William & Mary L. Rev.* 527 (1990); 1 Warren, *Harvard*, supra note 21, at 165–80. A trickle of efforts at programs of this sort continue to the present, but in general, the rise of the university law schools as separate professional schools and the shaping of the discipline of political science as a field centered on public law has largely excluded the study of private law and procedure from American undergraduate curricula.

83. In contrast to Sarah Pierce's female academy, which provided diplomas for its young women. One is reproduced in Vanderpoel, supra note 74, opposite 310.

84. E.g., "Mr. Henry Starr has read law in my office and constantly attended the lectures there delivered from the 24th day of October 1809 to the 10th day of August, 1810." Quoted by McKenna, *Litchfield*, supra note 27, at 59–60, further discussed, id. at 141.

85. Discussed in Reed, *Carnegie*, supra note 2, at 79–84.

86. Toward the end of its existence, the Litchfield Law School was conducting weekly learning exercises that were called examinations, but which were not tests in the modern sense. These sessions were described in an alumni publication in 1828:

> The examinations, which are held every Saturday, upon the lectures of the preceding week, consist of a thorough investigation of the principles of each rule, and not merely of such questions as can be answered from memory without any exercise of . . . judgment. These examinations are held by Jabez W. Huntington, Esq., a distinguished gentleman of the bar, whose practice enables him to introduce frequent and familiar illustrations, which excite an interest, and serve to impress more strongly upon the mind the knowledge acquired during the week.

"Advertisement to First Edition 1828," reprinted in Kilbourn, supra note 77, at 193, 194. We see in this practice some concession toward the recitation method of instruction then being practiced by Litchfield's competitors at Harvard and Yale, but the technique was so foreign to Gould that he delegated the work to a local practitioner.

87. Quoted in William P. LaPiana, *Logic and Experience: The Origin of Modern American Legal Education* 51 (1994).

88. Id. at 14, 57.

89. For a published list of Litchfield notebooks, see McKenna, *Litchfield*, supra note 27, at 183–86. Lynne Templeton Brickley has compiled a larger list, now containing 108 entries, for the Litchfield Historical Society (hereafter LHS). "Litchfield Law School

Student Law Notebooks," (Dec. 2001) Tapping Reeve Collection, Brickley Research File, LHS Archives.

90. Thayer remarked, following one of Blackstone's American editors, that as late as 1817 in a set of Litchfield lecture notes from that year, " 'references to Blackstone not only outnumber those of any other book, but may be said to outnumber all the rest together.'" James Bradley Thayer, The Teaching of English Law at Universities, 9 *Harvard L. Rev.* 169, 171 (1895), quoting (not entirely accurately) the preface to 1 William Blackstone, *Commentaries on the Laws of England* x. n. (William Hammond ed., San Francisco, 1890).

91. Bryson emphasizes that in Virginia, both George Wythe and St. George Tucker based their lectures on Blackstone. W. Hamilton Bryson, *Essays on Legal Education in Nineteenth-Century Virginia* 14–15 (1998).

92. Zephaniah Swift, *A System of the Laws of the State of Connecticut* (Windham, 1795–96). (Swift is reported to have operated a competing law school in Windham. Reed, *Carnegie*, supra note 2, at 431.)

93. James Gould, Law School at Litchfield, *United States L.J.* 400, 403 (1822–23) (letter report from Gould). In the afternoon the students consulted books from the school's library in order to read from "digests, abridgments, or treatises, on the title of which [the day's] lecture treats . . . ." Id.

94. Judges and professional books speak "not as school-masters to *novices,* but as instructors to the *profession.*" Id. at 402 (emphasis original).

95. Gould's plan of instruction, as he called it, echoed Blackstone in its aspiration to teach the common law "not as a collection of insulated [sic; isolated?] positive rules," but rather "as a *system of connected, rational principles* . . . ." Id. (emphasis original).

96. I discuss the text-and-recitation system in Lecture II, text at notes 8–22.

97. Describing his course in 1822, Gould spoke of his lifelong effort to update his "original digest" with new decisions. "From these notes" he delivered his Litchfield Law School lectures. Gould, supra note 93, at 401.

98. The practice is described in the so-called "Advertisement to First Edition 1828," of the Litchfield alumni catalogue, reproduced in Kilbourn, supra note 77, at 193, 194. A student's memoir:

> We had desks, with pen and ink, to record the important principles and authorities. The practice of Judge Gould was to read the principle from his own manuscript twice distinctly, pausing between, and repeating in the same manner the leading cases. Then we had time to note down the principle and cases. The remarks and illustrations we did not note. After the lecture we had access to a law library to consult authorities. . . . I . . . immediately returned home, and copied out into [my] lecture [book] all the principles and cases.

E. D. Mansfield, supra note 75, at 127–28.

99. Gould, supra note 93, at 402.

100. "Advertisement," discussed supra note 98, reprinted in Kilbourn, supra note 77, at 193, 194.

101. Id.

102. Gould, supra note 93, at 404. He explained that "there is kept up, in my lecture-

room, a *Moot-Court*, in which [the students], once in each week, argue before me, questions of law, on a case given out by myself, for the purpose. . . . [T]wo students [are] heard as counsel, on each side." Id. (emphasis original). Two volumes of manuscript notebooks containing arguments used in the years 1796–98 survive in the Litchfield Historical Society. See Tapping Reeve Collection, Research Box 1, LHS Archives. These sources have been examined in Donald F. Melhorn Jr., A Moot Court Exercise: Debating Judicial Review Prior to *Marbury v. Madison*, 12 *Constitutional Commentary* 327, 331 n.25 (1995).

103. Describing the Yale curriculum in 1831, Daggett replied to an inquiry from a prospective student that "we have no regular terms. . . . We receive students for 6 months or more. . . . [M]y course occupies about 14 or 15 Months." Daggett, Letter, supra note 40, at 1–2. At Harvard Law School, "[b]efore 1836, students came and went as they saw fit, exactly as they might have done in a lawyer's office. There was no regular time of entering or leaving." Roscoe Pound, "The Law School: 1877–1929," in *The Development of Harvard University Since the Inauguration of President Eliot: 1869–1929*, 472, at 490 (S. E. Morison ed., 1930).

104. LaPiana, supra note 87, at 14–15; Anthony Chase, The Birth of the Modern Law School, 23 *American J. Legal History* 329, 332 (1979).

105. See Charles C. Goetsch, "The Litchfield Law School: A Modern View" (unpublished paper presented to the annual meeting of the American Society for Legal History, fall 1979, copy on file with Litchfield Historical Society). Goetsch recently deposited his collection of photocopies of Litchfield notebooks with the library of the University of Connecticut Law School; see his account in *U. Connecticut Law School Report* (Win. 2002), at 27.

106. Speaking in 1821, Story already counted above 150 volumes of American law reports and was beginning to worry about the new "danger . . . that we shall be overwhelmed with their number and variety." Joseph Story, An Address Delivered before the Members of the Suffolk Bar, at Their Anniversary, on the 4th of September 1821, at 13 (Boston 1829) (Yale Law Libr. RB shelfmark TSt765ad 1829).

107. One set of Litchfield notes has been transcribed by Tracy Thompson (YLS '97) and deposited in the Yale Law Library rare book room. The manuscript, comprising seven bound volumes, is in the hand of Aaron Burr Reeve, the son of Tapping Reeve, and dates from 1802–1803 (Yale Law Libr. RB shelfmark MssB L71 1802).

108. Of course, constitutional questions arose in other settings. It is reported that Reeve commented on the power of judicial review of Acts of Congress in the context of lecturing on the construction of statutes. Melhorn, supra note 102, at 334–35 (drawing upon the student notes of Asa Bacon, 1794, now held in the Litchfield Historical Society).

109. James Kent, *Commentaries on American Law* (4 vols.) (New York 1826–30). The work was based upon a set of lectures that Kent presented at Columbia in the 1820s after retiring from the New York chancery bench. The circumstances are discussed in Langbein, *Kent*, supra note 12, at 564–66.

110. Indeed, Kent's chapters on American constitutional law were packaged as a one-volume work in North America, and were translated for German, Argentinean, and Mexican editions, cited id. at 585 nn. 179–81.

111. See 1 James Oldham, *The Mansfield Manuscripts and the Growth of English Law*

in the Eighteenth Century 223–44 (contract and quasi-contract), 450–78 (insurance) (1992) (2 vols.).

112. Id. at 223.

113. For a topical schedule of the curriculum, constructed from Litchfield notes of the period 1794–1829, see Samuel H. Fisher, *The Litchfield Law School, 1775–1833*, 6–8 (1933) (Tercentenary Commission of the State of Connecticut).

114. Gould, supra note 93, at 402.

115. McKenna, *Litchfield*, supra note 27, at 151.

116. 1 Warren, *Harvard*, supra note 21, at 182.

117. From as high as forty-four in 1823 to the teens in 1827 and low teens in the 1830s. In 1833 there were only six students. See the table in McKenna, *Litchfield*, supra note 27, at 151. (McKenna's student counts are not wholly reliable — see supra note 71 — but they are accurate enough to show the trend.)

118. It appears that the nascent Yale Law School was also competing for students who had merely intended to use New Haven as a transit center en route to Litchfield. According to Gould, more than three quarters of Litchfield-bound students made the trip via New Haven (mostly, one would assume, on account of the port of New Haven). Gould to Roger S. Baldwin, Nov. 15, 1828, Sterling M&A, Baldwin Family Papers, group 55, box 17, folder 195, at 1. According to Gould, these students were being subjected to "a *systematic* influence, exerted in New Haven . . . to induce them to remain at New Haven." Id. (emphasis original), which Gould viewed as "*war in disguise.*" Id. at 2 (emphasis original). Among the misrepresentations about which Gould complained was the report that he was ceasing to lecture. Id. at 3. Gould said had "no suspicions that the *teacher* of the New Haven School [presumably Samuel Hitchcock] has any concern in these measures," but he asked Baldwin to use his influence to stop this "*officious, systematic, undiscriminating* scheme of promoting one establishment, at the expense of others . . . ." Id. at 3 (emphasis original).

119. McKenna voices a somewhat contrary and in my view wishful account that all Litchfield needed to keep on going was a few good men. "If Litchfield had had dynamic young law teachers vigorously carrying on its course of study, it could have gone on indefinitely doing the work it had been doing," McKenna, *Litchfield*, supra note 27, at 174, but this begs the question of why there were none. McKenna does concede that "no unendowed private school could for long have maintained competition with schools supported by a permanent endowment, and forming part of an established university."

120. Id. at 160–65.

121. I discuss these events in Lecture II, text at notes 23–63.

122. Noted in Reed, *Carnegie*, supra note 2, at 131, who faults Litchfield for remaining in the lecture mode when the textbook was making the lectures obsolete. Simeon Baldwin was also alluding to that factor when he suggested that the appearance of published works such as Swift, supra note 92, and Kent's *Commentaries*, supra note 109, undercut the Litchfield model. See McKenna, *Litchfield*, at 174–75 & n. 91, citing Baldwin.

123. For a description of the Yale Law School curriculum as of 1826, see infra note 155.

124. Regarding text-and-recitation instruction at early Harvard, see Lecture II, text at note 11.

125. Id., text at notes 8–22.

126. See Hicks III:32, 2001 ed. at 148, quoting the Yale Law School catalogue for 1887–88: "The method of instruction . . . is mainly that of recitations [from] . . . standard text-books . . . ." *Yale Law School: 1887–88 Annual Calendar and Alumni Record* 7 (1887). Hicks quotes this passage, Hicks III:33, 2001 ed. at 149.

127. Hicks III:32, 2001 ed. at 148.

128. See Stevens, *Law School*, supra note 2, at 70.

129. Reed noticed how the resistance of Reeve and Gould to publishing their lectures contrasted with Kent and Story, who, by turning theirs into texts, facilitated the shift to the textbook-based system of instruction that characterized the early university law schools. Reed, *Carnegie*, supra note 2, at 131. Both Reeve and Gould did, however, publish specialized legal monographs that trace back to their lectures. Reeve wrote the first American treatise on domestic relations law. See Tapping Reeve, *The Law of Baron and Feme, of Parent and Child, of Guardian and Ward, of Master and Servant, and of the Powers of Courts [of] Chancery: with an Essay on the Terms, Heir, Heirs, and Heirs of the Body* (New Haven, 1816) (Yale Law Libr. RB shelfmark T R2598 1816). The work went through several editions in the hands of later editors. The third edition (Amasa J. Parker & Charles E. Baldwin eds., Albany, 1862) has been twice reprinted (in 1970 and 1998), reflecting the surge of interest in gender issues. The book collects authority from many states and was preoccupied with "the need to Americanize the English common law . . . ." Michael Grossberg, *Governing the Hearth: Law and the Family in Nineteenth-Century America* 21 (1985). Reeve also published a book on American intestacy law. Tapping Reeve, *A Treatise on the Law of Descents in the Several United States of America* (New York, 1825). Gould wrote a book on civil pleading that went through a dozen editions, the last in 1899. The first edition was *A Treatise on the Principles of Pleading in Civil Actions* (Boston, 1832). A photographic reprint was published in 2002.

130. 1 Warren, *Harvard*, supra note 21, at 304–7.

131. On the decisive role of Dane's contributions to the refounding of the school under Story, see Newmyer, supra note 50, at 240–41, 252–53. On the efforts of Story and the Harvard overseers to solicit books for the law library, see id. at 251–52.

132. See Lecture II, text at notes 26–35, 72–89.

133. Id., text at notes 92–115.

134. Franklin B. Dexter, *Biographical Notes of Graduates of Yale College* 310–11 (1885–1912) (6 vols.) (hereafter Dexter, *Yale Biographies*); Hicks I:4–5.

135. Hicks I:4.

136. Minus whatever he sold to Hitchcock when he disengaged from New Haven, Staples' collection as catalogued for auction by his estate in 1862 totaled 490 titles, embracing more than 1,000 volumes. See *Catalogue of the Private Law Library of the Late Seth P. Staples, Esq.* (Bangs, Merwin & Co., New York,1862) (Yale Law Libr. RB shelfmark BiblB B22).

137. "List of Students Who Have Entered the Office" (1819–24) (Yale Law Libr. RB shelfmark YL 14 1824) (photocopy of extract from Staples and Hitchcock law office cash and receipt book, 1817–27). This source is reprinted without attribution in Hicks I:12–14.

138. Simeon E. Baldwin, "Law School of Yale College," extract from the *Year Book of the City of New Haven for 1872–73*, at 3 (Yale Law Libr. RB shelfmark YL 111 1873). Hicks reports a slightly different version of this legend, Hicks I:9.

139. Tracy Thompson (YLS '97) has drawn attention to a cache of correspondence from Staples to his Yale College classmate, Thomas Day, beginning in 1797 and running, with gaps, to 1839. Six letters from the years 1797–98, all written from New Haven, allow Thompson to conclude that Staples "remained in New Haven almost constantly during the period in which he is reported to have studied with Reeve." Tracy L. Thompson, "The Correspondence of Seth P. Staples to Thomas Day" 4 (unpublished paper, 1996) (Yale Law Libr. RB classmark YL 31 St2 no.3). Thompson transcribes the Staples/Day correspondence, id. at 9–37, from the manuscript originals in Sterling M&A, Day Family Papers, MS 175, boxes 1, 4, 6, 10.

140. "Manuscript Notes of Lectures by Tapping Reeve at the Litchfield Law School" (Yale Law Libr. RB Room shelfmark MssB +L71 1798). Staples' source for this copy may have been the notes of Thomas Day, Staples' college classmate, who attended Litchfield during the 1797–98 year, and with whom Staples was in close contact, see supra note 139. Since Day's notebooks are not known to have survived, the comparison cannot be made. Day became the Connecticut law reporter; see his *Reports of Cases Argued and Determined in the Supreme Court of Errors of the State of Connecticut* (1814–43) (14 vols.). Day also produced digests to the Connecticut reports, noted in 2 Morris L. Cohen, *Bibliography of Early American Law*, entries 5475–77 (1998).

141. E.g., McKenna, *Litchfield*, supra note 27, at 168; Hicks II:3, 2001 ed. at 53 (but see id. at 5, 2001 ed. at 55, noting the possibility that Staples could have copied a notebook rather than attend the course, because Staples' notebook is not a complete Litchfield course and because it includes Staples' notes on other reading).

142. A manuscript account book from the firm of Staples and Hitchcock for the years 1811–34, hinting at some of the work of the firm, survives (Yale Law Libr. RB shelfmark MssB St27).

143. Dexter, *Yale Biographies*, supra note 134, at 257–59; Hicks I:15–16.

144. Hicks refers to Staples' involvement but misrenders Goodyear as Goodrich. Hicks I:18. On Goodyear see 7 DAB 413–15; see generally Richard Korman, *The Goodyear Story: An Inventor's Obsession and the Struggle for a Rubber Monopoly* (2002); on Goodyear's patent and the patent litigation see id. at 82–144 (discussing only the appearance of Daniel Webster, not Staples, on behalf of Goodyear). For accounts of the litigation mentioning Staples, see P. W. Barker, *Charles Goodyear: Connecticut Yankee and Rubber Pioneer—A Biography* 19 (1940); Ralph F. Wolf, *India Rubber Man: The Story of Charles Goodyear* 172 (1939).

145. Staples was counsel in *habeas corpus* proceedings. See *The African Captives: Trial of the Prisoners of the Amistad on the Writ of Habeas Corpus, before the Circuit Court of the United States for the District of Connecticut, at Hartford* (New York 1839) (Yale Law Libr. RB shelfmark Trials B Am57). Staples moved for the writ of *habeas corpus* on September 18, 1839. Id. at 1, 20–29, 34–37, 38. Staples' role is discussed in Howard Jones, *Mutiny on the Amistad: The Saga of a Slave Revolt and Its Impact on American Abolition, Law, and Diplomacy* 71–76 (1987); Christopher Martin, *The Amistad Affair* 105–6 (1970).

146. *U.S. v. Libellants and Claimants of the Schooner Amistad*, 40 U.S. 518 (1841).

147. Hicks I:17. Until 1842, the mayor sat ex officio as a judge of the city court. See Rollin G. Osterweis, *Three Centuries of New Haven* 165 (1953); Charles H. Levermore, *The Republic of New Haven: A History of Municipal Evolution* 165 (1886).

148. DAB 26–27, Hicks I:36.

149. Daggett's political writings are the subject of Michael T. Sansbury, The Political Pedagogy of David Daggett (1999) (unpublished paper, Yale Law Libr. RB shelfmark YL 19 H629 no. 5).

150. President Ezra Stiles of Yale was planning for this professorship in 1777. See 1 Warren, *Harvard,* supra note 21, at 165–69.

151. The event, and its entanglement in national politics, are discussed in Carl R. Fish, *The Civil Service and the Patronage* 32–58 (1905), cited by Carrington, supra note 82, at 543, n. 110.

152. Kelley, supra note 5, at 131.

153. Hicks I:40–42; on the Centum Millia Fund, see Peter Dobkin Hall, *The Organization of American Culture, 1700–1900,* at 163–72 (1982); Kelley, supra note 5, at 152–54.

154. See Frederick C. Hicks, *William Howard Taft: Yale Professor of Law and New Haven Citizen* 29 (1945).

155. I reproduce the description in full. Notice that the first paragraph refers to Daggett (but not Hitchcock) as "Professor of Law," hence invoking his College title.

> The Law School is under the instruction of the Hon. David Daggett, a Judge of the Supreme Court in Connecticut, and Professor of Law, and Samuel J. Hitchcock, Esq., attorney and counsellor at law.
>
> The students are required to peruse the most important elementary treatises, and are daily examined on the author they are reading, and receive at the same time explanations and illustrations of the subject they are studying.
>
> A course of lectures is delivered by the Professor of Law, on all the titles and subjects of the Common and Statute Law.
>
> A moot court is holden once a week, or oftener, which employs the students in drawing pleadings and investigating and arguing questions of law.
>
> The students are also called upon, from time to time, to draw declarations, pleadings, contracts, and other instruments, connected with the practice of law, and to do the most important duties of an attorney's clerk.
>
> They are occasionally required to write disquisitions on some topic of law, and collect the authorities to support their opinions.
>
> The students are furnished with the use of the elementary books, and have access, at all times, to the college libraries, and to a law library, comprising very important works both ancient and modern.
>
> The terms for tuition and use of library are $75 per annum. The course of study occupies two years, allowing eight weeks vacation each year. Students are however received for a shorter period.
>
> The Professor of Law will also, for the present, occasionally deliver lectures to the Senior class in College, until arrangements are made for a systematic course to be permanently continued.

Catalogue of the Officers and Students in Yale College 28–29 (Nov. 1826).

156. Kelley, supra note 5, 144–46.

157. Catalogue, supra note 155, at 28–29.

158. Kelley, supra note 5, at 131–32; Gerard N. Burrow, *A History of Yale's School of Medicine: Passing Torches to Others* 18ff (2002).

159. Hicks I:24.

160. This step was taken at Hitchcock's urging. Writing in 1842, he told the Yale authorities that Yale was losing students to Harvard because Harvard awarded degrees to its graduates and Yale did not. Hitchcock to President and Fellows of Yale College, Aug. 6, 1842, reproduced in Hicks I:24–25.

161. Yale Law School held a fiftieth anniversary celebration in 1874, with Chief Justice Waite and other dignitaries in attendance. See Hicks III:16–17, 2001 ed. at 132–33. Later in the century, the School's annual catalogue repeated this claim in its title, e.g., *Yale Law School: Sixty-Fourth Year 1887–88 — Annual Calendar and Alumni Record 1824–1886* (New Haven, 1887). The claim continues to be made, e.g., *Yale Law School 2002–2003*, at 20 (Bulletin of Yale University, series 98, No. 8, Aug. 10, 2002); Kelley, supra note 5, at 164n.

162. Catalogue of the Officers and Students in Yale College 5 (Nov. 1824).

163. Id.

164. Michael T. Sansbury (YLS 2001), "When Was Yale Law School *Really* Founded?" 5–8 (unpublished paper, May 17, 2001) (Yale Law Libr. RB classmark YL H629 no.7).

165. Supra note 162.

166. Hicks at I:14–15.

167. 1 Warren, *Harvard*, supra note 21, at 292–307. Stearns was also a part-time teacher; regarding his other employment, see supra note 50.

168. Because of his judicial duties in Washington and on circuit, Story insisted on having a colleague in residence to perform "the *drill* duty" and to look after the students. Newmyer, supra note 50, at 241, quoting correspondence from Story dated 1828 or 1829.

169. See supra, text at note 50.

170. Emphasized in Carrington, supra note 82.

171. Supra note 150.

172. I have discussed the circumstances and content of Kent's first lectures in Langbein, *Kent*, supra note 12, at 558–60. On Wilson's lectures at what became the University of Pennsylvania, see Carrington, supra note 82, at 546–50. Wilson's text has been published: *The Works of James Wilson* (R. McCloskey ed., 1967) (2 vols.).

173. Yale College (then the largest in the nation) had a student body of about 275 in 1817. Kelley, supra note 5, at 142. The finances were tuition-driven. The endowment as of 1817 (excluding land) stood at $54,440. Tuition was $33 per year. Id. at 143–44. Investment losses in the collapse of a bank in 1825 cost the College $21,000 of its endowment. Id. at 150. Between 1701 and 1830, Yale received a total of about $145,000 in gifts and grants. Id. at 151.

174. Hicks III:3, 2001 ed. at 119, discussed in Lecture II, text at note 60.

Law School in a University: Yale's Distinctive Path in the Later Nineteenth Century

JOHN H. LANGBEIN

In my previous lecture in this series,[1] I described the founding of the Yale Law School and undertook to place it in a broader setting as one of the earliest chapters in the history of university legal education in the Anglo-American world. I broke off in the 1840s with the Yale Law School as a proprietary venture operated from a "dingy" rented room over a downtown storefront.[2] Hitchcock and Daggett, the nominal professors, were practicing lawyers and part-time public officials, whose law school was a sideline. This enterprise became linked to Yale through Daggett's joint appointment as Kent Professor of Law in the College, which took effect in 1826. Not until 1843 did the University begin to bestow Yale degrees on the School's graduates. (When speaking of Yale as the University, I am taking a slight liberty. Yale University was known as Yale College until 1887,[3] even though, rather like today's Dartmouth, it was in function a university with several graduate schools.)

In this lecture I discuss the history of the Yale Law School across the middle decades of the nineteenth century. I first explore the text-and-recitation system, which was the School's main method of instruction. I then focus on the two episodes of near collapse in 1845 and again in 1869, when Yale considered washing its hands of this seedy little trade school, which the University had effectively franchised to operate under the Yale name. I conclude with a look at the years immediately following the 1869 rescue, when a remarkable change in the University's attitude toward the Law School took place. Yale ceased distancing itself from the School and began instead to bolster it, encouraging the Law School to develop an ethos that it has manifested ever since. I shall sketch what we know about how the Yale Law School came to develop its distinctive emphasis on the relationships between law and other disciplines and its special receptiveness to the study of public and international law, at a time when such tendencies were not in favor at other law schools.

Robert Stevens, in his opening lecture in this series, gave some reasons for thinking that the eminence of today's Yale Law School is quite recent.[4] Robert said that the place got really good just about when he and his cohort arrived, that is, in the later 1950s. Robert is surely correct to point to the renewal and enhancement of the faculty that occurred during the Rostow deanship (1955– 65) as the font of today's Yale Law School, but Rostow inherited a distinctive culture that had its origins in the second half of the nineteenth century, in the developments that I discuss in this lecture.

Both the near collapse of the School in 1845 and 1869 and the change in ethos in the 1870s are topics first identified in the work of Frederick Hicks, the Yale Law Librarian who in the mid-1930s undertook the first serious work on the history of the Yale Law School.[5] My account relies on Hicks for the main events, but there are significant differences of interpretation. Hicks wrote in a celebratory tone, long common to histories of law schools,[6] whose authors did not much tarry with any shortcomings of the institutions they came to praise. Hicks also had scant interest in the comparative dimension and the competitive pressures arising from events at Columbia and Harvard, a subject that I emphasize in this lecture. Because Hicks did not footnote or otherwise disclose most of his sources,[7] I have tried when citing Hicks to locate his actual or probable sources, but that has not always been possible.

I. The Text-and-Recitation Method

I resume with the Yale Law School in the hands of Hitchcock and Daggett, who ran it from 1826 into the 1840s.

How did two busy New Haven practicing lawyers, who were also part-time judges and civic officers, have time to do all the teaching at the Yale Law School, a law school successful enough to have driven Litchfield out of business in the 1830s?[8] The Litchfield proprietors lectured from their own knowledge, covering the entirety of private law. They constantly updated their lectures to keep abreast of developments in the American states and in England. By the 1820s, as the stream of law reports and treatise literature became a torrent, this work of updating became a considerable task. How could the part-timers in New Haven compete? The answer is that the Yale Law School from its earliest days[9] pursued a method of instruction quite different from the lecture-based pedagogy of Litchfield. This so-called text-and-recitation method also prevailed at Theodore Dwight's Columbia,[10] and at Harvard[11] until Langdell's reforms in the 1870s and 1880s. Yale emphasized text-and-recitation instruction ("the Yale System"[12]) into the early years of the twentieth century, before belatedly adhering to the case method pioneered under Langdell at Harvard. The Yale Law School catalogue for 1887–88 explains that the "method of instruction . . . is mainly that of recitations. It is the conviction of the Faculty of this Department, as well as the tradition of the University, that definite and permanent impressions concerning the principles and rules of any abstract science are best acquired by the study of standard text-books in private, followed by the examinations and explanations of the recitation room."[13]

A law school that operated under the text-and-recitation system would buy multiple copies of selected practitioner treatises, which would be lent to the students as assigned.[14] The instructor would assign particular chapters of a treatise to be read in advance for each class meeting. In the classroom students were called on to recite what they had learned and to answer questions about it. For a part-time faculty, the text-and-recitation system had a particular advantage over Litchfield-style lecturing: It effectively transferred the responsibility for coverage from the instructor to the treatise writer. The instructor simply assigned the stuff and then paced the students in recitation sessions, but he did not have to be a master of what he taught.[15] The text-and-recitation method did not wholly displace the older style of lecture — both Hitchcock and Daggett also did some lecturing,[16] as did the instructors at Harvard and Columbia[17] — but most of what passed for legal education at Yale throughout the nineteenth century was having students read and then recite from treatises. Among the works assigned for study in this way at Yale were Blackstone, Chitty's treatises on contract and on pleading, Cruise on real property, and Starkie on evidence.[18]

We see in the spread of the text-and-recitation method an instance of a deep and recurrent theme in the history of legal education, the connection between developments in legal literature and in legal education. The learning exercises of the inns of court at the end of the Middle Ages had been intimately linked to two forms of legal literature that were pioneered in that era, the yearbook reports of pleading practice in the courts, and the learned lectures called readings.[19] Litchfield, as I have explained, was made possible by Blackstone's *Commentaries,* which was itself a late manifestation of the European-wide phenomenon called institutionalist legal literature.[20] The text-and-recitation system was a curricular adaptation to the rise of the legal treatise. The university law schools of the early nineteenth century rooted themselves in treatise-based instruction. The nineteenth century began the golden age of the legal treatise, both in England and in the United States.[21] Although written for practicing lawyers, treatises lent themselves easily to being used in the text-and-recitation teaching format.

The new university law schools did not invent the text-and-recitation format — far from it. This technique had long been the standard mode of instruction in the undergraduate colleges[22] for subjects of all sorts — logic, metaphysics, geography, theology, natural science. The law schools seized upon the similarity between legal treatises and traditional college textbooks, in order to imitate the technique of teaching that had long typified the college classroom. In this curious way, the advent of the practitioner treatise facilitated the development of university legal education.

II. Rescuing the Law School in 1845 and 1869

The Yale Law School faced its first succession crisis in the summer of 1845, when Hitchcock died. Daggett was in his eighties and in no condition to carry on. Three prominent New Haven lawyers were found to do the teaching, including William Storrs,[23] in whose memory the Storrs Lectureship[24] was established decades later. This Storrs group carried the School for two years, until Yale could arrange for a new faculty. The Storrs team had such extensive outside commitments that its members were unable to cover many of the scheduled classes, which inspired the students to petition for a 50 percent tuition rebate. The Storrs group thought that this was a bit cheeky but reluctantly agreed to rebate one-third of a term's tuition[25] (leaving an interesting precedent of tuition refunds for deficient professorial performance).

A. RANSOMING THE YALE LAW LIBRARY

Soon after Hitchcock's death there turned up on Yale's doorstep none other than the executor[26] of Hitchcock's estate, with a message for Yale. He planned to auction off the Yale Law Library, since all the books belonged to Hitchcock. However, he was willing to sell the entire collection to Yale for $4,200, which was something of a discount to appraised value.[27] Yale showed no initial disposition to leap at this offer, signaling that Yale was willing to let this floundering proprietary law school be buried with its main proprietor.

The impetus to rescue the School came not from Yale, but from leaders of the New Haven bar. Their intervention had little to do with the advancement of legal education. They were concerned about losing the library, to which

Hitchcock had allowed them access. In 1845 two of their leaders, Storrs and Isaac Townsend, another member of the Storrs team of temporary faculty, petitioned the Yale authorities to save the library.[28] They argued that "the Study of Law is one of the proper branches of a University education,"[29] and that the most important prerequisite for a law school was "a good Law Library."[30] Law professors, by contrast, were a dime a dozen. "The College, if it owns a [law] Library, can always immediately and properly supply Instructors for any vacancies . . . ."[31] The leaders of the New Haven bar were quite correct about law professors being low-priority items. On account of the text-and-recitation system of instruction, virtually any practicing lawyer with a little time on his hands was a potential law professor. As Simeon E. Baldwin later said when he was suddenly called in to do the teaching during Yale's second succession crisis in 1869, "it is always easier to ask questions than to answer them . . . ."[32]

The New Haven lawyers of 1845 offered Yale a deal. They would raise part of the money that was needed to buy Hitchcock's library, in return for being allowed to continue using it. This was agreed, and almost half the $4,200 purchase price was raised in contributions from the bar.[33] Yale supplied the balance, and for years thereafter Yale carried its share of the outlay as a loan charged at interest to the Law School.[34] Yale now owned the Yale Law Library.[35]

In my earlier lecture, I spoke of the weaknesses of the Litchfield Law School. I emphasized that a university has certain comparative advantages over an unaided proprietorship such as that of Reeve or Gould at Litchfield. Yale's handling of the events following Hitchcock's death exemplifies two of those advantages, the ability to generate philanthropic support and the ability to manage succession problems.

Having bought itself a law library, Yale next needed a law professor or two. Theodore D. Woolsey, Yale's newly installed president, conducted the search. His attention focused for a time on a New York judge, but the offer was not extended. As one of Woolsey's advisors lamented, the Law School's finances were too meager to pay the person a serious salary. What Yale could offer, the advisor told Woolsey, "would exclude any but worn out or very young men."[36] We have in these deliberations a reminder that the Yale Law School had as yet no endowment. When the Corporation authorized the perpetuation of the Law School in 1846, it carefully quarantined Yale's finances from being used to support the Law School. The Corporation resolved that the compensation of the professors must be "derived exclusively from the proceeds of tuition fees paid by students under their instruction."[37] Yale saw no reason to subsidize this local trade school, and in any event Yale lacked the means to do very much for it. Yale was tuition-driven in these days. The entire Yale endowment at mid-century was only about $220,000.[38] Staffing the Law School with professors whose main income stream came from their earnings at the bar allowed the School to get a faculty on the cheap, but effectively limited the choice to practitioners from the area.

In 1847 Yale struck a deal with a prominent Norwalk lawyer, Clark Bissell, to take over the School. Bissell moved to New Haven, became professor in the Law School, and the next year, on Daggett's death, succeeded him as Kent professor in the College.[39] Bissell was a Yale College alumnus, a former state legislator, and a former judge of the superior court and the state Supreme Court. Not only was Bissell active at the bar, he was just then in the process of being elected governor of Connecticut. He took up both jobs in 1847, serving as governor until 1849 and as professor until 1855.[40]

To support Bissell, Yale hired in the same year, 1847, a second professor, Henry Dutton. Dutton relocated his law practice from Bridgeport to New Haven and thereafter served successively as a state legislator, county court judge, governor of Connecticut, and Connecticut Supreme Court justice.[41] From 1855 until his death in 1869, Dutton was the Kent Professor in the College[42] and the principal instructor in the Law School. He had the help of an associate, Thomas Osborne, a former congressman, for the decade from 1855 to 1865, but after 1865 Dutton was the only regular instructor. Reflecting on Dutton's last years, President Woolsey later observed that Dutton was "often called away by his private or professional business [and] was not able to give the due degree of attention to his professorial charge. The school, therefore, . . . greatly declined until there appeared a meager list of sixteen or seventeen students on the catalogues of 1867 and 1868, of whom a considerable part could scarcely be called students."[43]

B. THE SECOND BRUSH WITH EXTINCTION

At Dutton's death in 1869 the Corporation again brooded on whether this frail and undistinguished law school should be closed down.[44] Look at what they saw in the summer of 1869—a law school with no faculty, no endowment, and hardly any students. The law library had made no acquisitions since 1852, other than maintaining current sets of the Connecticut and United States reports.[45] The student body had deteriorated in quality as well as size; whereas in the 1820s, the students had all been college graduates, by the 1860s few were.[46] The only advantage that could be claimed for Yale as against the competing university law schools of Albany, Columbia, and Harvard was Yale's proximity to the New Haven bar for persons wanting to practice nearby. Indeed, in 1868, Dutton had succeeded in wangling the diploma privilege for Yale graduates;[47] that is, they were automatically admitted to the New Haven bar.

In 1869, as in 1845, the initiative to keep the Yale Law School alive came from the local bar. This time the moving figure was Simeon E. Baldwin,[48] an alumnus of both Yale College and Yale Law School, who had also attended Harvard Law School. Baldwin was a member of an illustrious Connecticut family[49] with long ties to Yale.[50] Baldwin became something of a guardian angel for the Yale Law School over the next half century, serving initially as rescuer, then as professor, administrator, and benefactor. He became the leading railroad lawyer of his day, made a fortune, and gave much of it to the Law School. It has been reckoned that he contributed upwards of $700,000 to the Law School across his lifetime,[51] stupendous sums for those days. While carrying the Yale Law School into the twentieth century, Baldwin would also serve as governor of Connecticut, justice and chief justice of the state Supreme Court, a founder and president of the American Bar Association, president of the Association of American Law Schools, president of the American Historical Association, president of the American Social Science Association,[52] and the author of dozens of works, including a text on railroad law[53] and a digest of Connecticut law.[54] (Baldwin is a fascinating figure, and I cannot do him justice here. He suffered a tragic misfortune in his personal life: His wife became deranged at an early age and was locked up.[55] He responded by redirecting his affections and his energy to the Yale Law School, candidly observing at one point that "[i]t has been a large part of my life — almost my child."[56] Baldwin finally retired in 1919, after fifty years of teaching at the School. He died in 1927.)

When Dutton fell ill in 1869, he brought in Baldwin, then aged twenty-nine and a solo practitioner at the New Haven bar, as his substitute. For a few weeks, Baldwin was the Yale Law School's only faculty member.[57] Following Dutton's death, with Yale poised to drop the ax on the Law School, Baldwin hustled up three young colleagues from the New Haven bar to join him in staffing the School.[58] President Woolsey later recalled their engagement as "rather an experiment than a permanent plan, both on their part and on [Yale's]."[59] As before, the Corporation insisted that the Law School's finances be quarantined from the finances of the University. Baldwin's group had to agree to operate the School "at their own risk."[60]

Although Yale began in the 1870s to provide some direct financial support for library and administration,[61] the Law School would continue to be a proprietorship into the early twentieth century. Among Baldwin's countless other duties, he served as the Law School's treasurer for decades. His account book for the School, which begins in 1874, survives in the University archives. It records a stream of payments to faculty members across the next thirty years that vary with current tuition revenue and are called "dividends."[62] In 1904, Arthur Corbin, the School's first full-time salaried faculty member, participated in the last of these distributions, which looks to have been in the nature of a liquidating dividend upon the occasion of the end of the old system. Corbin received $108.37.[63]

III. The Reforms of the 1870s and Beyond

The Yale Law School's second brush with extinction in 1869 provoked considerable soul-searching about the future of the School. There were two strands of this activity, a series of practical improvements, and a remarkable rethinking of the School's mission and its relations with the University.

Lurking in the background in Yale's deliberations about whether and how to revive the Law School was the spur of competition, not so much from Harvard as from Theodore Dwight's Columbia. The Harvard Law School in 1869 was at something of a nadir, smarting from a hostile report to the university overseers that triggered the resignation of the long-time professor Theophilus Parsons.[64] In 1870 Charles Eliot[65] would become the president of the university, and in 1871 he would install Langdell as the first dean of the Harvard Law School.[66] Columbia Law School, on the other hand, although founded only in 1858,[67] was ascendant. The growing importance of New York City as the nation's financial, transportation, and manufacturing center resulted in a boom in the demand for lawyers. Dwight's Columbia became an instant success, attracting the largest student body thus far seen at an American law school. Dwight opened his doors in 1858 to thirty-five students. By 1872 he had 371, a number more than three times the enrollment of Columbia College.[68] Dicey, visiting the United States in 1871, wrote back to England that Columbia "possesses the best law school in the United States,"[69] and Bryce reported in the same year that "it would be worth an English student's while to cross the Atlantic to attend [Dwight's] course."[70]

Woolsey was of two minds about Columbia's success. On the one hand, he thought that Columbia's location in New York City gave it an intrinsic advantage in attracting law students, which Yale could not hope to match. On the other hand, Columbia's success augured well for university legal education: It showed that something could be done if Yale could get its house in order.[71]

A. DEVELOPING A PHILANTHROPIC BASE

Among the series of practical steps that Yale undertook in the early 1870s to reverse the fortunes of the Law School was to authorize fundraising. Columbia, with its huge enrollment, could live from tuition, but if Yale wanted to escape its squalor and mediocrity, it would need philanthropic support. Attention turned to fund-raising, in the hope of breaking the School's dependence on tuition. Woolsey put his finger on the problem a few years before, corresponding with a concerned alumnus in 1867. He pointed out how hard it was for an undistinguished school to escape the vicious circle of its own mediocrity. He wrote, " 'The destruction of the poor is their poverty.' We could have raised the [Law School] by funds and men [by "men" Woolsey meant professors], but to get the funds we must have the men, and to get the men we needed the funds. There was no leverage."[72]

At a time when American law schools were all but completely tuition-driven and content to remain so, Yale recognized that a law school of the character being envisioned could not be financed from tuition alone. Yale began the work of developing a philanthropic basis for the School. In 1869, at the very meeting at which the Corporation authorized Baldwin and his three colleagues to continue the Law School on a proprietary basis, the Corporation also directed attention to the need to develop an endowment for the library, for a building, and "for the support of Professors . . . ."[73]

It will be recalled that the Yale Law School's physical plant consisted of one malodorous rented room located on the second floor of a downtown building over a storefront. The Law School needed bigger and better space but could not afford it. In the early 1870s, just as the School was being reorganized following the death of Dutton, a providential solution to the space problem appeared. Once again, the New Haven bar was the rescuer. A new county courthouse was to be built on the New Haven Green. A deal was struck that provided free space for the Law School on the third floor of this building. As in 1845, so in the 1870s, the *quid pro quo* was access for the bar to the Law School's library.[74] The Law School moved into the new courthouse in 1873 and remained there for the next twenty years.

The library's collection was in terrible shape, having had virtually no accessions since Hitchcock's time. A campaign was launched for funds to restock it, and about $20,000 was found to bring it up to date.[75] One of the leaders of this campaign, former Connecticut governor James English,[76] capped the drive with a donation of $10,000 for a permanent endowment to support future accessions. His gift was the largest sum ever given the Yale Law School to that time.[77]

The effort to obtain chairs to support a full-time faculty bore first fruit in 1880, when the Law School was given $60,000 under the will of Lafayette S. Foster.[78] The Foster chair could not be filled until 1903, however, because the devise took the form of a remainder interest subject to a long life estate.[79] The first chair to come into possession was the Edward J. Phelps[80] chair, funded in 1887 and 1891 by the Morgan family — J. Pierpont in New York and his father Junius in London.[81]

As we well know, gifts of this sort tend not just to plop in, even on deserving institutions. Who was doing the fund-raising to produce these gifts? The evidence is sparse, but it points to the Law School's first real[82] dean, Francis Wayland. Wayland joined the Law School faculty in 1871, replacing one of Baldwin's original group of four. He was named dean in 1873 and served in that position for almost 30 years.[83] Wayland was the son of the elder Francis Wayland, the president of Brown University from 1827 to 1855 and a prominent figure in the history of American education.[84] After graduating Brown and studying law at Harvard, the younger Wayland settled in New Haven to accommodate his wife's family. A man of independent means, Wayland served as a probate judge and became lieutenant governor of Connecticut before becoming a professor at the Law School.[85] From the beginning it was envisioned that his appointment might help the School raise funds,[86] and by the end of his career in 1903 he was lionized for his acumen in encouraging gifts to the School.[87]

In the 1890s, Wayland led the fund-raising for the Law School's first home on campus, Hendrie Hall. Mr. Hendrie, a Yale College alumnus with no ties to the Law School, became wealthy dealing in California real estate, then returned to Connecticut. He responded to Wayland's initial appeal by giving $5,000 in 1894; by the time the building was finished he had given $60,000 more.[88]

I must not leave the impression that the Yale Law School became well endowed in these years.[89] Wayland's fund-raising was only a start. But these early steps toward a philanthropic basis put the Yale Law School on the path of attempting to reduce dependence on tuition at a time when Columbia and Harvard were reasonably content to live on their more ample tuition income. By taking some of the pressure off tuition, philanthropy would ultimately enable Yale to remain small.

B. ENLARGING THE FACULTY

Another major change instituted in the period of rejuvenation of the Yale Law School immediately after 1869 was the enlargement of the faculty. In Dutton's last years the Law School was a one-person faculty. It will be recalled that Baldwin brought in a group of four young lawyers in 1869, one of whom dropped out and was replaced in 1871 by Wayland. Baldwin pressed Yale to make this larger faculty a permanent feature of the School, and in 1872 the Corporation confirmed four professorships in the Law School.[90] Baldwin became professor of constitutional law, contracts, and wills; Wayland was named professor of mercantile law (what we now call commercial law) and evidence. Johnson Platt became professor of pleading and equity jurisprudence. William Robinson was designated professor of elementary and criminal law and of the law of real property.[91] In case you are wondering what the professor of "elementary law" taught, you can consult his lectures, which for a time he dictated, Litchfield-style, but which he published in 1875 in a little book, *Notes on Elementary Law*, which he peddled to the students at seventy-five cents apiece. It is basically an abridgment of portions of Blackstone, together with some pointers to a variety of practitioner literature. Robinson helpfully recommended that students commit to memory all 150-odd pages of the book.[92]

The four law professorships that Yale recognized in 1872 were simply titles; there were no salary lines. The professors' only compensation for teaching continued to be their shares of the so-called dividends from the school's fluctuating tuition revenues. The professors remained part-timers whose main income came from their law practice. Apart from Wayland, the dean, the Yale Law School would not have its first full-time faculty member until Arthur Corbin in 1903, a generation after Eliot and Langdell began moving the Harvard Law School to the model of a full-time faculty.

In addition to these four professorships, the Yale Law School embarked on a course of bringing in adjunct faculty, mostly from Yale College, in circumstances about which I shall say more. This increase in the size of faculty for what remained a very small school with a few dozen students was the beginning of a tradition that abides to this day, and that has done much to shape the character of the Yale Law School — the exceptionally benign faculty-student ratio.

IV. Ethos

I have been speaking so far about the series of practical measures that were taken in the years following the Yale Law School's second brush with extinction in 1869: relocating the premises; restocking and endowing the library; renewing and enlarging the faculty; installing a dean; and raising funds.

In the same years that these steps were taken to stabilize the School and assure its survival, there occurred a profound and puzzling change in the ethos of the Yale Law School. In the 1870s the School began to fashion a vision of itself as a place quite different from the trade school that it and the other university law schools had thus far been. A law school that had grown up in a New Haven law office and was in so many ways the creature of the New

Haven bar began to project an image of itself as rooted in the academic and intellectual life of Yale College. The Yale Law School shifted its reference point from the law office to the University.

The aspiration to change the character of the Yale Law School was given its public voice by Theodore D. Woolsey. As president of Yale from 1846 to 1871, he had experienced the travails of the School after Hitchcock's death in 1845 and again after Dutton's death in 1869. Although Woolsey began his career as a professor of Greek, he had drifted into what would today be called political science, writing student books on political science and international law.[93] After retiring as president in 1871, Woolsey took up lecturing on international law at the Law School (he was the author of a student book on the subject that went through many editions).[94]

In 1874 Woolsey delivered a notable address to a gathering of Law School alumni, in connection with what was billed as the celebration of the fiftieth anniversary of the Yale Law School.[95] Woolsey remarked on the success of the Columbia Law School, and he conceded that Yale could not "in the best of circumstances"[96] hope to attract comparable enrollments. Instead, Woolsey said, the Yale Law School should take a different tack. It should undertake to "harmonize" itself "with the whole circle of study pursued at Yale College," using for this purpose "chairs already founded,"[97] that is, by drawing on faculty already on hand in the academic departments.

But how could the University faculty bolster the trade school that was the Yale Law School? Woolsey's bracing answer was that the Law School should change character and become more like the University. The Law School should cease being the mere trade school that it had been. "Let the [Yale Law School] . . . be regarded no longer as simply the place for training men to plead causes . . . . [Instead,] let it be regarded as the place of instruction in all sound learning relating to the foundations of justice, the history of law . . . the constitution . . . the law of nations . . . finance and taxation," political theory, and comparative law.[98]

Woolsey's message was: Do not compete with Columbia Law School on its terms, but try to do something different. Columbia under Dwight was the apotheosis of a model of legal education that had been shaped at Litchfield, and that had spread from there to the early university law schools, including Yale. The aspiration of these schools, powerfully reiterated by Dwight,[99] was to do a better job than apprenticeship had done at training students for the work of the law office. Woolsey was asking Yale to develop a version of legal education that would be oriented less to training for the profession and more to the study of cognate fields that were pursued elsewhere in a university.

There was an undertone of snobbery in Woolsey's message, perhaps a hint that the multitudes being trained at Columbia Law School were not quite the people whom Woolsey wanted for customers. He expressed the hope that his conception of legal education might appeal to "those young men of wealth, of whom there is an increasing number, who wish to cultivate themselves and take their appropriate place of influence in society."[100]

Woolsey's program was not some daydream of his own. As he observed in his 1874 address,[101] the Yale Law School had already begun to experiment with broadening its curriculum by drawing on professors from the College. Baldwin later recalled that soon after what he euphemistically called the reorganization of the Law School in 1869, "arrangements were . . . made with the University authorities by which law students could attend one or more of the special courses of graduate study in the philosophical department," including offerings in political science, economics, English history, and ethics.[102] Consequently, said Baldwin, at the Yale Law School in the early 1870s "instruction was given . . . (besides the topics then taught in law schools generally) in general jurisprudence, . . . English constitutional law, medical jurisprudence, international law, Roman law, [and] ecclesiastical law."[103]

In 1875 the Law School announced a graduate program that would offer advanced degrees in law, both a one-year master of laws and a two-year doctor of civil law.[104] The graduate curriculum would consist of a few extra offerings by the Law School faculty (for example, Robinson, the erstwhile professor of elementary law, would teach graduate students something called "forensic oratory and rhetoric"[105]). But the main added value would once again come from University faculty, who would teach Roman law, political economy, and so forth.[106] In 1876 the Yale Law School catalogue promptly boasted that "greater advantages are now offered at Yale . . . for following the study of public law, Roman law, comparative jurisprudence, . . . constitutional history, and political science, than have ever been afforded before at an American Law School, or [than] can be given at any school . . . where — from its want of connection with a University — the staff of instructors must be less numerous."[107]

Notice the twin emphasis in this manifesto on public law and on the linkage to the University. There was an inevitable public law skew to the curriculum that Yale Law School imported from Yale College. The College is not where you go to get expertise on civil procedure or commercial law.

There was a Potemkin village quality to the Yale Law School in the mid-1870s, with its claim to have become the nation's premier center of advanced interdisciplinary legal studies. The audacity, the sheer chutzpah, is breathtaking. Here we have a proprietary law school recovering from its latest brush with extinction, staffed part-time by four mostly young and undistinguished New Haven lawyers (including the self-styled professor of elementary law), and this place was passing itself off as a temple of advanced legal scholarship, on the ground that its students could also study with faculty from the classics department and elsewhere in the University. I am not at all sure that the Yale Law School of the mid-1870s could have withstood a probe by modern consumer protection authorities.

Indeed, the so-called graduate program was at its outset nothing more than a correspondence course for a handful of students, mostly Yale Law School graduates who had gone off to practice but who wanted to continue their studies. As Baldwin described it forty years later: "A course of reading was prescribed for each [such student] in view of his previous studies and circumstances. Moot cases, in which they were to draw the pleadings and prepare written briefs, and subjects for theses, were given out from time to time. [The students] were required to be present at New Haven, at least once a year, for oral examination on the works read . . . ."[108] Poignantly, the first recipient of one of these Yale graduate law degrees was named Alexander Hack.[109]

For the future, however, what would matter about these moves to enrich the curriculum and add a graduate program is not the tawdry reality but the resonance of the aspiration. By the second half of the twentieth century the Yale Law School would catch up with the wishful image projected in the mid-1870s. The Yale Law School would indeed become an incomparable center for public law, jurisprudence, international law, constitutional law, and political theory. Ultimately, the School would achieve this goal, not as Baldwin and Woolsey envisaged in the 1870s, by importing University faculty on lend-lease, but rather by developing genuinely cross-disciplinary fields of knowledge and instruction within the Law School, such as law-and-economics, legal history, constitutional theory, and international legal studies. To be sure, the older tradition of strong links to the University departments abides, and is reflected in scholarly collaborations and curricular ties, in the joint J.D./Ph.D. programs, and in the several workshops for the presentation of scholarly work in progress.

What caused the aspirations of the Yale Law School to take this unprecedented turn toward the academic departments in the 1870s? I do not have a satisfying answer to this puzzle, but I can point to some of the factors, which reflect both the weaknesses and the strengths of the School. I do not think that competition from Langdell's Harvard was a driving force. In the mid-1870s Langdell was new and embattled.[110] The model of Langdell's Harvard came to dominate American legal education only in the 1890s, when the Columbia trustees drove out Dwight and his followers, and brought in William Keener and an all-Harvard team to reshape the Columbia Law School in Langdell's image.[111] The package of innovations worked out at Harvard under Langdell would indeed become the industry standard, and by the early decades of the twentieth century, Yale and every other major American law school would accede to most of it.[112] The package included[113] higher entrance requirements, culminating in the requirement of a college degree for all students; the phased curriculum, in which certain subjects were identified as fundamental and had to be mastered in the first year before the student went on to more advanced subjects; course-level or annual examinations; a three-year curriculum; a faculty of full-time law professors specializing in teaching and in scholarship; and the so-called case method, which displaced the text-and-recitation system that the nineteenth-century Yale Law School so cherished. But in the early 1870s, when the Yale Law School was taking on its new coloration, all of this lay in the future. As Woolsey said in 1874 when he gave his address, Dwight's Columbia was the competitor that alarmed him, because he saw that Yale had no natural advantages over Dwight in the enterprise of running a better trade school.

Financial pressure was surely a precipitating factor in the Yale Law School's turn for strength to the College in the early 1870s. Using other Yale faculty to teach law students allowed the Law School to share faculty whom it could not support on its own. Furthermore, the Yale Law School's reorientation toward the academic disciplines in the 1870s occurred against a background of long-standing linkage between College and Law School through the Kent chair. I have suggested that what first joined Yale to the Hitchcock/Daggett law school was Yale's decision in 1826 to name Daggett as the professor of law in Yale College, the post that was later renamed the Chancellor Kent chair.[114] Daggett, Bissell, and Dutton successively held that appointment jointly with their Law School posts. They taught College seniors about constitutional and international law.[115]

The Yale Law School's effort to draw closer to the academic departments was a striking departure from the trend of the times at other American law schools, which emphasized the autonomy of law. To be sure, there was endless chatter in American law schools and at the bar about the importance of treating law as a science, but what was meant was mostly a science of private law, the effort to perfect legal doctrine. One important consequence of the Yale Law School's undertaking to tie itself more to the University's other disciplines was to encourage the study of public law and especially of international law at precisely the time when the emphasis on private law was reaching its zenith at Columbia and Harvard.

I conclude this lecture roughly where I began it, by reiterating that Robert Stevens got the Yale Law School of the nineteenth century about right. It did not amount to much, and if it had disappeared at any time before the 1930s, it (like so many other defunct law schools of the nineteenth century) would hardly have been missed. Yet, amazingly, this frail institution managed in the 1870s to articulate as an aspiration for itself a theme of great novelty: that the work of training for the legal profession requires participation in the full range of inquiry that a great university pursues. That conception of the mission of a law school came to define the intellectual life of the Yale Law School. Although long derided elsewhere, by the closing years of the twentieth century it had become the dominant ethos of American law schools.

Notes

I am grateful for the research assistance of Stuart Chinn (YLS '03) and Robert James (YC '05), and to Nancy Lyon, Yale University, Sterling Library, Department of Manuscripts and Archives, for help with the Yale archives.

1. John H. Langbein, "Blackstone, Litchfield, and Yale: The Founding of the Yale Law School," supra this volume (hereafter Lecture I).

2. Brooks Mather Kelley, *Yale: A History* 256 (1974).

3. Id. at 275.

4. See "History of the Yale Law School: Provenance and Perspective," supra in this volume.

5. Frederick C. Hicks, *Yale Law School: The Founders and the Founders' Collection* (1935; hereafter Hicks I); *Yale Law School: From the Founders to Dutton: 1845–1869* (1936) (hereafter Hicks II); *Yale Law School: 1869–1894: Including the County Court House Period* 32 (1937) (hereafter Hicks III; and *Yale Law School: 1895–1915: Twenty Years of Hendrie Hall* (1938) (hereafter Hicks IV). The pamphlets have been recently reissued in a collected photographic reprint edition as Frederick C. Hicks, *History of the Yale Law School to 1915* (2001) (hereafter 2001 ed.). That volume preserves the page numbering of the original pamphlets but also assigns continuous page numbers to the four pamphlets. When citing Hicks, I cite the original pamphlet, and I supply a parallel citation to the reprint edition for material appearing in Hicks II, III, or IV, for which the continuous pagination of the reprint results in a different page number.

6. Regarding the pathologies of the genre, see Alfred F. Konefsky & John Henry Schlegel, Mirror, Mirror on the Wall: Histories of American Law Schools, 95 *Harvard L. Rev.* 833 (1982).

7. Discussed in Lecture I, note 3.

8. On Yale's role in the decline of Litchfield, see id., text at notes 117–18 and n. 118.

9. As mentioned in Lecture I, text at note 138, it was remembered of the first proprietor, Seth Staples, that he "undertook the charge of a class of half a dozen law students, who recited to him in the intervals of business, generally before breakfast, every morning." Simeon E. Baldwin, *Law School of Yale College, extract from the Year Book of the City of New Haven for 1872–73*, at 3 (Yale Law Libr. RB shelfmark YL 111 1873) (hereafter Baldwin, *Law School*).

10. Julius Goebel, Jr. [& Samuel F. Howard], *A History of the School of Law of Columbia University* 36 (1955) (hereafter Goebel & Howard). Dwight was using the

text-and-recitation method of instruction in the 1850s at Hamilton College, before moving to Columbia. Walter Pilkington, *Hamilton College: 1812–1962* at 117 (1962).

11. Asahel Stearns, the principal instructor for the first decade of the Harvard Law School, reporting to the Harvard overseers in 1826 about the "regular exercises of the School," placed at the head of his list "[r]ecitations and [e]xaminations in several of the most important text books, such as Blackstone's Commentaries[,] Cruise on Real Property, Saunders on Uses, Fearne on Remainders, etc." 1 Charles Warren, *History of the Harvard Law School and of Early Legal Conditions in America* 334 (1908) (3 vols.) (emphasis deleted) (hereafter Warren, *Harvard*).

12. Hicks III:32, 2001 ed. at 148.

13. *Yale Law School: Sixty-Fourth Year 1887–88: Annual Calendar and Alumni Record 1824–1886*, at 7 (New Haven 1887) (hereafter *1887–88 Catalogue*), extracted in Hicks III:33, 2001 ed. at 149.

14. "The students are furnished with the use of the elementary books . . . ." *Catalogue of the Officers and Students in Yale College* 29 (Nov. 1826). This practice explains why at his death in 1845 Hitchcock (as proprietor of the school) owned the many copies of basic works noticed infra, note 18.

15. Text-and-recitation instruction had the same attraction at the undergraduate level, from which it was adapted. "A college with a prescribed course taught by recitation did not need a great variety of specialists . . . . The typical [New England college instructor] was the general scholar with a B.A. degree and, perhaps, some theological training." Richard J. Storr, *The Beginnings of Graduate Education in America* 3 (1953).

16. Daggett, replying to an inquiry from a prospective student, described regular lecturing. Daggett to James Dana, Dec. 9, 1831, David Daggett Papers, MS 162, series I, box 3, folder 88, at 1, Yale Univ. Sterling Libr., Dept. of Manuscripts and Archives (hereafter Sterling M&A), reproduced in Hicks II:51, 2001 ed. at 101 (spelling and punctuation modernized). A former student recalled Hitchcock "lectur[ing] . . . on the subjects we were studying," as well as conducting recitations. Hicks I:22, citing Theodore D. Woolsey, *Historical Discourse . . . and Oration* 19 (1874) (hereafter Woolsey, *Historical Discourse*). The Yale Law School catalogue for 1887–88, boasting of the School's adherence to the text-and-recitation method, admitted that "although certain subjects are separately taught by lectures, either because of the want of proper manuals or the constant and rapid advance of learning, or economy of time . . . , care is taken that the same topics shall be covered by recitation work . . . ." *1887–88 Catalogue*, supra note 14, at 7, cited in Hicks III:33, 2001 ed. at 149.

17. Stearns' report to the Harvard overseers in 1826 describes the use of lectures in addition to text-and-recitation instruction. 1 Warren, *Harvard*, supra note 11, at 334; regarding Dwight's lectures at Columbia, see Steve Sheppard, Casebooks, Commentaries, and Curmudgeons: An Introductory History of Law in the Lecture Hall, 82 *Iowa L. Rev.* 547, 583–86 (1997).

18. At his death Hitchcock owned thirty copies of Blackstone, thirty-four of Chitty on pleading, twenty-five of Cruise on real property, etc. Hicks I:29. The same works were used at Harvard, see supra note 11.

Judging from the surviving contracts notebook of Timothy Merwin, who studied at the Yale Law School in 1828, preparing for recitation classes involved a lot of copying from the textbooks. Merwin was studying Joseph Chitty Jr., *A Practical Treatise on the Law of Contracts, Not under Seal* (London, 1826). Peter Stern (YLS '97) has transcribed the notes with an introduction: "The Contracts Notes of Timothy Merwin: Earliest Evidence of Instruction at the Yale Law School" (unpublished paper, 1996) (Yale Law Libr. RB classmark YL 19 H629 no.3) (manuscript in Sterling M&A, Yale Course Lectures Collection, 1720–1980, YRG 47, RU 159, ACCN 19ND-A-394, box 3, folder 5). Daggett mentions some of the textbooks that were being used in 1831 in his reply to a prospective student, Daggett Letter, supra note 16, at 1–2.

19. See J. H. Baker, *Readers and Readings in the Inns of Court and Chancery* (2001) (Selden Soc. Supp. Ser. 13); S. E. Thorne, ed., *Readings and Moots at the Inns of Court in the Fifteenth Century* (1954) (Selden Soc. Vol. 71).

20. Discussed in Lecture I, text at notes 41–43.

21. A. W. B. Simpson, The Rise and Fall of the Legal Treatise: Legal Principles and the Forms of Legal Literature, 48 *U. Chi. L. Rev.* 632 (1981).

22. John C. Schwab, *The Yale College Curriculum: 1701–1901*, 2–11 (1901). Speaking of the text-and-recitation system, the Yale Law School catalogue for 1887–88 explains, in language quoted fully, supra text at note 13, that the text-and-recitation "method of instruction . . . is . . . the tradition of the University . . . ." See also supra, note 15.

23. Minutes of the Yale Corporation and the Prudential Committee (hereafter Corp. Mins.), Aug. 19, 1846, Sterling M&A, cited in Hicks II:24, 2001 ed. at 74. On Storrs see Franklin B. Dexter, *Biographical Notes of Graduates of Yale College* 710–11 (1885–1912) (6 vols.) (hereafter Dexter, *Yale Biographies*); Hicks II:22–24, 2001 ed. at 72–74.

24. On which, see Elizabeth Forgeus, *The History of the Storrs Lectureship in the Yale Law School: The First Three Decades, 1890–1920* (1940).

25. Corp. Mins., Aug. 19, 1846, Sterling M&A, Hicks II:7–8, 2001 ed. at 57–58.

26. He was Henry White, who also served briefly as one of the Storrs group of three provisional faculty in the interval after Hitchcock's death. See Corp. Mins., Aug. 19, 1846, Sterling M&A, cited in Hicks II:5–8, 2001 ed. at 55–58; on White, see Hicks II:18–22, 2001 ed. at 68–72.

27. Henry White to Yale Prudential Com., Aug. 19, 1846, Yale Corp. Recs., Sterling M&A, classmark RU 164, ACCN 92-A-83, box 2, reproduced in Hicks I:32–33.

28. Letter of William L. Storrs & Isaac H. Townsend to the Prudential Committee of Yale College, Dec. 23, 1845, Sterling M&A, Yale Corp. Recs., MS Vault I, Box 4, RU164 426 1-A ACCN 1993-A-083 (hereafter Storrs/Townsend Letter), quoted in Hicks I:30, at 31.

29. Storrs/Townsend Letter, supra note 28, at 1–2.

30. Id. at 2.

31. Id.

32. Simeon E. Baldwin, "The Graduating Class of 1898," *Yale Shingle* 68 (1898) (hereafter Baldwin, *Shingle*), quoted in Hicks III:2, 2001 ed. at 118.

33. The donors are identified in Hicks II:56–57, 2001 ed. at 106–7. For the favorable terms allowing donors, divided into annual and life subscribers, to use the library, and in the later case, "to take books to their offices," see "Rules of the Yale Law Library" (New Haven, Mar. 1847), Yale Law School Records, Sterling M&A, classmark RU 449 ACCN 1939-A-001, box 1, folder 3, reproduced in Hicks II:58–59, 2001 ed. at 108–9.

34. Hicks I:35. The Corporation stopped charging interest in 1856 because the Law School had inadequate revenue. Hicks II:34, 2001 ed. at 84.

35. Portions of the original collection bought from Hitchcock's estate survive in the Yale Law School rare-book room, designated (together with other books once owned by Staples and Daggett that have been subsequently acquired) as the Founders' Collection,

36. Daniel Lord to Woolsey, Feb. 9, 1847, Sterling M&A, Woolsey Family Papers, MS 562, series I, box 11, folder 168, quoted in Hicks II:15, 2001 ed. at 65.

37. Corp. Mins., Aug 19, 1846, Sterling M&A, quoted in Hicks II:4, 2001 ed. at 54.

38. Kelley, supra note 2, at 192.

39. Yale Corp. Recs., Aug. 15, 1848, noted in Hicks II:25, 2001 ed. at 75.

40. Hicks II:30–32, 2001 ed. at 80–82.

41. Hicks II:41, 2001 ed. at 91; 5 *Dictionary of American Biography* 555–56 (D. Malone et al. eds., 1928–37) (hereafter DAB).

42. Corp. Mins., Jul. 24, 1855, Sterling M&A, noted in Hicks II:30, 2001 ed. at 80.

43. Woolsey, *Historical Discourse,* supra note 16, at 11.

44. "The death, in 1869, of the last of the professors of the Yale Law School left the school without a faculty, without means, and with but few students. The Yale Corporation, it is understood, was not in favor of a continuance of the school and desired that it be closed." George D. Watrous, "Address before the New Haven County Bar Association," in *Records and Addresses in Memory of Simeon E. Baldwin: 1840–1927,* at 12–13 (1928), cited in Mark Bartholomew, The Relationship Between Yale's Law School and the Central University in the Late Nineteenth Century (unpublished paper, Feb. 18, 2000) (Yale Law Libr. RB shelfmark YL 19 H629 no. 8 c. 1). Woolsey feared a coming "collapse" of the school in a letter to an alumnus in 1867, saying that it would take a $100,000 endowment to make the school "respectable." Letter from Woolsey to Luther Maynard Jones, Yale Corp. Recs., Jun. 11, 1867, reproduced in Hicks II:36, 2001 ed. at 86.

45. Yale College: Needs of the University, Suggested by the Faculties 18 (1871) (Sterling M&A shelfmark Y51 1), noticed in Hicks III:7, 2001 ed. at 123.

46. For the decade of the 1860s the report shows a high of 39 percent college graduates in 1863 to none (in a class of sixteen students) in 1867. *Report of the President of Yale University . . . for the Academic Year, 1904–1905,* at 153 (1905) (Sterling M&A shelfmark HM 214). Hicks appears to be referring to this report, Hicks II:48–49, 2001 ed. at 98–99.

47. William C. Robinson, *An Address Commemorative of the Life and Character of Francis Wayland* 21 (New Haven, 1904) (Sterling M&A shelfmark Ycy 1 W365) (hereafter Robinson, *Wayland*); Hicks II:37, 2001 ed. at 87.

48. See generally Frederick H. Jackson, *Simeon Eben Baldwin: Lawyer, Social Scientist, Statesman* (1955); Charles C. Goetsch, *Essays on Simeon E. Baldwin* (1981) (hereafter Goetsch, *Baldwin*); 1 DAB 544–47; Hicks IV:63–85, 2001 ed. at 265–87.

49. Goetsch, *Baldwin,* supra note 48, at 93.

50. Baldwin's grandfather, also named Simeon (1761–1851), was a Yale College classmate (1781) of James Kent, the future Chancellor Kent. Dexter, *Yale Biographies,* supra note 23, at 178–80, 189–94. Kent maintained a lifelong friendship with the elder Baldwin. The two corresponded for sixty-five years, until they were the last survivors of the Class of 1781. Kent wrote the elder Baldwin in 1847, lamenting "the Devastation that

time has made in the wide circle of my collegiate Friends and acquaintances. You and I are the only spared monuments of God's Providence in our class . . . ." Sterling M&A, Baldwin Family Papers, MS 55, series I, box 26, folder 300, cited in John H. Langbein, Chancellor Kent and the History of Legal Literature, 93 *Columbia L. Rev.* 547, 551 & n. 18 (1993) (hereafter Langbein, *Kent*).

51. Hicks mentions this sum but does not attribute it. Hicks IV:80, 2001 ed. at 282. His source was probably *Reports Made to the President for the Academic Year 1930–31*, at 178 (1932) (exemplar in Sterling M&A, microfilm HM 214).

52. See 1 DAB 544–47.

53. Simeon E. Baldwin, *American Railroad Law* (1904).

54. Simeon E. Baldwin, *A Digest of All the Reported Cases in . . . Connecticut* (2d ed. 1900) (2 vols.) (1st ed. Boston, 1871–82).

55. Recounted by Goetsch, "Is There Any Woe Greater?: The Institutionalization of Susan W. Baldwin for Insanity During the Late Nineteenth Century," in Goetsch, *Baldwin*, supra note 48, at 186.

56. Id. at 44.

57. Baldwin, *Shingle*, supra note 32, at 68, cited in Hicks III:1–2, 2001 ed. at 117–18.

58. Corp. Mins., July 20, 1869, Sterling M&A; see also Hicks at III:3, 2001 ed. at 119.

59. Woolsey, *Historical Discourse*, supra note 16, at 11.

60. Hicks attributes this language to the Corporation. Hicks III:3, 2001 ed. at 119. I have not been able to trace the quoted passage in the Corporation records.

61. Hicks III:55–57, 2001 ed. at 171–73.

62. Yale University, Sterling Library, Manuscripts and Archives, Law School Treasurer's Accounts, 1874–1910 (classmark YL 122 B19).

63. Id. at 449.

64. 2 Warren, *Harvard*, supra note 11, at 358–59.

65. On the central role of Eliot in transforming American higher education to the science-centered model of the research university that had been developed in Germany, see Hugh Hawkins, *Between Harvard and America: The Educational Leadership of Charles W. Eliot* (1972); Henry James, *Charles W. Eliot* (1930) (2 vols.). On the importance of these developments to the changes at Harvard Law School in the 1870s associated with Langdell, see Anthony Chase, The Birth of the Modern Law School, 23 *American J. Legal History* 329, 332–43 (1979); David S. Clark, Tracing the Roots of American Legal Education: A Nineteenth-Century German Connection, 51 *Rabels Zeitschrift für ausländisches und internationales Privatrecht* 313 (1987) (hereafter Clark, *German Connection*); Mark Bartholomew, Legal Separation: The Relationship Between the Law School and the Central University in the Late Nineteenth Century, 53 *J. Legal Ed.* 368, 377–84 (2003).

66. Id., at 327.

67. Regarding Columbia's earlier experiments with legal education under James Kent in the 1790s and 1820s, see Goebel & Howard, supra note 10, at 11–25; Langbein, *Kent*, supra note 50, at 558–60, 564–65.

68. Goebel & Howard, supra note 10, at 62, 408 & n.111.

69. Albert V. Dicey, Legal Education, 25 *Macmillan's Magazine* 115, 127 (1871), quoted in Goebel & Howard, supra note 10, at 63, 409 n. 115.

70. James Bryce, The Legal Profession in America, 25 *Macmillan's Magazine* 206, 209 (1871), quoted in Goebel & Howard, supra note 10, at 63, 409 n.116.

71. Woolsey, *Historical Discourse*, supra note 16, at 22.

72. Woolsey to Luther Maynard Jones, Jun. 11, 1867, reproduced in Hicks II:36, 2001 ed. at 86. This document has not been located in the Yale archives, although Jones' response to Woolsey dated the next day does survive there. Jones to Woolsey, Jun. 12, 1867, Sterling M&A, Yale Corp. Recs., box 20, series I, group 652, folder 368.

73. Hicks III:3, 2001 ed. at 119. This concern was reiterated in 1871, see Hicks III:8, 2001 ed. at 124.

74. Writing at the time of the events, Simeon Baldwin described the deal:

> To secure the deposit of the Law School library where it would be most convenient of access to the members of the Bar, and the judges holding court in New Haven, it was suggested, when the erection of a new Court house for New Haven was determined upon, that it would be highly desirable to assign it a place in that building; and, this proposition being favorably received by the College, the architect was directed to plan the third story so as to provide suitable accommodations there for the use of the Law School.

Baldwin, *Law School,* supra note 9, at 6.

75. Hicks III:51–52, 2001 ed. at 167–68.

76. On whom see 6 DAB 165–66.

77. Hicks III:52, 2001 ed. at 168.

78. Corp. Recs., July 20, 1869, Sterling M&A. Regarding Foster, see 6 DAB 553.

79. Hicks III:37–38, 2001 ed. at 153–54.

80. On whom see 14 DAB 528.

81. Hicks. III:38, 2001 ed. at 154.

82. During the years 1869–73 the title was held solely as an honorific by Robinson, the most senior of the four instructors who comprised the Baldwin group. Hicks III:43, 2001 ed. at 159.

83. An acting dean replaced him 1901 when he became ill. Hicks VI:33, 2001 ed. at 235.

84. Hicks IV:17, 2001 ed. at 219; 19 DAB 558–60.

85. Hicks IV:18, 2001 ed. at 220.

86. The Corporation designated him to raise funds for the school at the time it hired him. Corp. Mins., Oct. 11, 1871, Sterling M&A; Hicks III:8, 2001 ed. at 210.

87. Robinson, *Wayland,* supra note 47, at 24–25; Hicks IV:22–23, 2001 ed. at 224–25.

88. Corp. Mins., Nov. 23, 1899, Sterling M&A; Hicks IV:10–11, 2001 ed. at 212–13.

89. As of 1917, a decade and a half after Wayland, the Law School's endowment stood at $720,000. *Report of the President of Yale University . . . for the Academic Year 1916–1817,* at 309 (1917) (Sterling M&A shelfmark HM 214).

90. Hicks III:7–8, 11, 2001 ed. at 123–24, 127.

91. Hicks III:11, 2001 ed. at 127.

92. William C. Robinson, *Elementary Law* v–viii (1875); Hicks III:44–45, 160–61. Robinson later quit in a huff about Yale's acceptance of case method instruction; see Robert Stevens, *Law School: Legal Education in America from the 1850s to the 1880s,* at 87 & n.34 (1983) (hereafter Stevens, *Law School*).

93. See generally George A. King, *Theodore Dwight Woolsey: His Political and Social Ideas* (1956); Theodore S. Woolsey, *Theodore Dwight Woolsey — A Biographical Sketch* (1912); 20 DAB 519–20.

94. Theodore D. Woolsey, *Introduction to the Study of International Law* (Cambridge, MA, 1860) (1st ed.).

95. The 1874 celebration may have been the occasion that established the convention of reckoning the Law School's founding from the entries in the College catalogue of 1824. I have explained why this account is unsound, and why I think that 1826 is the more likely date of the Hitchcock/Daggett school's affiliation with Yale. See Lecture I, text at notes 150–64.

96. Woolsey, *Historical Discourse*, supra note 16, at 22.

97. Id. at 23.

98. Id.

99. On Dwight's hostility to apprenticeship, see Goebel & Howard, supra note 10, at 43. His maxim was "principles before practice." Id. at 35.

100. Woolsey, *Historical Discourse*, supra note 16, at 23–24, cited in Hicks III:18–19, 2001 ed. 134–35.

101. Id. at 11–12.

102. Simeon E. Baldwin, "Yale's Graduate Course in Law and Jurisprudence," in *The Yale School of Law: An Account of Its Recent Progress and Expansion, Reminiscences of Its Earlier Days, Supplement to The Yale Alumni Weekly*, March 23, 1917, at 7–8 (Yale Law School RB shelfmark YL 19 Al8) (hereafter Baldwin, 1917 Essay).

103. Id. at 8. In the same period practitioners from outside the University were sometimes engaged to teach about their specialties. Id. at 9 (instancing insurance law).

104. For the suggestion that Baldwin was the architect of the program, see Bartholomew, supra note 65, at 396–402.

105. *Law Department of Yale College . . . 1876–77, Calendar for 1877*, at 8 (1876; hereafter 1876 Catalogue), cited in Hicks III:26, 2001 ed. at 142.

106. 1876 Catalogue, supra note 105, at 8–9, Hicks III:27, 2001 ed. at 143.

107. 1876 Catalogue, supra note 105, at 6, quoted in Hicks III:25, 2001 ed. at 141. (The word "than," bracketed in the extract, is misspelled as "that" in the original.)

108. Baldwin, 1917 Essay, supra note 102, at 8.

109. Hicks III:27, 2001 ed. at 143.

110. William P. LaPiana, *Logic and Experience: The Origin of Modern American Legal Education* 132–47 (1994).

111. See Goebel & Howard, supra note 10, at 135–58; James A. Wooten, Law School Rights: The Establishment of New York Law School, 1891–1997, 36 *New York Law School L. Rev.* 337 (1991).

112. See Stevens, *Law School*, supra note 92, at 51–64.

113. LaPiana, supra note 110, at 14–15; Anthony Chase, supra note 65, at 332. For the insight that Langdell's program in the Harvard Law School was part of Eliot's broader initiative to recast Harvard more on the model of the research university pioneered in nineteenth-century Germany, see generally Clark, *German Connection*, supra note 65.

114. See Lecture I, text at note 153.

115. The College chair was filled again in 1881 by Edward J. Phelps, who held it to 1900; and in 1913 by William Howard Taft, who resigned in 1921 to become Chief Justice. See Frederick C. Hicks, *William Howard Taft: Yale Professor of Law and New Haven Citizen* 29 (1945).

Professors and Policymakers: Yale Law School Faculty in the New Deal and After

ROBERT W. GORDON

John Langbein's lectures in this book, on the law schools at Litchfield and Yale in the nineteenth century, end the story around 1906, with the appointment of Arthur Linton Corbin to the Yale law faculty. At the urging of the New Haven bar, which wanted to save its law library, the administration of Yale College had preserved the struggling proprietary law school, staffed by part-time practitioners, from extinction. Yale had given it a small endowment, a modest building in Hendrie Hall, and a grandiose mission — to supplement a basic training in private law with studies in Roman law, international law, constitutional law, and political science. This high-flown academy, Langbein observes, was a Potemkin village. Yale had no real law school worthy of the name. Its only hope of attracting law students in competition with Columbia, and later Harvard, was to advertise courses taught by the regular Yale College faculty as if they had been designed to enrich pre-professional law studies with an interdisciplinary and public law approach. In the twentieth century, Langbein concludes, Yale Law School would gradually convert what had started out as a desperate advertising strategy into what became its genuinely distinctive institutional identity.

In this lecture I want to tell a piece of that twentieth-century story — but just a small piece. John Langbein has done heroic work in reconstructing the nineteenth-century history of the school from scarce and fragmentary materials. The problem for the twentieth-century historian is just the opposite, a massive overabundance of materials. This lecture will focus on a particular period, the late 1920s to the early 1950s, especially 1933–39, the period in which many Yale Law School professors went off to do part-time or full-time service for the New Deal; and then a brief period after World War II in which many of the school's faculty were actively involved in campaigns for civil rights and civil liberties. Any scholar working in this remarkably rich and exciting period of the Yale Law School's history is fortunate indeed to have the benefit of two first-rate books, Laura Kalman's history of legal realism at Yale and John Henry Schlegel's study of American legal realism and empirical social science.[1]

The main theme of this lecture is the law faculty's engagements with the outside worlds of law and politics, and the connections between these engagements and their teaching and scholarship. The lecture thus touches only incidentally on other important matters such as the changing character of the students, their law school experience and their careers; the school's curriculum and administration, and its relations with the university, alumni, and the bar. My theme is that of how the Yale Law faculty's scholarly projects, teaching priorities, and public engagements of this momentous and chaotic period contributed to some remarkable changes in the professional identities of law teachers, from deferential servants of the bench and bar to aggressive critics; from supposedly neutral expounders and simplifiers of the law on the books to remote social-scientific observers and empirical researchers of law in action; from rationalizers and organizers of existing law to engaged advocates, public policy entrepreneurs, administrative politicians, and crusading publicists.

Yale Law School in this period produced some faculty with virtuoso skills at juggling all these roles; but not even these magicians were able to perform them all without considerable strain and conflict with what always remains, however little we may like to think about it, the law schools' inescapable tasks—not their entire reason for being by any means, but the basic reason people are willing to pay them for their existence. These are the tasks of recruiting, teaching, certifying, and eventually raising funds from a corps of people largely aspiring to, preparing for, and eventually working at the private practice of law in a fairly conservative profession. These basic functions have a way of acting like a gigantic rubber band, which acts perpetually to drag the more adventurous experiments with legal education and the role of the law teacher back into the narrow confines of a set of basic routines—the private-law-centered, doctrine-centered, court-centered, case-centered curriculum, which accepts existing legal arrangements as given, and subject to only minor modifications. The generation of the 1930s also experienced the pull of the rubber band; but they also did much to stretch the band beyond its earlier limits and thus enlarge, for the benefit of law teacher and students, the conventional boundaries of the American law school's, and especially Yale Law School's, functions.

Yale as Harvard's Competitor and Rebellious Offspring

Let us begin by going back to where all histories of modern law schools start, to Harvard Law School after Dean Christopher Columbus Langdell's reforms of the 1870s and '80s.[2] Langdell aspired to a synthesis of English and German models of the lawyer's and law professor's roles. Harvard saw itself initially as preparing graduates for careers as "counselors." Langdell imagined these as something like the English barrister class, an elite corps of lawyers specializing in appellate advocacy (Langdell's own practice niche before becoming a dean) — a "scientifically" educated bar to act as advisors to an educated bench. This ideal American lawyer, like the English barrister, should have an undergraduate liberal arts education; but then a three-year course of graduate education in law on top of that, an education enabling him to understand law as a science of principles. Harvard's idea of the law professor's job, however, looked to Germany rather than England. English law teachers of that period had to struggle against an insular, ingrown, intellectually conservative profession of judges and lawyers who put no value on a scientific, or as we would now call it, a theoretical, training in law. Bright and ambitious young men entering the legal profession read classics rather than law; and got their legal educations from the course of dinners at the Inns of Court for barristers, or from crammers for the Law Society's exams for solicitors, and ultimately from apprenticeships. To validate their vocation in the eyes of a skeptical bench and bar, English law teachers presented themselves as a humble corps of clerks, whose job was to synthesize and simplify the decisions of the real makers of common law, the judges, for the benefit of aspiring lawyers. Their typical work product was the student textbook, usually published with a flattering dedication to an eminent judge; its function, as A. V. Dicey put it, was to "supply all the defects which flow directly or indirectly from a one-sided system of practical training. It is for law professors to set forth the law as a coherent whole . . . to reduce the mass of legal rules to an orderly series of principles . . . to [digest it] into a set of rules and exceptions. . . . [A] few principles which sum up the effects of a hundred cases . . . can thus be understood and remembered."[3]

To be sure, the English jurists hoped eventually to leverage this humble tutorial function into a much grander one as major expounders and reformers

of the law. In fact, they used the deferential role of textbook author as camou-
flage for some fairly ambitious critical and reformist work. But they looked
with envious longing to America, where the organized bar, which had been
destroyed by Jacksonian hostility to professional privileges and guild monopolies and was only in the 1870s beginning to rebuild itself, was too weak to
dictate to the emerging university law schools. The American schools were
thereby much freer to engage in institutional innovation. In America, in turn,
law teachers were looking back across the Atlantic, to German models of legal
science and the roles of law professors. Langdell's successor as dean, James
Barr Ames, noted that German law professors occupied the highest rank in
their profession — evidently a rational and agreeable arrangement — and that
the "influence of their opinions in the courts is as great or even greater than
that of judicial precedents." Ames thought that influence somewhat too great,
as it inhibited the development of a distinguished judiciary and body of case
law. But he greatly admired the capacity of the German full-time professoriate,
freed from the time demands and interest pressures of practice, to do original
research and produce monumental commentaries. Unlike the English jurists,
Ames did not view scholars simply as deferential butlers to the judges, working up compact Cliffs Notes or Gilbert's Summaries to their authoritative
output; but rather as their intellectual counselors and critics:

> The chief value in this new order of legal literature will be found in its power to
> correct . . . the principal defect in the generally admirable work of the judges. It
> is the function of the law to work out in terms of general legal principle the
> rules which will give the utmost possible effect to the legitimate needs and
> purposes of men in their different activities. Too often the just expectations of
> men are thwarted by the actions of the courts, a result largely due to taking a
> partial view of the subject, or to a failure to grasp the original development and
> true significance of the rule which is made the basis of the decision.[4]

The scholars' corrective was to be supplied by combining a historical
method, designed to trace the "original development" of misapplied rules,
with an analytic and comparative method, designed to locate the rules in their
proper places in the scheme of principles. This same scholarly function —
education in history and principles to correct and avoid mistakes — was also to
be applied to the work of legislatures, meaning principally legislative interven-
tions to revise private law rules, and especially to wholesale codifications of
private law fields. The Harvard scholars sought openly to appropriate for
Americans the German professoriate's control over code-drafting.

While looking to England and Germany for models of intellectual influence
over lawmaking and law reform, the Harvard scholars at the same time re-

nounced a well-established model that was distinctively American, although it too had counterparts in England and the European continent. This was the model of education to produce lawyer-statesmen, the lawyers who in public office, private practice, and as contributors to legal literature, expound the basic principles of Constitutional law, and as policy intellectuals reform public law and legislation to adjust them to the changing needs of a liberal commercial republic. This had been the most conspicuous and prestigious conception — Tocqueville's conception — of the American lawyer's role. It had led the cream of the American bar to high legislative, appointive, and judicial office; and it had generated a distinguished legal literature, the public law treatises of St. George Tucker, Peter DuPonceau, Joseph Story, Theodore Sedgwick Jr., Thomas M. Cooley, John Norton Pomeroy, Christopher Tiedemann, and Ernst Freund, to name just a few. But just as the English reformers of legal education avoided any contact with the "science of legislation" — the law-reform projects of political economists and lawyers such as Adam Smith, Jeremy Bentham, James and John Stuart Mill, and James Fitzjames Stephen — so too the Harvard private-law jurists steered their curriculum and their students clear of engagement with the rapidly growing output of the legislative and administrative state.

Why did Harvard, and the many schools after 1900 that adopted its model, turn its back on the republican tradition of public law, law as a branch of statecraft? While continuing to be vigorous and vital in the actual practice and careers of leading lawyers, as a mode of legal education the tradition had largely fizzled. Repeatedly throughout the nineteenth century, James Wilson's, James Kent's, and David Hoffmann's lectures in the grand manner and most similar ventures featuring law as a branch of statecraft had failed to attract students; in contrast, as Langbein has related, Litchfield taught exclusively private law as an autonomous subject, and succeeded. While languishing commercially, the science of public law was overtaken intellectually. To the late-nineteenth-century legal scientists, the old American lawyer-statesmen seemed like oratorical windbags; for serious scholars the new beacons of scientific rigor were English analytical jurisprudence and German Pandectist and historical jurisprudence. True, there were emerging new sciences of legislation that were moderately rigorous in their own right, but by the 1880s these had their own associations and disciplinary departments in the university, economics and political science. The new law schools wanted to monopolize their own distinctive disciplinary turf, which was law as an autonomous technical subject, and to keep intruders off.

Moreover, the great issues of public law were extremely controversial politically. Harvard Law School had been torn apart and lost many of its students in the convulsive national debates over slavery in the 1850s. After the Civil War, the national arguments shifted to such issues as the authority of the federal government in the postwar South, the legal supervision of capital-labor conflict, and the regulation of industrial accidents, business and labor combinations, and of rates and service of railroads and public utilities. Professors in other departments such as economics and sociology were fired for taking positions that trustees found too liberal on these subjects. A law dean trying to sell the practical virtues of a theoretical training to a skeptical and conservative bar might well want to avoid the swamp of interdisciplinary work and the third rail of public law and policy issues.

Now of course it was precisely this tradition of public-law and interdisciplinary forms of legal studies that Yale had identified — as we have seen, almost in desperation — as the distinctive element of its mission. Yale was not alone in its desire to continue and modernize this tradition. The study of public law was central to the new law school Woodrow Wilson planned, but never built, at Princeton. It had a beachhead in Chicago because of the presence there of Ernst Freund, the great administrative law scholar. It dominated the political science department at Columbia, where law students could take courses; and it was central to the curriculum of the upstart new law school at Stanford, set amid the pruneyards of the San Francisco Peninsula. But the Harvard model inexorably advanced, taking over one school after another after 1900, sometimes by means of dispatching Harvard's own professors to occupy, like viceroys, the deanships of rival schools, as William A. Keener did at Columbia and Joseph H. Beale at Chicago. As Harvardization advanced, the public-law tradition retreated and was often ousted altogether as incompatible with the private-law focus of Harvard and especially with the case method, which was ill suited to the study of legislation and policy.

Yale's faculty kept a close, even obsessive eye on Harvard's example, and at least through the 1960s were constantly divided over whether the school's best chances for improvement lay in imitating Harvard or resisting it. Eventually Yale determined to do both at once. It succumbed to the Harvard program of sequenced curricula, full-time faculty, regular exams, and the case method of teaching. The case method secured a beachhead at Yale with the appointment of Arthur Corbin — the great contracts scholar and most distinguished figure of the Law School's first third-century — in 1906. The method had been adopted in most courses by 1912, and became the school's official policy when Thomas W. Swan took over as dean in 1916. But Yale also gradually sought to develop and exploit comparative advantage in its differences from Harvard — smaller classes (in 1926 the faculty voted to limit total enrollments to five hundred), a greater emphasis on public law and policy, a growing interest in interdisciplinary and empirical legal studies, and opportunities for students to do supervised research work. By the 1930s, as we shall see, many of Yale's faculty made nationally visible another difference, their more openly skeptical attitude and tone toward law itself, the ideal of legal certainty, and the existing legal order.

But for the first third of the century, Yale Law School was not yet a serious rival to Harvard and Columbia, the powerhouse law schools it regarded as its chief competitors for students whose talents and attainments might recommend them upon graduation to the law firms of New York City. Yale was struggling to put itself on the national map. It was still mostly drawing students from, and bound for local practice in, Connecticut. Its main priorities in the period of the deanships of Henry Wade Rogers (1903–16) and Thomas W. Swan (1916–26) were to attract enough students for the school to survive while trying to raise their average quality, to attract and retain faculty, to raise an endowment, and to find space for its rapidly expanding library. In 1909 the school took a risk by joining Harvard, Columbia, and Stanford in requiring two years of college; by 1911 it required a B.A. Enrollments dropped immediately; but Yale Law School propped them up by allowing Yale College undergraduates to enroll in pre-law courses for which they could earn credit toward a law degree; by thus shortening their law school course Yale gave itself a leg up over other law schools in the competition for Yale College seniors. By 1927 for the first time Yale Law School had enough applicants to reject more than it admitted.[5] The school in this period also hired some distinguished scholars, but had a hard time holding on to them. Corbin stayed on, as did Ernest Lorenzen, Edwin Borchard, Wesley Sturges, and Charles E. Clark; but the jurist Wesley N. Hohfeld, who arrived in 1914, died in 1918; and Walter Wheeler Cook, Karl Llewellyn, Edmund Morgan, and Leon Green, among others, taught at Yale only briefly before moving on to other schools. The space problems, however, were finally solved with the completion of the Sterling Law Building in 1931.

All this strenuous activity of self-improvement, while the faculty held its breath every fall to see how many students would show up to register (the numbers seesawed wildly, varying from 176 in 1919 to 422 in 1925[6]) and tried to capture a larger share of students who would appeal to law firms, would seem to leave little scope for experiments in legal education. Indeed, the law school took some steps to define itself more clearly as a professional rather than a liberal arts school.[7] Yet Rogers's last report as dean strikes a different note: In the future Yale Law School should expand to provide

> not merely an opportunity as now to equip men to earn their bread and butter in the law, but to establish, what does not yet exist in America, a School of Jurisprudence — in which a comparative study of judicial systems can be

carried on and in which our system of law can be studied in the light of all other systems.[8]

And Swan's first report adds another mission:

> [N]ot only must law be studied as a science and not merely as an art, but the law schools of the land must pay greater attention to the solution of the many legal-political problems which the changes in our economic and social life are creating with unprecedented rapidity, if their graduates are to be adequately trained to play their part as judges and legislators as well as lawyers.[9]

A law school committee report of 1917 neatly synthesizes the two ventures, calling for "scientific and constructive" studies that will enlist "jurisprudence" in the service of legislative reform:

> the study of law and its evolution, historically, comparatively, analytically and critically, with the purpose of directing its development in the future, improving its administration and perfecting its methods of legislation.[10]

The hand behind these proposals is clearly that of the legal philosopher and new addition to the Yale faculty, Wesley Newcomb Hohfeld. In a widely quoted address as president of the Association of American Law Schools in 1914, Hohfeld had set out his plan for the ideal American law school.[11] The plan was a typical one of the Progressive genre, seeking to enlist scientific learning in the causes of efficiency, elimination of waste and delay, and the modernization of legislation. The task would require no fewer than six new "departments of jurisprudence": (1) legal history of the world's legal systems, to free law from the dead hand of useless survivals; (2) comparative study of other legal systems in their "actual functioning," to furnish examples for legislation; (3) formal-analytic jurisprudence of the type of Hohfeld's own, path-breaking work on "fundamental legal conceptions;" (4) "critical" jurisprudence, the testing of existing legal rules against their "ethical, psychological, economic, social" bases and purposes, with the object of "legislative modification or repeal" of "worn-out doctrines" (examples include "liberty of contract," the law dealing with "strikes and boycotts," and "the doctrine of Rylands v. Fletcher and evaluation of legislative results and experiments" (such as the incidence of taxation, capital punishment, indeterminate sentences and parole); (5) legislative or "constructive" jurisprudence (basically the same as 4); and (6) "functional" or "dynamic" jurisprudence, or "law in motion" studies, systematic empirical study of the "actual functioning of the various rules of law," and of sources of obedience and resistance to law. By such means law schools would produce a special class of "professional jurists," who through "constructive books, magazine discussions and proposals, appearances before legislative commissions and committees" would become activist law reformers on the public stage. As if that were not enough, Hohfeld added calls for detailed study, by way of history and general jurisprudence, of the Anglo-American legal system, to overcome the practicing bar's narrowness, the source of its "lethargy and indifference" to existing evils and reform proposals. Finally he called for courses in "office practice" — that is, document drafting.[12]

Where the funds, faculty, and student demand for so dramatically expanded a program for research and teaching would come from, Hohfeld did not say. At the time his plan must have seemed impossibly grandiose and utopian — rhetorically inspiring, perhaps, but dreadfully impractical.

Nevertheless, most of Hohfeld's proposals were in the next generation to become reality — though ironically not to any great extent, at least at first, at Yale. In the 1920s, most of the scholars who took up "functional" approaches to law, using empirical methods to study law by reference to its social purposes and social effects, who criticized existing doctrines and recommended reform of procedures and legislation, and who assumed the public roles of crusading law reformers, were located at Columbia Law School. Some even came from the bastion of orthodoxy, Harvard. It was at Columbia that a group of reformers, Herman Oliphant, Underhill Moore, Karl N. Llewellyn, Hessel Yntema, and William O. Douglas, initiated their famous experiment to reorganize the law curriculum around a "functional approach," a broad and vague label that roughly stood for the reclassification of legal fields and courses into social rather than doctrinal categories. (The premier example was Douglas's attempt to integrate the fields of agency, partnership, and corporations into a series of "Business Units" courses called "Losses," "Management" and "Finance."[13]) Columbia also produced the most famous and influential of all interdisciplinary empirical studies of a legal field, a collaboration between a law school professor, Adolf A. Berle Jr., and an economist, Gardiner C. Means: *The Modern Corporation and Private Property* (1932). From Harvard's deanship, Roscoe Pound used his influence to promote "sociological jurisprudence," an amorphous label for a general interest in the social forces that generate legal acts and the social consequences of adopting them, as well as a specific large-scale empirical study of criminal courts in Cleveland.[14] A small group of Harvard law professors in fact pioneered almost all the intellectual trends that Yale came to consider its peculiar hallmarks — the study of administrative law and public utilities (Bruce Wyman, Felix Frankfurter, and James Landis), empirical research in law (the Cleveland study, Frankfurter and Landis's study of the business of the federal courts,[15] Frankfurter and Greene's study of labor injunctions[16]). They pioneered some of the new social roles too: mocking critic of the decisions of the Supreme Court (Thomas Reed Powell), policy entrepreneur (Frankfurter again), defender of the civil liberties of unpopular victims of state persecution (Frankfurter on Tom Mooney, the Bisbee deportations, Frankfurter and Zechariah Chafee on the Palmer raids). Frankfurter also helped Roger Baldwin organize the American Civil Liberties Union, defended the Amalgamated Clothing Workers against an injunction, protested the convictions of Sacco and Vanzetti, conducted public-interest test-case litigation with Louis D. Brandeis and Florence Kelley on wages and hours legislation for the National Consumer's League, and worked up a snowstorm of articles of legal and political commentary for *The New Republic.*[17]

Yale's New Leadership in Progressive and Interdisciplinary Legal Studies

Columbia and Harvard pointed the way. Yet leadership in what we might loosely call "Progressive law-professoring" — a category that would include "sociological jurisprudence," the "functional approach" to teaching and researching law, "legal realism," empirical studies of "law in action," interdisciplinary legal studies, public criticism of court decisions and legislation, intervention as amici and expert witnesses in test-case litigation, drafting procedural or legislative reform statutes, and using the media to publicize critiques and reforms — ultimately passed to Yale. At Columbia a faculty majority and the university president defeated the radical reformers and turned back their experiments. From the resignations that followed, Yale's faculty picked up Underhill Moore and William O. Douglas. At Harvard, Dean Pound became steadily more conservative and stifled the innovative strivings of the tiny Progressive element on his faculty. Yale reached its new preeminence from a conjunction of fortunate events. The stock market boomed in the late 1920s. With the completion of the new Sterling Building in 1931, the Law School acquired a physical space worthy of its ambitions. James R. Angell, who became Yale's president in 1921, actively encouraged the school to expand its range beyond narrow professional training by means of novel interdisciplinary enterprises. To that end Angell recruited the boundless energy and imagination of Robert M. Hutchins, appointed acting dean of the law school at twenty-seven and dean at twenty-eight, and gave him authority and resources to hire new faculty and connect the law school with Yale's new social science research center, the Institute of Human Relations. Besides Moore and Douglas, Hutchins hired the psychologist Edward S. Robinson and the economist Walton H. Hamilton, beginning a tradition of non-lawyer appointments that has continued at Yale ever since. Finally — and indispensably for Yale's eventual success—Hutchins's successor, Charles E. Clark, wholly supported and continued the new experiments, even through the adversities of the Great Depression and unceasing attacks on faculty "radicals" from conservative alumni and the press. Clark was convinced that Yale courted only mediocrity if it aspired to be only another conventional law school, a Harvard in miniature; as he told the Yale Corporation in 1932:

> There is a distinct place in this country for a restricted experimental type of law school. There is no place for another school of professional type merely adding to the already excessive number of members of the bar, and particularly is there no place for such school at New Haven in a small community between the two large cities of Boston and New York, both well supplied with professional law schools.[18]

Yale was certainly anything but "conventional": the extraordinary faculty it recruited in the late 1920s and '30s saw to that. This faculty was much more than the sum of its parts. The new instructors struck sparks off one another and worked together to create a body of research, a set of teaching methods and materials, and a copious fountain of law reform and policy proposals, all marked with a distinctive Yale style. The key figures of this revival, besides Deans Hutchins and Clark, were Thurman Arnold, Wesley Sturges, Harry Shulman, William O. Douglas, Walton Hale Hamilton, Underhill Moore, Abe Fortas, Fred Rodell, and Jerome Frank. I will focus here on the four men who formed the core of the group: Frank, Arnold, Douglas, and Hamilton. Their work and personalities set the tone of the law school's most innovative and distinctive intellectual enterprises. Each, also, was to play a major part in the New Deal.

Jerome N. Frank (1889–1957) was one of the most prominent lawyers and legal intellectuals of his time.[19] A prolific writer on jurisprudence, legal sociology, and public policy, Frank was also a successful corporate lawyer, general counsel of the New Deal's Agricultural Adjustment Administration (AAA) and Reconstruction Finance Corporation (RFC), and a commissioner and chairman of the Securities and Exchange Commission (SEC) before being appointed as a judge to the Second Circuit Court of Appeals in 1941. The son of a German Jewish lawyer, Frank studied political science and psychology at the University of Chicago, was graduated from the Chicago law school, and took up corporate practice, specializing in corporate finance and reorganizations. He was active in the Chicago Progressives' (ultimately failed) attempt to take over the corrupt city street railway system and bring it under public administration. In 1928 he moved to New York and a partnership in Chadbourne, Stanchfield & Levy, and while commuting to work wrote *Law and the*

Modern Mind (1930). The book made him famous in intellectual circles and came to be widely, though very misleadingly, identified as expressing the central credo of American legal realism. Its thesis—to put it in a bald summary that doesn't do justice to the sparkling wit and insight of the book—was that the rules announced in legal decisions are rationalizations for results reached on other, idiosyncratic grounds. The decisions of courts are thus indeterminate and unpredictable and the ideal of the "rule of law" as based on consistent decision making is a myth and mirage; but the myth persists because humans desire the comforting illusion of a controllable universe as a substitute for their lost fathers. The book led to Frank's appointment as a lecturer at the New School for Social Research and a "Research Associate" at Yale Law School.[20]

Though a central figure of the Yale realist group, Frank never held a regular faculty appointment. Attempts to appoint him permanently were thwarted by the opposition of Arthur Corbin, whose objections were that Frank was intellectually undisciplined, more a propagandist than a scholar, left-wing, and Jewish.[21] At Yale Frank co-taught with Thurman Arnold and Edward S. Robinson a course on "The Judicial Process from the Point of View of Social Psychology"[22] (known by students as "The Cave of the Winds") and through the 1940s a course on fact-finding in the trial process. Arthur Schlesinger, Jr. described him as "an intellectual, omnivorous in curiosity, sharp and skeptical of mind, pungent in expression, forever worrying problems to their roots. . . . Of medium height, spare, with a high, rather austere forehead and lively blue eyes, his bearing volatile and gay, he seemed never to stop working, talking or thinking. 'Being married to Jerome,' his wife said, 'is like being hitched to the tail of a comet.' "[23]

Thurman Wesley Arnold (1891–1969) was another lawyer's son from Laramie, Wyoming.[24] He attended college at Princeton, where he excelled academically but was a social outcast, and the Harvard Law School. After a brief and unsuccessful practice in Chicago he returned to Laramie to practice with his father, and then went into politics, first in the Wyoming state assembly and then as a popular Progressive mayor of Laramie. A client who brought him to West Virginia on a business trip arranged his appointment as dean of the West Virginia Law School in 1927. There he led his new school to undertake a typical Progressive project of social research in the cause of reform, in this case the gathering of statistics on West Virginia courts in order to reform judicial practice and procedure. This project brought him into association with Charles E. Clark of Yale, who was embarked on a similar study of the Connecticut courts. Clark invited Arnold to Yale as a visiting professor in 1930 and then offered him an appointment. Roscoe Pound immediately offered Arnold a professorship at Harvard for more pay, but Yale met the competing offer and Arnold liked Yale better. He remained on the Yale faculty, in between frequent trips to Washington, until 1938, teaching among other things a course (with Clark and later Fleming James) on law administration and one (with Edward Robinson and Frank) on law and psychology, and publishing two best-selling books on legal and economic rhetoric as symbolism and ritual, *The Symbols of Government* (1935) and *The Folklore of Capitalism* (1937), along with an impressive quantity of law review articles, reviews, and occasional pieces for magazines. In 1938 (as I will relate in more detail) he resigned to become the head of the Antitrust Division, where he served until his appointment to the D.C. Circuit Court in 1943. Bored with being a judge, he left the bench in 1945 to found with Abe Fortas and Paul Porter the Washington, D.C., law firm that still bears his name. He had neither the patience for detail nor the skill at business or attracting clients that make a successful corporate lawyer; but Fortas fortunately had more than enough of both to ensure the success of the firm; and Arnold was an asset to the firm as a formidable advocate, both for business clients and for people accused of being Communists and subversives in the Cold War period. From Washington he continued to commute up to Yale to teach antitrust law.

A 1939 *Saturday Evening Post* profile described Arnold as a "large, somewhat paunchy, middle-aged man with a yellowish face and overflowing human gusto, who looks like a small-town storekeeper and talks like a native Rabelais. He also enjoys the distinction of being the only New Dealer who is also an Elk, and very likely the only Elk who is also an iconoclast. . . . His costume is disheveled. His voice is loud. His exaggerations are Gargantuan. His energy appears to be completely uncontrolled. He thinks so far that he rarely says more than a third of what he means, and commonly discusses three subjects at once. Indeed he seems at first to be another Marx brother, strayed into the Government by mistake."[25]

William O. Douglas (1898–1980) was born in Yakima, Washington.[26] His father died when he was only five. He and his sisters were raised by his strong-willed, self-reliant, and puritanical mother in a religiously and politically conservative town. His upbringing left Douglas with a lifelong sense of being abandoned and alone (despite, or perhaps partly because of, four marriages) and a social outcast, a fierce dislike of political and religious orthodoxy, and an ardent love of mountains and wilderness. After a spell as a high school teacher in Yakima, he determined to study law, and rode the rails east to arrive, completely broke, at Columbia Law School. To pay the fees he tutored the dull and idle sprigs of the rich to help them get into fancy colleges. At law school he attracted the attention of the dean, Harlan Fiske Stone, and did research for the brilliant and unorthodox commercial law scholar Underhill Moore. After graduating second in his class, Douglas was recruited in 1925 to the New York law firm of Cravath, Henderson & de Gersdorff, then a firm of about fifty lawyers specializing in corporate reorganization practice. Columbia invited him back as an assistant professor in 1927 to teach commercial law. He allied himself with the "realist" reformers such as Underhill Moore and Herman Oliphant, who were trying to remake Columbia's curriculum. The reformers lost their struggle when their candidate for dean was not selected. Several of the losing side resigned, some to found a new research institute in law at Johns Hopkins. Moore and Douglas were recruited by the young Dean Hutchins to Yale. Hutchins became president of the University of Chicago shortly afterward and offered young Bill Douglas, whom he called "the outstanding professor of law in the nation," to come to Chicago for a salary of $20,000—an almost unimaginable sum for a professor in Depression America. Douglas accepted; but changed his mind when Hutchins's successor, Dean Clark, arranged for him to become Sterling Professor of Law at Yale at a salary of $15,000. He was thirty-three years old and had been in law teaching for four years.

Was he worth it? From this observer's perspective some seventy years later, he was. In the few years he had before public office claimed him, Douglas wrote seminal articles on business tort liability, corporate reorganizations, and the operation of the Securities Act of 1933; put together casebooks radically restructuring the field of business associations; instituted a joint law-business program with the Harvard Business School; and undertook massive empirical studies of bankruptcy administration and business failures, which required huge commitments of time commuting to New York in order to interview bankrupts and processing the data that emerged. He was probably the hardest working and most productive of this remarkable group of Yale scholar-activists. But his work is not impressive only for its quantity: He also had a strikingly original, penetrating, and powerful mind.

His subsequent career is, of course, well known. After directing a study of reorganization committees for the SEC, he was appointed chairman of the SEC in 1937, where he served until Roosevelt appointed him to the U.S. Supreme Court in 1939. Roosevelt seriously considered choosing him as his running mate in 1944, but passed him over in favor of the better-known Harry Truman. Truman actually did ask him to be his running mate in 1948, but Douglas turned him down, possibly because he hoped that the liberal wing of the Democratic Party would draft him as the presidential candidate. He remained on the Court—surviving an attempt inspired by President Nixon to impeach him—until resigning, most reluctantly, in 1975.

Walton Hale Hamilton (1881–1958) was another émigré from small-town America, born in Hiwassee College, Tennessee.[27] He received his B.A. from the University of Texas in 1907 and his Ph.D. in economics from the University of Michigan in 1913. Before Hutchins recruited him to Yale Law School in 1928, Hamilton had taught at the University of Michigan, Chicago, Amherst College, and the Robert Brookings Graduate School in Washington, D.C.[28]

Hamilton came to Yale as an institutional economist in the tradition of Thorstein Veblen and the sociologist Charles Horton Cooley. The method of institutional economics was to break down abstract universals of classical and neoclassical economic theory into concrete historical and sociological descriptions of particular trades, industries, and markets for goods and services.[29] "Hammy's" specialty was the study of how different industries set wages and prices, which in turn led him to the historical study of costs, path-dependent customs, and other sources of price rigidities and wage stickiness, including local monopolies like patent pools and informal price-fixing agreements. He and his disciples wrote dozens of such monographs, with titles like "Milk," "Whiskey," "The Automobile Tire," and "Dresses."[30] (Boris Bittker, who worked with Hamilton both as a law student and in the government, and a friend once produced a hilarious parody of the genre and of Hamilton's gentle, graceful, leisurely narrative literary style, called "Beer—The Broth with a Froth."[31]) Once he arrived at a law school, Hamilton applied his historical-evolutionary, thick-descriptive method to legal abstractions. Some of his finest work—"The Ancient Maxim Caveat Emptor," "Businesses Affected with a Public Interest," "The Path of Due Process of Law"—shows how phrases or concepts get lifted out of historical or social context, misapplied through casual generalization across time and place, and then frozen in place with the status of revered traditions or, worse, abstract universal laws.[32]

When he arrived at Yale he had no legal training; but unlike many scholars appointed from other disciplines he adjusted immediately to the new milieu and became one of the most energetic members of the school's innovative core. He taught many different subjects, including trade regulation, constitutional law, public service law, torts, public control of business, judicial process (with Clark), and a course called "The Frontiers of Public Law." He collaborated in teaching and writing ventures with all his principal colleagues, and the influence of his institutionalist approach can be detected in all their work.

As will be seen, Hamilton was treated by Roosevelt's administration as a consultant and all-purpose wise man on economic policy, and in the 1930s was often called away from New Haven on a variety of New Deal assignments. He took leave from Yale to work full time as a deputy on Arnold's antitrust staff; and after the war, left the school to join the firm of Arnold,

Fortas and Porter. Once at the firm Hamilton was finally admitted to the bar and was lead counsel in much of the firm's litigation practice. He was a gentle man of unusual grace, charm, and good humor, though his life was tinged with travail and tragedy. His first wife killed herself on the day that her divorce from Hamilton became final. He was chronically afflicted with bad health; he broke down from nervous exhaustion in 1934; and by the 1950s his deteriorating eyesight had rendered him legally blind, so that the massive documentary records of the cases he undertook had to be read to him.

The animating spirit of this group was their revolt against formalism.[33] Formalism was a many-headed hydra. The antiformalists' motto might have been Justice Holmes's, "Think things, not words." They were suspicious of the categories, concepts, principles, and rules of the classical doctrines of both private and public law, the formidable body of legal constructs and reasoning methods that had been assembled in great treatises and leading court decisions of 1870 to 1930; and of classical and neoclassical political economy. They insisted on trying to describe the legal-economic system in pragmatic terms, as "facts" rather than "words," "results" rather than "principles," the "activities of officials" and of private law-interpreters and law-appliers rather than the rules governing officials, the "law in action" rather than the "law on the books" — and perhaps most distinctively, the operations of concrete and particular institutions and organizations rather than the decisions of featureless abstract individuals, the A's and B's and "reasonable persons" of legal theory, the rational maximizers of economic theory.

In some respects, of course, they carried on the work of an earlier generation of legal critics.[34] Holmes, one of the group's intellectual heroes, had pioneered in breaking down doctrinal formulations of "rights" and "principles" into "predictions of what the courts will do in fact" — to designate the scope of property "rights" or contract and tort-based "duties" in terms of specific remedies injured parties would have for breach. Holmes pointed out that sometimes the law gives the owner of "property" the remedy of an injunction or bringing a criminal complaint, sometimes only a remedy in damages (the violator may continue to violate, if he is willing to pay), and sometimes no remedy at all, because the harm to property is privileged — actually encouraged by the legal system — such as the economic injuries inflicted by competition to a competitors' profits.[35] The actual "right" is coextensive with the remedy, the practical consequences of violating it: Hence, a contracting party has an option to perform or pay damages. Wesley Hohfeld elegantly synthesized this disaggregation of basic legal concepts into specific remedy-types in his "Fundamental Legal Conceptions."[36] Arthur Corbin was a leader among the many realist critics who checked classical principles against the facts of cases that supposedly supported them, and found substantial variation and departures from principle in the actual case law. When Samuel Williston, the great classical contracts scholar, argued that a fundamental principle of common law was that promises, to be enforceable, must be supported by "consideration"—that is, promises or performances bargained for in exchange for such promises—Corbin produced bundles of cases in which the courts had enforced gratuitous promises relied upon by the promisee.[37] Leon Green studied thousands of tort cases to discover that the regular patterns of decision gave the term "negligence" markedly different practical meanings depending on the factual context or parties (such as railroad accidents, farm machinery accidents, or auto accidents; or suits against railroad companies by shippers, passengers, employees, or bystanders).[38] In field after field, the realists argued, there was not one governing doctrinal principle, but many, and which doctrine would be given force and effect depended on usually inarticulate premises of policy and factual context.

The purpose of "realist" critique and scholarship was to dredge up the submerged bases of fact and policy actually informing legal decisions. If these underground policies and facts were valid and defensible—as most realists believed of the decisions of the common law courts—they could and should become the explicit ground of legal decision, so that lawyers and clients and officials could predict results more certainly and argue for them directly rather than covertly. If, on the other hand, the grounds were debatable political prejudices or dubious economic theory or erroneous empirical assumptions—as most realists believed of decisions of constitutional courts invalidating Progressive social legislation—the critiques would bring the premises into the open air and discourage judges from acting on them.

Another strand of critical inquiry was sociological. It asked how legal rules were actually applied by those with discretion to enforce them; how much slippage there was between paper rules and actual compliance; and how much those subject to laws voluntarily obeyed, resisted, or simply ignored the law.

The Yale Progressives adopted all these kinds of critique. They then went far beyond them, drastically extending their substance and intensifying their critical tone, sometimes to the acute discomfort of the earlier critical jurists like Corbin and Pound. Despite much variation in approach and topics of interest, the writings of the group converged on some common clusters of basic assumptions and operating methods:

The delusiveness of words. The Yale scholars were relentless critics of verbal formulae in legal, political, and economic discourse. They claimed that the textual analysis of words divorced from social context and function was almost always delusive. Hamilton and Douglass Adair wrote a book critiquing the idea that the word "commerce" in the Constitution's clause giving Congress power to regulate interstate commerce, could plausibly be interpreted by modern courts to mean what it meant in 1787.[39] They reconstructed the original context to show that the Framers were giving effect to a body of "mercantilist" views and policies, which moderns, especially the "economic individualists" who appeal to original meanings, have long since rejected. The Framers, they argued, used general words, and those words have been given fresh meanings by "fact" — for instance, the development of the "industrial system," which had moved economic activities that were once confined within single states into organic relations with the rest of the nation and the world.[40] Frank pointed out — repeatedly, since he was inclined to repetition of his favorite ideas — that debates over public policy were prone to using buzzwords such as "competition," "monopoly," "government policing," and "regulation" that have a vague and shifting content and tend to substitute slogans for facts and analysis. He proposed that analysis of appropriate government policies to address the many different degrees and types of imperfect competition might proceed more effectively if "ugwug" were to replace "public utility" and "agwag" to replace "regulation." In the same spirit, asked to define "Property" for the *Encyclopaedia of Social Sciences,* Hamilton wrote:

> PROPERTY is a euphonious collocation of letters which serves as a general term for the miscellany of equities that persons hold in the commonwealth. A coin, a lance, a tapestry, a monastic vow, a yoke of oxen, a female slave, an award of alimony, a homestead, a first mortgage, a railroad system, a preferred list and a right of contract are all to be discovered within the catholic category. Each of these terms, meaningless in itself, is a token or focus of a scheme of relationships; each has its support in sanction and repute; each is an aspect of an enveloping culture.[41]

The power of words and symbols. While the Yale critics aimed to expose the emptiness of legal forms and the delusiveness of legal language, at the same time, taking a more anthropological approach to law than most of their Progressive-realist contemporaries, they recognized the power of legal forms as myths, rituals, ceremonies, symbols, and ideologies. Legal forms and language might not realistically describe the "concrete realities" of economy and society they pretended to reflect and regulate, but by structuring perceptions of the world, the symbols soothed fears of a disorderly and anarchic world, imparted illusions of control, enabled people to assimilate new phenomena to familiar descriptive and moral categories. Thurman Arnold wrote his two best-selling books[42] on the magic power of words, such as the use of "private property," with its associations of individual persons holding on to their treasured belongings, to rationalize the power giant industrial organizations held over others and their legal immunity from public regulation.[43] This emphasis on the power of symbols and language, as Mark Fenster has valuably emphasized, marks an important departure of the Yale school, particularly Arnold, from legal realism.[44]

From principles to functions. The Yale group asked not only, How can we reanalyze legal doctrines and decisions so as to make them more predictable to litigants and judges? but also, How can we reanalyze them so as to assess whether they effectively serve valid social functions and purposes? In a brilliant pioneering article on vicarious liability in tort, for example, Douglas asked whether the doctrinal tests distinguishing acts of agents for which businesses were liable from acts for which they were not (such as whether the agent was on his boss's business or a "frolic and detour," or whether the agent was an employee or independent contractor) made sense from the point of view of businessmen managing risks (by avoidance, prevention, or shifting), or of legislatures or courts deciding how to distribute risks and losses. He answered that the existing doctrinal distinctions were arbitrary and mostly irrelevant to both the business job of administering risks and the social issue of resolving what costs businesses should bear. This did not necessarily mean that the tests should be abolished, but that they needed reevaluation in light of their social functions.[45] In the same vein, Douglas's radical restructuring of the teaching and study of business law proposed to sweep away the division of the field by forms of organization (agency, partnership, corporation, etc.) to focus on "a consideration of the phenomena observed in the organization and operation of a business . . . of the things men attempt to do . . . when engaging in a business . . . that would discard at one sweep the theological refinements of the concepts."[46] The main new topics of such an approach, using nonlegal as well as legal materials to explore them, would be (1) assembly of resources, especially attracting capital through short and long-term financing; (2) actual (rather than notional or formal) control or direction of the business enterprise ("If 'control' or 'direction' be taken to mean the legal and non-legal devices for forcing certain members of the group to act in certain ways and for effecting certain policies . . . practically no business unit today exists in which the phenomenon of allocation of 'control' among labor, creditors, employees, investors and the state is not present."[47]); and (3) the allocation of losses. Even more ambitiously, Douglas's large-scale empirical studies of bankrupt debtors were meant to study the problem of bankruptcy through its causes and roots, by asking why businesses fail and wage earners declare bankruptcy, with a view to adjusting bankruptcy administration to the varieties of causes of insolvency.[48]

In these studies, Douglas went well beyond the traditional realist technique of reexamining cases and the rationales of case law. He relocated the legal element as incidents and instruments of larger ends—the ends of persons seeking compensation, businessmen managing risk, government decision-makers allocating costs and distributing losses and addressing problems of insolvency by trying to prevent its incidence as well as cope with its results.

From doctrines to institutions. One of Walton Hamilton's main contributions to the team was to impart the methods and focus of institutional economics, which had conducted parallel antiformalist campaigns against orthodox economics. In economic theory, prices and wages are set by the intersection of supply and demand curves in markets created by the preferences of abstractly described self-interested individuals. To institutionalists, they are determined by complex social processes—collusion or price leadership among dominant firms, restrictive practices or trading rules sanctioned by professional or trade associations, or deals struck with regulators or agreements imposed by investment bankers, by bureaucratic job-description and wage-classification schedules, by formal or informal agreements with unions, by the discretion given to salesmen, and by historically derived customs. Such processes vary considerably from industry to industry and even firm to firm. In the spirit of Hamilton, Arnold believed that the people who had caused and then misdiagnosed the catastrophe of the Great Depression were people like classical lawyers, orthodox economists, and financial experts, who understood the economy and industrial world by its symbols—abstract market theory, stock prices as indicators of value, corporations as owners of private property competing for profits. They had failed to grasp the practical realities of enterprises as professional managers (and presumably unillusioned observers such as Arnold) saw them, as organizations actually involved in the production of goods and services.[49]

Jerome Frank applied something resembling the institutionalist method to the trial process—again adventuring beyond the conventional legal scholar's domain of appellate cases—to analyze how the key outputs of the judicial system, "law" and "facts," are actually produced. The work he was always best known for, which made him the (in)famous symbol of the legal-realist movement, was his picture of judicial decisions as inevitably influenced by the backgrounds, ideologies, and personalities of individual judges.[50] But his more substantial and enduring work is about how the "facts" are generated that supply the material for decision in the first place. The formal model of the trial is one in which the jury distills findings of facts from adversary presentation and applies to them the law as given by the judge. Frank's penetrating account of fact-production underlined the inherent unreliability of witness and documentary evidence and the many distortions that evidence undergoes in partisan preparation and presentation, the incomprehensibility of judges' instructions to juries, and the discretionary breadth and unpredictability of jury decisions. What makes legal prediction difficult even under apparently clear legal rules, Frank pointed out, is that the facts triggering the legal result you want may not be the facts the trial process will find.[51] Moreover, the institutionalists liked to emphasize the important point — to this day often forgotten even by lawyers and judges who should know better from experience — that legal words and rules are not self-enforcing. People in organizations — agencies, law firms, companies, prosecutors, stockholders — who are delegated the job of interpreting and enforcing rules can also ignore or distort or evade them. Unless one understands the structures and incentives and interests of the organizations whose agents act on the words, one cannot understand or predict the effects of legal enactments.[52]

The public-private distinction. The Yale group also expanded on one of the key points of Progressive realism, its critique of the public-private distinction in classical law and political economy. The classical model divided the legal-social world into a "private" realm in which individuals voluntarily ordered their affairs by contract, and a "public" realm of law that coercively regulated such private relations. In this model market, transactions, governed and structured as they were by common-law rules of property, contract, and tort, were private; whereas state action in the form of legislation and administrative rulings that went beyond common law was public. Progressive critics like the philosopher Morris Cohen, the Columbia lawyer-economist Robert L. Hale, and the contracts scholar Arthur Corbin attacked this distinction at the root. Property was sovereignty, a legal delegation of the right to use state force (to exclude others or enforce conditions on their use of the property) to private owners.[53] Contracts gave parties the right to call on the state for enforcement, and the state put its force behind policies favoring one party or the other.[54] Common-law rules defining torts, duress, and the privileged infliction of economic harm made up the coercive system of rules governing labor conflicts. These rules, by granting or denying powers to organize, to refuse access to valuable resources, and to coerce or resist coercion, distributed bargaining advantages and wealth to private actors.[55] In short, state coercion was an omnipresent element in supposedly private consensual transactions. Private law was a regulatory system as much as public law. The clear implication was that if the private-law regime were not a fair or efficient regulatory system, it could and should be modified by public law.

The stakes of this debate escalated during the New Deal years. Business critics of the New Deal and their lawyers regularly denounced the tyranny of bureaucratic government and the dangers to liberty and efficiency of government regulation and taxation of private business activity. The Yale group devoted a good deal of its energy attacking the "private activity good/government interference bad" premises of such critics. The powers and evils attributed to government, they pointed out, are just as characteristic of private corporations. Although personified as individuals, corporations are organized as bureaucratic hierarchies; they regulate, tax, and coerce those subject to their power; and although their subjects in theory consent to such exactions, as a practical matter they are often less able to influence their corporate rulers or hold them accountable than they are many acts of democratic governments. Frank made such points a regular feature of his public writings and testimony.[56] Hamilton incorporated them into his "institutionalist" descriptions of business practices.[57] Arnold produced two classic works for a popular readership, *The Symbols of Government* and *The Folklore of Capitalism,* developing variations on these themes. A typical passage comes from a chapter on "The Benevolence of Taxation by Private Organizations":

> It was ... bad for men to become dependent on government organization; but it was a good thing for employees to become completely dependent on industrial organization, which was supposed to foster initiative and independence down to the lowest worker. ... [W]hen the government wasted, it was wasting the taxpayer's money. When a railroad, or public utility, wasted it was wasting its own money — which, of course, every free individual has a right to do unless you are willing to change your "system of government" and adopt "Socialism." Of course, the great industrial organizations collected the money they spent from the same public from which the government collected. However, in the case of a public utility, or textile concern, or a building corporation, the collection was voluntary, since men could go without clothes, light or houses. ... When the government collected, the collection was an involuntary tax, which in the long run fell upon the poor, because of the great principle that it is unjust to tax the rich any more than you happen to be taxing them at the time, and that the rich will refuse to hire the poor if taxed unjustly.[58]

The defense of administration. While legal Progressives were insisting that private groups regulated through bureaucratic hierarchies and restricted freedom as much or more than governments did, they also energetically defended administrative agencies against the charge that they were arbitrary despots. Such charges were frequently made by anti–New Deal groups such as the Lawyer's Committee of the American Liberty League and given extra weight by Roscoe Pound, reporting for a committee of the American Bar Association.[59] The best-known work of the time defending agency discretion was *The Administrative Process,* by James Landis, Douglas's predecessor as head of the SEC and Pound's successor as dean at Harvard.[60] The Yale group contributed substantially to the argument that agencies were not only equal to judges in the procedural protections they afforded to regulated groups, but in most respects superior: Their process was speedier as well as more scrupulous, it was spared the expense, delays, and uncertainties of adversary litigation, and administrators could work more efficiently with industry because they understood its problems.[61] The worship of courts by the established bar was only superstition. To quote Arnold again:

> The distinction between bureaus and courts is important. Courts are bound by precedent, and bureaus are bound by red tape. Of course courts are forced to follow precedent even when it leads to absurd results because of their solemn obligation[s]. . . . But bureaus in allowing themselves to be bound by red tape do so out of pure malice and disregard for the fundamentals of freedom. . . . The distinction between a bureau which is a very bad sort of thing and a commission with quasi-judicial powers . . . is that the commission . . . is more like a court than it is like a bureau. Therefore if we are very watchful of these commissions and see [that their work] occurs only on lower levels, and in comparatively minor matters such as the valuation of railroads, the fixing of rates, workmen's compensation, banking, taxation, trade regulation, zoning, immigration, irrigation of arid lands, drainage, insurance, and similar things which do not involve the great principles of freedom — as for example a suit for libel and slander, replevin or criminal conversation — we may escape this new form of despotism.[62]

Attitude and tone. The Yale group, as we have seen, borrowed eclectically from all the main contemporary strands of critical jurisprudence and social thought. They added a distinctive voice of their own. Perhaps what set them most apart from other realist and Progressive lawyers was attitude — a heightened and intensified critical spin coupled with a manner of huge satirical amusement. They not only criticized bodies of case law, but also took aim at individual judges and scholars and particular decisions and texts; they held up to ridicule the prevalent manner of judicial and scholarly reasoning. Their broadsides were pointedly — and ungratefully — directed at the classical generation itself: Their main targets were the "high priests" (a term they often used) of what they perceived, and caricatured, as legal orthodoxy: Harvard doctrinalists such as Langdell, Williston, and Joseph Beale and the treatises they wrote synthesizing thousands of cases into internally consistent systems of principle; the Harvard method of teaching exclusively from appellate cases; the conservative majority of the U.S. Supreme Court and the conservative leaders of the bar; the American Law Institute, which periodically assembled the entire priesthood for the particularly sterile enterprise of producing Restatements of the Law,[63] and the American Bar Association, more often than not a redoubt of attacks on the New Deal.

Perhaps Harvard's most important contribution to the development of Yale was to give it something solid to define itself by, a heavy successful father both to emulate and to hurl itself against in rebellion. Harvard's was a dogmatic tradition that inspired antidogmatism, a disciplinary isolation that inspired interdisciplinary experiment, a grave condescension and assumption of superiority that inspired the urge to ridicule and destroy.[64] Ironically, in its own heyday, the Harvard-based classical tradition had itself been a critical one. It aspired to analyze and synthesize the doctrinal output of courts and shape the cases into a manageable order by use of generalizing categories — theory. In the process large numbers of cases (and virtually all the reasons the judges themselves gave for their decisions) had to be discarded or ignored as mistakes, outliers, and anachronisms, and many others tortured into submission to the theoretical scheme. Doctrinal legal science is not an intellectually conservative enterprise; it remakes the legal-conceptual order. Its virtues of simplicity, theoretical elegance, and ultimately even some predictability, if the courts and bar buy the treatise and buy into its conceptual order and categories, require some ruthless iconoclasm. The significant works of that generation — Williston on contracts, Thayer and Wigmore on evidence, Holmes on torts, Gray on perpetuities — were anything but reverential toward the output of the courts. Nonetheless their critiques were mostly restrained and respectful; and they rarely claimed do be doing more than simply setting in order the work of judges.

The Yale crowd by contrast were — at least in their rhetoric — showy iconoclasts, destroyers of the temple. They blasted away at the pillars of the bench, bar, and legal academy with a tone of high-spirited mockery, ironic detachment, and sweeping overstatement that had rarely been heard before in established legal circles. Frank's *Law and the Modern Mind* characterized the belief in law as a body of certain and predictable rules as the product of a childish impulse to preserve the illusion of an orderly and morally just world controlled by an omniscient father-substitute, the judge. Thurman Arnold analyzed the meetings of the American Law Institute as a form of ritual, the incantations of a priestly caste reassuring the legal world of its orderliness and predictability, among other means through the use of charming parables (the "Illustrations" of Restatement principles).[65] And surely only at Yale could anything have been written like Fred Rodell's *Woe Unto You, Lawyers* (1939), a broadside attack on legal "words and concepts and principles" as meaningless mumbo-jumbo that "float in a purgatory of their own, halfway between the heaven of abstract ideals and the hell of plain facts and completely out of touch with both of them."[66] The main social function of law, said Rodell, was to enable lawyers to collect high fees for protecting interests of the conservative and wealthy. It would be better to abolish lawyers and their law altogether and replace them with a body of technical experts armed with common sense and practical knowledge of the field of dispute.

Even at Yale few others ever went quite so far as Rodell, but they egged him on, as they all egged one another on to ever wittier and more slashing critiques of the formalist establishment. They collaborated on empirical research, policy projects, articles for law reviews and magazines, talks on radio shows publicizing their ideas, and new teaching ventures. This was a high-spirited and hard-drinking body of companions (apparently Frank brought the bootleg liquor up from New York). Even the gruff loner Douglas warmed up in their company. They were constantly trying out new ventures and between long workdays and nights out on the town together seem to have rarely slept. But for all their perpetual mood of slightly manic hilarity, their basic aims were serious, earnestly pursued, and for the most part intensely practical.

The collection of ideas a later age has come to call "legal realism" was, as the English legal theorist Neil Duxbury has said, "more a mood than a movement,"[67] and though united in their critique of "formalism" its various factions were very divided. Some divisions have already been noted. Older realists such as Corbin wanted to reconnect the study of doctrine to the evolutionary forces and folkways underlying law; but their method was relatively conservative, to stick to the study of cases but to show how general abstract categories like "offer and acceptance" were applied differently in different commercial contexts. Other realists, such as the newer Yale group, wanted to go outside doctrine to study the "law in action." These were, however, divided on whether if you do go outside, you find order or an arbitrary jumble. The party of order — which would include Hamilton, Clark, Douglas, and Moore — assumed there were regularities in legal decision making and the social effects of law. These were discoverable through social-scientific investigation — such as court studies and industry studies. Scientific (or at least well-informed) policymaking could be based on knowledge of such regularities. If you found the pattern, you would also know the path to reform. The party of jumble or chaos is probably best represented by Jerome Frank's law- and fact-skepticism, with its emphasis on the wild variety of influences that go into the production of legal outcomes. Between these camps was a latent conflict, with contrary implications for the practical purposes of legal studies. For if the party of chaos were right, the study of law in action would reveal its contingency, variety, unpredictability, and uncontrollability. It would not be susceptible to scientific policymaking. All you could predict about law in action was that the effect of law on social action was unpredictable. What helped to mediate this conflict between approaches were two things. One was the spirit of inquiry: It is always better to try to understand the world, even if that should unsettle old truths and produce new uncertainties. The other was the spirit of pragmatic experiment: To find out what works, try it. If that doesn't work, try something else. This latter spirit was to prove, needless to say, deeply congenial to the programs of the New Deal.

Some realists saw themselves as insiders, others as outsiders. Insiders saw themselves as actual or potential players within the system: They took existing legal institutions and doctrines as their starting point for the enterprise of legal rationalization and reform. Outsiders started from a point of alienation from the existing system, or aspects of it. Some assailed and ridiculed it from without, seeking to expose its intellectually threadbare foundations. Others, like the Yale activist labor and immigration lawyer Walter Nelles, viewed the legal system as largely the instrument of capitalist exploitation and saw their job as trying to use its formal protections of rights to shield dissenters or minorities from harassment. Still others, like the Columbia scholars who went off to found the short-lived Johns Hopkins Institute, viewed the law from an Olympian scientific detachment or purely anthropological interest, as visitors from Mars, or Papua New Guinea. The factions differed sharply on what law schools were for and whom they should train — research scholars, policy scientists, private practitioners alert to the social effects of law, or all three. These differences eventually sank the Columbia experiment, because many of Columbia's faculty and the university's president could not see a bright future for a law school that organized itself primarily as an institute for disinterested research rather than as a school for training lawyers.

Most of the leading Yale faculty were protean in their approaches: doctrinalist and interdisciplinary, pattern theorists and chaos theorists, insiders and outsiders, sober policy analysts, and mocking or detached anthropologists. Their derision toward classical legal science, classical Constitutional law, and classical economics and economic policy was compensated for by an equally intense confidence in the potential of objective fact-investigation to yield solutions to policy problems, of objective social science to reveal regularities in legal and social experience, and of well-trained lawyers to solve basic legal and social problems. Indeed even an historian who generally admires, as I do, the brilliance and iconoclastic spirit of this band of law teachers will often be irritated by their blithe assumption that, once the formalist scales of illusion have been scraped from their eyes, clear-headed sensible fellows immersed in the technical facts of policy problems will briskly arrive at the appropriate practical solutions. Even at its best, this attitude led them toward a naïve faith in technocracy. At its worst, as occasionally in Arnold's work, it led toward an admiration of extremely antidemocratic and even fascist administration if it proved itself "efficient."[68]

On balance the aims of the Yale pioneers were more worldly than academic. Their immediate aim was the reform of legal scholarship and education. We cannot understand them without understanding that they viewed law schools as key platforms from which to launch the cadres of a new legal profession, which would be equipped to reform society by reforming its laws and their administration. Yale Law School in particular, freed from the ingrown stuffiness and inertia of the Harvard model, and fitted up with a new curriculum and new methods of research and teaching, could be the vanguard of the reform movement to produce more competent and socially responsible practitioners, more informed and effective judges and administrators, more carefully framed and efficient proposals for the reform of legal policies and the legal system.

Frank might have been a skeptic to the point of nihilism, but his aim was to produce activists, not paralyzed doubters. He wound up his studies of chaos in fact-production with a slew of practical proposals for reforming the trial process so as to make it a more reliable fact-finder.[69] He lobbied strenuously for changing law schools into "clinical-lawyer" schools on the model of medical schools. The case method was too divorced from actual practice, especially because it accepted the "facts" of cases as given in appellate opinions, far away from the messy indeterminate processes that produced them. Law teachers should have years of practice experience and should train students in practice skills in real and simulated practice settings.[70]

None of his colleagues adopted Frank's ideas about legal education (partly because few of them had as much practice experience as he would have required[71]), but their aims too were practical. Arnold adopted the pose of the disinterested observer, seeing his own legal culture through an anthropologist's eyes. At his confirmation hearings to become Roosevelt's antitrust chief in 1937, he blandly asserted that none of his books contained "any [particular policy] recommendation whatever."[72] But of course his work on law as symbols and folklore has a serious policy-directed purpose. It is meant to enable the lawyer and citizen to pierce the veils of myth and illusion surrounding public policy discussions. The lawyer should free himself of the fictions that corporations are like individual property-owners and that unlike government bureaucracies they do not regulate or coerce; and, once having freed his mind to perceive and pursue practical ends, should manipulate the symbols to bring those ends about. In 1936 Arnold told Harold Laski that:

> I have now, as you know, come to believe that a completely skeptical position means only a futility, that a sincere humanitarian must formulate a philosophy in words if he is to move people about or even maintain his own morale and that leadership consists in skill in formulating such a philosophy and getting people to respond to it. . . . When young men cannot listen to you

without being intensely moved and when the only result of Walter Wheeler Cook [a prominent critical realist] is to make them extremely hardboiled, I began to see what was wrong with the realist's position. And so I tried to express a philosophy which permitted an idealistic use of the opinion which can only be obtained in a skeptical frame of mind. In it was, I am aware, all the inconsistency between the position of an observer and the position of a reformer but I have, so far as my own spiritual comfort is concerned, been able to jump from one platform to another without feeling logically inconsistent.[73]

Hamilton turned to the long view of history to put in context some of the main doctrines of contemporary conservative legalism, such as "due process of law," "caveat emptor," and "business affected with a public interest"; but his purpose was critical, not antiquarian. He sought to sheer these doctrines of ancient pedigree and show them up as rooted in distortions and misunderstandings of their development.[74] Hamilton's economic writings were even more immediately policy-directed — proposing restructuring of employment relations, and regulation of competition and prices, in industries such as bituminous coal whose internal structural evolution had produced dysfunctional rigidities.[75]

Douglas was overtly vocational in his aims. Among other things, he wanted his school to train more competent business lawyers, lawyers who understood business methods, finance, and documents. His course materials were crammed with financial statements, legal documents such as debenture indentures, and reorganization plans.[76] He helped to institute and teach (along with Abe Fortas, who briefly joined the faculty in 1935) a joint law-business venture with the Harvard Business School. But he did not just want to turn out lawyers who would continue, albeit more expertly, to do the bar's jobs as the bar was currently doing them — for example, to enable trustees under corporate indentures to wriggle more adroitly out of their fiduciary duties and engage in self-dealing. "[I]f we are to make measurable progress in effecting more adequate social control over finance we must undertake seriously the training of enlightened corporation lawyers. . . . This . . . entails training for law in the sense of training for government."[77] Private lawyers who understood the social functions and effects of business units, and the policymaking and governance functions of business lawyers, would make more socially responsible corporate counsel.

When they arrived at Yale in the 1920s, the group shared the Progressives' belief of the time that the path to the understanding of social "facts" and "functions" that would lead to efficient reform of legal policy lay through law professors' collaboration with social scientists in the empirical study of legal and social institutions. Clark, Douglas, and Arnold collaborated on important studies of Connecticut state criminal courts for the Wickersham Commission and of federal courts in the diversity jurisdiction.[78] Douglas undertook an enormously ambitious empirical study of bankruptcy administration, which expanded into a study of the causes of business failures.[79] The young Abe Fortas, recruited to this venture as a student, spent the summer of 1932 researching wage assignments (the practice by which consumer debtors assigned creditors a right to part of their wages as security for debts) in Chicago.[80]

By the early 1930s, however, the research projects had run out of energy and funds. As Schlegel's excellent study has shown, the promise of empirical research had been hugely oversold. The studies were often unable to yield either solidly reliable materials for scientific generalization about the effects of law on social change or facts pointing unequivocally to the need for reform and to the directions reform should take. Arnold and Douglas were later to take the line that the whole empirical research venture had been a waste of time.[81] That was ungenerous and untrue; some of the studies yielded novel, counterintuitive results; promoted fruitful interchanges with other disciplines and some understanding of social science methods; and involved select students such as Fortas in close faculty-student collaborations. Even when results were clear, however, if they disappointed sponsors they were likely to be ignored. The studies of trial courts, for example, were undertaken to illustrate the bar establishment's cherished belief that the problem with judicial process was delay and inefficiency. What the court studies actually showed was the vast majority of cases being processed all too rapidly, through plea bargains or settlements.[82] At worst the empirical projects were naive Baconianism run riot, a piling up of data without any theory at all to structure them, or else of unelaborated and unexamined theory.[83] The social scientists recruited as collaborators invariably found the law professors lacking in rigor, patience, and attention span, and far too quick to generalize from inadequate data. In any case, the Depression effectively wiped out research funds, which went from $18,000 in 1929, the beginning of Robert Hutchins's deanship, to $3,400 in 1936.

It was always difficult to retain faculty for any ventures requiring long-term commitments of time, in view of competition from private practice, government service, and other law schools — the more prestigious Harvard, the higher-paying Chicago. Yale had helped solve the problem by hiring young Yale graduates attached to the school and New Haven; it had also (either admirably or desperately given the prejudices of the time) considered the solution of hiring young Jewish lawyers, cheaper and less mobile because less in demand by firms. Except for Underhill Moore, who grimly persisted into the 1940s with his famous parking studies, the leading Yale Progressives abandoned large-scale long-term empirical research projects and began rest-lessly looking around for the next big thing to move on to. The next big thing turned out to be the New Deal.

The Professors Go to Washington

The New Deal swept through the Yale Law School faculty like a cyclone. This was in large part due to Jerome Frank. Felix Frankfurter recruited Frank for the New Deal, initially as general counsel of the Agricultural Adjustment Administration. Frank later served as a special counsel to the Reconstruction Finance Corporation and to Interior Secretary Harold Ickes. He became an SEC commissioner in 1938 and succeeded Douglas as chair the next year, where he served until his appointment to the Second Circuit in 1941. Like Frankfurter, Frank became one of the principal recruiting officers of lawyers for the New Deal. He brought in many of his Yale friends and colleagues. President Angell's 1934–35 report lists eight Yale law professors on part or full-time loan to the government. Arnold, Fortas, and Sturges were working for Frank at the AAA; Douglas was running a study for the SEC; Hamilton was chairing the Consumer Advisory Board for the National Recovery Ad-ministration; J. Howard Marshall was a member of the Petroleum Admin-istrative Board.[84] Yale Law School's Washington branch maintained a close tangle of connections with one another, and arranged for a whole phalanx of prize former students such as Boris Bittker and Gerhard Gesell to come to work for them. Frank at AAA and Douglas at the SEC fought a polite but in-tense tug-of-war for the services of Fortas — which Douglas eventually won.[85] Douglas later brought Frank himself over to the SEC as a commissioner.[86] When Arnold became antitrust chief in 1938, he brought Hamilton into the division. Such alliances persisted after the New Deal was over, when Arnold, Fortas, and Hamilton practiced law together in postwar Washington.

Yale Law School became thoroughly identified in the public mind with the New Deal, to the perpetual consternation of many Yale College alumni. Dean Clark and Presidents Angell and Charles Seymour spent an inordinate amount of time fending off conservative complaints that Yale Law School was just an outpost of Roosevelt's Red Revolution. Some alumni protested furiously when the Law School appointed Rexford Tugwell, of Roosevelt's controversial "brain trust," to be a research associate.[87] The high tide was probably the moment in 1939 when the *Chicago Tribune* illustrated a series about the school with a cartoon showing the Yale law faculty hoisting the hammer and sickle over the Sterling Law Building.[88] An accompanying story said students were more likely to read Karl Marx than William Blackstone.[89] (In fact, Yale students had not read Blackstone since the introduction of the case method, and by 1939 they were much more likely to read orders of the Bituminous Coal Commission than anything by Marx.) Clark had also to placate the sizeable conservative wing of his own faculty, which successfully resisted the appointment of Jerome Frank. While stoutly defending the New Dealers on his faculty, he also feared that Yale Law School professors would grow too closely associated with the New Deal program, telling Angell in 1933:

> I recall that you have expressed warning that our group should not become too greatly responsible for the new program. I [think] that most of us are well aware of its uncertainty and even those who are working upon it of our group do not wish to sponsor it further than as an experiment. It would seem to me that they have been and will be able to preserve a consistent attitude wherein they will not be compelled to believe in all the details of the program but they will do what lies in their power to make it operate.[90]

This was diplomatic, but futile. By Roosevelt's second term the New Dealers at Yale, including the dean himself,[91] had become unabashed cheerleaders for his programs. A majority of Yale's faculty (11–8), again including Clark, publicly supported FDR's court-packing plan, for example; while Harvard's went the other way.[92] While serving as consultants, lawyers, or agency heads, Arnold, Hamilton, Clark, Sturges, Douglas, and Frank were anything but unobtrusive bureaucrats: they were aggressive publicists for the Administration's programs and critics of its opponents, writing for periodicals like *Harper's* and *The New Republic* as well as the law reviews, giving speeches all over the country and on the radio. Angell's last report as president in 1937 mused that "law faculties tend to harbor relatively more men of leftward-looking political tendencies than are found in academic groups generally. It is at variance, I should say, with the prevailing trend in bar and bench and probably reflects the theoretical, as contrasted with the practical, attitudes of mind."[93]

The main questions I want to ask here are about the compatibility between the Yale Law professors' roles as scholars and teachers and as policymakers, politicians, and publicists for the New Deal. In what ways were the roles continuous? In what ways in conflict? Did the New Deal experience ultimately strengthen Yale Law School as an intellectual center and professional school or weaken it?

Let us look at some of the principals: Frank, Arnold, Douglas, and Hamilton.

Jerome Frank illustrates in some ways the smoothest continuity between certain versions of legal realism and New Deal policies. In other ways he illustrates the inadequacy of the realist perspective, or at least his own realist perspective, as a preparation for the tasks of government lawyers. Frank, as we have seen, was both an extreme rule-skeptic and fact-skeptic. Doctrinal principles were after-the-fact rationalizations of results reached on other grounds. The "facts" of appellate records were like ice sculptures: artifacts of litigation strategies and an irrational trial process. His ideal law school was a clinical school in which students would master complex factual records, not just appellate cases, and learn to manipulate factual and legal arguments in simulated practice settings. Such a training, plus experience in actual practice, would produce the ideal government lawyer, who was, like any other lawyer, an advocate for a client.

In a 1933 speech, "Experimental Jurisprudence and the New Deal," Frank singled out those "realist" or "experimentalist" attorneys as most efficiently serving the government's needs. These attorneys shared the Realist's general skepticism by being "critical students of institutions . . . committed not to mere detached study but . . . devoted to action on the basis of their tentative judgments." But that skepticism did not prevent them from loyally serving the government. They instead used tne insights afforded them by realist doctrine as a tool toward the completion of their client's desired ends, ends which themselves embodied realist experimentalism by representing an attempt to "find new principles, new guides for action, which will tend to produce happiness and security in the place of anguish and confusion." A lawyer must start by focusing upon the desired aims and ends, then "work backward in [his] search for adequate generalizations." Toward this purpose, the lawyer acted best when he saw "clearly that his role is to justify, if possible, what his client desires." Confronted with a New Deal statute with a new approach to relief, "Mr. Try-it" says: "This is a desirable result . . . essential in the existing crisis . . . it means raising the standard of living to thousands. The administration is for it and justifiably so. . . . The statute is ambiguous. Let us work out an argument . . . so to construe the statute to validate this important program." The lawyer schooled to think law was a science of immutable bedrock principles — "Mr. Absolute" — would be at a comparative disadvantage. Refusing to consider the validity or lack thereof of the statute's policy aims, he would approach the problem as one of pure legal interpretation. Eventually, Frank thought, Mr. Absolute would produce the same brief as Mr. Try-it, but take ten times as long. Both opinions would "preserve the "Jovian fiction" of legal autonomy, neither revealing on its face any concern with social and economic policy objectives."[94]

Frank made it sound as if taking traditional doctrine too seriously, as a conventionally trained lawyer would be prone to do, was like dragging around a hundred-pound weight. An education appropriately skeptical toward doc-

trinal formulae would eliminate the handicap and produce — what? A hired
gun, apparently, an advocate flexible enough to come up with effective arguments for the client who retains him — including, when strategically appropriate, entirely traditional-sounding arguments.[95] That is one lawyerly talent, to
be sure — but it seems hard to believe that, in its cheerful agnosticism toward
substantive norms and results, it suffices to define the ideal Progressive lawyer.
Frank himself as a government lawyer was anything but a passive and quies-
cent servant of his bureaucratic superiors. At the AAA, Frank carved out a
considerable independent discretion for his role as the agency's lawyer: he and
his staff were to interpret the statute in the light of its "declared policy," and
argue that such interpretations bound the agency as law. By expanding his
mandate to interpret the policy purposes of legislation, as Robert Jerome
Glennon has pointed out, Frank was able to use his position as lawyer to take
positions on many important policy issues facing the agency; and in particular,
to take positions trying to protect sharecroppers, tenant farmers, and consumers.[96] The agency heads, however, believed the mission of the agency was
to promote the interests of farmers and nobody else. Which was the legal
realist position? Both, clearly. A cynical or purely sociological realist who
thought law was just the sum of the interests producing it would have to agree
with the Administrators: the AAA was farmers' legislation, enacted to benefit
farmers. A normative realist, or legal Progressive, would argue instead that
laws serve immanent functions and purposes, including social functions and
public purposes as well as private interests, and that the lawyer is an expert
on — and creative construer of — such purposes and functions. Frank and his
staff adopted the second view. In a famous showdown with Administrator
Chester Davis, Frank's Legal Division wrote an opinion, which it sent out to
AAA field offices, that the Act required Southern cotton farmers undergoing
acreage reductions not to evict their tenants. The opinion enraged cotton-belt
senators and led to Frank and most of his legal staff being fired.[97]

Frank went on to other New Deal posts, including chairman of the SEC; and
in those roles he was directly responsible for making policy. Oddly enough,
however, he never had much to say about how lawyers were to acquire the
knowledge, skills, and wisdom to become policymakers, except that they
should have enough experience of corporate practice to learn all the slippery
tricks corporate lawyers would use to evade regulations. In fact, Frank was an
intellectual radical, but a political moderate. Like most New Dealers, he was
out to save capitalism, "to give the profit system . . . a fair trial," as he put it.
"As I see the New Deal, it is to be an elaborate series of experiments which
will seek to show that a social economy can be made to work for human welfare by readjustments which leave the desire for private financial gain still

operative."[98] While Frank had plenty of substantive policy views of his own —
he was strongly attached to the "underconsumptionist" theory that lack of
wage-earner purchasing power was the main cause of the Depression, and in
the late 1930s urged an isolationist course for American foreign policy[99] — as
an SEC commissioner he saw his role as largely that of a technician, loyally
implementing and only to a limited degree shaping government policy. The
SEC's task, he said, "is not primarily creative. Its role is a physician's role. It
plays the doctor to our financial system — not to the bankers and brokers who
operate within the system, but to the financial system itself."[100]

Thurman Arnold worked part-time through the 1930s on a miscellany of
New Deal consulting jobs until he took on the full-time job of assistant attorney general for antitrust in 1938. His introduction to the New Deal came
through Jerome Frank at the AAA, whom Arnold assisted in 1933 by representing the agency in litigation. In 1933–4 Arnold and Clark worked together
on an amicus brief in *Nebbia v. New York*.[101] In the summer of 1934, Rexford
Tugwell persuaded Arnold to travel to the Philippines to help the local government administer the Jones-Costigan Sugar Act.[102] (Arnold apparently gave
Clark little notice of his trip, causing the latter some concern and embarrassment regarding his unawareness of faculty activities.[103]) Arnold was offered a
spot on the new National Labor Relations Board in 1935; like Douglas and
Clark he declined the honor,[104] but took a year's leave from Yale to serve as
special assistant to the attorney general. In 1937, the same year as he was
offered the unexpired term of James Landis on the SEC,[105] Arnold became
special assistant to the attorney general in the Tax Division. In this capacity,
Arnold argued several cases before the U.S. Supreme Court. That year, he also
began to work with the Antitrust Division,[106] of which he assumed command
one year later.

For most of his New Deal service, then, Arnold was still on the Yale faculty,
and even after taking leave hoped and expected to return.[107] Yale finally had to
terminate his appointment, though he was kept on as a lecturer and in later
years returned frequently to teach antitrust. "Thus," Arnold was later to remi-
nisce in his inimitable style,

> [T]he Yale Corporation inflicted an injury on the cause of legal education
> from which it has not yet recovered. But one can hardly blame them. They
> were so obsessed with the narrow idea that a Yale professor should spend a
> little time at Yale that they were blind to the broader consequences of what
> they were doing. I felt sad and dispirited at the news. I had lost my tenure at
> Yale, a place I loved, and at which I had spent seven of the happiest years of
> my life. The chances of ever getting back did not seem to be particularly
> bright.[108]

Arnold is often viewed as an example of sharp discontinuity between professorial and policy personae, the realist critic and the activist bureaucrat. In *The Folklore of Capitalism* (1937), Arnold had described the antitrust laws as one of the symbols by which government promotes the fiction that the United States remains a society of small competitive individual producers, while papering over, and actually helping to produce, the reality that it is an economy of giant firms and administered prices. Antitrust prosecutions, like prosecutions of prostitutes and bootleggers, symbolically condemn bigness as a sin while discreetly aiding it to flourish.[109] Arnold did not expect when he wrote this to become the antitrust chief; and in fact was offered the job because it happened to be available. At his confirmation hearings some senators like William Borah (whom Arnold had described in the book as having built a political career on the symbolic cause of antitrust) asked if he could take the antitrust laws seriously. Arnold said he could, that the book was one of detached analysis and not policy proposals; and that he would try to make the best of a flawed policy instrument.[110] He was as good as his word: Arnold was the most aggressive antitrust enforcer in history. As head of antitrust enforcement he enlarged the staff from 55 to 300 lawyers, increased the budget fivefold. In 1938 the division had brought 11 new cases; in 1940 it brought 92. In 1938 it conducted 59 investigations, in 1940, 215. His division not only won almost every case; it transformed itself from a prosecutor's office to a proactive administrative agency. Guided by the expertise of Walton Hamilton, it conducted industry-wide investigations of pricing practices; it brought industry-wide prosecutions and settled most cases with consent decrees; and by these means converted the clumsy tool of criminal litigation into one of structural remedies.[111]

Was this a turnabout in attitude? I do not think so. While restructuring the division to make it more instrumentally effective, Arnold also promoted a new symbolic conception of the antitrust laws. The original impulse behind the antitrust laws — Senator Borah's impulse, for example — was a political and moral attack on concentrated power so as to "restore authority to individuals and communities."[112] The Brandeisian gospel that various New Dealers, including to a limited extent William O. Douglas at the SEC, helped to spread was that institutions of the economy should be accountable to democratic control, especially that of small producers. Arnold had one criterion, the price to the consumer. Arnold had no critique of bigness, and thought those who did had "religion" criticizing "economic sin." Unlike Brandeisians who wanted to restore competition in order to limit the role of the state, Arnold thought government had to play an active role in creating the framework of competition, restructuring the economy, then patrolling and monitoring. He trusted in experts, agencies, and bureaucratic power to do this, and — what may seem an incongruous view for a legal "realist" — to do it independently of politics. Arnold started out by prosecuting unions as well as corporations for antitrust violations, and was genuinely taken aback when both the Supreme Court and the president instructed him that, given labor's long experience with the Sherman Act as a union-busting strategy, criminal prosecutions directed against this important wing of the New Deal coalition were out of bounds.[113] As the historian Alan Brinkley has described it, Arnold's was an "antimonopoly ideal largely stripped of its populist and democratic content."[114] The professor and the policymaker here seem to me the same person. Arnold never deprecated the symbolic functions of law and government, indeed saw them as promulgating useful myths. But the myths could also distract from the practical work of government. As antitrust administrator he sought to refashion the symbol of the government's role to protecting "consumer welfare" while directing prosecutions at "bottlenecks" — localized concentrations impeding competition.[115]

William O. Douglas had involved himself with government-sponsored projects well before the advent of the New Deal. Along with Clark, he completed a legal trends report as part of the President's Research Committee on Social Trends.[116] In the early 1930s Douglas served as assistant director on the Wickersham Commission on Law Observance and Enforcement.[117]

When the Roosevelt administration came to power, Douglas eagerly anticipated his opportunity to participate in the New Deal experiment. In April 1933, the special counsel to the Senate Committee on Banking and Currency asked Douglas and Wesley Sturges to develop a report on various social and economic aspects of stock market operations.[118] (For various reasons, Douglas and Sturges never undertook this project.) Then, in 1934, Douglas was asked by SEC chair Joseph P. Kennedy to direct a study of protective committees in corporate reorganizations for the commission.[119] He began his work on the study in 1934, juggling trips to Washington with his teaching duties at Yale Law School.[120] What would become an enormous eight-volume report (of which Douglas himself would later say that only one person, Vern Countryman, had ever read through it) was slow in coming, and would only be fully released in 1938.

In 1936, Douglas joined the SEC as a commissioner. While on the commission, Douglas also found time to give speeches defending New Deal policies and attacking "financial termites" seeking to promote personal profits at the public expense,[121] and to ingratiate himself deftly with the president.[122] When Landis returned to Harvard in 1937, Douglas was appointed SEC chairman.[123] Douglas was by all accounts an exceedingly able and effective leader of the SEC. "[H]is chairmanship," comments the leading historian of the SEC, Joel Seligman, "was the most accomplished in all the SEC's history, in part because it articulated a coherent policy framework for federal corporations law that was to guide the next two generations of corporate reform efforts."[124] The most notable success of his tenure was, by an adroit strategy of bullying, diplomacy, and use of political opportunities opened by scandal, to induce the New York Stock Exchange to reorganize itself from an insider's club of gentlemen prone to secrecy and self-dealing to a relatively accountable, transparent, and rule-bound body.[125]

Douglas had taken a leave of absence from Yale beginning in February 1936, but planned on occasional trips back to New Haven to supervise certain graduate student projects.[126] This loss to Yale was tempered by the fact that Douglas had already expressed his intention to accept a partnership with a private New York firm at the close of the 1935–36 academic year.[127] In 1939, however, Clark resigned as dean to become a judge on the Second Circuit. The Law School faculty were virtually united in wanting Douglas as his successor. Douglas accepted the offer of the deanship, but a few days later was appointed by Roosevelt to the U.S. Supreme Court.[128]

How did Douglas's government career fit together with his academic work? More than most young New Deal lawyers, who were often tossed into the middle of fields like agricultural policy where they were initially clueless, Douglas at the SEC was able to draw on his special knowledge and experience. The continuities and discontinuities between his academic and government work are best illustrated by his contributions to corporate bankruptcy law. In practice with the Cravath firm, Douglas had specialized in corporate reorganizations. As a young scholar, Douglas wrote on reorganizations from the point of view of a disinterested observer. When a company went bankrupt, as for example virtually all the railroads in the country did at some point, "protective committees" formed consisting of small groups of stockholders or bondholders purporting to represent and protect the interests of their class of investors. These committees were accused of many abuses, especially self-dealing at the expense of the investors they supposedly represented. In a 1934 article, Douglas defended the control of protective committees by institutional investors, calling proposals for protective committees controlled by small investors and supervised by the federal government a utopian fantasy, failing which, it was best to have savvy investors with a big stake in control.[129] Around 1934 there was a marked shift in the tone and direction of his scholarship: he began to denounce insiders' control of reorganizations and to be an advocate for the little shareholder. The 1933 Securities Act, he wrote, "is symbolic of a shift of power. That shift is from the bankers to the masses; from the promoter to the investor. . . . [T]he government is taking the side of the helpless, the suckers, the underdogs. It signifies that the money-changers are being driven from the temple."[130] (The "money-changers" image was a favorite of Brandeis, the chief critic of manipulation of corporate finance by insiders.) He also criticized the 1933 Securities Act as practically toothless, a relic of nineteenth-century approaches to regulation, and urged the creation of a new agency. There is no secret about the reasons for this shift: Douglas was angling for a job with the New Deal, preferably as a commissioner with the new agency.[131]

Douglas was first appointed to direct a giant research project, the SEC study of Protective Committees in Reorganizations. Arnold and Fortas were among the other lawyers Douglas recruited for the study. This study was a dream opportunity for a legal-realist with policy aspirations; it was empirical research, amply funded by the government, and armed with subpoena power. If you really want to know the effects of the law in action, put the people who are supposed to comply — in this case Wall Street lawyers and bankers — under oath and cross-examine them. The resulting eight-volume study is a fascinating piece of work — part social science, part muckraking exposé, part polemical advocacy for new legislation. It is a powerful and impressive document, as government reports go, lucidly narrated and monumentally thorough. Its sometimes dramatically overstated conclusions could not be called wholly disinterested social science, but that was not its purpose. The facts were drafted as soldiers for the cause of proposing new regulatory legislation, and all marched in that direction. As SEC commissioner and later chairman, Douglas used the study he had directed to campaign for legislation (Chapter X of the Chandler Act of 1938) prohibiting Wall Street bankers and their lawyers from serving as or advising trustees in charge of corporate reorganizations for large, public-held corporations. That role had to be performed by an independent, "disinterested" trustee. The SEC itself had to scrutinize every proposed reorganization. As the bankruptcy historian David Skeel has summarized the reforms:

> Under the new system . . . a trustee would take over when a large corporation filed for bankruptcy, and the current managers would be sent packing. The firm's Wall Street underwriters and lawyers could neither serve as trustee, nor attempt to organize its bondholders while everyone waited for the trustee to propose a reorganization plan. Looking over everyone's shoulders to make sure there were no surprises was the SEC. Out were private negotiation and the wiles of Wall Street, in was pervasive government oversight.[132]

The Chandler Act destroyed the elite Wall Street lawyers' reorganization practice (except for railroads) in which the young Douglas had labored years before. Its insertion of the SEC in the procedure for approving reorganizations also reflected the Yale and New Deal Progressives' distrust of the common-law judge and greater confidence in administrative agency scrutiny.[133] But Chapter X proved to be a Pyrrhic victory for the legal Progressives. Practitioners slyly avoided it by filing reorganizations under the 1938 Bankruptcy Act's Chapter XI, supposedly designed for small business firms; and federal judges — including Supreme Court Justice Douglas himself in important decisions — indulged them in this practice.[134] In 1978 the new Bankruptcy Act wiped out the SEC's supervisory role and returned reorganizations to dealing in the back room.

Later in his life Douglas rewrote the history of his early years in practice and at Yale to make himself out to be more of a populist than he really was at the time.[135] His populist rhetoric actually dates from the time Roosevelt was beginning to denounce "economic royalists." But very likely the Protective Committee study itself had something to do with the change in Douglas's attitudes toward Wall Street: it unfolded a tale of insider manipulation, self-dealing, and the most respectable lawyers of New York outdoing one another to grab for huge fees wholly out of proportion to the work they had put in. It gave Douglas and his staff direct exposure to the high-handedness and arrogant complacency of Wall Street's bankers and lawyers. At the SEC, however, Douglas, though tough in negotiating with the financial community and resisting the political pressures it brought to bear on his agency, was generally far from radical in his substantive regulatory views. Government regulation to produce transparency and effective self-policing of the financial services industries were his principal goals. The militant liberalism for which he eventually became famous, in his opinions fiercely defending the civil liberties of minorities, dissenters, and social outcasts, did not emerge until his service on the Supreme Court.

Walton H. Hamilton, like other prominent New Deal advisors, was shuttled from agency to agency. Unlike Arnold, Douglas, Frank, and Fortas, however, he had no particular administrative talent or political skills; but he was enormously respected and much in demand by agency heads and policymakers. His work provided intellectual ammunition — research and policy arguments — for the senior administrators. When New Deal policies stalled, or when chief advisors locked in conflict over what to do next, Roosevelt was fond of creating advisory or study commissions to work out differences. These would buy time to assess which way the political winds and economic trends were blowing while the principals wore each other out. Hamilton was a natural for appointment to such bodies.

In 1933, the Department of the Interior requested his counsel on matters regarding the coal industry.[136] That summer, Hamilton was appointed to a three-member Emergency Board mediating a labor dispute concerning the Louisiana, Arkansas and Texas Railway Company.[137] During the 1933–34 school year, Hamilton continued to serve on the Emergency Board under the Railway Labor Act; was appointed a member of the Consumers' Advisory Council of the National Recovery Administration; and became a member of the Advisory Committee to the Coordinator of Railroads. In 1934 Hamilton began work on a price study for the government, which would eventually provide him material for a book.[138] In March 1934, he was also recruited for a month's duty on a mediation board weighing a dispute concerning the Delaware and Hudson Railroad.[139] In September 1934, he was named to the newly constituted National Industrial Recovery Board, which assumed former NRA head High Johnson's administrative duties.[140] He balanced these duties with his teaching responsibilities, commuting frequently to Washington, and further impairing his already precarious health.

In early 1935, Hamilton's government work consisted, as he wrote to Dean Clark, of "attending Board meetings and scribbling a memo on price policy."[141] "I need," he added plaintively, "to do some writing to get back my intellectual self-respect."[142]

That summer, Hamilton served as one of two U.S. government delegates to the International Labor Organization conference in Geneva. In this role, Hamilton focused on the issue of the reduction of hours[143] and spoke in favor of collective bargaining and a worldwide forty-hour week.[144] Almost immediately afterward, when after the *Schechter* decision President Roosevelt reorganized the National Recovery Administration, Hamilton was named one of six members of the advisory council in aid of the NRA.[145] Later that summer, Hamilton was given sole control over consumers' problems; as "adviser on consumers' problems" he reported directly to the president. Hamilton was simultaneously appointed a member of the National Emergency Council.[146] Not long afterward, Hamilton became head of the NRA Consumers' Division. This Division, a "thin disguise" attempting to unite "a number of worthy ventures which otherwise would have been completely lost,"[147] assumed the workload of the NRA Consumers Advisory Board, the consumers' division of the National Emergency Council and the cabinet committee on price policy. Hamilton's major duties were outlined as (1) field service to two hundred county consumer councils set up under the National Emergency Council; (2) advisory direction to the Division's headquarters staff; and (3) research.[148]

Back at Yale, an unhappy and skeptical Dean Clark wondered what his itinerant colleague could be accomplishing to take him so frequently away from New Haven.

I have not seen or heard from [Hamilton] and must rely for my information on the newspaper account of his new appointment, but I did read of it somewhat differently than apparently you have. Frankly, I thought it a bit of a cushion by which the President was letting both himself and Mr. Hamilton down easily, as, I think, he has been doing with respect to the N.R.A. generally. I reached this conclusion because, in spite of all the high-sounding titles and activities which Mr. Hamilton was now supposed to have, I could see nothing real beyond what he was already doing, including the Price Study (the research into prices upon which he has been engaged with a staff for some time for the Cabinet). Of course he has been supposed to represent the consumer from the beginning, although all representation of the consumer seems to me actually to have been but sounding brass and cymbals. Except for the Price Study and except for an official name, I doubt if there is anything of substance in the appointment.[149]

By 1936, the Dean's patience was running out with Hamilton's commuting. As Clark wrote Yale Provost Charles Seymour in April 1936:

For his own good and for that of the School generally, [Hamilton] ought now to return to Yale or to sever his connections completely. He is fast losing touch with the student body and with his work here, and I doubt if his work in Washington, even his new work in connection with the organization of research for the Social Security Board, is sufficiently worth while to demand his remaining in Washington. I doubt, however, the utility in forcing his return in September. . . . He is likely to be unhappy indeed, in part because his family life is unsettled and personal difficulties have arisen which he has not yet thoroughly faced. I doubt if, under the conditions, his work with us would be very happy.[150]

Hamilton did in fact return to the school for the spring 1937 semester, having resigned as director of the board. That same year, he divorced and remarried.[151]

Meanwhile, Hamilton also became a special assistant to the attorney general in 1938, serving as such through 1945,[152] working both as Arnold's deputy at the Antitrust Division and as one of the principal directors of the studies of the Temporary National Economic Committee, the huge joint Congressional-Executive study commission Roosevelt and the Congress devised to iron out conflicts over monopoly policy and formulate a plan to deal with the 1937 recession.[153] He also commented frequently in magazine articles and public speeches on current issues facing and personalities within the Supreme Court, Congress, and other branches of the government.[154] While a special assistant, Hamilton continued to spend several days a week in Washington.[155] Though overcommitted and exhausted, Hamilton published prolifically in this period, producing *The Power to Govern* (with Douglass Adair, 1937); *Price and Price Policies* (1938); *The Pattern of Competition* (1940); *Anti-Trust in Action* (with his new wife, Irene Till, 1940); and *Patents and Free Enterprise* (1941). In a memorandum to Seymour, he defended his dual residency with a thorough discussion of his role as a professor, and how Washington experience benefited his academic work.

> A professor of law, at Yale, I take it, has a kind of three-in-one office.
> He owes a duty of instruction to the students, through courses, honors work, and personal conference.
> He is expected to serve the academic community, by pushing beyond the current frontiers of his subject and publishing the results of his work.
> He is under obligation to blaze trails which public policy may later follow.
> Economy demands that the three lines should be fused into a unified program. If the three activities are to be kept alive, each should support the other two. . . .
> From the first the great difficulty has been with materials. It is easy enough in New Haven to work with the stuff in the law reports. It has not been easy to supplement these materials with "the recitations of fact" with which the law has been concerned. Nor is real raw material available. A year-on-leave in Washington with the NRA opened to me government files and provided an opportunity to use a small group of persons to make clinical reports of a number of industries. A chance to continue this work, after the NRA was liquidated, led to a second year's work along the same line. Without this work, the course in Public Control I could never have been formulated along its present lines. And access to the files of the Department of Justice and an opportunity to get two studies financed by the TNEC, has led to a connection which has meant two months of the summer in Washington and two days a week there through the academic year.
> Out of the work in Washington, in addition to a number of articles in various legal periodicals, have appeared the following books:
> Price and Price Policies . . .
> Antitrust in Action . . .
> Patents and Free Enterprise . . .
> A number of pieces of work, using the files of the government, are currently in various stages of completion.
> Evidence and Business Activity . . .
> The Habits of Industry . . .
> The Cost Formula for Price . . .
> The Corporate Estate . . .
> Case Histories on Various Industries . . .
> . . . It must be admitted that, since my wife is with the Bituminous Coal Control, personal values enter the equation. Yet Washington alone can supply

Jim McElholm, Tapping Reeve Law School Interior. Courtesy of Litchfield Hills Visitors Bureau and Litchfield Historical Society.

(above) Portrait of Seth
Staples, by Jared Bradley
Flagg. Collection of Yale Law
School.

(right) Portrait of Samuel
Hitchcock, by Jared Bradley
Flagg. Collection of Yale Law
School.

Portrait of David Daggett, by Ulysses Dow Tenney, 1874. Collection of Yale Law School.

Heublein Building on Church Street, viewed from the New Haven Green, c. 1900. Courtesy the New Haven Colony Historical Society.

Portrait of Simeon E. Baldwin, by Frank Weyland Fellowes, 1901.
Collection of Yale Law School.

The New Haven County Court House, c. 1870. The Yale Alumni Weekly, March 13, 1925. By permission of Yale Alumni Magazine.

Interior of the New Haven County Court House Library, c. 1870. Photos of Yale Collection, Manuscripts and Archives, Yale University Library.

Engraving of Theodore Dwight Woolsey as President of
Yale College, by Thomas H. Pease, engraved for the
Class of 1858. Pictures of Yale Individuals Collection,
Manuscripts and Archives, Yale University Library.

HENDRIE HALL · ELM STREET

Hendrie Hall on Elm Street. Manuscripts and Archives, Yale University Library.

Construction of 127 Wall Street Building, c. 1930. Manuscripts and Archives, Yale University Library.

Portrait of Charles E. Clark, by Franklin Chenault Watkins, 1959. Collection of Yale Law School.

Photograph of Thurman Arnold, by Gilbert J. Vincent. Manuscripts and Archives, Yale University Library. By permission of the *New Haven Register*.

Portrait of William O. Douglas, by Bruno Beran, 1961. Collection of
Yale Law School.

Jerome Frank. Yale Law Report vol. 3, no.1.
Courtesy of Yale Law School.

Walton Hale Hamilton. The Yale Reporter
1946 Supplement. Courtesy of Yale Law
School.

ANOTHER COLOR ON THE CAMPUS

(above) Parrish, "Another Color on Campus," Chicago Tribune. Copyrighted January 21, 1939, Chicago Tribune Company. All rights reserved. Used with permission.

(right) Portrait of Thomas Emerson, by Joseph Funaro, 1992. Collection of Yale Law School.

Portrait of Alexander Bickel, by John Norton, 1975. Collection of
Yale Law School.

Portrait of Louis Pollack, by Joseph Hirsh, 1973. Collection of Yale Law School.

Hydrant with "Create Two, Three . . . Many Yale Law Struggles." Yale Law Reporter, 1970. Courtesy of Yale Law School.

the material for a research program outlined in general terms some time ago. My access to files is at the courtesy of a group of officials who happen to be "intellectuals." Since personnel changes constantly, I want to exploit the materials while they are open. For the immediate future a disturbance of this 2-day arrangement would necessitate an abandonment, or at least a complete reorganization, of my current program.[156]

In most of his government jobs, in short, Hamilton did pretty much the same thing, and the thing was what he did as a professor — he supervised, or wrote, narrative and statistical studies of the variables that went into pricing policies in various different industries. The New Deal for Hamilton was a grand seminar. In one year he instituted an externship program that brought eight Yale Law School students down for the semester to work for various New Deal agencies. Hamilton convened them every week in a seminar. For others government work may have meant a sacrifice in academic productivity; for Hamilton it was a godsend.

Professors as Policymakers: Productive Symbiosis or Damage to Both Roles?

From these examples and others, what can we conclude about the effect of the New Deal on legal scholarship and teaching? In many ways the New Deal was enormously beneficial to the new generation of liberal-progressive legal-realist scholars. It brought liberal-progressive legal academics in from the cold. It gave scholars who had of necessity been outsiders to the orthodox legal order and its culture — and perforce assumed the roles of mocking critics of the system, smashers of its idols, exposers of the vacuity, and the indeterminacy or reactionary political foundations of its principles — the positions of insiders, often high positions at that. Historians have noted[157] that many of the leading New Deal lawyers were socially as well as intellectually marginal in the elite legal culture; this was true of the Yale lawyers as well. Frank, Fortas, and Shulman were Jewish; Arnold, Hamilton and Douglas from small towns in the Midwest and West; though some had practiced in Wall Street, they felt ill at ease in that social milieu. Nothing gave young marginals like Fortas and Douglas more satisfaction than their SEC work, which put them in positions of authority to subpoena, sharply question, threaten with sanctions, and expose the self-dealing of the haughty managers of the financial world's clubs — Wall Street law partners like John Foster Dulles, New York Stock Exchange barons like Richard Whitney, whom they had the satisfaction of seeing ruined and going to jail for using clients' money to finance his own speculations.[158]

More important and enduring than cultural revenge was the new insiders' advance in what the sociologist Ronen Shamir has called the realists' "collective mobility project" and status competition for cultural capital.[159] Works such as Arnold's *Symbols of Government* and *The Folklore of Capitalism* and James Landis's *The Administrative Process* are overt bids for social respect for bureaucratic administrators equivalent to that accorded judges, law partners, and heads of corporations.

The New Deal rescued Yale's experimentalism just as it was beginning to flounder for lack of research funds, lack of sustained faculty interest, and lack of obvious application to policy change or relevance to professional careers. It validated the claim that research and theory combining legal with social science could be a practical training equipping graduates for important legal jobs; and broke the identification of the "practical" with the old doctrinal/dogmatic curriculum. It established at the highest levels of government a counter-elite to the traditional elites of private practice — a body of officials, advisors, judges and administrators who were themselves versed in and accustomed to new "discourses" of policy argument, which then ipso facto became "practical." It certified the practicality of policy argument, not only for government lawyers but also for the private lawyers representing clients before them. (A similar service was later performed for Chicago law and economics by the Reagan administration, which suddenly alchemized what had been viewed as the off-the-wall theoretical speculations of academics who had been exiled to the wilderness into official government policy.)

It remains, however, a little uncertain what the linkages were between law graduates' academic training and their government work. Did Yale methods actually produce lawyers better suited to the New Deal? Frank, as we saw, suggested that lawyers less hampered by formal Harvard-style principles might do a better job; but, like Frankfurter, hired many Harvard-trained lawyers and had a preference for lawyers with a background in corporate practice, because they had more experience in all the tricks of evading government orders. On the other side, Boris Bittker has suggested to me that much New Deal work called for imaginative answers to new questions — for example, what sort of documents should be prepared to transfer control over Lend-Lease materiel? — which experienced business lawyers had no preparation to address; for such problems, a mind uncluttered by standard ways of doing things was often better suited. Law students who had worked closely with their professor on an empirical research project — as when Fortas went to Chicago to study wage-assignment practices — got some valuable experience in the kind of intensely fact-based studies that the New Dealers used to document their administrative initiatives and legislative proposals, and to overwhelm the opposition to their policies. There were many different kinds of New Deal legal jobs — policy entrepreneur, legislative draftsman, negotiator and deal-maker, publicist, bureaucratic rule-maker and enforcer, constitutional litigator. For some of these jobs, such as devising litigation strategies to protect legislation from being struck down in the courts, cautious craftsmanship in the Harvard mold was clearly an asset,[160] in others just as clearly a liability.

The New Deal helped law school graduates as well as faculty by opening up new careers for both graduates and teachers through involvement with government service. Like other progressive lawyers of the time, Yale's dean and faculty hoped that the expanding administrative state would create a demand for what Dean Clark called "public counsel" in private practice, lawyers who would advise their corporate clients to comply with the spirit of regulatory programs in their long-term interests.

The faculty's involvement in government work also considerably enriched the curriculum. In the 1930s the school added courses in Labor Law (Rodell), Public Control of Business (Hamilton and Shulman — which in 1937 became, along with Borchard's Constitutional Law, a basic required first-year course), Law Administration (Hamilton, Clark and James), The Psychology of Modern Judicial and Legislative Institutions (Arnold, Frank, Robinson and George Soule), Douglas's new courses on Business Units, New Deal Legislation (Arnold, Robinson and Soule), Administrative Law (Fortas and Shulman), History of Constitutional Decision on State and Federal Powers (Nelles), The Utilization of Land for Public Purposes (McDougal), and Judicial Process (Clark and Hamilton). By 1940 the school had four courses on Public Control of Business, including Public Utilities, Unfair Competition, The Control of Competition, and Industry and the Law of Patents.[161] Among the major schools only Columbia's curriculum registered similar changes in response to the legislative and administrative innovations of the New Deal. Harvard Law School in the same period moved the administrative law course from the graduate to the undergraduate program and added courses in legislation, taxation, antitrust, and regulatory law; otherwise, its settled, almost entirely required, curriculum was substantially unaffected by changing times.[162] At Yale, exam questions were taken from pending constitutional and antitrust cases and administrative proceedings. Regulatory statutes and the practical means of implementing them moved into course materials, as did contemporary debates over basic economic policy. Hamilton, Arnold, and Frank recycled research and insights gained from their New Deal jobs into new books. Thus, distracted though they undoubtedly were by their public jobs, the Yale New Dealers kept their missions of 1930 — developing an institutional perspective beyond case-law analysis, and reforming the law school to produce cadres of reform lawyers — steadily and clearly in focus. They took students from Yale and moved them to Washington; but they also took materials and examples from government service and brought them back to New Haven.

On the negative side, the New Deal necessarily drained intellectual energy away from theory and research, and tended to convert scholars into politicians and propagandists. Accession to policy influence made the professors' approach to law relevant, even glamorous; but was hardly conducive to carrying on any sustained project of research or intellection. On the contrary, their experience in government reinforced the traditional lawyers' disposition to think that their generalist training equips them to flit from field to field, handle any problem in any specialty, picking up as much superficial knowledge as they need along the way. The New Deal also lured away some young graduates who might have become faculty into government service, and — because it had helped soften up the old ethnic barriers — into private practice as well. The faculty were physically out of town much of the time, commuting either on the train or by car along Route 1 to Washington and back. Frequent leaves often made it hard for the school to staff basic courses.

More subtly and profoundly, engagement with the actual world of policy had an inevitably muting and deflating effect on the progressive lawyers' theoretical and progressive agendas. The massive government research projects on which they labored, such as the SEC Study of Protective Committees and the TNEC studies of economic concentration, which they hoped would generate major legislative initiatives, languished unread and unheeded, and produced either legislative action rapidly unraveled by regulated interests (in the case of the SEC Study's godchild, Chapter X of the Chandler Act) or no action at all (in TNEC's). Jurisprudential radicals like Frank and Arnold had in practice, as they perfectly well realized, to tailor their arguments narrowly to sway conservative courts. And ultimately, the most ample policy-reform ambitions of the great New Deal experiment were disappointed. "Public control of business" in any and all the various meanings New Deal policies gave to it — corporatist planning, stringent direct regulation of wages and prices, aggressive antitrust policies — proved to be much harder to implement than anyone had supposed. One after another the main goals were modified or abandoned; corporatist planning and direct regulation were displaced by Keynesian fiscal policy and countercyclical uses of spending powers; the aggressive trustbusting program ran out of steam when Thurman Arnold was not allowed to prosecute unions, and, more important, when business interests moved en masse into government war production agencies and successfully negotiated exemptions to the antitrust laws.[163] The resourcefulness of business in evading controls and capturing the agencies that would be their controllers was not lost on the Yale observers. Thus Thomas Emerson:

> [We] were discouraged by the high degree of noncompliance in many areas of industry. [W]e were impressed by the degree to which business firms . . . engaged in violations. . . . The atmosphere of willingness to evade regulation and the general attitude that such evasions are not unethical but rather to be expected, will make any attempt at control of the economic structure through the regulatory process difficult. . . . [E]conomic regulations inevitably become extremely complex [in part] due to the constant and ingenious efforts that were being made to avoid [their] impact. . . . At a certain point, the effort to control from the outside will collapse if the task becomes too complicated. Those subject to the regulations cannot understand them, the courts cannot understand them, and they become much too technical for practical operations. The only alternative would seem to be some simplification in terms of government ownership or direct government operation. That raises other problems, but at least it is much simpler.[164]

And Walton Hamilton:

> The members of a regulated industry are not indifferent as to whom their overlords are to be. . . . They constitute a compact group with every incentive to unified action, and capable of massing their power at the point where decision is to be made. They have their connections in the White House and on Capitol Hill. Against this group, the general public is too numerous to have a single voice, too widely scattered to be easily organized, and too little informed to become articulate. . . . [P]ersons after a discreet interval . . . become attorneys in corporations whose affairs they had been called upon to regulate. . . . [P]laying it safe means another little shift in the balance in favor of the private, as against the public interest.[165]

These are truisms today, but then they were truths in the process of being discovered.

By the 1940 elections, it was clear that the liberal moment in government was over, at least for the time being. Emerson's New Deal experience had turned him into a socialist, but socialism was not on the American agenda anytime soon. The more radical lawyers of the New Deal chose the emerging specialty of labor law, either as lawyers for the NLRB, for unions, or for labor-side law firms. The federal judiciary was now dominantly liberal, and some New Dealers joined it, including Jerome Frank, William O. Douglas, and (for a brief spell) Thurman Arnold. Most New Deal lawyers were not radicals, had worked to save capitalism, and were entirely comfortable working the other side of the street. After leaving the bench, Arnold with Fortas and Paul Porter founded a famous Washington law firm, which Walton Hamilton eventually joined.

Shulman, Sturges, Roscoe Steffen, Fleming James, Edwin Borchard, and Eugene Rostow, however, returned to Yale Law School, where soon they were joined by an influx of young ex-government lawyers. The New Deal—and, it goes without saying, the wartime agencies and services[166]—withdrew many lawyers from the academy, some for good; but then deposited many more: Thomas Emerson, Boris Bittker, Ralph Brown, Quintin Johnstone, Myres McDougal, and Grant Gilmore, among others.

The Postwar Public Law Agenda— Civil Liberties and Civil Rights

The new generation of ex-government servants on the faculty had for the most part a different set of public concerns and public involvements. This is the postscript to my lecture—the "and After" in the title. Broadly speaking, the change in faculty focus is from public control of business to civil rights and, especially, civil liberties.

Back in New Haven, Yale Law School's faculty became as identified with civil liberties and civil rights as it had been with the New Deal. Consider this brief inventory of faculty involved in civil liberties and civil rights: Charles Black, a consultant to the NAACP Inc. Fund and writer on segregation; Ralph Brown, member of the ACLU board and author of the leading critical analysis of the government's loyalty-security programs; Eli Clark's work for the Connecticut Mental Health Association; Vern Countryman, with his colleagues Fred Rodell, Fowler Harper, and David Haber, among the leading crusaders against McCarthy and anticommunist congressional committees; Charles Black, John P. Frank, Louis Pollak, Eugene Rostow, and Wesley Sturges, and intermittently Alexander Bickel, all active in the antisegregation cause; Boris Bittker took time off from being the leading tax scholar to write a book defending the feasibility of black reparations. The professors often spoke collectively as well as individually: twenty-two out of twenty-seven members of the faculty signed a "Manifesto" in 1947 urging the abolition of the House Committee on Un-American Activities. Several joined in signing an amicus brief of 188 law professors in *Sweatt v. Painter,* the Texas law school segregation case,[167] the largest collective intervention of law faculty in any case to date. The brief was actually drafted by Yale's John Frank and Thomas Emerson and Harvard's Dean Erwin Griswold. Through Dean Sturges, Yale Law School as an institution lobbied for years to try to get the Association of American Law Schools to deny membership to schools that discriminated on the basis of race.

Indisputably the central and most conspicuous figure of the Yale faculty's new public engagements was Thomas Emerson. Just out of school, Emerson worked for the Scottsboro Boys' defense team, then for the National Recovery Administration, National Labor Relations Board, and Office of Price Administration in the New Deal; became president of the National Lawyers' Guild; ran as the Henry Wallace Party candidate for governor of Connecticut in 1948; produced a classic treatise on the First Amendment, *The System of Free Expression,* and, in his portion of the *Sweatt* amicus brief, the first developed legal theory that separate education of the races was necessarily unequal. "Tommy the Commie," as he inevitably came to be called, was also a major headache for a succession of deans and Yale presidents, most of whom defended him, while others, like President A. Whitney Griswold, treated him as a "cross to bear."[168]

As in the New Deal years, there were important members of the faculty whose public engagements pulled them in different directions. Alexander Bickel, a distinguished scholar and cautious Harvard-trained advocate of restraint amongst the reckless and raucous Yalies, partially dissented from the liberal wing over a long complex career, eventually becoming a major critic of the Warren Court's school-integration orders. There were also many faculty who carried forward the New Deal agenda of public control of business — as Eugene Rostow did in a 1948 book proposing a national policy for the oil industry.[169] Fleming James and Friedrich Kessler, having given up on the national government as a plausible source of social insurance, subtly rechanneled their efforts into private law reform, the project of expanding enterprise liability through the common law courts. (This story has been brilliantly told by George Priest.[170]) But the major trend in shift of focus of the public lawyers is unmistakable.

This shift was common of course to liberals generally, and liberal lawyers especially. It tracks the shift in the principal emphasis of constitutional law — foretold in the famous *Carolene Products* footnote — from protecting business liberty and property (*Carolene Products* was an unsuccessful due process challenge to milk-content regulation) to protecting the rights of "discrete and insular minorities."[171] Out of power, liberals were less concerned about promoting government regulation of business than defending minorities and dissenters from government. The Red Scares and the return of business conservatives to government also reminded liberal intellectuals, especially if Jewish, of their precarious status in American society, after their heady interlude of power. On the Supreme Court, Douglas, with his colleagues Black and Murphy, became the judicial pioneer in such cases as *Skinner v. Oklahoma, Dennis v. U.S.* (dissenting) and *Griswold v. Connecticut*[172] of a far-reaching theory of constitutionally protected individual liberty — while incidentally carrying on

Yale's feud with Harvard caution and stuffiness, as personified on his Court by Mr. Justice Frankfurter. Arnold and Fortas became famous as private lawyers for their pro bono representation of clients like Owen Lattimore, charged by government loyalty boards or Congressional committees with subversion or disloyalty (though they would not represent actual Communists).[173] Eventually, of course, it was the courts, led by Warren's Supreme Court, that inaugurated the so-called Rights Revolution, while left-liberal professors cheered, and centrist liberals, while often favoring the results, deplored the reasoning.[174]

One of the small ironic consequences of the end of New Deal and the shift of public engagements to civil rights and civil liberties was that liberal-social activist lawyers reverted to relatively conventional lawyers' intellectual materials, styles, and roles — writing briefs, defending people in court; and when the Warren Court came along, providing rationalizations for judicial decisions. The liberal lawyers still represented outsiders, but to the highest of established tribunals. Meanwhile the lawyers with reservations about the Court's Rights Revolution, like Bickel, reenacted the role that Progressive academics such as T. R. Powell, Thurman Arnold, Fred Rodell, and Walton Hamilton had played in the 1920s and '30s, that of public critic, both in scholarly works and in *The New Republic,* of activist courts. Law professors are never happier than when they are talking about the courts, especially from the inside player's perspective that is possible when the courts are on their side. The 1960s and '70s would, however, also see a brilliant revival of interdisciplinary studies, with Guido Calabresi's pioneering integration of law and economics in *The Costs of Accidents* (1970) and Joseph Goldstein's integration of law and psychiatry, among many others; and a resurgence of public engagements on behalf of outsiders. But I will leave that story for Laura Kalman's lecture in this volume.

At the start of this lecture I described how the law school's core functions of professional training have a way of acting like a gigantic rubber band, which acts so as perpetually to drag the more adventurous experiments with legal education and the role of the law teacher back into the relative narrow confines of a set of basic routines — the private-law-centered, doctrine-centered, court-centered, case-centered curriculum, which accepts existing legal arrangements as given, and subject to only minor modifications. The Yale faculty of the New Deal era and their immediate successors also experienced the drag of these constraints; but instead of yielding to them helped stretch them way beyond previously accepted limits. They expanded, for the benefit of all of us now teaching and studying here, the conventional boundaries of the American law professors' possible roles. They brought the techniques of social science, the task of social analysis of the effects of law, and the concern to use law as an explicit tool of social policy, from the periphery into the heart of law teaching and scholarship. Some of them allowed their political partisanship to overpower their critical judgment; some lacked intellectual discipline and the capacity to sustain interest in any new method or project; and of all their work, only Thurman Arnold's and Jerome Frank's books are much read today. But they made it acceptable for law teachers to be searching — and, perhaps even more subversively, amusing — critics of established legal doctrines and policies; and to speak to and collaborate with wider audiences in the rest of the university and the public world beyond it, in both elite and popular languages. They created the romance of Yale Law School as a center of intellectual experiment and heterodoxy, and incidentally helped make it glamorous and famous. They bequeathed to us a sense of intellectual adventure and critical daring. They took the risks that have helped later generations live in the legal academy as something it had never been before, a safe haven for critics and reformers, visionaries and rebels.

Notes

When I began this project, I was greatly fortunate to have the benefit of the research assistance of Kyle Graham (YLS '01), a genius for spying and retrieving the documentary nuggets in the cavernous reaches of institutional archives, and for synthesizing and reflecting on the significance of what he found there. His work was indispensable to this project. Allegra Hogan (YLS '02) provided valuable additional research assistance in the revision phase, and Emily Gordon and Kate Gordon expert copyediting of the manuscript. I would also like to thank Michael Widener, Head of Special Collections, Tarlton Law Library, University of Texas School of Law; the staffs of the Manuscript Division, Library of Congress, and the American Heritage Center, University of Wyoming; and Nancy Lyon and the endlessly cooperative and helpful staff of the Manuscripts and Archives Division, Yale University Library.

1. Laura Kalman, *Legal Realism at Yale, 1927–1960* (1986; hereafter Kalman, *Legal Realism*); John Henry Schlegel, *American Legal Realism and Empirical Social Science* (1995; hereafter Schlegel, *Empirical Social Science*).

2. Langdell's reforms are ably treated in Robert Stevens, *Law School: Legal Education in America from the 1850s to the 1980s,* at 35–64 (1983; hereafter Stevens, *Law School*); and William LaPiana, *Logic and Experience: The Origins of Modern American Legal Education* (1994).

3. A. V. Dicey, *Can English Law Be Taught at the Universities?* (Oxford Inaugural Lecture 1883), cited in David Sugarman, "Legal Theory, The Common Law Mind, and the Making of the Textbook Tradition," in William Twining, ed., *Legal Theory and the Common Law* 26, 30 (1986).

4. James Barr Ames, *The Vocation of the Law Professor* (1901), reprinted in Steve Sheppard, ed., *The History of Legal Education in the United States: Commentaries and Primary Sources,* 1000, 1006–7 (1999).

5. Report of Acting Dean Robert Hutchins, 1926–27, at 117.

6. These figures include Yale College undergraduates taking pre-law courses for credit toward a law degree. They exclude derisory enrollments during World War I (104 for 1917 and 90 for 1918–19).

7. In 1912–13, for example, Yale eliminated its BCL degree, which had required Roman Law and allowed students to substitute courses in political science for courses in law; and reorganized the graduate program to drop all the "non-legal" subjects such as Constitutional History and Sociology. Eventually, of course, such subjects would creep back in, but this time as an integral part of *legal* studies.

8. Report of Dean Henry Wade Rogers, 1914–15, at 319.

9. Report of Dean Thomas W. Swan, 1916–17, at 307.

10. "A Program for the Expansion of the Yale School of Law into a School of Law and Jurisprudence, Committee Report, 1917," printed in Swan Report, supra note 9.

11. Wesley N. Hohfeld, "A Vital School of Jurisprudence and Law" (Presidential Address to Association of American Law Schools, December 1914).

12. Id. at 1–47.

13. For the Columbia curricular experiments, see Brainerd Currie, "The Materials of Law Study," 8 *J. Am. Leg. Edu.* 1 (1955); Kalman, *Legal Realism,* supra note 1, at 68–78; Schlegel, *Empirical Social Science,* supra note 1, at 15–17; Stevens, *Law School,* supra note 2, at 112–25.

14. Roscoe Pound and Felix Frankfurter, eds., *Criminal Justice in Cleveland* (1922).

15. Felix Frankfurter and James M. Landis, *The Business of the Supreme Court: A Study in the Federal Judicial System* (1928).

16. Felix Frankfurter and Nathan Greene, *The Labor Injunction* (1930).

17. For Frankfurter's early career as a crusading public-interest lawyer, see Michael E. Parrish, *Felix Frankfurter and His Times: The Reform Years* (1982).

18. Charles E. Clark, "Outline of Proposed Remarks Before the Educational Policy Committee of the Corporation," April 8, 1932. Charles E. Clark Papers, Manuscript and Archives Division, Yale University Library (hereafter Clark Papers), Box 19, Folder 244.

19. Frank is the subject of an excellent intellectual biography, Robert Jerome Glennon, *The Iconoclast as Reformer: Jerome Frank's Impact on American Law* (1985; hereafter Glennon, *Iconoclast*). His papers are deposited in the Manuscript and Archives Division, Yale University Library.

20. For Frank's early life, see Glennon, *Iconoclast,* at 15–22. Frank was also active in political and social causes. He was a co-founder of the National Lawyers Guild, set up to be a liberal counterweight to dominantly conservative bar associations such as the ABA, though he left the Guild in 1940 when he thought it had become dominated by radicals. An isolationist in the 1930s, he strongly supported the war effort after 1941. An assimilated reform Jew, he spoke out against Zionism in 1941, but changed his mind and supported a Jewish state in 1947. Id at 26, 30–31.

21. Corbin's letter to President Angell in opposition to the appointment is worth quoting in full:

> The name of Mr. Jerome Frank is being proposed as a candidate for a professorship of law. It now appears that in opposing this suggestion I shall be a minority member of the faculty committee appointed to consider such proposals. I therefore

desire to lay before you in writing the exact reasons for my opposition, before the question shall be presented for even a preliminary vote. . . .

My objections are:

He seems to be a propagandist and an agitator rather than a teacher and investigator.

His matured opinions are so personal and particular as to justify and require agitation to propagate them. . . .

It seems probable to me that as a member of a law faculty he would always occupy an exaggerated place as its assumed public representative . . .

It is now publicly represented that he has been forced out of the government service as an extreme "left-winger."

I have never voted against any man because of his race or nationality, although racial background and education are not matters that can be disregarded. We have already proved our tolerance and appreciation. At the same time, I am sure that the service that this school can render will be rapidly reduced if we appear to become an asylum for the oppressed of less tolerant nations or to be flying the flag of a social propaganda. Special weight is given to this fifth point in the case of Mr. Frank, by reason of the four preceding points listed above.

Corbin to Angell, Feb. 8, 1935. Records of James Rowland Angell as president of Yale University, 1921–1937, Manuscript and Archives Division, Yale University (hereafter Angell Papers), RU-24, RG 2-A.

22. *Yale University Bulletin 1932–33*, at 320. This seminar had various titles in its career.

23. Arthur Schlesinger Jr., *The Coming of the New Deal*, 49–50 (1959).

24. Arnold wrote his own charming autobiography, *Fair Fights and Foul* (1965). A good biographical sketch may be found in the editor's introduction to Gene M. Gressley, ed., *Voltaire and the Cowboy: The Letters of Thurman Arnold* 1–94 (1977; hereafter Arnold Letters). His papers are deposited in the American Heritage Center at the University of Wyoming. As this lecture was going to press I read the manuscript of an exceptionally brilliant and penetrating critical essay on Arnold's thought: Mark Fenster, *The Symbols of Governance: Thurman Arnold, Post-Realist Legal Theory, and Social Criticism* (2003).

25. Joseph Alsop and Robert Kintner, "Trust Buster: The Folklore of Thurman Arnold," *The Saturday Evening Post*, Aug. 12, 1939, at 5–6.

26. A fine biography is James F. Simon, *Independent Journey: The Life of William O. Douglas* (1980; hereafter Simon, *Independent Journey*). Douglas covered this period of his life in the first volume of his autobiography, *Go East, Young Man* (1974), lively and engaging reading but often unreliable. A useful collection of letters is Melvin U. Urofsky, ed., *The Douglas Letters* (1987; hereafter Urofsky, *Douglas Letters*), which excerpts selected letters from the collection in the William O. Douglas Papers in the Manuscript Division, Library of Congress. A new biography has just appeared: Bruce Allen Murphy, *Wild Bill: The Legend and Life of William O. Douglas* (2003).

27. There is unfortunately no biography of Hamilton. Some biographical information can be gleaned from the memorial tributes in 68 *Yale L. J.*, especially Fred Rodell, "A Sprig of Rosemary for Hammy," 68 *Yale L. J.* 401 (1959). His extensive papers are in the

Archives of the Tarlton Law Library, University of Texas Law School. I am grateful to Hamilton's son and daughter-in-law, Professors Robert W. Hamilton and Dagmar Hamilton of the University of Texas at Austin, for sharing with me further personal letters and reminiscences.

28. In 1926 and 1927, he also helped organize the Committee on the Costs of Medical Care. This committee's report, issued in 1932, discussed the effects of changes in medicine and medical practice on consumers.

29. Hamilton himself wrote the leading manifestos of the American school of institutional economics: "The Development of Hoxie's Economics," 24 *J. Polit. Econ.* 855 (1916) and "The Institutionalist Approach to Economic Theory," 9 *Am. Econ. Rev.* 309 (1919). For useful secondary accounts of American institutionalism, see Ben B. Seligman, *Main Currents in Modern Economics: The Revolt Against Formalism* 129–253 (1962) and Herbert Hovenkamp, "The First Great Law and Economics Movement," 42 *Stan. L. Rev.* 993 (1990); for an explanation of its eclipse, see Heath Pearson, *Origins of Law and Economics* 130–61 (1997).

30. See, e.g., Walton H. Hamilton and Stacy May, *The Control of Wages* (1923); Walton H. Hamilton and Helen R. Wright, *The Case of Bituminous Coal* (1926); Walton H. Hamilton, ed., *Prices and Price Policies* (1938).

31. Copy (courtesy of Boris Bittker) in possession of author.

32. "The Path of Due Process of Law," 48 *Ethics* 269 (1938); "Affectation with Public Interest," 39 *Yale L. J.* 1080 (1930); "Property — According to Locke," 41 *Yale L. J.* 864 (1932); "The Ancient Maxim *Caveat Emptor*," 40 *Yale L. J.* 1133 (1931).

33. This apt phrase comes from a classic early treatment of Progressive social thought: Morton White, *Social Thought in America: The Revolt Against Formalism* (1949).

34. For good accounts of the various strands of realist-Progressive legal thought, see Kalman, *Legal Realism,* supra note 1; Schlegel, *Empirical Social Science,* supra note 1; Edward Purcell, *The Crisis of Democratic Theory: Scientific Naturalism and the Problem of Value* (1973); William Twining, *Karl Llewellyn and the Realist Movement* (1973); Morton Horwitz, *The Transformation of American Law, 1870–1960* (1992); Joseph William Singer, "Legal Realism Now," 76 *Calif. L. Rev.* 465 (1988); William W. Fisher III, "The Development of Modern American Legal Theory and the Judicial Interpretation of the Bill of Rights," in Michael J. Lacey and Knud Haakonssen, eds., *A Culture of Rights* 266–365 (1991); Neil Duxbury, *Patterns of American Jurisprudence* (1995); Fenster, *Thurman Arnold,* supra note 24.

35. See O. W. Holmes Jr., *The Common Law* (1881); O. W. Holmes Jr., "Privilege, Malice and Intent," in *Collected Legal Papers* (1920).

36. Wesley N. Hohfeld, "Some Fundamental Legal Conceptions as Applied in Judicial Reasoning," 23 *Yale. L. J.* 28 (1913).

37. This was the debate that led to the recognition of reliance as an alternative to bargained — for exchange as a basis for enforcing promises in the First Restatement of Contracts, §90. See Grant Gilmore, *The Death of Contract* 62–65 (1974).

38. Leon Green, *The Judicial Process in Tort Cases* (1931).

39. The book responded to the opinion of the U.S. Supreme Court (per Sutherland, J. for a 5–4 majority) invalidating the Guffey Coal Act in *Carter v. Carter Coal Co.,* 298 U.S. 238 (1936) (manufacture of a commodity, wages, and labor conditions are "local in nature" and hence beyond the scope of the federal power to regulate commerce).

40. Walton Hamilton and Douglas Adair, *The Power to Govern* 184–92 (1937).

41. Walton H. Hamilton, "Property," *Encyclopaedia of the Social Sciences* 12:528 (1934).

42. *The Symbols of Government* (1935) and *The Folklore of Capitalism* (1937).

43. For this example, see *The Folklore of Capitalism,* Ch. 5.

44. See Fenster, *Thurman Arnold,* supra note 24, at 14–17.

45. William O. Douglas, "Vicarious Liability and Administration of Risk I," 38 *Yale L. J.* 584 (1929).

46. William O. Douglas, "A Functional Approach to the Law of Business Associations," 23 *Ill. L. Rev.* 673 (1928–29).

47. Id. at 678.

48. See, e.g., William O. Douglas, "Wage-Earner Bankruptcies — State v. Federal Control," 42 *Yale L. J.* 591 (1933).

49. Arnold, *The Folklore of Capitalism,* supra note 42, at 121–35.

50. Jerome Frank, *Law and the Modern Mind* (1930).

51. For the fullest statement of his views on the trial process, see generally Jerome Frank, *Courts on Trial* (1949), which synthesizes articles Frank had written on the subject from 1931 onward.

52. See, e.g., Jerome Frank, *If Men Were Angels* 155 (1942).

53. Morris R. Cohen, "Property and Sovereignty," 13 *Cornell L. Q.* (1927)

54. Arthur L. Corbin, "Offer and Acceptance and Some of the Resulting Legal Relations," 26 *Yale L. J.* 204 (1917).

55. Robert L. Hale, "Coercion and Distribution in a Supposedly Non-Coercive State," 38 *Pol. Sci. Q.* 470 (1923).

56. See, e.g., *If Men Were Angels,* supra note 53, at 148–78.

57. For a typically Hamiltonian account of the large corporation, see, e.g., Walton H. Hamilton, "Book Review," 55 *Harv. L. Rev.* 551, 553 (1942):

> Once the will of the Titan was the will of the corporation; now discretion is set in a matrix of folk-ways and decrees, habits and vested interests. The individual recedes; the institution, with its permeating compulsions, comes into ascendancy. Within the stereotype of legalism, a clash attends the going concern. One official refuses to be disturbed in his ways; another seeks to enlarge his power; a third attends to personal irons in the fire. . . . Men with interests vested in their own habits, resist change; tolerant of the ossification of the enterprise, they fear the obsolescence of their own skills. As its anatomy has become rigid, the authority of the corporation has become enlarged. In the good old days, the business unit was a private affair. For the concern was small, there were many to an industry, its contracts were made at arms [length], it was one of two parties of equal power in shaping the terms of the bargain. . . . But, as the business unit has become the corporate estate, it has gone far to usurp the office of the market. Where goods are trademarked, put up in standard packages, passed along routine channels, made notorious by advertising, detail cannot be left to the impersonal operation of economic forces. A flexible price . . . hardly accords with the rigidities of intricate organizations. Decisions in respect to cost, design, promotion, volume of product must be made months before goods are ready to be sold. . . . [The] market, when its chance comes, can only confirm or rebut managerial judgment. Where a concern,

singly or in concert with its fellows, enjoys a sheltered market, it decrees price, and between itself and its customers becomes both party and judge. Thus one of the two parties to the bargain has been catapulted into a public office.

58. Arnold, *Folklore of Capitalism,* supra note 42, at 263–64.

59. American Bar Association, Report of Special Committee on Administrative Law (1938).

60. James M. Landis, *The Administrative Process* (1938).

61. See, e.g., Jerome Frank, *If Men Were Angels,* supra note 53, at 316–49 (defending SEC procedures and attacking Pound); William O. Douglas, "Virtues of the Administrative Process," in *Democracy and Finance* 243–47 (1940).

62. Thurman W. Arnold, "The Role of Substantive Law and Procedure in the Legal Process," 45 *Harvard L. Rev.* 617, 624–25, 626 (1932).

63. See Thurman W. Arnold, "Institute Priests and Yale Observers — A Reply to Dean Goodrich," 84 *U. Pa. L. Rev.* 811 (1936).

64. Like many rebellious children, they did their fathers less than justice. But for the classical generation's projects of legal science, the treatises and articles of Langdell, Ames, Beale, Williston, and Scott, and the Restatement projects that came about as close as American common lawyers could get to comprehensive codifications of private law, there could have been no legal realist movement. But for the classics' heroic work of generalization, doctrinal rationalization, and synthesis — and, I should add, the fifty years' work of classical lawyers, judges, and treatise-writers in building up the imposing structures of classical constitutional law — there would have been nothing to critique as "empty formalism" and "transcendental nonsense" — as sterile, oppressive, over-abstract, indeterminate, and removed from life.

65. See, e.g., Arnold, "Institute Priests," supra note 63.

66. Rodell, *Woe Unto You, Lawyers* 201 (1939).

67. Duxbury, supra note 34, at 69.

68. This critique was leveled against the realists, especially Arnold, in their own time, was revived in a fine article by Douglas Ayer, "In Quest of Efficiency: The Ideological Journey of Thurman Arnold in the Interwar Period," 23 *Stanford Law Rev.* 1029 (1971), and is developed at length in Fenster, supra note 24.

69. Jerome Frank, *Courts on Trial,* supra note 51, 80–146.

70. Jerome Frank, "Why Not a Clinical Lawyer School?" 81 *U. Pa. L. Rev.* 907 (1933).

71. Arnold, who had the requisite practice experience, had another reservation about Frank's proposals: "Most practicing attorneys are more conservative in their attitudes than even the law teachers as you yourself know from experience. . . . Certainly the Yale Law School has developed in the way it has over the dead bodies of many prominent alumni." Arnold to Frank, May 26, 1932. Jerome N., Frank Papers, Manuscripts and Archives Division, Yale University Library (hereafter Frank Papers), Box 1, Folder 8. Dean Clark had a still more basic practical objection: "I cannot get the able teachers we want even without practice, and . . . it seems absolutely impossible to get good men who just at that time would be getting ahead. Here you and I are scrapping for the body of one Fortas, who has had two months of practice. . . . Moreover it is interesting to note that some of the men with the most practical training react most violently against practical

training later on. A good example is your own model Thurman Arnold, who is now getting the most joy out of being philosophical and as far from the students' every day needs as is conceivable, and whose own choices for the faculty tend to favor those without law training at all." Clark to Frank, Sept. 5, 1933, Frank Papers, Box 10, Folder 39.

72. Nomination of Thurman W. Arnold: Hearings before a Subcommittee of the Committee of the Judiciary, United States Senate, (75th Congress, 3rd Session) March 11, 1938, at 11. Arnold had not always been particularly shy in recommending government programs. See Thurman W. Arnold and Wesley A. Sturges, "The Progress of the New Administration," 32 *Yale Rev.* 656 (1933). Upon its completion in March 1933, Arnold and Sturges submitted this plan, which advocated the limitation of farm production, the refund and reduction of farm debts, and the control of farm credit, to Secretary of Agriculture Wallace, the Farm Loan Board, and Henry Morgenthau Jr., chairman of the Federal Farm Board. See Yale University News Statement, March 18, 1933 (copy in Angell Papers).

73. Arnold to Harold Laski, Jan. 9, 1936, in Letters, supra note 24, at 217.

74. See Hamilton, writings cited supra note 30.

75. See Hamilton, writings cited supra note 32.

76. See, e.g., William O. Douglas, Materials prepared for the private and confidential use of the students in the course known as Business organization I, given in the Yale University School of Law in the year 1928–29 (1928).

77. William O. Douglas, "Education for the Law," in *Democracy and Finance* 278, 286–87 (1936). See also William O. Douglas, "The Lawyer and Reorganizations," 1 *Nat'l Lawyer's Guild Q.* 31 (1938) (describing the large discretionary power the lawyer has to make policy as counsel for protective committees in corporate reorganizations).

78. See Schlegel, *Empirical Social Science,* supra note 1, at 82–98.

79. Id. at 99–105.

80. Laura Kalman, *Abe Fortas* 20–21 (1990).

81. Simon, *Independent Journey,* supra note 26, at 118–19.

82. American Law Institute, *A Study of the Business of the Federal Courts, Part I, Criminal Cases* (1934) at 12:

> Current literature and thought would lead us to expect that the serious obstacles to criminal law enforcement consisted of technicalities, delays and continuances, irrational juries, a cumbersome grand jury system, long trials, appeals on obsolete doctrinal points, and in general the widely advertised results of what is generally called "the sporting theory of justice." The picture drawn by these figures fails to reveal the presence of any of these difficulties which are usually assumed without argument. On the contrary, doubts arise, not because the system is inefficient, but because it seems almost too efficient; because it presents the spectacle of a long line of orderly offenders, few of whom it is necessary to commit to jail, pleading guilty with systematic regularity because reasonably accurate estimates of the sentence seem possible; raising few technical objections, and so far as the records show, rarely complaining about invasions of their constitutional or other privileges.

For the legal establishment's cool reception of this report, see Schlegel, *Empirical Social Science,* at 94–97.

83. Arnold said of the statistical report on the Federal courts on which he had labored: "Much of the material in it is unquestionably useless. Some of it is interesting. Nonetheless I feel that it is worth while because the limitation of this type of study is one of the things that had to be proven. We have made the most elaborately objective study of the courts which, I think, has ever been made, and it shows, among other things, that there is no particular object in counting anything until you have an idea what you want the information for." Thurman Arnold to Felix Frankfurter, Feb. 23, 1933, reprinted in Arnold Letters, supra note 24, 195, 195–96.

84. Kalman, *Legal Realism,* supra note 1, at 130.

85. Simon, *Independent Journey,* supra note 26, at 140.

86. Apparently one of Douglas's few diversions after bruisingly long workdays at the SEC was to meet Arnold in East Prospect Park to play an "antic version of hide and seek." Simon, *Independent Journey,* at 178–79.

87. See Kalman, *Legal Realism,* supra note 1, at 132–35.

88. "Another Color on the Campus," *Chicago Tribune,* Jan 21, 1939.

89. William Fulton, "Reveal Radical Doctrin [sic] Taught in Law Schools," *Chicago Tribune,* Jan. 15, 1939, at 1; "New Deal Ideas Influence Yale School of Law," *Chicago Tribune,* Jan. 16, 1939. Dean Clark wrote a detailed response at the request of Yale's Secretary, pointing out the diversity of political views on the law faculty and the fact that several members of the faculty had opposed New Deal measures and represented private companies against the government. Clark to Carl A. Lohmann, Jan. 24, 1939. Charles Seymour Papers, Records of the Provost's Office, Yale University 1914–1964, Manuscripts and Archives Division, Yale University Library.

90. Clark to Angell, Sept. 26, 1993, Angell Papers.

91. Clark had previously been a lifelong Republican who voted for FDR for the first time in 1936.

92. The story of law professors and the court-packing plan is told in fascinating detail in Kyle Graham, "A Moment in 'The Times': Law Professors and the Court-Packing Plan," 52 *J. Leg. Educ.* 151 (2002).

93. Quoted in Kalman, *Legal Realism,* supra note 1, at 134.

94. Jerome Frank, "Experimental Jurisprudence and the New Deal," Speech to Am. Ass'n. of Law Schools, Dec. 30, 1933, 31 *Handbook of the Am. Ass'n. of Law Schools* 101 (1934), reprinted at 78 *Cong. Record,* pt. 2, 73d Cong., 2d Sess. 12412–14 (1934; hereafter Frank, "Experimental Jurisprudence").

95. Frank spelled out these views in a revealing correspondence with Felix Frankfurter, who had worried that Frank might appear too unconventional an advocate to the judges before whom he defended New Deal programs: "My notion in brief-writing has always been that one must use the particular kind of jargon and articulate one's ideas in terms of the particular kind of precedential language that, so far as one can conjecture, will be most pleasing to the particular tribunal to which the argument is addressed." Frank to Frankfurter, Dec. 4, 1935, quoted in Glennon, *Iconoclast,* supra note 19, at 88.

> I don't say [as Frankfurter had accused him of saying] that "most law is bunk" . . . I think "law" is damned real. But I do not believe that it works the way it appears, on the surface, to work. I think that many legal ceremonials could be eliminated. But

> while they exist, they play an important part in their effects on human lives. Therefore, as a lawyer, I want to be well up on them and meticulously practice them. To use high-brow terms, I think that, pragmatically, practice, procedure and substantive law inter-mingle or, to put it differently, "substantive law" is merely one of the implements used in a court fight, — one of the implements of persuasion used to induce a court to issue an order which will be backed by armed force, if necessary, to compel some one to do what your client wants him to do.

Frank to Frankfurter, Dec. 9, 1935, quoted in Glennon, *Iconoclast,* supra note 19, at 89.

96. Glennon, *Iconoclast,* at 94–101.

97. For good accounts of the AAA conflicts and purge, see Arthur Schlesinger Jr., *The Coming of the New Deal* 49–80 (1959); Glennon, *Iconoclast,* at 98–101; Peter Irons, *The New Deal Lawyers,* at 156–80 (1982).

98. Frank, "Experimental Jurisprudence," supra note 94 at 12414.

99. For his vigorous expression of these views, see Jerome Frank, *Save America First* (1938).

100. Jerome Frank, speech to University of Buffalo Alumni, May 28, 1938 (transcript in Frank Papers).

101. *Nebbia v. N.Y.,* 291 U.S. 502 (1934).

102. Id.; *Nomination of Thurman W. Arnold: Hearings before a Subcommittee of the Committee of the Judiciary, United States Senate, (75th Congress, 3rd Session) March 11, 1938* (GPO 1938). Wesley Sturges served in a like capacity during the summer of 1934 in Hawaii, apparently kicking up quite a fuss among Hawaii's Yale alumni in the process. See 1933–34 Dean's Report at 122; Clark to Hamilton, Sept. 20, 1934, Angell Papers.

103. Clark to Angell, Sept. 10, 1934, Angell Papers.

104. Clark to Angell, Aug. 13, 1935, Angell Papers.

105. Arnold to Mr. and Mrs. C. P. Arnold, Sept. 18, 1937, reprinted in Arnold Letters, supra note 24 at 265.

106. Id.

107. To President Seymour, explaining his request to extend his leave for another year, Arnold wrote:

> I regret this situation has developed. I accepted my present leave with no political career in mind, with no desire to enter private practice, and I have not changed my mind. My principal reasons for preferring Yale to any other career are two. In the first place, I am enthusiastic about teaching, and feel I have the ability to catch the imaginations of the students. In the second place, I have two more books that I wish to write and which could not be written without the time for research which I would have as a teacher. I have had an unusual bird's eye view of the impact of legal institutions upon economic organization from my present office. I believe I can produce an objective analysis of governmental problems which will be extremely relevant in the field of public law.

Arnold to Seymour, July 4, 1939. Records of Charles Seymour as president of Yale University, 1917–1956, Manuscripts and Archives Division, Yale University Library (hereafter Seymour Papers), RU-23, RG 2-A.

108. Thurman W. Arnold, *Fair Fights and Foul* 136 (1965).

109. Arnold, *The Folklore of Capitalism,* supra note 42, at 207–29.

110. Senate Judiciary Committee, Nomination of Thurman W. Arnold, 75 Cong. 3 Sess. 3–5 (1938).

111. For accounts of Arnold's leadership of the Antitrust Division, see Ellis Hawley, *The New Deal and the Monopoly Problem* 420–55 (1966); Alan Brinkley, *The End of Reform* 106–22 (1995).

112. Brinkley, id., at 113.

113. Id. at 119–20.

114. Id. at 122.

115. Thurman W. Arnold, *The Bottlenecks of Business* (1940).

116. Charles E. Clark and William O. Douglas, *Law and Legal Institutions* (1933).

117. Urofsky, *Douglas Letters,* supra note 26, at 3.

118. See Douglas and Sturges to George Parmly Day, April 7, 1933, Angell Papers, Box 121, Folder 1250.

119. Urofsky, *Douglas Letters,* supra note 26 at 27.

120. Douglas to James Landis, July 18, 1934, reprinted in Urofsky, *Douglas Letters,* at 29.

121. See footnote 1 to Douglas to Robert Hutchins, May 6, 1936, in Urofsky, *Douglas Letters,* at 34.

122. See Douglas to Franklin Delano Roosevelt, July 7, 1936, in Urofsky, *Douglas Letters,* at 36.

123. Id. at 27.

124. Joel Seligman, *The Transformation of Wall Street* 157 (rev. ed. 1995).

125. See id. at 156–212; Michael E. Parrish, *Securities Regulation and the New Deal* 209–19 (1970).

126. Clark to Angell, Jan. 24, 1936, Angell Papers.

127. Clark to Seymour, Jan. 9, 1936, Angell Papers.

128. Kalman, *Legal Realism,* supra note 1, at 140. The next most popular candidate with the faculty, Dean Acheson, declined the deanship. The realist faction favored Arnold, but he was too controversial. The same faction opposed Harry Shulman, Frankfurter's protégé and favorite, apparently because of his Harvard connections. In the ensuing deadlock, the dean chosen, Peyl Gulliver, was, ironically, intellectually more conservative than Shulman. Shulman finally did become dean in 1954 but died soon thereafter of cancer. Kalman, *Legal Realism,* at 141–43, 197–98.

129. William O. Douglas, "Protective Committees in Railroad Reorganizations," 47 *Harv. L. Rev.* 565 (1934).

130. William O. Douglas, "Protecting the Investor," 23 *Yale Rev.* 521 (1934).

131. Simon, *Independent Journey,* supra note 26, at 133–36.

132. David A. Skeel Jr., *Debt's Dominion: A History of Bankruptcy Law in America* 122 (2001).

133. See William J. Bratton, "Berle and Means Reconsidered at the Century's Turn," 26 *Iowa J. Corp. Law* 737, 746–47 (2001).

134. Skeel at 162–68.

135. Douglas's romantic reinvention of his life story in his autobiography, *Go East Young Man*, is deftly documented in Simon's *Independent Journey*, supra note 26.

136. Clark to Seymour, July 25, 1933, Angell Papers, Folder 1238.

137. 1933–34 Dean's Report at 122.

138. 1933–34 Dean's Report at 122.

139. Samuel E. Winslow, Chairman, United States Board of Mediation, to Charles E. Clark, March 6, 1934. JRA.

140. "Roosevelt Picks 2 Boards To Redirect Reorganized NRA; He, Himself, Has Last Word," *New York Times,* Sept. 28, 1934, at A1.

141. Hamilton to Clark, March 13, 1935, Angell Papers.

142. Id.

143. See, e.g., Clarence K. Streit, "American at I.L.O. Hedges on Hours," *New York Times,* June 4, 1935, at 40.

144. Clarence K. Streit, "American Assails I.L.O. Employers," *New York Times,* June 8, 1935, at 7.

145. "NRA Executive Orders," *New York Times,* June 17, 1935, at 2.

146. "Dr. Hamilton Heads Consumers' Survey," *New York Times,* Aug. 1, 1935, at B:5.

147. Clark to Angell, Sept. 9, 1935, Angell Papers.

148. Oliver McKee Jr., "Consumers' Agency to Get Price Data," *New York Times,* Aug. 18, 1935, at E:7. An article published soon thereafter identified five activities and objectives for the Division: (1) Inquiries by economists into prices and price-determining structures of specific industries to develop means of eliminating those "trouble spots" in production-distribution systems which keep products out of the consumers' reach; (2) Education of the public to recognize and encourage wider use of quality standards and grade labeling; (3) Studies of the consumers' cooperative movement both here and abroad with a view to making information on organization and administrative methods available to American groups interested in cooperative purchasing; (4) Further organization of consumers' county councils on a nationwide basis to gather data and distribute educational information on problems; (4) The recognition of the interests of the consumer in all matters dealing with production, price, and trade practices; and (5) Review of current legislation and public policy from the consumers' viewpoint. "New Agency Acts for Consumers," *New York Times,* Sept. 9, 1935.

149. Clark to Angell, Aug. 6, 1935, Angell Papers.

150. Clark to Seymour, April 15, 1936. Id.

151. 4 *Yale L. Rep.* at 16.

152. Hamilton's work here consisted primarily of research, making it sensitive to budget cutbacks. See Gulliver to Edgar Furniss, Oct. 30, 1942 (discussing Thurman Arnold's termination of Hamilton-led research for the Anti-Trust division because it was "too academic in character to warrant its continuation under a reduced budget."). CS.

153. On the TNEC, and its work, see Hawley, supra note 113, at 456–71; Brinkley, *End of Reform,* supra note 113, at 123–32.

154. See Walton Hamilton, "Justice Cardozo: The Great Tradition," *The New Republic,* July 27, 1938, at 328–29; Walton Hamilton, "Mr. Justice Black's First Year," *The*

New Republic, June 8, 1938, at 118–22; Hamilton and George Braden, "The Supreme Court Today," *The New Republic,* August 5, 1940, at 178–80; Walton Hamilton, "The Smoldering Constitutional Crisis," *The New Republic,* January 18, 1943, at 73–76; Walton Hamilton, "Blueprint for a Virile Congress," *New York Times Magazine,* Sept. 10, 1944, at 12, 34–35.

155. Seymour to Gulliver, June 7, 1941, Seymour Papers.

156. Hamilton to Seymour, June 16, 1941, Seymour Papers.

157. See Jerrold Auerbach, *Unequal Justice* (1976) at 184–88.

158. Kalman, *Abe Fortas,* supra note 81, at 56–58.

159. Ronen Shamir, *Managing Legal Uncertainty: Elite Lawyers in the New Deal* 131–57 (1995).

160. See generally, Irons, supra note 99, at 226–53, discussing the strategy devised by New Deal "legal craftsmen" to save the National Labor Relations (Wagner) Act.

161. *Yale Law School Bulletin,* 1929–40.

162. *Harvard Law School Bulletin,* 1929–40.

163. See generally Brinkley, *End of Reform,* supra note 113.

164. Thomas Emerson, *Young Lawyer for the New Deal* 271–72 (1991). Emerson's experience was surely exceptionally frustrating, since his job was enforcement of wartime price and wage controls for the Office of Price Administration.

165. Walton H. Hamilton, *The Politics of Industry* 156–57 (1957).

166. The Yale faculty's wartime service is concisely summarized in a 1943 report to the alumni:

> The Dean reported on the war time activities of the members of the faculty. [Edwin] Borchard has been consultant to various government departments; [Peyl] Gulliver has acted as Chairman of the Alien Enemy Hearing Board for Connecticut, is a member of the Connecticut Post-War Planning Board and Chairman of the University Post-War Planning Committee, and has done work locally for the O.P.A.; [Walton H.] Hamilton and [Roscoe] Steffen are engaged in part-time work for the Department of Justice; Underhill Moore has been a mediation representative for the National War Labor Board. The majority of the resident faculty have served in civilian defense as air raid wardens or otherwise. [George] Dession is Special Assistant to the Attorney General of the United States, and has a responsible position in the Criminal Division of the Department of Justice in the formulation of policy with respect to war crimes. [Harry] Shulman is in Detroit most of each week, acting as Umpire of Labor Disputes for the Ford Motor Company and U.A.W., and has also been an associate member of the National War Labor Board and a member of the Alien Enemy Hearing Board for Connecticut. [Abe] Feller is Deputy Director and General Counsel of the Office of War Information, and is serving on several board and committees operating under that office. [Fleming] James is Director of the Litigation Division of the Enforcement Department of O.P.A. [Myres] McDougal is General Counsel in the Office of Foreign Relief and Rehabilitation Operations of the State Department. [John F.] Meck is a Lieutenant in the United States Navy, his work being principally in connection with the naval training programs at schools and colleges throughout the country. [Eugene V.] Rostow has served as Assistant General Counsel of the Office of Lend-Lease Ad-

ministration, Executive Assistant to Dean G. Acheson, Assistant Secretary of State, Executive vice chairman of the North African Economic Board, and Acting Director of Economic Operations in the North African Theatre; he has now returned to New Haven in order to enter the army. [Wesley] Sturges was at the head of the O.E.W. Mission to North Africa, and is currently serving as Sub-Area Director of Economic Operations for Sicily for the State Department.

Minutes of the Meeting of the Executive Committee of the Yale Law School Association, Oct. 29, 1943. Yale Law School Association Minutes of the Executive Committee, 1923–84. Manuscript and Archives, Yale University Library (RU 183 YRG 26-H ACCN: 995-A-056 Box 1, Folder 3.)

167. *Sweatt v. Painter,* 339 U.S. 629 (1950).

168. Emerson, quoted in Kalman, *Legal Realism,* supra note 1, at 195.

169. Eugene V. Rostow, *A National Policy for the Oil Industry* (1948).

170. George Priest, "The Invention of Enterprise Liability: A Critical History of the Intellectual Foundations of Modern Tort Law," 14 *J. Legal Stud.* 461 (1985).

171. *U.S. v. Carolene Products,* 304 U.S.144, 154 n. 4 (1938).

172. *Skinner v. Oklahoma,* 316 U.S. 535 (1942); *Dennis v. U.S.,* 341 U.S. 494, 581 (1951) (Douglas, J. dissenting); *Griswold v. Connecticut,* 381 U.S. 479 (1965).

173. For the Arnold Fortas & Porter firm's representation of clients accused of Communism and "disloyalty," see Kalman, *Abe Fortas,* supra note 81, at 125–51.

174. Doing his part to keep the Yale-Harvard feud going, Arnold defended the Warren Court from Harvard scholars' attacks on its inadequate reasoning. See Arnold, "Professor Hart's Theology," 73 *Harv. L. Rev.* 1298 (1960), responding to Henry M. Hart Jr., "Supreme Court 1958 Term, Foreword: The Time Chart of the Justices," 73 *Harv. L. Rev.* 84 (1959).

Politics and the Law School:
The View from Woodbridge Hall, *1921–1963*

GADDIS SMITH

The Yale Law School in the middle years of the twentieth century was a problem for successive university presidents ensconced in nearby Woodbridge Hall. The difficulty stemmed both from disagreements over the role of a law school within the university and from presidential fears that the association of the Law School and particular faculty with left/liberal positions would deprive Yale of sorely needed financial support from alumni. It was exacerbated by the anti-Semitic and anti-New Deal prejudices of one president (James Rowland Angell, 1921–1937) and the conviction of another (A. Whitney Griswold, 1950–1963) that all Yale faculty should concentrate on "pure" scholarship and teaching uncontaminated by contact with living issues in society. The relationship between the Law School and Woodbridge Hall illustrates both the complexity of power within Yale and political and intellectual connections with the external world.

During the first two decades of the twentieth century, the Yale Law School ceased to be a local institution requiring only a high school diploma for admission and with part-time faculty including some men of talent from the bench and bar but not active scholars. Yale President Arthur Twining Hadley (1901–1921) feared that by requiring a college degree for admission, the profession of law (and of medicine) would be monopolized by the privileged rich. Otherwise, he paid slight attention to the Law School and showed little interest in the aspirations of Deans Henry Wade Rogers (1903–1916) and Thomas Swan

(1916–1927) and the new full-time faculty to create a "School of Law and Jurisprudence" dedicated to a scientific, philosophical, and ameliorative rather than simply vocational approach to teaching and research.

The retirement of President Hadley and the inauguration of President Angell was a mixed blessing for the Law School. Angell believed in a university with strong, modern graduate and professional education — not just an undergraduate college with weak, outlying postgraduate schools. He was a crisp, outwardly unruffled administrator fully in sympathy with the law faculty's belief "that university law schools must play a larger and larger part in the adaptation of our legal system to the needs of modern life."[1] Beneath the surface he struggled with conflicting ideas about human character, political principles, and the purposes of the university. He was simultaneously a bold thinker and a man crippled by prejudice.

On one hand, he had a broad, modern attitude toward the social sciences and to trends in legal education. On the other, he was captive to racist eugenics, that cluster of ideas that sought to protect the United States from "genetically inferior" races capable of destroying the superiority of the "best stock" of English descent. This duality was startlingly expressed in a major speech Angell delivered in 1922 on the subject of legal education. First, he said, the study of law must

> make students feel that . . . law is . . . but one part of the development of our social fabric, that it cannot . . . be treated as a whole isolated group of problems without doing violence to the facts and without distorting the fundamental understanding of human nature and human institutions. This broad historical and social conception of the law is one of the characteristics of the best modern legal education.

Precisely the sentiments of the Yale Law faculty. Then Angell said the legal profession was threatened by Jews:

> [T]here has been a very considerable invasion of the profession of law by men wholly alien through lineage and training to our entire Anglo-Saxon tradition, to the conception of the English common law, and to all that is involved in our ideal of the relation of the law to the life of the community. . . . Thus far it is apparently chiefly the bar and not the bench which is affected, but the bar of today will supply the bench of tomorrow. . . . It is not merely that the bench and the bar are being thus recruited by men of foreign race and alien tradition . . . [but that they are also] undermining the finer professional spirit and feeling which characterizes the professional training of the American lawyer.[2]

The Secretary of the University in Angell's first years was Robert M. Hutchins, Yale College '21, a boy wonder who in 1925 earned his Yale Law degree through part-time study. In 1927 Hutchins, having done some teaching in the

Law School, resigned as Secretary of the University and became a professor of law and acting dean when Swan became a judge. In 1928 the "acting" was dropped. He and some of the faculty soon provoked a complaint from a weighty external source, a former faculty member and before that president of the United States, and now Chief Justice of the United States Supreme Court: William Howard Taft. The Chief Justice began a letter to President Angell with a fulmination against Felix Frankfurter of Harvard for claiming that judicial prejudice and flimsy evidence led to the murder convictions and death sentences of the Italian immigrants and political anarchists Nicola Sacco and Bartolemeo Vanzetti and for urging the Massachusetts high court to reverse. No criminal case of the decade was so widely covered by the press and so ideologically charged. Frankfurter, said Taft, "seems to be closely in touch with every Bolshevistic communist movement in this country." Taft then complained that Dean Hutchins and some Yale law faculty had sided with Frankfurter and joined a protest concerning litigation outside of Connecticut that originated in a conviction "when Hutchins must have been a boy." The Chief Justice urged Angell to admonish and restrain Hutchins. "I haven't read the evidence in this case, and I know nothing about it, but there are certain limitations that should surround the conduct of a great Law School." Angell replied that he would bring the letter to the dean's attention but "the case is not quite as you assume" and many men of "absolute sobriety of judgment share in the feeling that it is in the public interest to have the case retried and are joining in an appeal to the governor to bring this to pass."[3] On this occasion Angell was defending a protégé.

Angell, Hutchins, and Milton C. Winternitz, the imaginative dean of the Medical School, combined in an effort to change the university in a profound way. They envisioned a holistic approach to all aspects of human behavior under the organizational umbrella of an Institute of Human Relations. Law and medicine would be the monarchs surrounded by the behavioral sciences and perhaps even the Divinity School. Under the direction of the Institute, faculty research would address specific problems such as juvenile delinquency while seeking an all-encompassing set of principles governing human behavior. The Rockefeller Foundation was persuaded to provide millions of dollars for research and for a grand building as the Siamese twin to the Sterling Hall of Medicine.

Angell asked the trustees of the Sterling estate to pay for a new law building near the Medical School in order to cement the marriage of the monarchs of the science of human behavior and save the Law School from the frivolity of Yale College and the undergraduate residential colleges soon to be financed by Harkness millions. But in a clear illustration of the strings attached to money, the Sterling trustees — with the support of a faction of the Yale Corporation — said that if Yale wanted Sterling money for law, the new law building must be on what was called the Hopkins School site adjacent to the Sterling Memorial Library.

Angell and Hutchins failed to change the decision of the Sterling trustees and thereby lost the architectural keystone of the grand design. Hutchins's frustration may well have contributed to his decision to accept the presidency of the University of Chicago. The next dean, Charles E. Clark (1929–1939), a faculty member since 1919, thought the grand design was nonsense and a threat to the independence of the Law School. He angered Angell by refusing to commit the school to a binding relationship with the Institute of Human Relations. Soon the Institute of Human Relations became an embarrassing failure. Except for psychology, the social sciences were not heavily involved in part because Graduate School Dean Wilbur Cross rightly sniffed a threat to his school. The research funds from Rockefeller supported some worthwhile but uncoordinated studies. No overarching understanding of human behavior was ever discovered or seriously pursued. In the meantime, the Sterling Law Buildings occupying the entire block of Wall, York, Grove, and High were built on the grand scale ordered by the Sterling trustees. At the time the faculty would have preferred a simpler structure and more money for endowment.

As Laura Kalman has so well described, the deanship of Charles Clark was the high tide of exuberant "legal realism,"[4] an eclectic and irreverent approach emphasizing the subjective, man-made characteristics of law and especially of judges, the need for legal scholarship to gather facts in the real world rather than mouth old pieties, and the responsibility of lawyers to battle for change in a liberal direction. Professor Arthur Corbin, the first of the new breed of faculty in 1903, had been a pioneer, but now he was turning conservative at the end of his career. The leaders were Clark, Underhill Moore (brought from Columbia as Sterling Professor in 1929),[5] William O. Douglas (on the faculty since 1928, promoted to Sterling Professor in 1932 at age thirty-two), Thurman W. Arnold (recruited as full professor in 1931), Wesley Sturges (on the faculty since 1924, full professor in 1928); and economist Walton H. Hamilton (recruited as full professor in 1928). In 1933 they were joined by an especially provocative assistant professor, Fred Rodell; and in 1936 briefly by another assistant professor, Abe Fortas.

President Franklin D. Roosevelt's New Deal — brash, experimental, dismissive of tradition — was top gallant delight for the realists and a boon for the railroad on which several of the law faculty shuttled to Washington in service to the New Deal's proliferating agencies. President Angell disapproved. He felt that the political views and involvement of left-liberal faculty were an embarrassment to the university and should be curbed. Angell and university officers regularly denied university space to speakers whose views they disliked and in one notorious case terminated Divinity School associate professor Jerome Davis, a critic of capitalism and apologist for the Soviet Union who had been on the faculty for fourteen years and an increasingly embarrassing annoyance.

On the economic side, at a time when general faculty salaries were frozen, Provost Charles Seymour in 1932 objected strenuously to a salary of $15,000 for Douglas because it was larger by many thousands than that of Yale's most senior faculty in the arts and sciences, and more than twice that of a professor in the Divinity School. He refused to present the salary to the Corporation and let Angell do it.[6] Three years later, when underpaid Fred Rodell asked for a raise, President Angell asked if Rodell knew there was a depression and warned that the style of his protest might endanger his academic career.[7] The dean and faculty also said the president's insistence on increasing enrollment to bring in more revenue had prevented innovations in teaching.[8]

The political dimension was more serious. In April 1933 Ferdinand Pecora, the special counsel to the Senate Committee on Banking and Currency, asked Professors Douglas and Sturges to write a report on "various social and economic aspects of stock market operations." Angell said the project could be embarrassing to the university. Pecora's hearings were exposing the unregulated malpractices of New York banking and securities trading and tarring men and institutions important to Yale. Douglas and Sturges took no for an answer.

When New Dealer Rexford Tugwell—a *bête rouge* for those who hated FDR—was named a research associate in the Law School in order to make an occasional appearance, alumni protested and Angell was furious. Nor was he happy that Jerome N. Frank, another New Dealer much admired by the legal realists, had a similar minor appointment. Dean Clark told Angell that "the reaction is developing that our brightest ideas are likely to meet rather severe condemnation at the President's Office and it is this reaction which I regret and would like to avoid."[9]

Corbin was Angell's ideological ally within the law faculty. In 1935 he sent Angell a memorandum he had circulated among the Law School's governing board (the full professors) in order to block the possibility that Jerome Frank would be recommended for a professorship. It bears quoting at some length for the way Corbin blended political considerations, anti-Semitic prejudice, and concern for Yale's image. Corbin had five objections to Frank:

> 1. He seems to be a propagandist and an agitator rather than a teacher and investigator.

2. His matured opinions are so personal and peculiar as to justify and require agitation to propagate them. . . . [Especially objectionable are] his social, political and economic opinions, and also his opinions concerning his own race and religion.

3. It seems probable to me that as a member of a law faculty he would always occupy an exaggerated place as its assumed public representative. . . .

4. It is now publicly represented that he has been forced out of government service as an extreme "left-winger." . . . Our election of Mr. Frank . . . will be taken as a political gesture rather than an adventure in scholarship, and also as an expression of the political attitude of Yale Law School and Yale University. [In a policy dispute, Frank had been shifted from general counsel to the Agricultural Adjustment Administration to general counsel to the Reconstruction Finance Corporation.]

5. I have never voted against any man because of his race or nationality, although racial background and education are not matters that can be disregarded. We have already proved our tolerance and appreciation. At the same time, I am sure that the service this school can render will be rapidly reduced if we appear to become an asylum for the oppressed of less tolerant nations or to be flying the flag of a social propaganda. Special weight is given to this fifth point in the case of Mr. Frank.[10]

Corwin's comment on "asylum for the oppressed of less tolerant nations" referred to Jewish scholars driven from Nazi Germany. Angell in 1934 had already discouraged the Law School from pursuing a possible appointment of displaced scholar Ernest Levy, whom Clark called "the most distinguished Romanist in the world." Angell told Clark that Yale had only appointed one displaced scholar "on a basis involving the financial responsibility of others and not our own," and he warned against the "moral risk" of bringing in people who might expect a continuing appointment.[11] Levy was not offered a position.

Angell was succeeded as president by Charles Seymour (1937–1950), an equally conservative but more timid man. That year Professor Thurman W. Arnold published his best-selling (and reviled in business circles) *The Folklore of Capitalism*.[12] Arnold applied a scalpel to the "folklore" that corporations were legally "persons" and as such held an inalienable constitutional freedom under the Fourteenth Amendment to acquire property and use it any way they wished. "Men have come to believe that their own future liberties and dignities are tied up in the freedom of great industrial organizations from restraint, in much the same way that they thought their salvation in the future was dependent on their reverence and support of great ecclesiastical organizations in the Middle Ages."[13] In 1938 Arnold took a leave of absence to head the antitrust division of the Justice Department and send shivers into many a corporate boardroom, thereby strengthening the opinion of conservatives that the Yale Law School was to the New Deal what West Point was to the Army.[14] In the same era, Fred Rodell's Menckenesque tirade against law and lawyers as a vast conjuring game, *Woe Unto You, Lawyer,* infuriated those who cherished the majesty of the law and added still more to Yale's ill repute among conservatives.[15] In Chicago, Yale alumnus Robert R. McCormick made matters worse by ordering a lurid front-page attack in his *Chicago Tribune* on the Law School as a nest of Communists.

Meanwhile, a strong-minded Washington lawyer, Dean Acheson, had joined the Yale Corporation — where he would serve for twenty-five years and exercise a large influence on the university and the Law School. Clark turned to Acheson for sympathy and complained to Seymour "that the future is not very bright for the School unless we have more support in the Corporation or more sympathy with our general point of view." He was angry over Yale's prohibition of faculty leaves of absence of more than one year because of the effect on colleagues serving in Washington, especially Professors Douglas and Arnold.[16] Acheson, however, was no friend, but a critic of a tendency of legal realists "to exude vaguely and warmly toward the subject matter without organizing it into such shape that it could become the basis of an intellectual discipline."[17]

In 1939 Clark was appointed to the federal Second Circuit, and the school had to find a new leader.[18] Douglas, on leave in Washington, was favored by the majority of the faculty, but became unavailable when named to the Supreme Court. Acheson was the next choice, but he declined, and pushed for the selection of Harry Shulman, a Harvard Law graduate and superb teacher, but not a "jazzy" legal realist or a commuter to agencies of the New Deal. Acheson told President Seymour that the law faculty's involvement with national politics colored their preferences for dean. The Law School should have a man like Shulman in order to restore a focus on teaching. "The discussion really comes down to the question of race. . . . In view of what has happened in the last month [the German attack on Poland and outbreak of World War II] . . . I should like to see some of us act upon . . . the old decencies which everyone professes, even though there may be some who won't like it."[19] There was sufficient opposition to Shulman to block his selection, and soon the Law School turned to Assistant Dean Ashbel (known as Peyl) Gulliver, who presided uncontroversially for six years while the school came almost to a halt during World War II. The military took over the student rooms of the Sterling Law Buildings and enrollment dropped below one hundred, a high proportion of whom were women.

While the United States was allied with the Soviet Union in the war against

Germany, broad ideological attacks on the Law School were suspended, but one incident in 1941 revealed President Seymour's sympathy for the concerns of wealthy, right-wing donors. In November 1941 the university easily broke the first strike by organized labor in Yale's history. The issue was the union demand for a closed shop. William Robertson Coe, a wealthy and ultraconservative benefactor being assiduously courted by Seymour, congratulated the university but complained about the pro-union statements and behavior of two law professors — Fred Rodell and Abraham Feller — who had cancelled their classes out of respect for the union picket line:

> [V]iews as they expressed tend to alienate the friends and benefactors of institutions of learning and I hope we shall not see any more of it at Yale. It is difficult for many of us to understand the reason for the serious spread of the teaching of subversive doctrines in institutions of higher learning. If its outcome results in the acceptance of the theories so frequently advocated, it would mean the destruction of the system and wealth which made and makes the continuance of these institutions possible. . . . A friend of mine who had responded on a number of occasions to appeals from the President of one of the large colleges, in response to another request, wrote him that he would send no more money to the college until they cleaned house of the teachers of subversive doctrines.

Coe's warning to Yale was clear. Seymour replied that he was "deeply heartened by your understanding."[20]

Gulliver was succeeded by Wesley Sturges (1946–1954), a champion of legal realism. Sturges inherited a crisis. The right-wing radio columnist Fulton Lewis Jr. broadcast that the law faculty had recommended professorships for Thomas Emerson, Abe Fortas, and Harold Lasswell.[21] With U.S.-Soviet relations freezing into Cold War, Lewis's report was widely heeded and as disturbing to conservatives as the *Chicago Tribune* article in 1939. A shaken Yale Corporation and president tabled the recommended professorships of Emerson, Fortas, and Lasswell for further consideration, although they came with unanimous faculty support. Dean Acheson was down in the State Department handling the Russians, but his closest friend and colleague on the Corporation, Wilmarth Lewis (no relation to Fulton) rallied support for the appointments: "We must meet it squarely. Woodbridge Hall has been pelted with letters from our reactionaries. . . . The officers are cowering in the corner, green with fright."[22]

Two of the pelting letters came from John Dempsey — an influential alumnus, contemporary and friend of President Seymour, and Cleveland lawyer — who was about to wage a sustained campaign against the school. The longer letter, designed for circulation in the Corporation, expatiated on the radicalism of Emerson, Lasswell, and Fortas and challenged the Corporation to assert its authority:

> Yale can very well face — in fact should welcome and be proud of criticism by extremists and in the end will gain in public opinion by rejecting the appointments of these three men and of all like them. . . . This is not an issue which can be compromised. It must be faced and settled once and for all. In my opinion, if any of these appointments are confirmed, the reaction among the alumni . . . will be so strong and so critical as to adversely affect the future of Yale for many years to come.

A second private letter to Seymour focused on Fortas as a Jew. "I have some very good Jewish friends for whom I have the highest regard. . . . Nevertheless, I believe that there are too many Jews on the Yale Law School Faculty, and especially that there are too many of the wrong kind. . . . Mr. Fortas would add one more of the wrong kind."[23]

On the other side, dean-designate Sturges and former dean Judge Clark voiced the outrage of the faculty. Clark warned Judge Thomas D. Thacher, venerable member of the New York bar and fellow of the Corporation, that if the appointments were rejected Sturges would probably refuse the deanship and the school might descend into chaos. Thacher was sympathetic, and in the end the Emerson and Lasswell appointments were approved after Fortas withdrew from consideration in order to stay in Washington.[24]

Two years later there was a flurry over a book by Eugene V. Rostow, a political centrist recently promoted to full professor. In *A National Policy for the Oil Industry*,[25] Rostow argued that the domination of the oil industry by a few integrated companies was wasteful, expensive, and a threat to national security. He urged breaking up the big companies into separate producing, transporting, and marketing entities; less wasteful management of oil fields; and greater reliance on foreign oil. An uproar followed. One protestor was W. S. S. Rodgers, an alumnus who had rowed in the same freshman shell in 1904 with Charles Seymour, but, more important, had been president and then chairman of the board of the Texas Company (Texaco) since 1933. This book, said Rodgers, "has injured the prestige of Yale, particularly the Law School, very materially . . . [although it] may have gained for Professor Rostow considerable prestige and increased stature among the extreme liberals." Another letter came from Malcolm Aldrich, the head of the Commonwealth Fund, the family foundation of the Harknesses, whose vast fortune flowed from the family patriarch's backing of John D. Rockefeller almost a century before, a foundation to which Yale looked for continuing support. Rostow, said Aldrich, is "alienating the feelings of many good people toward Yale, which is not a good thing for the University. . . . [What he advocates] is far from the preservation of our present system of free enterprise."[26] Seymour had already asked Provost Edgar S. Furniss for a report to use in reply to criticism. Furniss noted that Rostow in fact argued that present practices in the petroleum industry were suppressing competition and could destroy free enterprise. That storm blew over, probably because Rostow's proposals had no impact on policy and only the most ignorant could sustain the charge that he was an extreme liberal.

The Law School was still in rough water. Dempsey intensified his attack on what he and like-minded alumni considered the dangerous radicals on the school's faculty and other professors who had slight experience in the practice of law. More serious from President Seymour's perspective were Dempsey's allegations that the school's curriculum did not teach what good lawyers must know. Dempsey assembled an imaginary horrible selection of courses from the list of electives to argue that a student could get the degree without taking any of the basic courses in torts, contracts, estates, and so on. He believed there was no place in a law school for the study of economics, psychology, political science, or anything other than law taught in a traditional way.

Seymour and the Corporation asked a committee of the new University Council to investigate the Law School with specific reference to Dempsey's charges.[27] William Dean Embree, senior partner in Milbank, Tweed, Hope and Hadley,[28] chaired the committee. The committee reported that the students were quite capable of dealing with radical political views and that the issue of "questionable private and public utterances by members of the faculty should be left to the Corporation." Embree received detailed rebuttals to Dempsey's criticism from Dean Sturges and the faculty. They said that traditional subjects were well taught and heavily enrolled, noted the success of students in passing bar examinations and in finding jobs, and denied that there was any ideological indoctrination in the classroom by the faculty. Former Dean Clark said that acceptance of Dempsey's line would "spell the death of the School in the form in which I have seen it grow to a unique success." The committee's principal evidence came from 496 responses to detailed questionnaires sent to law graduates of the previous decade, beginning with the class of 1939 (an excellent 46 percent response rate). The verdict was positive.

President Seymour's conclusion was a limited vote of confidence. He agreed with the Embree committee that teaching in the school was good and that students found themselves well equipped for the practice of law. But he warned that the school could not count indefinitely on support from the general budget and would have to meet its own expenses. "Expansion into new

fields . . . must be carefully watched and probably for a time restricted."
Seymour then turned to the question of radical views of the faculty. On one
hand, he said that the opinions of the faculty should not be "subject to external
pressure of any sort. But, on the other hand:

> The Dean and the Faculty must realize that this freedom . . . also involves
> responsibility on their part. The good name of Yale is involved whenever they
> speak and it must not become involved in opinions lightly conceived or inade-
> quately supported. . . . As St. Paul said, "All things are lawful unto me, but all
> things are not expedient."[29]

Seymour retired in 1950. The selection of forty-three-year-old history professor A. Whitney Griswold (1950–1963) as Seymour's successor had been
rather deviously orchestrated by Acheson and Wilmarth Lewis. They wanted
someone as unlike Seymour as possible. Griswold was humorous, stubborn,
short-tempered, beloved by his friends, unforgiving to those who challenged
him or failed to behave according to his code of civility, and a liberal Democrat
in personal politics, but a fierce believer in John Henry (Cardinal) Newman's
idea of a university. In his inaugural address Griswold lauded Archimedes,
who, in the words of Plutarch, "placed his whole affection and ambition in
those purer speculations where there can be no reference to the vulgar needs
of life." Griswold's ideal scholar was the "dreamer, the questioner . . . [who]
is seldom at home in the present or with the practical men of his generation. . . . The voyage is lonely, for great scholarship is an individual experience."[30] Griswold's relations with the Yale professional schools were mutually
uncomfortable.

Griswold set out from his first day in office to rid the university of all
academic activities falling short of this ideal of scholarship. He dropped his
guillotine where he could — on the Institute of International Studies, the Department of Education, Engineering as a separate school, and several research
centers. He also inherited a financial crisis for the university and had the
misfortune to become president one week after the start of the Korean War
and in the midst of the era of Joseph McCarthy, when William F. Buckley Jr.
was about to rally the dinosaurs with his *God and Man at Yale: The "Supersti-
tions" of Academic Freedom.* The combination of Griswold's philosophy and
the tensions of the times led quickly to difficulty with leftist faculty in the Law
School, and above all with Thomas Emerson.

In 1951 Griswold lamented that Emerson's agreement to defend a group of
second-tier Communists indicted under the Smith Act would seem to "prove"
Buckley's case. "I shouldn't, and don't mean to, cry on your shoulder," he
wrote his confidant Wilmarth Lewis, "but I don't mind telling you I am *pro-*

foundly discouraged."[31] And to law professor Ralph Brown, Griswold denounced Emerson for not despising what his clients had been convicted of doing; and because by defending them he imposed burdens on others and on Yale as an institution. "I believe the welfare of the faculty is far more important to the civil rights and liberties at stake than the welfare of a group of individuals who advocate and conspire for the destruction of those rights and liberties. . . . If you want the true purposes of Yale, I give you teaching and scholarship. And whether you want it or not, I give you greeting from this beleaguered fox-hole."[32]

Griswold was a stronger defender of academic freedom than Angell or Seymour, but he also was captive of the times. He needed the generosity of wealthy alumni and resented faculty whose statements and behavior embarrassed the university. He also looked to Acheson — now a ranking member of the Yale Corporation and Secretary of State — for magisterial advice on the Law School and many other things. All of these elements came together in 1953–54 in the simultaneous selection of a new dean and the denial of tenure to associate professor Vern Countryman.[33]

Countryman had joined the faculty in 1948. His scholarship was substantial in volume and generally well regarded. Students said his teaching was excellent. In April 1953, near the end of Wesley Sturges's deanship, Countryman was recommended for tenure by unanimous vote of the professors — but significantly without future Dean Harry Shulman present. President Griswold withheld the recommendation from the Corporation pending discussion with Sturges's as yet unselected successor. Griswold was responding to the urgings of Acheson to pick Shulman as dean and to apply new standards in selecting faculty. Shulman was supported for the deanship by faculty vote in October 1953. He would take office in July 1954. Acheson then gave Griswold his version of the history of the Law School since the 1920s:

> [T]here developed the belief on the part of some that they were more advanced, more daring, more radical, in the pedagogical sense, than elsewhere. To prove it an element of the bizarre entered, the desire to startle and shock the old fogies. This soon led to the conception of the faculty as beleaguered knights surrounded by the hosts of reaction of which the Corporation was a formidable part. . . . A schism occurred between the beleaguered knights and the rest, with different standards of excellence and scholarship. When new appointments were made, a situation arose like the pre-Civil War admission of states, for every free state a slave state must come in. The great need . . . is to restore standards of excellence, to apply them quietly, persistently, and mercilessly to the work of faculty and students and to promotion and appointments. I believe Shulman could and would do this. . . . Shoddiness and

foolishness would have the garb of pioneering and daring removed, and excellence would be firmly insisted upon day in and day out.[34]

Meanwhile, Griswold had received a disturbing report about Countryman. Charles F. Clise in Seattle, a 1911 graduate of the Yale Sheffield Scientific School, was at the center of Yale's efforts to raise a large amount of money from alumni in the Pacific Northwest. Clise wrote that the activities of Emerson and Fowler might cost Yale several millions from potential donors in Seattle, but Vern Countryman, well known in the state of Washington, was a real danger.[35]

> [He] may not be a Communist, but if not, it is simply because he thinks it is safer and more effective to work without taking on the risks and responsibility that are involved if he joins up with the Party. He goes with the wrong people and has always done so. He operates "in the woodwork," but it is quite effective and is dangerous.[36]

At Griswold's request, Yale's general counsel Frederick (Fritz) Wiggin gathered more opinions from Clise, and looked at Countryman's involvement with the Emergency Civil Liberties Committee, an entity condemned by McCarthyites as a Communist front. Griswold scrutinized Countryman's testimony before the Senate Internal Security Subcommittee on the subject of Communist influence in labor unions and read Countryman's book *Un-American Activities in the State of Washington: The Work of the Canwell Committee.*[37] The Canwell Committee, a state version of the House Un-American Affairs committee, had been responsible for a purge in the University of Washington faculty. Countryman had nothing good to say about it.

Thus, two streams were merging in Griswold's deliberately delayed consideration of the faculty's recommendation of tenure for Countryman. In December 1954 Dean Shulman, supported by Eugene Rostow and with President Griswold present, told the faculty that he was withdrawing the recommendation of tenure for Countryman and offering a three-year extension as associate professor, after which tenure might be reconsidered. Griswold said he had read Countryman's book and considered it bad scholarship — period.

The furor over the case at Yale and nationally was equal to that over Jerome Davis in the Divinity School a generation before. Justice Douglas wrote Griswold that Countryman had been the best clerk he ever had and offered to come to New Haven to plead reconsideration. Griswold managed to be unavailable. Scores of Countryman's present and previous students including future New Haven mayor Frank Logue said he was the best teacher they had ever had and that he never introduced political ideology into the classroom.

The majority of the Yale Law faculty was furious. Former Dean Sturges told Shulman that he could not dismiss the suspicion that something more than judgment of scholarship was involved. Sturges asked Griswold to reconsider, noting that not only the faculty and students but "our alumni in the law teaching profession and law teachers generally are stunned and shocked. What is the profit to Yale—to the Yale Law School—from all of this?"[38] Fred Rodell, outrageous as always, accused Shulman of hiding his opinion of Countryman in order to gain the deanship and then betraying the faculty under pressure from Griswold. Shulman showed Rodell's letter to Griswold. Griswold in turn told Rodell that the letter was "so offensive in both tone and substance that it is difficult for me . . . to believe the assurances you have given me either as to your friendship, your confidence in me, or your devotion to Yale or the Law School."[39] Case closed.[40]

It was now 1955. Joseph McCarthy had self-destructed during Senate hearings on alleged Communist influence in the U.S. Army. The Korean War was over. At Yale Harry Shulman died in March and was succeeded as dean by Eugene Rostow, a close friend of Griswold's since the 1930s and ally in the Countryman affair. A few left-liberal faculty were not happy, but no one had as much support as Rostow. Alumni of the stamp of Robert R. McCormick, John Dempsey, and Charles F. Clise were passing from the scene. In 1963 Griswold died and was succeeded in Woodbridge Hall by a former professor of law at Harvard via a stint as Yale provost—Kingman Brewster Jr. Although Brewster may have been appointed provost by Griswold with an eye toward succession, Brewster as president led Yale in directions Griswold had blocked, tearing down the ivory tower, calling for teaching and research directly relevant to improving the world, welcoming dissent, tolerating the obstreperous, demonstrating a practical respect for civil rights and academic freedom far deeper than Griswold's. The Law School maintained the growth that had begun under Dean Rostow. A much larger faculty pursued a wide range of subjects from many philosophical points of view. Fowler Harper and Tom Emerson, favorite targets of the old anticommunists, contributed to establishing a constitutionally guaranteed right to practice birth control. There would continue to be outside critics of law faculty and some disagreements between the Law School and Woodbridge Hall, but never as intense and even venomous as in the Angell, Seymour, and Griswold years. As Brewster said, times had changed.

Notes

This essay is adapted and excerpted from my forthcoming book on "Yale and the External World: The Shaping of the University in the 20th Century."

1. Report of Special Committee of the Faculty on the Development of the Law School, January 21, 1925, Angell papers, 121:1246 (hereafter Angell Papers). This is a comprehensive statement of the needs and emerging philosophy of the Yale Law School.

2. Address of January 30, 1922, Angell Papers, supra note 1, MS group 2, 28a:319.

3. Taft to Angell, May 1, 1927, and Angell to Taft, May 3, 1927, Angell Papers, supra note 1, Yale Archives and Manuscripts, Box 119, Folder 1231.

4. Laura Kalman, *Legal Realism at Yale, 1927–1960* (Chapel Hill, 1986).

5. Moore, who retired in 1947, was an obsessive empiricist who, among other things, sat at street corners gathering statistics on the behavior of motorists in response to traffic and parking regulations. See John Henry Schlegel, *American Legal Realism and Empirical Social Science* (Chapel Hill, 1995).

6. Seymour to Angell, Feb. 9, 1932, Angell Papers, supra note 1, record group 3-A, Office of the Provost, 39:390.

7. Angell to Dean Charles E. Clark, May 20, 1935, Angell Papers, supra note 1, at 127: 1252. On the other hand, the Corporation in 1937 readily increased the salary of an assistant football coach and law student from $3,000 to $3,500 — more than starting instructors with Ph.D.s. The coach's name was Gerald Ford. Cabinet minutes, Seymour Papers, 35:310 (hereafter Seymour Papers).

8. Memorandum to the President and Fellows of Yale University, June 1, 1935, Angell Papers, supra note 1, at 120: 1252.

9. Clark to Angell, Nov. 27, 1933, Angell Papers, supra note 1, at 121:1250.

10. Corwin memorandum: "To the Members of the Governing Board of the School of Law," Feb. 8, 1935, copy in Angell Papers, supra note 1, at 121:1252.

11. Clark to Angell, Feb. 9, 1934 and Angell to Clark, Feb. 10, 1935, Angell Papers, supra note 1, at 120:1239.

12. Thurman W. Arnold, *The Folklore of Capitalism* (New Haven, 1937).

13. Id. at 185. Arnold, perhaps without realizing, was echoing William Graham Sumner, one of Yale's first and great social scientists, who explained behavior as the evolution of "folkways" rather than ordained by God. The alumni who fumed over Arnold's treatment of capitalism were the ideological descendants of those who despised Sumner's attack on the protective tariff a half century before.

14. Arnold, having exhausted the time allowed by Yale to be on leave, resigned from the Law School in 1939. He served briefly as a judge and in 1945 was a founder of the powerful Washington law firm of Arnold, Fortas & Porter.

15. Fred Rodell, *Woe Unto You, Lawyers* (New York, 1939).

16. See the Clark letters to Acheson and copy of Clark to Seymour, Nov. 9, 1938, in Dean Acheson papers, manuscript group 1087, box 6: 73 and 74 (hereafter Acheson Papers).

17. Acheson to Provost Edgar S. Furniss, May 6, 1939, Papers of the Provost, record group 3-A, 1:2.

18. Kalman, *Legal Realism*, supra note 4, at 140–43.

19. Acheson to Seymour, September 19, 1939, Seymour Papers, supra note 7, at 1:3.

20. Coe to Seymour, Nov. 14, 1941 and Seymour to Coe, Nov. 15, 1941, Seymour Papers, supra note 7, at 126:1069. Coe donated his rich collection of Western Americana to Yale and in 1950 gave generously to the fledgling American Studies program in the belief, encouraged by Seymour, that it would inculcate students against socialist doctrines.

21. Emerson, a graduate of Yale College (1928) and the Law School (1931), was a

New Deal lawyer and supporter of groups and causes on the left of the American political spectrum. Fortas had gone to Washington after his two years as an assistant professor. Harold Lasswell was not a lawyer, but an iconoclastic political scientist known for his studies of the manipulative power of words and psychological roots of behavior.

22. Wilmarth S. Lewis to Dean Acheson, January 3, 1946, Farmington, Connecticut (hereafter Lewis Papers).

23. Dempsey to Seymour, both letters January 10, 1946, copies in the papers of Thomas D. Thacher, manuscript group 757, 49:609 (hereafter Thacher Papers).

24. Kalman, *Legal Realism*, supra note 4, at 148–49.

25. Eugene V. Rostow, *A National Policy for the Oil Industry* (New Haven, 1948).

26. Rodgers to Seymour, June 30, 1948, and Aldrich to Seymour, June 16, 1948, Seymour Papers, supra note 7, at 96:822.

27. The University Council was in large measure the brainchild of Wilmarth Lewis. It organized committees of knowledgeable persons, mostly alumni, to investigate and report on different schools and activities of the university, especially when there was a perceived need for improvement. The committee reports, confidential for the President and Corporation, could be very critical.

28. Hadley was Morris Hadley, son of President Arthur T. Hadley, and fellow of the Corporation from 1940 to 1962.

29. Documents on the Embree committee and Seymour statement of Jan. 3, 1949, are in Seymour Papers, supra note 7, at 164:1388.

30. A. Whitney Griswold, *Essays on Education* 2–3 (New Haven, 1954). See also Josephine Broude, ed., *Inaugural Addresses of the Presidents of Yale University* 153–54 (New Haven, 2001).

31. Griswold to Lewis, August 22, 1951, Lewis Papers, supra note 22.

32. Griswold to Brown, September 25, 1951, at 137:1246 (hereafter Griswold Papers).

33. Kalman, *Legal Realism*, supra note 4, at 196–99.

34. Acheson to Griswold, Dec. 18, 1953, Yale Archives and Manuscripts, Acheson Papers, supra note 16, at 14:174.

35. Clise to Griswold, Nov. 27, 1953, Griswold Papers, supra note 32, at 2:14.

36. Clise to Reuben B. Holden (Secretary of the University), Dec. 1, 1953, Griswold Papers, supra note 32, at 2:14.

37. Vern Countryman, *Un-American Activities in the State of Washington: The Work of the Canwell Committee* (Ithaca, 1951).

38. Sturges to Griswold, January 10, 1955, Griswold Papers, supra note 16, at 2:14.

39. Rodell to Shulman, Jan. 3, 1955, and Griswold to Rodell, Jan. 10, 1955, Griswold Papers, supra note 16, at 2:14.

40. Countryman chose to leave Yale at the end of the academic year for a brief stint in private practice, then the deanship of the University of Arizona Law School, and soon a professorship at Harvard, where he completed his career. Had Countryman stayed for the offered three years, would he have gained tenure? Who knows? I think the answer is no, given President Griswold's stubborn streak.

The Dark Ages

LAURA KALMAN

Prologue: The Dream

As a historian of the Yale Law School, I have suffered from a recurring dream over the past twenty years. In it, I have died and gone to heaven. (The dream entails a leap of faith.) Almost as soon as I enter the pearly gates, I am handed a summons to appear before a tribunal. There is no information about what will take place, but I infer it will not be pleasant. Arriving, I find that I am facing a group of Yale Law professors from the 1930s headed by their dean, Charles E. Clark. I realize at once that when they checked my book, *Legal Realism at Yale*,[1] out of the heavenly library, they were displeased. Clark speaks first. "Laura," he says, "you got it all wrong."

As both the dream and the book indicate, I regard Yale as Clark's law school. His deanship witnessed the launching of the most ambitious challenge anywhere ever to the hegemony of Harvard and Langdell. Leave aside the question of whether the Columbia and Hopkins professors can lay a better claim to realist jurisprudence, as another historian of Yale, Robert Stevens, maintains.[2] Though the attempt to apply legal realism to education began in New York, the Columbia well had run dry by 1928. The focus shifted to New Haven, where Clark and Robert Maynard Hutchins had drafted a plan for their law school to become "the first honors or research school in America." It would restrict its enrollment to three hundred (no sacrifice, for Yale had always been small);[3] increase its endowment; require students to engage in research; "discover the actual operation of the law," advancing "beyond the classical study of the Harvard type;" and offer a way by which "law could be coordinated with the social sciences."[4] The insistence that students engage in interdisciplinary scholarship justified the school's smallness and selectiveness: The point of selective admissions was to establish what Clark, as dean, called "an intellectual aristocracy,"[5] and what later generations would call a meritocracy. It was the Yale faculty under Clark's guidance in the 1930s — and building on his legacy in the 1940s and 1950s — which tried most concertedly to make legal education "realistic" by making casebooks functional; "integrating" law with the social sciences; focusing on the role of idiosyncrasy in judicial decision making; tolerating some experimentation with clinical education; and training students to see law's potential as an instrument of justice. And it was during the Clark years, as both Robert Gordon and Gaddis Smith remind us in this volume, that, in Gordon's words, the "New Deal swept through the Yale Law School faculty like a cyclone," giving the institution an enduring reputation for progressiveness that appealed to students who wanted to change society for the better.[6] Under Clark, Yale found its niche. It would become the boutique law school for both intellectuals and activists.

One might contend that the Yale realists were principally motivated by the need for product differentiation. Stuck between New York and Cambridge, they had to claim they turned out something unique, if ever they were to attract better applicants and bring the Yale student body up to par with Columbia and Harvard's.[7] One might concede that the realists did not successfully realize the promise of interdisciplinarity through "integration" of law with the social sciences. And one might conclude that legal realism at Yale never posed that serious a threat to Harvard and Langdell, inasmuch as the Yale faculty always placed the case method at the center of legal education. As Grant Gilmore said, though realism symbolized a revolution, it proved "a palace revolution, not much more than a changing of the guard."[8] Yet for all its flaws and limitations, the Yale experiment stands out as arguably the most significant development in American legal education in the century following 1870. And thanks to the realists, Yale did edge out Columbia for second place. Further, it was the realists who imbued Yale with a mystique that, as students and faculty ever after have emphasized, has endured to this day.

Thus I cannot agree with Robert Stevens that the modern Yale Law School is the creation of its dean from 1955–1965, Eugene Rostow.[9] True, Rostow is crucial to the school's history for curricular, institutional, and jurisprudential reasons. He introduced the tradition of one seminar-style course for each first-termer, guaranteeing beginners a "small group" experience in one of the school's only mandatory courses: Contracts, Constitutional Law, Procedure, and Torts. Here was another important moment in the school's history. Small-group instruction during the first semester, like the lack of requirements afterward, made it distinctive. Rostow also ushered in the divisional program, requiring each student to choose a specialty for serious scholarship. Time-consuming for professors, it was abandoned within a decade — after the dean had used it, with small groups, to justify doubling the size of his faculty.

Rostow took a school that had lost a third of its professors over a fifteen-month period between 1954 and 1956 and both rebuilt and expanded it. He organized what he called a "great talent hunt" between 1955 and 1959. As Rostow said, using a phrase that I anachronistically find irksome, "several hundred men and several women" were seriously considered for professorships.[10] "Gene's boys and girl" included people who would have a lasting impact on the school: Alexander Bickel, Charles Black, Guido Calabresi, Abraham and Joseph Goldstein, Leon Lipson, Ellen Peters, and Harry Wellington. In one five-year period, Rostow hired and/or promoted the school's next four deans.[11] His creative financing enabled the Law School to thrive by bleeding the central administration.

During Rostow's deanship the school's identity became further bound up with legal liberalism, the trust in the potential of courts, particularly the Supreme Court, to bring about "those specific social reforms that affect large groups of people such as blacks, or workers, or women, or partisans of a particular persuasion; in other words, policy change with nationwide impact."[12] As an alumnus of, and professor at, Clark's Yale, Rostow believed that *Brown v. Board of Education* signaled the "triumph of legal realism,"[13] and he and his colleagues volubly defended both *Brown* and the Warren Court.[14] To the irritation of old realists, such as Clark,[15] Rostow also broadened the school's intellectual horizons by reaching out to Felix Frankfurter, nemesis of the realists and sometimes the Warren Court, and hiring two legal process theorists the justice had shaped, Alexander Bickel and Harry Wellington. Indeed, during Rostow's deanship, the jurisprudential blend of process theory and interdisciplinarity evident in the work of so many Yale professors today began to percolate through the school.

Rostow secured for Yale Law School the place in the hierarchy to which Clark, who had set its shape, projected it. This was no small achievement, but Yale still played Avis to Harvard's Hertz. So clearly established was its standing as second-best that on the day that Rostow's successor entered the dean's office, he found a sign bearing the slogan Avis had made popular: "We Try Harder."[16] The joke was not wholly appropriate. Yale *was* the first choice of some students, who believed it the country's best law school and appreciated its small size, its favorable faculty-student ratio, its emphasis "on the social policy and interdisciplinary approach to the study of law, the 'policy' orientation," which some thought would prepare them to become better lawyers; others, better public servants; and still others, better law professors.[17] But as Rostow himself had lamented in 1957, when he asked his colleagues whether Yale Law was "still known as a country-club" in the nation's colleges, "if the LSAT Ranks have even prima facie meaning, and they do . . . they show that Harvard probably has a better class than we do—a much better class."[18] And as an internal memorandum five years later declared, Harvard was still ahead.[19] Further, most Yale Law graduates were headed for law firms: "Myths to the contrary notwithstanding, upwards of 75% of Yale LL.B. recipients go into private practice. . . . Perhaps 15% go into government, at all levels; and the small balance are widely scattered—on the bench; in teaching; and a few out of the profession." Interdisciplinarity was another myth. His successor was well aware that "our students and faculty have much to gain from the books and people looming on the shores dimly seen across Wall and High Streets, and vice versa."[20] Rostow left a law school still overshadowed by Harvard and one less distinctive than its administrators liked to insist.

Assuming I am right and Yale is Clark's law school, who brought the "contemporary" Yale Law School into existence? By "contemporary," I refer to the law school that dwarfs its rivals. It is both most and least competitive: Yale attracts students because it is the most selective *and* because they know they will pass their first-term courses, which are graded credit-fail, and need only worry about whether they receive Honors or Pass afterward.[21] It is a school distinguished by its celebrity. (When a magazine entitled *M: The New He-Man* publishes an article about the Law School entitled "The Yale Plot to Take Over America," it seems clear that Yale has assumed a distinctive place in popular culture.[22]) It is a school that is "the nearest thing the United States has to an École Normale Superieure."[23] It is a school that is considered ideologically slightly left of center, but not too much, having avoided hiring a Critical Legal Scholar until well after the movement had peaked. It is a school that mostly produces corporate lawyers. But it is also a school that is a breeding ground for public servants. (Its administrators thoughtfully destroy statements on "The Wall" inside the Law School building—the forum for written expressions of opinion about the school and external affairs—every two months, so that their student authors need not fear that their former views will haunt them in future confirmation hearings.[24]) Further, it is a school known for its academic and interdisciplinary approach to law. Yale does not just produce a disproportionate number of its own professors, but of other schools as well.[25] It is the humane and interesting school. As the *New York Times* once observed, "When it comes to choosing law schools, students favor Yale for the same reason nondrinkers favor screwdrivers: it's the most palatable way to swallow something you don't really want."[26]

In short, who created the law school that reflected Clark's vision in full flower? Insofar as the answer is decanal, my candidates are Harry Wellington and Guido Calabresi. But as is usually the case,[27] the answer is not simply decanal. Students also built the contemporary school. In this essay, I focus on an especially important group of them, those who comprised the generation of "the sixties," a period that did not begin at Yale (as elsewhere) until well after the mid-1960s.[28] During this time, Yale's young included future public servants, including a First Lady and U.S. senator,[29] professors, and lawyers. Inspired by the social unrest around them, a vision of democracy and citizenship, and a sense of their school's historic importance as innovator in legal education, its students branded their law professors hierarchical; accused them of racism and sexism; and threatened to leave the school en masse. They were a part of a social movement calling for "student power."[30] Yale students during the late 1960s possessed an extraordinary range of concerns and proved extremely vocal in articulating them.

Yale's close connection with legal realism and legal liberalism, its faith in meritocracy and turning the running of society over to the "best and brightest" that "Gene's boys" exemplified, and the Law School's sense of itself as an intellectual hothouse in which carefully chosen elites interacted in close quarters, almost guaranteed that the 1960s would hit the school hard. The school's emphasis on its realist legacy ensured that students entered with high hopes. Yale was the obvious place for a smart college graduate with a social conscience to go precisely because the faith that law could promote a more equitable society lay at the core of both realism and the liberalism of the Warren Court and the Great Society.

By the late 1960s, however, left-leaning students were coming to question whether law necessarily made matters better. In the early 1960s, "to be trained in the law, for those with a social conscience, was to be trained to create change," one member of the class of 1970 said. "In 1964 we elected a liberal President, pledged to a Great Society and to a peace in the Vietnam War." But in the "six long years" since that election, "[t]he best of a whole generation of Americans have been gassed in the streets."[31] Strikingly, the young often made an exception for members of the Warren Court. Indeed, it helped provide the glue that would hold the Yale Law School together. Dissatisfaction with the

Court there sometimes was.[32] Nevertheless, the editors of the *Yale Law Journal*, like law students elsewhere,[33] would maintain that Earl Warren "made us all proud to be lawyers."[34] The Warren Court never came in for the opprobrium heaped upon its partner in liberalism, the Johnson White House.[35] For all the Court's imperfections, those studying law at Yale and elsewhere saw it, and more generally, the federal courts, as symbols of hope during the late 1960s and 1970s. Yet although their professors saw themselves as part of an "interlocking directorate" with the Supreme Court justices whose work their scholarship bolstered,[36] students viewed teachers more critically. Familiarity bred suspicion.

Yale students of the late 1960s, then, saw themselves as at once unique and representative. They worked to unlock the democratic vision of law and social change that they associated with the legal realists at Yale during the 1930s. They appealed frequently to the sense of the school's special history that they shared with the faculty.

But the young were also creatures of their time. Open the newspapers published at elite law schools during the period, and you will find common themes beneath the dust. United in the condemnation of their education as sterile, dissatisfying, and needlessly competitive, law student agitators sought to eliminate hierarchy and alienation and to achieve community, citizenship, democracy, and relevance. Though more focused on their immediate world than undergraduates, activist law students did care about American politics, as well as academic politics. They worried constantly about the draft; they grappled with racial injustice; they confronted sexual inequality (though it chiefly concerned women); they saw their professors as symbols of a sick "system" and society; and they wondered how, once they became lawyers, they could serve the larger world.

The issues on which law student activists concentrated were similar too. They involved grade reform and often, as a corollary, law review participation; student participation in Law School governance; increased enrollments of, and an end to discrimination against, students of color and all women. Students also shared professional concerns. They condemned the lawyer as "hired gun." At a time of "huge demand for law grads,"[37] corporate law firms were forced to expand pro bono programs and raise salaries to attract the best and brightest.[38] But that appeared to do no good. Indeed, law students saw the firms' behavior as a sign of weakness[39] and complained that the corporate bar was immorally trying to lure future lawyers away from serving the public interest.[40] The *American Bar Association Journal* carried articles about law students entitled "Will They Enter Private Practice?"[41] and reported that none of the thirty-nine *Harvard Law Review* editors planned to do so.[42] Association of American Law Schools President Albert Conard mourned that "law schools are up against the wall."[43]

Of course, all of higher education was. Like undergraduates, law students did not confine themselves to talk. In the spring of 1968, after the faculty voted to convene classes during the undergraduate occupation of the campus, Columbia law students acceded to the pleas of two third-years, Robert Cover and David Kairys, and mounted an effective strike.[44] The following year, a Boalt student was tried for inciting a riot because he had urged students to destroy the fence around People's Park.[45] Thirty African American law students forced major concessions from the Columbia administration when they occupied the law library and held a "study-in" to protest the "intransigence of the law school on certain matters respecting an institutional commitment to black and other minority students, and the manner in which this institution chooses to respond to years of good faith on our part."[46] Annoyed by the paternalism and "implicit faith in the efficacy of the law as a remedy" they saw in the faculty's decision "to deal with the outrageous lack of Black representation in the state's legal profession" by graduating one hundred minority students in five years, the Association of Black Law Students at Rutgers-Newark circulated an "indictment of the Rutgers Law School Community" and demanded that "the law school offer courses which are relevant to Black students [and] that these courses be taught by Black instructors, which are selected by the Black students in this law school."[47] Howard law students seized their school, chained its doors, and locked the faculty out,[48] as they called for, among other things, student participation in faculty committees and meetings and pass-fail grading.[49] In the spring of 1970, someone placed a Molotov cocktail on a shelf in the Columbia International Law Library, lit it, and disappeared. It did little damage; a suspicious fire that broke out late at night in the Yale Law Library two months later caused more.[50]

At each institution, of course, the story developed differently. At Harvard, for one example, the faculty proved fairly successful in battening down the hatches. "Never has there been more pressure for reform at the Law School, yet what reforms have been effected this year?," the *Harvard Law Record* queried sadly in 1969.[51]

Yale students' efforts and achievements were among the earliest and most considerable of the "law student power" movement.[52] That was at least in part because Yale's particular intellectual history made students already stirred up by the "the sixties" more eager than ever for change; Yale's smallness contributed to engagement;[53] more of its students entered public interest law upon graduation and were, at least temporarily, committed to the vision of the "left" it represented;[54] and unlike activists at other elite law schools, the young at

Yale were consistently urged on, rather than reined in, by the student press.[55] And where students at other elite schools did not always produce lasting reforms — with most, for example, reverting to multitier grading systems by the mid 1970s — those of Yale students were more likely to endure. Their actions thus profoundly troubled their professors.

As some Yale professors perceived it, "left-wing" students were destroying the Law School in a Kulturkampf that reflected their desire to bring the faculty to its collective knees. And even after the members of Yale's sixties generation had opted for more traditional careers in the very law firms they had once condemned as the "worst piece[s] of shit I ever saw,"[56] memories of their disdain continued to affect the school they left behind. Senior professors re-affirmed scholarly and ideological "standards" as soon as what one future dean reportedly disparaged as the "dark" ages had ended, and students had turned their attention elsewhere. Junior faculty members who had recently witnessed their seniors wringing their hands over student demands were deemed inferior scholars by those same seniors during the early 1970s and dismissed. And the faculty proved intolerant of Critical Legal Studies in the late 1970s and the 1980s as it rebuilt: Having suffered through one bruising battle with the "left," Yale law professors may have been fearful of becoming embroiled in another. Critical Legal Studies was born in part out of the Dark Ages, and "Dark Agers," such as Duncan Kennedy (Yale Law School '70) played a key role in its formation. But Yale Law School, which had embraced forward-looking legal realism in the 1930s, rejected realism's descendant, Critical Legal Studies, at the same time that Harvard Law School, which had once turned its back on realism, made a home for realism's child. Ironically, Yale law students of the sixties helped to create a school that embraced a culture of timidity. Indeed, the contours of the modern Yale Law School that appeared in the late 1970s, I argue, were shaped by a desire to avoid conflict. For Yale, the "sixties" was not just a period, but a complex of events as well.

The Sixties Come to Yale

Our story begins with a journey into the lost world of liberal good intentions. Louis Pollak, who was appointed Rostow's successor in 1965, was a thoroughly decent man, with exceptional liberal credentials. The son of an eminent civil liberties lawyer,[57] Pollak worked with the NAACP in *Brown*, was on the brief in *Cooper v. Aaron*,[58] and stood with King in Montgomery at the end of the march from Selma. But just as the Selma–Montgomery march represented the last gasp of liberal interracialism, so Pollak's deanship suggested that liberalism would face problems in confronting militancy.

The "Dress British, Think Yiddish" meritocratic mindset of the faculty Pollak inherited was in some ways epitomized by Alexander Bickel, one of its leading intellectual and political forces. The son of scholars, Bickel fled Romania with his family in 1938 and served as a machine gunner in World War II before enrolling in CCNY. Unlike most of his colleagues, he had not attended Yale Law School. In Cambridge, where he remembered being "a trouble maker" and "a real bad guy," he was treasurer of the *Harvard Law Review.* "I think my frame of mind was screw you guys, if I'm going to get anywhere here it's going to be in spite of what you think I am and it's going to be because you just can't help it."[59] Perhaps it was his clerkship with Frankfurter that somewhat tamed him. It certainly helped give him his judicial philosophy. With Harry Wellington, he departed from the Yale pattern of applauding judicial activism and the Warren Court. Bickel liked to needle students that "federal judges were not inevitably 'little Earl Warrens in black robes' " — to which they responded that he could not make them into "little Alexander Bickels in blue jeans." [60]

Bickel appeared in class in impeccably tailored three-piece suits, "Phi Beta Kappa key displayed prominently,"[61] hair slicked back. Status mattered to him, as it did to many of "Gene's boys." He disliked student challenges to his authority. He wrote with elegance and could talk that way too, though friends also found him witty, acidic, and, at times, undiplomatic. A disastrous, brief marriage to a woman apparently on the rebound from another relationship,[62] who left Bickel to resume it, may have intensified an inner insecurity and a fragile ego. But if it did, Bickel hid them behind a self-assured exterior.

Traditionally an anticommunist Democrat, he joined a growing number of former Cold War liberals who had begun to speak out against the war in Vietnam by mid-1967. As Bickel put it, "We are the most powerful nation on earth, and are savagely fighting one of the smallest and poorest, and ruining it from the air with increasingly indiscriminate . . . bombing."[63] He jumped Lyndon Johnson's ship at the beginning of 1968. "I know that it is very risky to abandon an otherwise liberal, sitting democratic President, and I am proud to this day of never having been tempted to desert Truman in 1948, but I am sick at heart with the Vietnam War and with all it has done to the country," he told a friend.[64] At first, he supported Eugene McCarthy.[65] But Robert Kennedy's mounting opposition to the war won over the Yale professor. By the spring of 1968, Bickel was characterizing Kennedy as "our best hope"[66] and comparing him to Brandeis.[67] Professor gave himself to candidate "heart and mind" with a dedication that outstripped "any prior political commitment," believing, Bickel wrote in *The New Republic,* that Kennedy "above all other public men would . . . stop war and heal suffering because he had the trust of those whose trust we so desperately need."[68] Like most of his colleagues, with the notable exception of Rostow, the number three man in Johnson's State Department,[69] Bickel was vocal about his hatred for the war.[70]

The students shared that hatred. For members of the class of 1970, such as Duncan Kennedy, the Vietnam war permeated everything. Theirs was the first class to face the end of graduate school deferments and the omnipresent threat of the draft.[71] Still, other issues also moved them.

Consider, for example, Kennedy's infamous critique of legal education, "How the Yale Law School Fails," which began to circulate around the school and the central university administration in Woodbridge Hall as a pamphlet in 1968.[72] Kennedy condemned the "boring and dead" classes, which meant that "the Yale Law School fails miserably to live up to its academic and intellectual pretensions."[73] "What is altogether absent from the Law School is the feeling of intellectual tension which comes of the confrontation of ideas in the process of growth," a quality Yale "notoriously had" in the 1930s.[74]

But the classroom was not just boring, Kennedy and others said — it was also unpleasant. Indeed Robert Stevens, then a Yale law professor, found that "the most frequent complaint" registered by Yale first-years was the "perceived tendency" of "the case class and Socratic method" to "demean and degrade students," and reported that teachers characterized the instructor as "a 'fearful trial court judge,' 'an inquisitor,' or a 'pounding' . . . adversary."[75] Kennedy scorned the "truly extraordinary narcissistic phenomenon" of the Yale law professor, who "preen[ed]" before his classes.[76] He reported most of his classmates repeatedly asked themselves one question about their professors: "Why am I taking this shit from them?"[77] He predicted a breakthrough only when the "psychic territory" was changed and "students and faculty treat each other decently."[78]

Student efforts to achieve that seemingly modest goal had begun when Kennedy's colleagues in the class of 1970 entered Yale. Its members argued about the right goals for social change. Should they concentrate on the war, civil rights, and poverty, concerns they shared with their professors? Or were the "radicals" among them right to insist transformative change must begin locally? The debate ended when the radicals found the perfect issue — grades.[79]

Imagine 160 first-year students, more than 90 percent of them men, all of whom have graduated college at the top of their class, returned to an adolescent setting. Six days a week, often dressed in coat and tie, 1Ls marched in lockstep from one class to another. When called upon, they often stood. Yale preserved a gentlemanly atmosphere by providing waiters in the dining hall to serve all meals.[80] But inside the classrooms, the atmosphere was tense. One's entire career depended on how one performed the first semester on the eight-point grading scale ranging from A downward.

So when the first years held a referendum on grades in 1967, more than 80 percent of their number voted for a pass-fail or honors-pass-fail grading system.[81] But the faculty did little, spurring more complaints.[82] According to an editorial in the student paper, *The Yale Advocate*:

> A malaise pervades Yale Law School like the smell of formaldehyde masking decay in a morgue. Everyone senses it at first, and then soon becomes accustomed to it. It exists because Yale Law School is not the pioneering institution which its myth would have one believe. It exists because of the almost grade-school-like relationship between most faculty and students. It exists because students cannot meet as equals with faculty. . . . It exists because for most people education here is merely floating on a gutterlike stream of courses until their momentum turns them into lawyers and empties them into the sewer of Wall Street.[83]

The "sixties" had arrived at New Haven's Wall Street.

In fall 1968, the new first-years raised the grades issue again. They organized a referendum, which brought well over 90 percent of their number, 183 of them, to the polls. Eleven supported the current grading system; a resounding 93 percent did not.[84] Further, the referendum revealed that pass-fail was far and away the most popular grading system among students for first-year courses, garnering 55 percent of first-preference choices. Less than 16 percent supported the distinction-pass-low pass-fail system that the Curriculum Committee, chaired by Thomas Emerson, was considering.[85] That news made Emerson, one of the professors closer to the students, unhappy. "It seems pretty clear to me that we'll just have to start over again," he told the *Yale Daily News*.[86]

But the faculty did not want to start over. With final examinations scheduled for January, it met three days into Christmas vacation to decide the issue. Emerson and some committee members liked the idea of taking a step toward better faculty-student communication by putting current first-years on a pass-fail system for three years as an experiment. [87]

Bickel was appalled. "Pass-Fail is not an experiment," the faculty minutes had him telling his colleagues. "[I]t's adopting a different system. That new system (of personal evaluation, conferences, e.g.) is one he wants no part of: it's not what he understands as the function of a law professor."[88]

The following morning, the Yale law faculty nevertheless adopted its current grading system.[89] First-semester courses would be graded credit/fail. Thereafter, with the exception of a limited number of advanced courses that instructors could offer on a credit-fail basis, courses would be graded "Honors," "Pass," "Low Pass," and "Fail."[90] Prominently highlighting the comment of one Yale student that "I didn't study less — but I worried less," the *Harvard Law Record* and Michigan's *Res Gestae* reported the faculty vote as a triumph for the students.[91] Grade reform had not yet begun to sweep elite law schools, and when it did, beginning the following year, few faculties were willing to make credit-fail grades mandatory.[92] Yale law students, however, did not view the faculty vote as a victory so much as the minimum change acceptable. "Stand together, not on top of each other!," members of the class of 1970 would joke in their yearbook. "Abolish Grades! Remember — Richard Nixon was third in his class at Duke Law School!"[93] Further, professors had just traded off one problem for another. At the same meeting the faculty decided on the new grading system, Black Law Students Union members demanded a hearing.[94]

Believing the LSATs culturally biased, the Yale faculty had given "less weight to the LSAT and the rest of the standard academic white apparatus in assessing black applicants" since 1948,[95] when it had decided to admit any African American who, "in our judgment, was qualified in the sense that he or she could successfully complete the three years required to obtain a degree. All other applicants competed on a best-qualified basis, with the exception that, as a 'national' law school, we guarded against overrepresentation of particular regions of the country." The statement was not quite accurate. As an internal memorandum admitted, "we should be fooling ourselves if we refused to acknowledge" that "Yale connections" could give children of Law School alumni and those strongly supported by faculty members an edge in the admissions process too.[96] The Yale admissions committee did not keep the African American track of its special admissions program, which had traditionally yielded up to six black students, secret, but it never advertised it.[97]

The winds of change began to blow in 1968–69, when a push by the admissions office in response to student demand after Martin Luther King's assassination ensured that the first year included the highest percentage of black students of any class yet.[98] There were twelve students, many from working-class families and/or the South. One of them, Otis Cochran, organized the Black Law Students Union, which he chaired, and made it the "most active group in the law school."[99] And on December 10, the BLSU delivered its "presentments" to the Law School administration. They included the demand for an increase in the number of African Americans in the student body to 10 percent (up from 4 percent) and the proposal that "presently enrolled Black students serve as advance men" to help the school achieve the goal. Black students also sought the establishment of separate facilities in the Law School for the BLSU's use and a separate table for black students in the dining hall. They appealed to the Law School to fund a permanent chair for a black professor. They demanded that Yale award more financial aid to black students and sponsor a Council on Legal Education Opportunity Institute during the summer to prepare black students for law school. African Americans also insisted that the curriculum be revised to include courses focusing on topics relevant to lawyers who sought to serve the black community, such as poverty and discrimination. They called for a halt to campus police harassment.[100]

A week later, on December 16, the BLSU received Pollak's reply. The dean reported that he and his colleagues shared students' interest in "recruiting more qualified black students and qualified black professors," but objected in principle to a target of a specific percentage of black students because "that would smack of a quota." Pollak denied the demand for a separate dining table (one took root anyway), but provided for an office. He made vague, but encouraging "we'll have to study this but we're all people of good will here" noises about everything else.[101]

Unappeased, the BLSU quickly responded that the "general insensitivity and unwillingness of the Dean of the Law School to respond to our previously stated demands clearly demonstrates his ineffectiveness in responding to the needs of the black students." It called for a meeting with the faculty. And the BLSU warned that while it was making "every effort to approach this grave situation with fairness and restraint, we cannot allow our unanswered demands to wallow in committees and discussion. We must have positive answers by the time we return from the Christmas break, or we must seek avenues other than discussion and debate."[102]

The BLSU had thrown down the gauntlet, and Cochran appeared by invitation at the faculty meeting to discuss grades. "These are demands — not for discussion," he announced. The BLSU reiterated its needs. When Pollak replied that the faculty found the airing of student views useful, that more conversation was necessary, and that he was establishing a faculty committee to discuss these matters further with the BLSU, Cochran answered that he wanted action. The students then departed. "Let's not buy peace at a price that may haunt us," Charles Black and Alexander Bickel urged.[103]

Bickel's response was less surprising than Black's. As his statement on grades indicated, Bickel was no supporter of student-initiated changes. But Black, who had "found his voice" working with the NAACP Legal Defense Fund in *Brown*,[104] maintained that "we've always had affirmative action, whether for alumni children or football players" and pointed out that the fairness of affirmative action was challenged only when it involved African

Americans.[105] It was not the substance of BLSU demands that bothered Black so much, apparently, as the fact that Cochran thought he had a right to make them. As the lines between students and professors hardened, Black often argued with Bickel and others not inclined toward concessions that the faculty must retain unilateral control over affirmative action and every other policy it had traditionally set.[106] And he confessed publicly that as he and many of his colleagues confronted the student activists of the sixties they felt not "discontent," but "panic."[107]

The dean himself sounded near panic as he reported to the president and provost. "[T]here is a very substantial likelihood that . . . the Faculty will not, at least as of now, be disposed to go any substantial distance beyond most of the positions outlined in my letter . . . of December 16, and that . . . the BLSU will not enter into real discussions of these issues with Mr. Simon's committee," Pollak said. "With matters in this posture, the BLSU rhetoric of post-Christmas threat may be a very serious matter."[108]

That was enough for Woodbridge Hall, which promptly sent the provost to a luncheon meeting of the faculty. By now, the faculty had drafted a reply to the BLSU, which affirmed its commitment to change in the vaguest of fashions. "Specific questions in Black demands are not plainly answered," the provost complained. "What about 10% demand?" According to the central university administration, the Law School might be "right in rejecting a quota," but it must "increase the intake of Blacks."[109] (Actually, the administration probably did not believe the Law School was correct. It had recently welcomed the Singer Report, which advocated raising the proportion of African Americans at Yale College to a point at which it would equal that of African Americans in the general population.[110]) The provost cautioned faculty members "to decide how far we're willing to go . . . before a confrontation so as not to appear to be yielding under pressure."[111]

On Christmas Eve, President Kingman Brewster was brought in. By this time, the faculty was certain the BLSU "may be unwilling to discuss differences and want to do something active." With finals approaching, professors were worried that the BLSU would picket or bar entry to exam rooms.[112] After affirming his faith in Pollak, Brewster turned to the faculty's draft response to BLSU demands. Stressing "Yale's responsibility to adopt a posture that's meaningful in other universities," Brewster urged the professors to make "some positive assertion of total University position, for the benefit of *all* students," and to insist that they could not "drop standards, for sake of Blacks — students or faculty." What Brewster wanted, probably, was for the faculty to adopt the students' demands *and* reiterate its commitment to "standards," lest African

Americans be stigmatized—that is, to emphasize the need for more imaginative admissions criteria and how much African Americans added to the school.[113]

But the faculty was not buying. "We're using a double standard now," Bickel replied. The double standard could not be avoided, Harry Wellington added: "We're taking people who are not only not qualified but whose interest is in bringing the system down. We must come to grips with this dilemma."[114]

To the relief of the President's Office, the faculty came to grips by accepting most of the black students' demands. By New Year's Eve, the Law School faculty had confirmed that the admissions policy would *continue* to give "substantial weight to past educational disadvantage and cultural difference." Significantly, while refusing to commit itself to "a given percentage or a given number of black law students or, for that matter, any other group of law students," the school extended the application deadline for black undergraduates. It announced a program to expand recruitment, which would make use of black alumni, led by Leon Higginbotham. Most important, it promised that an extra ten to fifteen places would be reserved for "black and other minority or disadvantaged students who meet the admissions criteria. Any students thus selected will be in addition to the roster of students who apply and are admitted during the normal period—a roster which should itself include a number of black students." In effect, the school promised to commit 10 percent of its positions in the first-year class to minority groups; and also to increase financial aid for African Americans; contribute financially to the BLSU; participate in the Council on Legal Opportunity Institute; make additions to the curriculum that would allow students greater exposure to the community; and combat campus police mistreatment of black students.[115]

Here was an example of black student power. Though the faculty had not accepted all BLSU demands, it had agreed to a number of them. Pollak vigorously defended its action in a widely publicized exchange of private letters, subsequently published in *The Public Interest*. Emphasizing that "long before such skepticism was fashionable," the Admissions Committee had doubted "the predictive value (with respect to ultimate professional distinction) of the LSAT, and even of the college record" for *all* "whose childhood and family backgrounds are remote from the experiences and aspirations of (primarily white) middle-class America," Pollak reiterated that the Admissions Committee had for some time accepted "numerous black students" it otherwise would have rejected. Few had failed, and "[a] few" had received high grades—even achieved membership on the *Law Journal*. "Not surprisingly," though, "given their lesser academic preparation[,] most of these students have not achieved academic distinction at the Law School." What was important, however, was that "so many black alumni have, entering upon the profession, speedily demonstrated professional accomplishments of a high order." What was new about the admissions practice was only that the Admissions Committee would seek a higher number of students of color—and Pollak emphasized—disadvantaged whites. Thus "the real question is whether the School was warranted in enlarging its numeral commitment to this objective." The dean reasoned that the country needed more African American leaders, and lawyers were surely leaders. There was no down side.[116]

The faculty's action seemed impressive to students at Michigan, whose student body was only 3.6 percent black, whose dean was defensive,[117] and where faculty complained it could not find the cash for more minority scholarships.[118] Indeed, though one might have expected Pollak's suggestion that few law students had done well academically to elicit charges of paternalism, student reporters at the University of Michigan Law School's weekly singled the dean out for praise. "It is time to understand that one comes to law school not to get good grades or make law review, but to become an accomplished lawyer."[119] At Yale, though black students criticized their professors' unwillingness to go further, they seemed, for the moment, largely satisfied.[120] "[W]e got through last year rather well," Associate Dean Ralph Brown acknowledged after admissions season had ended in 1969. "The first interest of our black students was, I think, that their numbers be increased. In this we have been very successful, in that perhaps 15% of the entering class are from racial minority groups."[121] A more effective affirmative action program had taken root at Yale.

To the discomfort of some professors, so did more emphasis on relevance. Yale's student-run legal services program, in existence since the 1930s, when legal realist Jerome Frank breathed vitality into the clinical movement with his call for a "clinical lawyer-school,"[122] had long placed students in legal aid work and the public defender's office. It possessed too few openings for the many who hoped to work with clients in the fields of urban and poverty law during the late 1960s.[123] Now, the clinic became "one small arena for the broader social and cultural struggle, and one battleground in the war between the faculty and students at Yale Law School."[124]

With some anxiety, on the grounds that clinical education was insufficiently "academic," the faculty successfully applied for a Ford Foundation grant for clinical education in 1969. That year, the school hired Daniel Fried to develop the clinical program; launched the Danbury Project, in which students provided legal services to inmates; and appointed Dennis Curtis to become supervising attorney of the new in-house clinic. The following year, Steven Wizner left Mobilization for Youth to become his colleague. At a time when litigation was touted as the best tool of social reform, the program demonstrated responsiveness to students' pleas that they learn skills enabling them to fight racial discrimination and poverty.[125]

The skeptic might say that the Yale faculty was trying to buy off white and black students in the sixties generation with such "accommodation."[126] Yale professors, for example, specifically cited the "proposed Legal Services Clinic (a storefront center)" in their New Year's Eve letter to the BLSU.[127] Perhaps faculty members hoped that the clinical program could absorb the demand for relevance, enabling them to be left alone. Perhaps they also hoped that clinicians would prove so happy to teach bright Yale Law students that they would infuse the warmth into the institution that students said their professors withheld. But clinics still made "regular" professors nervous and suspicious, with one warning that "clinical programs may themselves be escapism for some people, escape into what is sometimes called 'real life.'"[128] At first, students could receive only "forensic," not "academic," credit for clinical work.[129] As at other schools, there was a tension between the academic and the non-tenured clinical faculty, reflecting the academics' anxiety that clinical education was insufficiently theoretical and too expensive. "We are probably a little more obsessed than we should be with a fear of such programs," Professor Abe Goldstein admitted.[130]

White student groups supported the BLSU and expanded clinical education and demanded their own place at the table. After three months of internal deliberations, the Student Negotiating Committee unveiled its plan for change in February 1969 — "joint student-faculty rule."[131] The committee envisioned governance by a Law School council, which would replace the faculty as the school's primary deliberative body, and on which elected student representatives and the faculty would possess equal voting power. In addition, all committee meetings would be open, and students and professors would possess equal voting power there.[132] This student utopia was itself hierarchical: The proposal gave no power to staff.

The student press liked it anyway. *The Advocate,* whose editor, Richard Hughes, was a Student Negotiating Committee Member, applauded the SNC for trying to bring faculty and students together and characterized the plan as "ideal."[133] The *Yale Daily News* celebrated the "peaceful revolution" at hand. Superficially, the committee's proposal seemed "as radical as any in the nation's most troubled universities," it reported. "But given the friendly spirit of the 'revolutionaries,' the smallness and cohesiveness of the Law School, and its recent history of controversial issues, 'radical' hardly seems a fitting description."[134]

Wishful thinking. Now, in the hundred days following Nixon's inauguration at the beginning of 1969, the Student Negotiating Committee faced a series of meetings with its faculty counterpart.[135] And the SNC's first meeting with faculty negotiators was inauspicious. Professors representing the faculty maintained that the university's bylaws required the faculty to serve as the Law School's governing body.[136] (Students subsequently heard that Black, Bickel, and Wellington had circulated a memorandum damning their proposal as unconstitutional.[137])

Of course, the bylaws could be changed, professors acknowledged, but the dean insisted that "the Bylaws are right." The professors expressed sympathy with the students' ideal of greater "community." Nevertheless, according to the notes of student negotiator Richard Hughes, Abe Goldstein insisted that the faculty was "not prepared to give up the vote — but assuming that, cannot community still be achieved? — & the burden is on the students to show where communication, etc., has broken down."[138] Eugene Rostow, recently returned from the State Department, raised the lawyer's "parade of horribles" and contended that concessions might lead to a revolution at Yale comparable to the one that had given students control of Latin American universities. Hughes, doubtless dressed more casually, was struck by the former dean's appearance: "& lo and behold — he wears garters!" Rostow's insistence surprised Hughes too: "[H]e draws the line rather harshly — the faculty will maintain its authority over policy 'against all comers' — & he has the audacity to speak of striving towards community."[139]

From this meeting, it was downhill. "Why not vote?" Bickel asked the SNC at another meeting. "I'll tell you why not. We're professionals and as Mr. Rostow says, we have professional responsibilities. You wouldn't vote on a surgeon's techniques." The students were simply future graduates, or what Bickel called, "premature alumni." No current interest of the young could match that of the (tenured) faculty, who had a "lifetime interest" in Yale.[140]

With spring recess approaching, students suspected faculty negotiators of trying to run down the clock.[141] In March 1969, just after the break, the faculty finally acted. It approved a resolution Pollak had written in which he attempted to find a middle ground between faculty opponents of "student power," such as Goldstein, Bickel, and Rostow, and supporters. (One of them, labor lawyer Clyde Summers, compared the faculty-student negotiations to the conversations that must have occurred when Walter Reuther demanded codetermination for workers at Ford. Here, too, Summers said, the faculty employed "the arguments of generous and benign management who could not understand why those on the other side, who were treated so well, should be making such demands — a management with such a sense of institutional responsibility that they felt it would violate the underlying principles of the institution to surrender any measure of management prerogatives."[142]) In it, professors formally rejected the Law School Council on the grounds that faculty decision-making powers should not be "diluted, or delegated (whether in whole or in part) to another body."[143] There could be no compromise on one principle. Pollak contended that the power to govern the school legally and rightfully belonged to the faculty. The resolution reflected the dean's conviction that it would be "insulting to ourselves" and to the students to give them the "appearance" of sharing in authority.[144]

Still, Pollak tried to dress up the faculty's action as a victory for students. In their resolution, professors insisted that they were "impressed" by the need for student representatives to participate in some faculty meetings. Students had been sitting on some committees on an experimental basis since the fall, and according to the resolution, they had made a convincing case that on occasions when the faculty considered matters students had helped shape as committee members, there should be "student participation in discussion (although not decision) at the level of the Faculty itself." Consequently the faculty hoped "to explore with the Student Negotiating Committee arrangements which look in this direction (provided, of course, that such arrangements would guarantee the Faculty's right to meet by itself on any issue at any time").[145] Professors thus gave students a pat for persuasiveness and signaled their willingness to contemplate continued student membership on selected committees and limited participation in some faculty meetings, at the same time they announced their refusal to give students either a vote at faculty meetings or a regular place at the faculty table.

Following the example of the BLSU, the white activists on the Student Negotiating Committee rejected the faculty resolution. A week after SNC members had stormed out of their April Fool's Day meeting with the faculty negotiators and resigned from all committees in protest against the faculty resolution, the SNC committee published an open letter to the faculty. In attempting to codify the "inadequate procedures created this year," it alleged, professors proposed a model "of co-optation and supplication" that institutionalized "the subordination of student views and interests." The end product was a "disheartening statement about the courage and intellectual integrity of those faculty members who require the cloak of secrecy to shield their views from others in this community."[146]

As they often did, students flung history and expectations at their professors. The episode "explode[d] the myth of the 'progressive,' adventuresome Yale Law School that you purport to embody." The failure of this "effort at liberal reform through rational discourse" pointed up "the conservative, establishment character of this faculty and the Yale Law School of 1969 — whatever it may once have been."[147]

Refusing "to continue to be treated as children," Student Negotiating Committee members grandiosely announced that they were releasing all the information about "this fiasco" to the media and darkly predicted "collective action by students to bring about a reversal of this decision."[148] The faculty's action "fatally undermines those of us who would seek to move forward by means of rational discourse among men of mutual trust and good will," they said.[149] It demonstrated that radical students, who had predicted SNC failure from the beginning, warning that the "Christians had a better chance against the lions," [150] had been right all along.[151] The editors of *The Advocate* piled on, inveighing against a faculty "[c]linging blindly to the privileges and power of professorial status" that had obviously decided to "meet the students head-on in combat." Professors were on a fool's errand. "The faculty may be patting itself on the back for its smooth disposition of the grading issue and black students' demands, but they have seen nothing yet." With "increasingly concerned and aware students" entering the school, the paternalism at its core would be challenged and, perhaps, subjected "to violent shaking. Yet the faculty has blocked the one avenue open to it by which it could very likely meet and overcome those and other challenges which the school must face." Students would not go to "the barricades" over "the issue of participation," the newspaper conceded. "But when the proper issue arises — and it will — the breakdown of orderly processes at the law school will be directly traceable to the faculty resolution."[152]

For an instant, it looked as if the "breakdown" might occur over the March 1969 faculty resolution. More than 300 law students attended an open meeting to protest the Yale faculty's action.[153] ("Tired of being ——' by the Faculty?" one sign advertising it read.[154]) After Pollak warned that "if you pursue as the only issue before you the question of voting on the faculty, I don't suppose that you will succeed," the floor was opened. "I thought it was a dumb idea in the fall," Duncan Kennedy said of the move to increase student participation in faculty governance, because he was sure that the faculty would "figure out a real cooptative, chummy scheme. I was wrong." Because so few professors "had a brain in their head on this," there was "a real opportunity" to make the most of student dissatisfaction. "The impasse [is] . . . precipitated by a system of administration that is based on anti-human relationships," Kennedy concluded. "Shut this school down — or burn it down," black activist Don Howie exhorted. Someone else urged students to form a group called S.H.I.T.F.A.C.E., "Students to Help Increase the Faculty's Authority and Control over Everything." It could hold an organizational meeting "as soon as it gets the faculty permission."[155]

In the end, students and faculty drew back from the abyss. When both groups went back to the table and the student negotiators proposed regular, rather than limited, student non-voting representation at all faculty meetings, save those in executive session, they were astonished. "Yoicks!" Hughes noted. "Goldstein comes out in favor of our point — says let's try it — things couldn't be worse than they are now."[156] The faculty would allow the Law Student Association to hold elections for ten representatives each fall. Elected representatives and "a number" of appointed student representatives would serve on standing faculty committees,[157] save Appointments and Promotions.[158] The extent to which students would participate in disciplinary matters was fuzzed over.[159] The elected representatives also would serve as non-voting participants in all faculty meetings except when the dean or three other professors decided the faculty was meeting in "executive session."[160]

Pollak rightly forecast that he could sell the deal to his colleagues, though he told the University administration that "some faculty, though not a majority felt that the resolution he supported could be taken by students as a sign of weakness."[161] And he predicted correctly again that the Student Negotiating Committee would agree to the resolution.[162] None of its student negotiators liked it. Even the six publicly most supportive advised the larger student body that "we are disappointed in the outcome of the negotiations," and with the faculty's treatment of them, which demonstrated that "a majority of the faculty still clings to its prerogatives with persistence."[163] But they accepted the compromise, and in yet another referendum in the spring of 1969, the student body did too.[164] The Yale faculty had more clearly maintained the upper hand in its fight with white activists than it had in its struggle with African American students. Students had won greater representation, but they had not been enfranchised. Professors still ran the school and remained, in students' words, "the distinct, controlling caste."[165]

Faculty dominance fostered fragmentation. The culture clash was not just reflected in conflict between white faculty members and black activists and between liberal professors and reformist or "radical" white students. 1968–69 also witnessed the rise of a counterculture and women's movement at the Law School. Instead of a "community," the Law School was becoming the site of communities — black activists, white activists, yippies, and feminists.[166]

Thanks to members of the class of 1970, the counterculture came to the Law

School in early 1969 to give a sound and light show for a mixer. Sixty members of the Hog Farm Commune, a group affiliated with Ken Kesey's Merry Pranksters and including the notorious "Wavy Gravy," began making visits to Sterling Law Dorms. Though the Hog Farmers believed mixers a relic of the past, they made the first of many visits to New Haven, arriving in their psychedelic bus, wearing brightly colored jumpsuits, and staying with law students.

After they left, their hosts created Cosmic Laboratories, a group of some thirty-odd law students that used huge inflatable plastic portable structures, including one in the shape of a whale, to house "happenings" at Yale. A tube to the fan in Thomas Emerson's office kept the inflatables inflated when Cosmic Labs held events in the Law School courtyard. Designed by architecture students, they could hold as many as three hundred. Inside the inflatables, sound and light shows and collective exercises created an alternative reality. Members of Cosmic Labs wore jumpsuits of their own on which they sported a symbol particularly appropriate for 1960s law students, the scales of justice held up by a lightning bolt.[167]

They were not legal hippies, though they were more attracted to "William Burroughs than Earl Warren."[168] They did not withdraw from politics; they supported the white activists pressing for shared governance. Cosmic Lab members were analogous to Yippies such as Abbie Hoffman and Jerry Rubin. The "S.H.I.T.F.A.C.E." proposition, for example, combined left politics with the counterculture theater of protest.[169]

Like the Hog Farmers, women thought that the Law School should adopt more enlightened attitudes. The faculty had pleased women (and probably campus police, who, the records sometimes seemed to suggest, had spent most of the sixties investigating parietal violations)[170] by approving coed dorms in 1968.[171] Women who wished to live in dorms were no longer confined to one of Yale's most dreadful buildings, Helen Hadley Hall, a long trek from the Law School.[172]

But Yale Law women, many of them active in both the white student and feminist movements, wanted more. The class of 1970 was typical in that it included only seven of them. "This was not simply a product of disinterest on the part of women; the law school limited its recruiting and advertising efforts to men's schools from which most of its students came."[173] Largely because women students pressed the administration,[174] the next year witnessed a noticeable jump in numbers. In the fall of 1968, one year before Yale College became coeducational, twenty-five women entered the Law School. And they possessed a full plate of issues. "Mixer," one *Advocate* notice announced soon after school began. "Smith girls and Kentucky Fried Chicken in the Courtyard. Plenty of legs and breasts."[175]

Now that women approached a critical mass, they placed feminist matters front and center. They persuaded the Dean that Yale needed to offer a "Women and the Law" course.[176] Three of them wrote the celebrated *Yale Law Journal* article on the Equal Rights Amendment with Thomas Emerson.[177] Two of the authors active in New Haven Women's Liberation, Ann Freedman and Gail Falk, formed the Yale Law Women's Association, which began life in part as a consciousness-raising group.[178] Yale Law women also joined with local New Haven women to file *Women v. Connecticut,* the suit that overturned Connecticut's statutory prohibition against abortion.[179] They charged that there were too few women law students and persuaded the Admissions Committee to agree "to adopt a policy of affirmative recruitment" of women, which resulted in a doubling of applicants. Women soon regularly constituted about 16 percent of the first-year class.[180] They contended that law firm members discriminated by holding recruitment dinners at Yale's male eating club, Mory's — where the law women staged a sit-in — and by openly telling women, "they were better situated in fields other than law."[181]

As at other law schools,[182] some of their accusations were not new. Betsy Levin, the first woman to become a dean of a major law school, and civil rights activist Heywood Burns had lodged charges that law firms discriminated against women and minorities when they were Yale students during Rostow's deanship.[183] The Yale women who followed understood the problem as one of enforcement. Their school circulated a pamphlet to all employers who used its facilities prohibiting any form of discrimination in hiring based on race, sex, or religion. But there were no specific guidelines about implementation or imposition of sanctions. To make matters worse, the dean's designee for investigating complaints was also charged with alumni relations and financial contributions and apparently received no instruction about what he should do in the event of violation.[184] The women did not believe he much cared about discrimination. "It was up to the female students to apply the pressure."[185]

At least, Yale women received lip service from the placement office, which warned firms against interviewing at Mory's and did not permit those that "actively discriminate in their hiring practices" to use school facilities for interviews.[186] Yale Law School was quick to avow support for equal rights in the workplace. Women at the University of Chicago, on the other hand, who alleged that its placement office permitted firms that did not hire women to use its services, received so little satisfaction from administrators that they filed a Title VII action against it. "Our law school never even pretended," one woman at Chicago told a reporter from Yale's newspaper.[187]

The currents of discontent surfaced and converged at Yale's Alumni Weekend in the spring of 1969. Alumni were treated to a harangue by the Student

Negotiating Committee against "the inertia and self-satisfaction" of the faculty. Committee members protested that Yale had not turned out to be the "very progressive institution on the frontiers of legal education" they had expected and complained that their dream of interdisciplinary work, urban law programs, and "a real community" languished unfulfilled.[188]

Then Judith Areen, who would become the first woman dean of Georgetown Law Center, took her turn. The popular professor Friedrich Kessler had called on her during virtually every class her first term — because she was a woman, Areen thought, and focusing on her "was a way of capturing the class's attention."[189] That, at least, represented an improvement over Harvard, where professors generally ignored women altogether.[190] Soberly, Areen called attention to "the serious underrepresentation of women in the Law School and in the profession."[191]

Then Black Law Students Union Chair Otis Cochran spoke. He lamented that "the great liberal faculty of this great liberal institution could find no way to make black enrollment at Yale Law School more than a token." On the same day that more than eighty African American militants stood in front of Cornell's student union brandishing guns and wearing ammunition belts, Cochran warned that "you can go on for only so long and there's going to be a fire."[192]

Meanwhile, other students, including members of Cosmic Labs, celebrated alumni weekend by showcasing a photograph of one of their number, Dennis Black, complete with gun and cartridge belt, lounging under a poster advising "Hands Off the Vietnamese Revolution!" in an *Advocate* article entitled "Students Provide Welcome for Alumni Weekend."[193] And students supporting the Student Negotiating Committee had indeed pretended to form a group called "S.H.I.T.F.A.C.E: Students to Help Increase The Faculty's Authority and Control Over Everything." As alumni prowled the halls, they could see signs declaring S.H.I.T.F.A.C.E. support for some of the most controversial faculty policies. Alumni could see everywhere, too, the partially playful signs the student negotiators had circulated at the time of their walkout: "Create Two, Three . . . Many Yale Law Struggles"; "Support Class Struggle at Yale Law School"; "All Peoples Support Heroic Struggle of Yale Law Students."[194]

Activists topped off the Alumni Weekend event by building a gallows in the Law School courtyard.[195] Graduates were treated to the sight of hearing one student informing a drunken alumnus who came to stare at the gallows and to ask repeatedly what the students "really" wanted: "We want a law school that graduates nobody like you ever again."[196]

In retrospect, the theater of Alumni Weekend might seem funny. But at the time, faculty and many alumni would not have laughed. A gallows was a fearsome addition to a courtyard that had long been the site of the civil conversation on which the school prided itself. There was a world of difference between the friskiness of "S.H.I.T.F.A.C.E.," which was simply impertinent, and a scaffold with a noose. And when Cochran spoke, one alumnus complained to the dean, he was "surrounded by eight colleagues on the platform who did not speak but merely sat with folded arms."[197]

Quite understandably, by this time, Pollak was "tired."[198] One of his colleagues reported that "for the whole of the past academic year, we were in no small degree engaged in a struggle for survival" and said that he feared the "threats" of black and white activists departing for the summer "that they would see us in the fall."[199] The Dean told Yale's president he did not want another term.[200] Brewster agreed the school would install a new dean, come summer, 1970. That still left Pollak with the next academic year, which would prove the worst one yet.

As the 1969–70 school year opened, Cosmic Lab members, some of whom had worked at Woodstock over the summer, and other law students established a "tent city," a commune of twenty-odd tents in the Law School courtyard.[201] Students camped out part of the fall in an attempt "both to establish a sanctuary in which students could escape the law school atmosphere, and to demonstrate to other members of the law school a counter-community with new values."[202] Unlike Woodstock, Yale's tent city discouraged drug use. Though marijuana, at least, was generally as much a staple of law school as college life,[203] participants carefully avoided using drugs there, lest they be busted. Each night, they would sing songs and declare the courtyard a "people's park."[204]

Charles Reich sometimes joined them. That professor had spent the Summer of Love in San Francisco and Berkeley grooving to the sounds of Big Brother and the Holding Company and the Grateful Dead.[205] "I was much too conventional . . . [to have] dreamed of having an encampment in the courtyard," Reich stressed later, characterizing himself as just curious enough to visit.[206] Still, he apparently viewed the development as such a hopeful sign that he alluded to it in the conclusion of *The Greening of America*: "When, in the fall of 1969, the courtyard of the Yale Law School, that Gothic citadel of the elite, became for a few weeks the site of a commune, with tents, sleeping bags, and outdoor cooking, who could any longer doubt that the clearing wind was coming?"[207] Reich's occasional presence, the students believed, kept the tent city alive, since no one powerful "wanted the embarrassment of a faculty member being arrested."[208] As the students carried on outside, many professors looked on in horror.[209]

The dean was not among them. Years later, he did not even remember the tent city "camp-in." Pollak provided eloquent testimony to the difficulty of deaning during this period when he remarked, "Probably at the time, it seemed like a minor irritant."[210]

The Vietnam War was major. Draft calls had shrunk to a tenth of their size under the Johnson administration, and Nixon had changed the selective service system from an oldest-first to youngest-first order of call when he introduced the lottery.[211] Though they were no longer at such risk, Yale law students continued to protest American policy. In an early faculty meeting, Pollak welcomed "symbolic" student participation because the Yale Law School Student Association had not yet formally elected its representatives. The students present then asked their professors to suspend all classes on October 15, 1969, the day of the national moratorium against the war, "to symbolize our protest at the continuation of the Viet-Nam War and to allow students, faculty, and staff to participate in the activities planned for that day."[212] President Brewster opposed that position on the grounds that "Yale should not forfeit its institutional neutrality for a political cause, no matter how widely backed,"[213] as did Pollak, who nevertheless expressed his strong sympathy with "student hostility towards the Vietnam war." Junior faculty members Richard Abel and John Griffiths argued that the gravity of war outweighed the importance of "academic neutrality."[214]

To the unhappiness of Abel and Griffiths, the faculty proceeded to defeat the student resolution overwhelmingly.[215] Yale students saw their professors' action as additional evidence that that their professors did not get it. And the fact that Bickel and most of his colleagues began their performances at the meeting with "a personal, cathartic, denunciation of the war" did not impress the young. For them, this was another indication of their professors' "blindness."[216]

The students had little care for the importance of institutional neutrality to Bickel and his colleagues. Writing of Friedrich Kessler, who had been "powerfully influenced" by Max Weber, Anthony Kronman, who was himself powerfully influenced by Weber, eloquently testified to Kessler's staunch defense of "the ideal of academic neutrality — the ideal of the university as a place apart from the pressures of politics and the demands of partisan allegiance." Here, Kronman maintained, Kessler consciously followed Weber, who "understood, with far more clarity than most, the role that values play in scholarly research and teaching." Kessler realized it too, Kronman added, but "like Weber, he has fought against the argument that research and teaching are merely politics by other means. He has fought to keep the academy separate from the world."[217] It was a laudable aim in many ways, all the more so when those who embraced the goal understood it was unrealizable. The impossibility of achieving an ideal can make the act of working toward it even more worthwhile.

Still, the students did not see institutional, or academic, neutrality as a

valuable goal. They observed that "institutional neutrality" was itself a political position, with political consequences.[218] They focused on the political
impossibility of achieving it: In a society in which large institutions played
such an important role in decision making, how could the "university," any
more than "the corporation," retain its neutrality? Too often, they claimed,
their professors seemed guilty of "intellectual schizophrenia . . . accepting, but
defining as nonpolitical, those academic enterprises which support the interests of the government."[219] And why had "neutrality" suddenly become so
important? "Who decried the politicization of American institutions of higher
learning when they made total accommodations in mobilizing for the Second
World War?"[220]

Fifty thousand gathered at the New Haven Green on October 15 for "the
second largest Moratorium demonstration in the nation." Both Brewster and
Mayor Richard Lee denounced the war.[221] A surprise occurred when the mod-
erator of the Black Students Alliance at Yale, Glenn DeChabert, interrupted
the proceeding. He inveighed against "police brutality" against African Americans by New Haven and Yale law enforcement and condemned Yale's president and New Haven's mayor for permitting it to continue.[222] The same day,
the Yale Law School Student Association delivered a statement to Brewster
declaring itself "highly disturbed by the administration's evasion of its direct
responsibility to Yale students and of its moral obligation to the New Haven
community at large . . . to take any action to eliminate the unjustified harassment and abuse to which Black people are subjected daily by New Haven
police."[223]

Few at Yale openly backed the war; DeChambert had raised a more divisive
issue. In August 1969, Black Panther Chairman Bobby Seale had been charged
with six counts of murder, conspiracy to murder, and kidnapping in connection with the death of Alex Rackley, another Panther. Police found Rackley's
body soon after Seale had given a speech at Yale Law School the previous May.
According to the indictment, the victim had been tortured and murdered at
Seale's behest by Panthers who suspected Rackley of having acted as a police
informer. Seale and his followers countercharged that the New Haven arrests
reflected part of a nationwide police conspiracy to destroy the Black Panther
Party.[224]

Many at Yale worried that Seale would be denied a fair hearing when his
trial began the following May. Even New Haven Police Chief James Ahern
subsequently acknowledged that Seale's indictment had "astonished" him.
"Although the New Haven Police Department had evidence that Seale had
visited the Orchard Street apartment while Rackley was there, we had no solid

evidence to link him to Rackley's death or torture," the chief recalled. But at the time, Ahern kept his doubts to himself.[225]

With Yale students anxious about Seale, attention turned naturally to the impact of law on African Americans in the fall of 1969. As the BLSU had indicated in its presentments, black Yale students were frequently stopped for questioning by campus police, who suspected they were outsiders up to no good. Here they were in "an oasis of privilege," Cochran said later, and African Americans "were being jerked around as if they were in the Delta."[226] And their experience with New Haven police proved no better.[227]

On Tuesday, October 14, a black student in Visiting Associate Professor George Lefcoe's property course at Yale Law School asked Lefcoe to discuss police harassment. Lefcoe replied that it was not germane. As distressed students stood discussing their teacher's response after class, BLSU member Eric Clay, who was not in Lefcoe's course, happened along. After hearing what had happened, he later testified, "I said to Mr. Lefcoe that if he didn't stop messing over black people in his classes, he might get his ass kicked." Taken aback, Lefcoe asked Clay for his name. Refusing to identify himself, Clay warned the professor to remember what he had said. Lefcoe reported the matter to Associate Dean William Felstiner. The memories of Lefcoe and Clay about what had been said diverged. According to the professor, the student had threatened to "beat the shit out of" Lefcoe.[228]

Lefcoe, a Law School alumnus, was no stranger to racism. As an Orthodox Jew growing up in the segregated school systems of South Florida, he had regularly engaged in fistfights with the "rednecks" with whom he debated integration in schoolyards. As a high school student, he had given talks in black churches and visited the separate, unequal black high schools. And as a USC professor, Lefcoe lived in the racially mixed community of Baldwin Hills. Yale had offered him a three-year contract, presumably a "lookover" to determine whether it would offer him a permanent position.[229]

In the view of some, the visit had not gone well. One professor remembered that at Yale, Lefcoe had a reputation for nastiness to students.[230] Some black students had branded him "insensitive" and later complained that he had been "demoralizing black students in that class in a number of ways" even before the exchange with Clay.[231]

From Lefcoe's perspective, of course, the situation seemed entirely different. Lefcoe had always maintained that "teachers owe their students the moral obligation to secure the integrity of the classroom." When Clay made the comment to him, Lefcoe remembered fearing for academic freedom. Still, he acted cautiously, consulting with a number of colleagues before lodging a formal complaint with Felstiner. He was, after all, a visitor, which meant that he did not even attend important faculty meetings. And Lefcoe felt in no physical danger. Had he considered his personal safety at issue, he would have contacted either the campus or the New Haven police: "The only reason I considered filing a complaint with the law school was because this threat was uttered in an attempt to coerce me to open my classroom to an intimidating diatribe by a few black students about the New Haven police." And "[t]o a man," the professors he consulted urged Lefcoe to lodge the complaint.[232]

Here was another emergency. The following Monday, between sixty and eighty African Americans, many of them law students, marched into the school.[233] Dividing into several groups, they entered three large classrooms. Chanting "Stop the cops!" they marched around each for five minutes. The students then proceeded across the street to the plaza in front of Woodbridge Hall. Intercepting them, Pollak climbed atop a car and warned that the Law School would not "tolerate further interruption of classes. Any students will be subject to discipline." As the Dean tried to speak, the cry of "Stop the Cops!" continued. When the demonstrators refused to listen, *The Yale Daily News* reported, Pollak "jumped onto the tractor part of the [plaza's] Olden-burg sculpture and shouted: 'Does anybody in this group have enough real interest in this problem to listen to me?'"[234] His office soon posted a warning that "Yale students who interfered with the equal rights of other students, instructors, or members of the staff, to engage in their regular academic pursuits" through "demonstrative activity" interrupting classes or "other aspects of the work of this school," would be "subject to academic discipline."[235] And sure enough, Dean Felstiner then informed three law student participants in the demonstration that they might be disciplined. Felstiner also referred Clay's case to an ad hoc disciplinary panel, which like others at the time, included no student representatives.[236]

By the weekend, the entire Law School community was in an uproar over the three law-student protesters and Clay. Students considered it arbitrary to single out the three for discipline; Felstiner maintained they were the only ones he could identify. Worse still, from the professors' point of view, the BLSU was making menacing noises and had sent them a telegram summoning them to a meeting. Upon receipt, several professors immediately demanded a faculty meeting in executive session, which Pollak held at his house.[237] And while the Student Association believed it had won a promise to notification of executive meetings before they occurred, none was forthcoming. As the dean later explained to association members, some of his colleagues had insisted it was unnecessary since the Student Association had not yet held its election.[238] The students, however, had learned of the gathering anyway, and they appeared at Pollak's house to protest. When the faculty refused to grant them a hearing, they left in anger.[239] Professors — who still seemed more willing to conciliate white than black student activists — then agreed to hear the BLSU the following day.[240]

But the long meeting with African American students did not go well. The faculty was intimidated. Reich recalled two BLSU members "standing at the door looking for all the world like they were guards."[241] For his part, Cochran told the *Yale Daily News* that although "[w]e tried to convey, as honestly and sincerely as we could, the disaffection of black students," professors "took notes, then tried to feed us legalistic generalities which are completely inadequate when our presence in this University is threatened." [242]

The following day, two weeks after the confrontation between Clay and Lefcoe, white and black law students walked out. The *New York Times* reported on "a picket line of placards depicting the scales of justice severed in two by a lightning bolt."[243] And Pollak backed down, announcing that he would not discipline the three African American law students who had interrupted classes.[244]

Yet the disciplinary committee action against Eric Clay for "threatening a member of the faculty with violence" still hung fire. The faculty apparently hoped to resolve the issue quietly.[245] But Clay had selected an African American third-year, Mel Watt, as his student attorney. Perhaps Clay and Watt knew each other before Yale. Both had attended the University of North Carolina. Perhaps Watt's Law School record also impressed Clay; Watt was a member of the *Yale Law Journal*. Clay and Watt now proceeded to insist on a "trial." And because the disciplinary panel was not going to include students, it would have been difficult for its faculty members to insist on an ex parte proceeding. Joe Goldstein, the chair of Clay's panel, refused to open the show to the public[246] — perhaps, Watt speculated, because it would mean he and other committee members would have "to treat Clay, a student, as an equal."[247] Goldstein did agree, however, to allow access to the Law School community.[248]

The trial, which was held in the school's largest classroom, "attracted an overflow audience which spilled into the aisles and onto the windowsills," historian Anne Standley reported.[249] For some reason — perhaps a strained attempt either to convey an atmosphere of informality,[250] or to comply with some notion of due process by replicating the office in which disciplinary hearings normally took place[251] — the panel required its members, Clay, and Watt to sit on the couches and overstuffed chairs brought in just for the occasion. The atmosphere was charged. Though the audience was "well behaved" and treated the complaining witness, Lefcoe, well enough, it was clearly skeptical of the disciplinarians.[252]

Watt and Clay had crafted a neat defense. The imminent threat of violence against Lefcoe did not justify the abridgment of Clay's own right to free speech because the phrase, "get your ass kicked" had to be taken in context. The Supreme Court had recently affirmed the validity of doing just that when it vacated the conviction of an antiwar protester found guilty of violating a statute that prohibited anyone from making a physical threat against the president of the United States.[253]

Here the context was Clay's background. Where Clay had grown up in North Carolina, the words, "get your ass kicked," constituted a prediction, not a threat, and not necessarily one to worry about either. It was simply "the hyperbole of street talk," whose meaning depended on the circumstances that surrounded its utterance. Watt insisted that Clay was engaged in "theoretical expression" and intended no violence.[254] Perhaps that was correct. When Otis Cochran was called, he said Lefcoe could not have grasped Clay's meaning and contended that Clay had been "restrained."[255]

Yet street talk was hardly Clay's only argot. Lefcoe remembered hearing that Clay had grown up in an inner city housing project. He was the first person in his family to attend college. Still, at the University of North Carolina, where Clay and Watt had both graduated Phi Beta Kappa, Clay had been chairman of the Carolina Political Union and president of the Dialectic and Philanthropic Societies.[256] Lefcoe considered Clay, and all other Yale law students, for that matter, "splendidly articulate."[257]

By suggesting there was miscommunication, the defense shifted the spotlight from the accused, Clay, to the complaining witness or accuser, Lefcoe. A prosecutor might have helped Lefcoe. Yet although students complained that the panel engaged "in a mixture of prosecutorial and judicial functions which in itself makes a fair hearing difficult,"[258] there was no formal prosecutor. A colleague skilled in litigation or administrative hearings could have volunteered to stand by during the hearing, to make sure the trial did not become an instance of "blaming the victim." But no one did. From Lefcoe's perspective, the Law School administration and most of his colleagues, including some of the very individuals who had advised him to file a complaint, hung him out to dry.[259] Lefcoe thought he was put on trial. The disciplinary action against Eric Clay, which might have been entitled *Yale Law School v. Clay,* became *Clay v. Lefcoe.*

Because of the nature of the proceeding, no one examined Lefcoe. Watt, however, cross-examined him at length about his prior experiences with African Americans in an apparent attempt to demonstrate that Lefcoe had little and had not comprehended Clay's words. Watt assumed Lefcoe's contact had been limited to interchanges with servants, a supposition that Lefcoe found amusing in light of his background and status as an underpaid young professor. "The notion that somehow I had misunderstood Mr. Clay's meaning, though a clever assertion, was one that I am sure Mr. Clay and Mr. Watt knew to be without merit," Lefcoe said later. Yet Clay and Watt "were just students at the time and I could appreciate how they played their hand."[260]

Elaborating on the point of cultural difference, Watt asked Clay to "tell the panel what the words 'get your ass kicked' means where you come from?" Clay responded, "it could mean a number of things, from 'Now you die,' to 'Good morning,' or 'Good afternoon.'" He had "intended for the statement to mean that unless Mr. Lefcoe reformed his behavior, he would in fact suffer consequences," Clay explained.[261]

Then, however, Clay undercut the argument.[262] The line of questioning had created the chance for him to claim that he had not threatened Lefcoe with violence. Watt now asked him about the myriad meanings of the remark, "If you continue, you are going to get your ass kicked," in the context of his exchange with Lefcoe:

> Q [WATT]: Did that include a threat that you personally were going to kick Mr. Lefcoe's ass?
> A [CLAY]: I don't know that the consequences would necessarily follow, be dependent on whatever action I would take. The statement was intended to mean that such occurrence — and I still do think — that such occurrence will come to pass if Mr. Lefcoe does not alter his behavior. Whether I would do it or someone else would do it, I don't know.
> CHAIRMAN GOLDSTEIN: Could you tell us what consequences you have in mind?
> THE WITNESS: No.
> CHAIRMAN GOLDSTEIN: You are refusing to, or you don't have any idea in mind? I didn't understand the answer.
> THE WITNESS: I am refusing to.[263]

The defense had nearly accomplished the impossible. It had demonstrated the chasm between the culture of Yale Law School and that of the inner city while creating the chance for Clay to back down without apologizing. Years later, one BLSU officer still recalled the "bravura performance by Mel Watt,"[264] who "seemed to be making the statement that we were lawyers and had these tools at our disposal, as well as demonstrations."[265]

While Watt and Clay had shown that their legal education had served them well, they had convinced few of the faculty members in attendance that Lefcoe had misconstrued Clay's meaning.[266] Had Clay seized the opening his counsel had created for him, the incident might nevertheless have been dismissed as a misunderstanding in the interest of moving forward. But Clay had underlined the political nature of the trial in his reply to Goldstein and his insistence that his conduct was right. In a dramatic moment, he had *appeared* to depart from the script after the stage had been set.[267] That made his words seem more menacing than ever.

Consequently, the disciplinary panel proved ill disposed to be gracious. It unanimously agreed that all the language variations, ranging from "beat the shit" to "suffer consequences" constituted threats of violence. Nor did the panel find persuasive any of the arguments offered as defense or in mitigation, including the contentions that Lefcoe had not appeared frightened; that the episode reflected the need for increased white sensitivity to black culture; or that assuming, arguendo, Clay *had* made a threatening statement to Lefcoe, "it was a very deserved statement." Yet the panel could not agree on a recommendation. A minority recommended Clay's immediate suspension for the remainder of the year,[268] the majority that Clay first be given the chance to show he understood his remark conveyed a threat of violence and to disclaim violence.[269]

But for Pollak, the majority's solution was unworkable. What the dean did not say was that BLSU members had privately warned him all African Americans students would quit school if he chose either option.[270] White students had let him know they would be "mighty unhappy" too.[271] What Pollak said was that after consulting with Clay and others, he had determined no assurances would be forthcoming because Clay would view their rendering "to be degrading." So the dean put Clay on probation and let him stay in school.[272]

Pollak shrewdly decided against making Clay a martyr, especially because the student had violated no explicit strictures of the school. The dean could have damaged Clay's career, or, at least, caused trouble for him with a bar committee later. But had he done that, he would have lifted the lid off the kettle at a dangerous moment. Had the administration proven completely unyielding on grades, affirmative action, or student participation in governance, the school might have reached its boiling point sooner. The *Advocate* had predicted that the issue of governance would not radicalize students the previous year,[273] but when it arose within the context of a disciplinary proceeding, it acquired explosive potential. Yale College allowed students to sit on its Executive Committee, which disciplined students.[274] Suspension of Eric Clay on professors' recommendation, amid an atmosphere of concern about police harassment, racial injustice, and free speech, and in a way that could have created the impression that even more than Yale College, Yale Law School treated its students as children, might well have brought students to the barricades.

Instead, while Mel Watt was becoming one of the two African Americans elected to Congress from North Carolina in the twentieth century, Clay was making his own way. He clerked for U.S. District Judge Damon Keith when he graduated from the Law School. Clay then became one of three African American lawyers to establish one of the first and largest law firms in the nation founded by minorities, one that combined corporate law with public interest law.[275] When Bill Clinton appointed Clay to the Sixth Circuit in 1997 to fill the vacancy created by Keith's retirement, Keith administered the oath to Clay in front of an audience that included Clay's Yale Law School classmates Clarence Thomas and Lani Guinier.[276] Among other things, Judge Clay wrote an opinion striking down school vouchers as a violation of the Establishment Clause that was subsequently reversed by the Supreme Court and issued a concurrence strongly defending the constitutionality of race-based affirmative action at the University of Michigan Law School.[277] Lefcoe later maintained that Pollak had done the right thing.[278]

At the time, though, no one was satisfied. As the dean said, his decision "came closer to dividing the faculty than any other issue."[279] The tensions had been manifest for some time, as Pollak tried to hold together those with some sympathy for the students, such as Emerson, Summers, Reich, Boris Bittker, and some junior faculty members, and those, such as the Goldsteins, Bickel, Black, and Rostow, who thought the dean should take a harder line. In the Clay case, the process, along with the solution Pollak selected, poisoned the atmosphere further by angering professors who opposed concessions to students. As the dean recognized, Joe Goldstein considered his action so "grossly improvident" that Pollak could only comfort Goldstein by reminding his colleague that he would not remain dean much longer.[280] Pollak did just that.[281] It was a gracious gesture that may also have been spurred by rumors that Joe Goldstein, Bickel, and others were talking about decamping from Yale to establish their own research institute.[282] Bickel, Guido Calabresi, Kessler, and Ralph Winter circulated a memorandum insisting that the school's disciplinary standards had always been clear and that the dean's action with respect to Clay jeopardized academic freedom.

> The student himself has simply and forthrightly maintained, and continues to maintain, that he has an absolute right to adhere to his personal code of conduct, no matter how it impinges on the School's educational mission or how it violates the established qualifications for membership in this academic community.
>
> The freedom to teach and to write according to the dictates of one's conscience is the cornerstone of any academic institution worthy of the name. A threat to use physical force to change the manner in which a faculty member conducts his classes, much less to compel discussion of a non-related matter, should offend all — students and faculty alike — who value the academic

commitment. It is an affront to free scholars everywhere. And the assertion that this has not always been well understood within the Yale Law School community is unacceptable.[283]

Without a doubt, the Clay case, like the times themselves, proved especially hard on refugees. Calabresi had fled fascist Italy; Kessler and Joe Goldstein's wife and Yale Law School classmate, Sonja, Hitler's Germany. Just as Kessler had fought "the politicization of the universities in Nazi Germany," Anthony Kronman recalled, so, "in the 1960s, with equal courage, he opposed the demand for relevance and social engagement that threatened American universities from a different direction."[284] Bickel, whose uncle had lost hope for a position at Berlin University when the Nazis came to power,[285] explicitly likened the actions of campus radicals to the deeds of those bewitched by "fascist romance" and exhorted their professors to resist intimidation.[286]

While Pollak had gone too far for such disgruntled colleagues, he had not gone far enough for many students. Clay had "won," but only because the dean had stayed a sentence handed down by a body many students considered unjustly constituted. The sound and fury of the clash between the Student Negotiating Committee and the faculty the previous year had signified nothing. Though Clay had gotten off, it was a hollow victory. Watt recalled feeling "empty" after the trial and certain that graduation could not come quickly enough.[287]

Only May Day restored some measure of unity. With ten thousand people due to converge on New Haven for the Seale trial at the beginning of May 1970, the Law School community drew together. On April 21, after four to five thousand attended a mass meeting at Ingalls Rink, Yale College students voted to assist the thousands of protesters expected to descend on New Haven for May Day weekend and themselves to engage in a nonviolent "strike."[288] Two days later, their professors met. "God knows, the tension was high, because it was just the kind of issue on which other institutions like Cornell, Harvard, and so on had split wide open, not only between faculty and administration, but within the faculty," Brewster recalled.[289] He, the African American faculty, and student activists carried the day.[290] While a crowd of undergraduates roared outside, and in an atmosphere that reminded one professor of 1789,[291] the faculty voted overwhelmingly in support of a resolution introduced by African American professors to "modify . . . the normal expectations of the University." There would be a temporary change in the regular academic schedule, so as to give "all those concerned and interested a chance to discuss the issues and ramifications of the issues and to plan what direction we should take in this crisis." Classes would still meet, but professors and students could address the Panther trials and related issues. That limited the possibility that professors would create crises by turning down the requests of students like Eric Clay to discuss the situation in the community. Further, Yale would open its campus to the protesters.[292]

And Brewster made his famous declaration: "I personally want to say that I am appalled and ashamed that things should have come to such a pass that I am skeptical of the ability of black revolutionaries to achieve a fair trial anywhere in the United States." That sparked Richard Nixon's vice president to urge Yale alumni to demand that a "more mature and responsible person" head the institution.[293] But notwithstanding Spiro Agnew's rage, preparation for the strike continued. "The only major university that had not yet experienced a serious disruption, Yale was now expected to be at the center of the worst such storm in history."[294]

Following Brewster's lead, and with the faculty's support, the university had pledged to aid students and outside protesters alike. Thus what was happening, as the *Washington Post* editorialized, did not really constitute a strike against Yale. "Rather, it is a sort of joint testimony to Yale's sense of responsibility toward the black community, a joint response to a feeling of crisis aroused by the Black Panther trial in New Haven." What distinguished campus unrest in New Haven from upheavals elsewhere was "that university administration, the faculty and most of the student body are firmly united. There is an exhilarating, perhaps unique, solidarity on the Yale campus today." To the *Post*, it was obvious that Brewster deserved the credit for transforming "seeming division and discord" into unity and purpose. "Of course, he owes an incalculable debt to Vice President Spiro Agnew. . . . He [Brewster] said yesterday that he has never been so proud of Yale; it is patent that Yale has never been so proud of a president."[295]

Over at the Law School, it was not so patent. Opinion there about the trial ran a gamut. At the first large meeting on the subject, a second-year law student had proposed, apparently seriously,[296] that one hundred members of the Yale community make a suicide pact. Each day, one of them, chosen by lot, would kill himself in an orgy of self-destruction that would continue until Seale and the other Panthers on trial were freed and would enable participants "[t]o die like a Panther, to die like a man."[297] Claiming that the Law School's response to the trial would show the world "whether Yale Law School possessed concerned and active civil-libertarians, or know-nothings who will turn their backs to the use of courts for genocide," BLSU member and Yale Law Student Association representative John Doggett had called on every member of the faculty to work to guarantee the Panthers a fair trial, lest New Haven and the Law School "burn as black people vent their fury on the system you represent."[298] During the second half of April, some white and black students had done research for the Panthers' defense counsel,[299] while others joined some professors in educating the nonlawyer public about the trial.[300] Pollak, who publicly compared Agnew to Joe McCarthy, was on Brewster's side.[301]

But Bickel, who was coming to regret his vote in support of the strike, was wavering.[302] With Charles Black, and several others inside and outside the Law School, Bickel privately asked Yale's president what he had been thinking when he made his declaration about black revolutionaries: "We are aware of no evidence that the responsible legal and judicial officers of the state of Connecticut are unable or unwilling to see to it that the defendants receive a fair trial."[303] Behind the statement was a question. Was this "official welcome"[304] of protesters evidence of the "institutional neutrality" to which Brewster had pledged allegiance?

A few were bolder than Bickel. What he said privately as the Yale community waited for thousands to converge on the New Haven green and publicly afterward in *The New Republic,* dean-designate Abe Goldstein was declaring now. As the work week leading up to May Day weekend began, Goldstein, an expert in criminal procedure, announced that he could "see no evidence yet that the New Haven Panthers cannot get a fair trial here."[305]

At 1:04 the next morning, law student Paul Gewirtz telephoned the Yale University Police Department to report that he and others smelled smoke in the basement.[306] Rushing to Sterling Law building, Yale Police found a fire "of suspicious origin" in the International Law Library. Some five hundred books had been destroyed and some structural damage sustained. The police sergeant on the scene reported that law students "did a very commendable job in forming a bucket brigade to salvage as much as they could" and that "some girls also took part."[307]

Pollak rushed to the scene. Indeed, the fire reminded students that the dean was someone of "gentleness and wit," who "preserved a sense of community in the law school when confrontation was the prevailing mold."[308] One student subsequently recalled:

> Around 2 a.m., after the fire was extinguished and a brigade of students had removed the smoldering books, a mass meeting, chaired by Dean Pollak, began in Room 115. Several suggestions were offered about ways to prevent future incidents. Finally, at 3 a.m., one of the more lawyerly among us proposed that we obtain a T.R.O. to stop an onslaught of what he called "a bunch of crazies" who were presumably planning to disrupt the law school the next morning. Lou Pollak paused a moment before giving his answer. "It may be a bit late in the day to tell you this," he said, "but I have absolutely no idea how to get a T.R.O."[309]

Pollak himself later characterized the fire as the event that had made his deanship worthwhile. He thought it had revealed students' commitment to the institution, and the library as its heart.[310] "The one gratifying aspect of all this," he said at the time, "is the marvelous way in which our students sensed the insult to the School and the profession—more than a hundred of them gathered at 2 a.m. to start cleaning up the stacks and maintaining a security guard from then forward."[311] The dean was exultant "to discover that our students were as deeply shocked as we elderly Faculty members were at the mere possibility that anybody could be sick enough (either as a matter of ideological motivation or otherwise) to burn books."[312]

Abe Goldstein believed that the fire had returned law students to reality. "It was not a major fire, but it was dramatic because there were these burned books, water-soaked lying on High Street," he recalled. "Many of us at the time felt that event more than anything else suddenly tamed the order of the firebrands, tamed the order of our homegrown student radicals. They calmed down because it looked like things might be getting out of hand."[313]

Goldstein's appointment as dean was also obviously intended to tame the "homegrown student radicals." The son of a pushcart peddler, he had grown up in New York's Lower East Side and Brooklyn. "It never occurred to me that I would ever get here," Goldstein reflected later, private universities such as Yale being "the stuff of dreams and storybooks."[314] But World War II intervened after his graduation from City College of New York. After serving in the Army as a demolitions man, a military policeman, and military counterintelligence agent, Goldstein enrolled in Yale Law School and found "what seemed to me a new meritocracy which was emerging as a result of the GI Bill." He was articles editor of the *Yale Law Journal* and the first clerk of David Bazelon, "who had a reputation as a radical judge of that period,"[315] and who played a pivotal role in reshaping the insanity defense.[316] Then, as a Washington lawyer during the McCarthy era, Goldstein had established his civil liberties credentials when he defended Val Lorwin in an important challenge to the government's loyalty program. A distinguished scholar of criminal law and procedure, who had recently declined a professorship at Harvard because at Yale "the existing ties of loyalty and friendship are too strong to be set aside,"[317] Goldstein described himself as "a specimen Yale" in integrating law with the social sciences.[318] Though an innovative creator of educational policy, he personified toughness. He had not been "in the group that wanted to give the students everything they ask for whenever they ask for it," Goldstein told the *New York Times*, which announced the appointment of this "immigrant's son" in a front-page article that called attention to the school's recent unrest and highlighted the disappointment over Goldstein's appointment among "white radicals and blacks [who believed] that he was not sympathetic to their goals."[319]

Now, despite the fact that the Law School seemed to be coming together, Pollak and Goldstein decided to cancel the upcoming alumni weekend anyway.[320] As the weekend approached, Professor Ralph Winter informed a reporter that "if ten percent of the rumors spreading around here are true, there will be no New Haven on Monday."[321] A number of law professors, who lived close to campus and had already been worrying about whether their homeowner's policy covered riot damage,[322] rushed to buy fire extinguishers.[323] Bickel removed his papers from his office and had them microfilmed.[324] "We thought this was Armageddon," Lefcoe recalled.[325]

Against the background of the approaching May Day, then, the Law School fire represented unity and chaos. Because it had been detected early, the fire had done relatively little damage. Still, as Pollak said at the time, "the symbolism bulked large."[326] A front-page *New York Times* story about the incident included a photo of Bork pondering the books left outside the Law School to dry. "Fire at Yale," the caption read. "Burned books cover the sidewalk outside the Law School Library, . . . where an arsonist set fire to the basement, destroying property worth $2,500."[327]

In fact, police had reported the cause of fire "undetermined,"[328] and two months later, Pollak still awaited the official verdict on whether the blaze had been deliberately set.[329] Officials subsequently told him the fire had been accidental, and he believed them. As the dean knew, the library basement had been in such disarray that fire easily could have broken out there.[330]

Nevertheless, the fire went down in collective memory as a case of arson. When Hillary Clinton spoke at Yale's Class Day some thirty years after the event, she joked about "a cottage industry of folks" claiming she had set it. "But actually I joined the bucket brigade of students to save the books and it was an odd feeling to be in one of the greatest institutions in our country saving books from people who were so frustrated and so angry and so outraged that they . . . [followed] the traditions of fascists and others of oppressive political beliefs and burned books."[331] When Bork wrote his memoirs, he maintained that arson had hit the library; compared students to Nazis and Fascists; and deplored the surrender of Yale and other elite universities.[332] That was the view Bickel, as a refugee from World War II Europe, held too. Writing in *The New Republic,* he described the fire as "obviously set."[333]

To those such as Bickel, who viewed the events at Yale during the late sixties as assaults on their life's project, May Day weekend must nevertheless have seemed anticlimactic. It proved relatively tranquil, with law students working to help the protesters; putting out another fire in the Moot Court room; and guarding the Law School. But there was no time to celebrate. Nixon's April 30 announcement of the American invasion of Cambodia caught everyone by surprise. On Monday, May 4, just as Yale was celebrating the successful completion of the weekend with "a surfeit of self-congratulation,"[334] and announcing the resumption of "normal expectations,"[335] the National Guard killed four students at Kent State. The antiwar movement that had reemerged with the Moratorium against the war the previous fall gathered great, renewed force.

Thus began yet another crisis of the "1960s" at Yale Law School. Graduate students, law and medical students who had largely surrendered May Day to Yale College now moved out front.[336] Law students gathered Monday night, intending to be at the forefront of the effort to launch a nationwide student strike to protest the Cambodian invasion. One reported that Senator Fulbright "urged student moderation in order to forestall a backlash against Senate doves." Those who wanted no part of "student political gurus" assailed him. "No one here knows how the country feels, so let's act according to our own consciences for once," another replied.[337] The motion to strike carried by a vote of 239–9–12.[338] Only two students voted against the next motion, which urged the faculty to give them credit for their courses without requiring them to sit for final examinations.[339]

If students lacked interest in "political gurus," they did nevertheless possess a grandiose faith in their own ability to shape politics through rational discourse and moderation. Declaring that they would "educate the public and actively support the campaigns of progressive candidates for national office," they displayed "great concern . . . for the effect on public opinion of the action taken at the nation's leading law school." With most students certain that their action would make the newspapers' front pages, they told a *New York Times* reporter in attendance to "get the story right."[340]

Just as the *Times* gave Yale law students no coverage, so the faculty paid them little heed. At another meeting on the morning of May 5, students turned to proposals to modify the academic calendar that fall in order to provide time for political involvement prior to the midterm elections. Princeton had adopted a plan to postpone the beginning of school until after the November elections, which Brewster was promoting,[341] and two younger Yale professors, Larry Simon and Richard Abel, thought the law school should follow suit.[342] To the disgust of one of its organizers, "much of the initial emotional power" of the meeting was lost in debate over the professors' proposal, which went nowhere and which they regarded as unimportant anyway.[343]

At 3:30 that afternoon, the faculty met to consider students' motions about the spring 1970 calendar. The student representative, who himself had been one of the lone voices against the movement for credit without final examinations, had predicted that "many, probably most, faculty members will be opposed. And thus, once again, the Law School 'community' will fall to bickering-bickering between student and teachers about matters which should be secondary to a unified faculty-student effort to turn this country around."344 He was right.

At the beginning of the meeting, Pollak asked student representatives to present their proposals. One informed the professors there were three alternatives: "(1) continue as scheduled; (2) take incomplete and make up later; (3) certify substantial completion of work in course activities and get a Satisfactory." The students, of course, preferred the third possibility, to which Charles Black immediately objected. At this point, Abe Goldstein introduced a motion, on which he and Pollak had clearly collaborated, aimed at mitigating "the effect upon students of the extraordinary confusion and dislocation of events of recent weeks in New Haven and elsewhere." In courses and seminars where it proved "reasonable" for a professor to give the student a grade or credit "on the basis of written work already submitted or, in [first-year] small groups where it is possible fairly to do so on the basis of already-existing work of those groups," no final examination or paper would be required. To this extent, the faculty would work with the students. "In all other offerings, while examination or paper will be required, instructors are urged to be as flexible as reasonably possible in working out delays in examination or paper requirements or modification in examination arrangements in response to individual requests." In any event, students should normally complete alternative arrangements by mid-September. "Third year students may arrange to have the award of their degrees deferred to enable them to delay completion of degree requirements."345

The reaction varied. While concurring, Bickel wanted the unusual nature of the circumstances stressed. Student representative Ben Stein urged the faculty to issue a statement "supporting the students." Meanwhile, Tom Emerson maintained that "[w]e're sticking too closely to normal academic procedures. [Nixon's Cambodia "incursion"] [s]hould be treated as a national emergency and [the law school faculty should] be willing to waive the rules." After much discussion, Emerson moved to amend Goldstein's motion, so that third-year students, at least, could have all their work graded on a credit-fail basis. His amendment was defeated. With Pollak emphasizing that Goldstein's motion reflected university policy anyway, it then carried, with only two professors in opposition.346

The faculty's motivation was unclear.347 Possibly professors worried that they would jeopardize third-years' eligibility for the New York Bar Examination if they agreed to students' credit-without-examination proposal. A week after the faculty meeting, the New York Court of Appeals issued an order declaring that no graduate could take the bar examination "unless he or she had taken and passed an authentic examination in each of his courses of study in accordance with the previous practice of the school." Only when law schools begged the court to reconsider did the court soften just a bit and agree to permit take-home examinations, even if the school had not previously administered them.[348]

So, as Goldstein said, unlike many schools, Yale refused to call off finals. "We were liberal as we often had been in letting people take them at different times, but we never let our students have the experience which some others had, which was to be denied admission to the New York Bar because they had been given passes in courses in which they were not examined. . . . We spared them that travail by standing fast against their pressures."[349] Professors may also have reasoned that since the fire, they had regained the upper hand in their struggle with the students and should not yield anew. Whatever moved them, the students read the resolution as a commitment by the faculty to "business as usual."[350]

By the morning after the faculty meeting, almost all students had returned to class. The strike had collapsed. Bitterly, the graduating Student Association president railed against "the hypocrisy of fellow students and faculty." According to him: "The failure of Yale Law Students to honor the goals they set for themselves only two short days ago signals a further decline in the prestige of their school and may be symptomatic of the gradual disappearance of the traditionally reformist role of American students in this nation's political system."[351]

Of course, to others, the episode symbolized students' return to the "reformist politics" of the mid-1960s from the politics their professors labeled "far left,"[352] and augured the ascendance of "student political gurus," such as Bill Clinton, who would enter the law school that fall. Yale law students still worked against the war. During the last week of classes in May, some went to Washington to lobby their representatives about it,[353] on occasion joining forces with Bickel.[354] An impressed Mary McGrory reported, "Among the thousands of students learning to lobby for peace on Capitol Hill, the Yale Law Students Lobby Group has moved out front." Up to forty students at a time took to the halls of power in a "glossy" and "high-powered operation," which, their leader freely admitted, involved "shameless . . . name-dropping." Predictably, "Senators who can't find time for Franklin and Marshall make time for Yale, when they hear that Burke Marshall, Cyrus Vance, Paul Warnke, or

Edward Burling, former Republican finance chairman and senior partner of Covington and Burling, will be in the group." Politicians "respectfully" pored over the Yale students' brief, "complete with quotations about Congressional powers in foreign policy going back to Thomas Jefferson."[355]

And, Pollak informed the alumni, there was more good news to report about the reading and final examination periods. The crisis atmosphere had "substantially diminished." Further, despite the faculty's "flexibility" about examination and term paper deadlines, "most students have in fact taken examinations and submitted papers in accordance with the prevailing schedule; and all students appear to understand and appreciate the School's insistence that regular academic standards are to be observed."[356]

Summing up his deanship, Pollak pointed to the increased enrollment of women and minorities and called attention to the development of student participation in faculty governance. It had sometimes seemed that "disputation between students and faculty was the dominant motif," he acknowledged, and "vast quantities of decibels, petitions, graffiti, statements of quasi-nonnegotiable demands, and elaborately orchestrated moral posturings were expended on a bewildering array of issues: *e.g.*, the grading system; the admissions system; disciplinary procedures; student participation in faculty decision-making; and faculty responsibility for (a) police brutality and (b) the Vietnam War." But once again, he focused on progress by term's end, insisting that by May Day, "the great majority of our law students" had demonstrated "their determination to master the law and use it as an instrument to advance the values of the democratic order."[357]

The events of spring 1970 ended the intense student turmoil at Yale.[358] And at the Law School, one group of visitors Brewster sent to report on its condition reported, calm abruptly descended. "Its crisis of confidence, its period of hesitation about basic values, appear to be passing."[359]

Yale's new dean agreed that "faculty and staff morale is recovered from the troubles of 1969–70 and students are more serious than they had been for many years.[360] He thought, Goldstein told the graduating class in 1971, that students might have learned that liberals had been right all along; radicals, wrong; and what he allegedly called "the dark years" or "the dark ages" had ended.[361] It had turned out, Goldstein said, that the university was "not a microcosm of the larger society and its problems." Bringing the university to heel did not guarantee that the rest of society would fall into line, he told the students. Reminding them that he and his colleagues shared many of their goals, he asked them to consider "how plain it has been that university people are opposed to the war and want to cut it short; or that faculty and students in overwhelming numbers want more personal freedom, more experimentation in life style and politics, more radical reform of many aspects of our lives; . . . *and* how deeply resistant — politically and emotionally — the larger society had been to those preferences." He believed "even activist students" now possessed "a soberer sense of where the problems are." But during the time it had taken the young to learn this lesson, he told them, they had alienated many professors. "In the university, more than elsewhere," Goldstein said, "we had the seeming collision of cultures, the suspicions of foot-dragging, the impugning of motives."[362]

Others interpreted history differently. To some students, the "sixties" proved that the university was indeed a microcosm of society. The problem had been that "sixties liberalism" could not remedy the problems of either society or the university and had not opened the door wide enough to allow in those with better solutions. As one activist later stressed, even when the young did not achieve their specific goals, the issue had never been the issue. Their movement did not just aim at achieving individual objectives, such as grade reform, but was "always 'about' the deepest identities of the participants . . . who . . . stoke[d] it."[363]

That was why Yale Law School graduates of 1970, 1971, and 1972 continued — ironically, proudly, and nostalgically — to trumpet their association with the "Dark Ages" or "Dark Years" long after some of them had become corporate lawyers.[364] The disagreement about whether the activists had wasted their time underscored another "truth" too: The "sixties" and Yale's "Dark Ages" were to be marked off as contested terrain for years to come. They had not ended, either.

After the Fire

In the early 1970s, the tenured professors who constituted the school's Governing Board declined to promote or advance six junior faculty members who had been at Yale during the "Dark Ages." In 1970, the Governing Board decided against making assistant professor John Griffiths an associate professor without tenure. It denied tenure to Robert Hudec and David Trubek in 1972. It declined to promote Larry Simon in late 1973. Soon afterwards, the Appointments Committee decided against bringing the case of associate professor Richard Abel before the Governing Board for a tenure vote. The last to go was Lee Albert in 1974.

Had Yale's growing deficit affected the Law School, as it did other parts of the university, these decisions might be explained on financial grounds. Yet though the university's budgetary problems did leave a scar, the Law School was not involved in Yale's personnel reduction program.[365] "We have, in fact, 'made out' better than all of Yale," Dean Goldstein acknowledged.[366]

To him and others, there was nothing unusual about any of the decisions with respect to the six junior faculty members denied promotion in the early 1970s.[367] "I don't think we were acting on political grounds," Goldstein maintained.[368] Those in his interpretive camp can point to the fact that not all the professors dismissed identified with the left. Further, not all junior faculty members were denied tenure during this period. John Ely, Arthur Leff, and Michael Reisman were promoted from within between the end of 1970 and 1972.[369]

Those who see nothing odd about the failure to advance the other six junior faculty members reason further that many of "Gene's boys," who voted on tenure, had first arrived at Yale in the 1950s after another failed promotion and advancement — that of Vern Countryman to professor and David Haber to associate professor.[370] Senior professors, the argument goes, would therefore not have considered tenure automatic. Tenure had not been assured for them, though in a highly unusual step, the Governing Board had promoted eleven of "Gene's Boys" — including Bickel, the Goldsteins, and Harry Wellington — in one swoop.[371]

And as long as senior faculty members helped those they decided against keeping to find good jobs elsewhere, they believed it appropriate to stick to the same "absolute standard" of scholarly excellence they maintained had been applied to evaluating themselves.[372] Eugene Rostow explained later that unlike Harvard, which usually promoted to tenure automatically after three years, Yale required applicants to write *something* to be tenured. "We usually appoint to the junior ranks for a period of five, six or even seven years, and then promote if we are satisfied that the candidate's published scholarly work gives serious ground for believing that he has promise of 'scholarly distinction.' This is supposed to be, and I think really is the sole criterion for appointment to tenured rank at Yale."[373]

Rostow was responding to a chart showing that everyone considered for promotions during his administration and during most of Pollak's received them, with the pattern then changing dramatically under Goldstein. Some junior faculty members during the 1950s and 1960s had taken the hint and departed before their promotions could be considered, he explained. And during the year before he became dean, Rostow added, "we had a promotion controversy about two . . . professors which stirred the dovecotes from here to there."[374]

Those who disagreed with Rostow and Goldstein about Yale's reasons for letting the six go during the early 1970s maintained that the early 1970s witnessed the second "slaughter of the innocents" at Yale.[375] They saw the dismissals as the successor to the first slaughter, that of Countryman and Haber, which they blamed on Countryman and Haber's left-leaning politics during the McCarthyite 1950s.[376] To such individuals, the faculty's resolution of the six cases between 1970 and 1974 reflected an unfair change in the rules and standards.

Whatever the interpretation, there was something peculiar about the six decisions. They contradicted expectations. With characteristically self-deprecating wit, Pollak explained that the negative vote against David Haber in the 1950s had "[a]pparently" rested on the judgment that he had not yet written enough to justify advancement. "But I have been told by one of my most senior and respected colleagues that if Dave had been judged by the standards of productivity which just a few years later were applied to my faculty generation, Dave would unquestionably have been promoted. Thus have we little men come into our own."[377]

Of course, "high quality" was a fuzzy and contingent term. Even so, young law professors hired — particularly those who looked to history and saw that all those of Rostow's recruits considered for tenure by the Governing Board had received it, including some who published very little before and after their promotions — would have anticipated tenure: Some "little men" had indeed come into their own. (As Rostow said, some junior faculty members obviously had taken a hint and departed before the Board had to vote on their promotions.[378]) "If we could not hold out the hope of permanency, we simply could not hope to draw top-flight young lawyers into law teaching," Pollak stressed.[379]

So why did the hope of permanency shrink? During Pollak's deanship, senior faculty members had worried about standards. Were they willing the grades battle of the 1960s onto the professorial front in the 1970s? In the grades battle, they had fought against pass-fail after the first semester. Did they transform the tenure evaluation system from "pass-fail," in which virtually everyone passed, to one in which only "honors" recipients won tenure? And, if so, what factors entered into their decision to award or withhold an "honors?" Was the only criterion the "promise of scholarly distinction," and was it applied uniformly?

Did the decisions between 1970 and 1974 to deny permanent positions to Griffiths, Hudec, Trubek, Simon, Abel, and Albert constitute a "purge"?[380] Not in the conventional political sense:· None had radical politics. Nor is there evidence of a conspiracy to fire the six. Can we say, nevertheless, that the dismissals of all at once constitute more than mere coincidence? Griffiths maintained that what "happened was a *structural firing* by an *institution* of a whole group of people, not just some isolated instances that happen to add up to a group."[381]

Did the failed promotions have something to do with the "Dark Ages"? Did tenured professors get rid of their younger colleagues because they perceived their juniors as more tolerant of the "barbarians at the gate" during the late 1960s?[382] Did tenured professors act because they could not tolerate having had the young (and most of those let go were not significantly older than the students) witness the faculty's anxiety as it had struggled to confront the students of the 1960s? Did senior professors make their juniors surrogates for the students, "the barbarians," of the 1960s? Charles Reich thought so: "They were angry, they were intimidated, they were threatened," he said of his Governing Board colleagues in the aftermath of the 1960s. In his view, the experience of warring with the students "skewed their judgment," rendering them unable to make the distinctions between candidates they would have made otherwise.[383] David Trubek added that though he and the others let go supported the Dark Age students to various degrees, most seemed more sympathetic than the tenured professors, many of whom proved "incredibly hostile towards the students." In his view, he and his peers were "caught in a tremendous culture clash" between old and young. Unable to "fire the students," he theorized, senior faculty members fired their juniors.[384] That was also the opinion of Richard Abel, who saw the outcomes as "calculated to appease the faction of the faculty who felt that 1960s attitudes and styles were threatening the school's quality."[385]

Some of the faculty's actions do seem odd. Abel, for one example, had produced so much work that as his vote approached, the Governing Board was warned that because Abel's "writings are quite extensive, an early start in reading is advisable."[386] It was outside the doctrinal mainstream and in the emerging field of Law and Society scholarship. The faculty had hired him because it wanted such work.[387] Abel had also consistently and strongly sided with the students during the "Dark Ages," as, for example, when he supported their resolution in favor of the moratorium.[388] He had long hair and a beard. Some members of the Governing Board remembered that Goldstein, as one put it, had taken a "scunner," or dislike, to him.[389] Nor did Abel have much to do with his colleagues. He did not play the game the Yale way. He wanted to help his wife with childcare, and, he said, "I felt a profound sense of alienation from the senior faculty. I didn't dress like them (and didn't want to), couldn't entertain like them."[390] Abel's case did not even make it out of committee. No Governing Board vote was ever taken.[391]

On the other hand, of the five considered for tenure, the faculty found Larry Simon's case closer. Simon had greatly impressed his professors during his days as a Yale law student.[392] Arriving back at Yale Law School to teach in 1968 after clerkships with Edward Weinfeld and Earl Warren, he had plunged into matters involving race and education. Though he had little involvement in the faculty-student conflict, he had much to do with bolstering the Law School's reputation with African American and white student activists and the black community of New Haven. He served on a task force that conducted hearings around New Haven and developed a plan for ensuring community control of the schools. He became director of Yale's Summer High School, an Upward Bound program designed to give underprivileged students of color an intensive summer precollegiate experience. Simon, who had himself traveled round the country to hand-select its 120-odd students, considered Summer High "probably the best thing I've ever done" and pointed with pride to the roster of distinguished instructors that included one future president of Yale, A. Bartlett Giamatti. But, like participating in hearings on public education, running Summer High took time. His senior colleagues encouraged him to take on such obligations. "Though my stance on race was pretty strong, I wasn't picketing," he stressed. "I was helping the law school with what I did."[393]

Simon was a popular teacher,[394] and his "tenure article," focusing on which legally permissible systems of school financing were politically viable, fell squarely within the liberal realist tradition.[395] Many thought it excellent, but it was not large in size, and it did not appear until the eleventh hour. Some also remember that Simon had said he did not intend to publish anything again.[396] Others, Simon included, deny that he — or anyone else who sought a promotion, for that matter — would have said anything so stupid.[397] In fact, apparently all Simon had done was say that he wanted to turn from school finance to urban law.[398] But whatever his plans, Simon had given the faculty relatively little published work. His case therefore seems as if it should have been among the easiest to turn down. Yet oddly, it turned out to be the hardest. Simon almost made it: He fell one vote short of the two-thirds majority he needed for promotion.[399] His decision was characterized as a postponement,[400] and Goldstein offered him a two-year contract. But given his hesitation about publishing what he had written, Simon wondered whether he could satisfy his colleagues in two years, particularly after Bickel told him that although the school finance article was quite good as far as it went, Simon must now produce "big-think" constitutional law work. When he received an excellent offer from USC, Simon took it.[401]

What of the failure to promote John Griffiths to associate professor? Generally, the candidate needed only be able to fog a mirror to become an associate professor at Yale Law School — and Griffiths had already done far more than that. The one instance during the 1960s when some *hesitated* to promote an individual from assistant to associate professor had occasioned a storm of controversy.[402] Like Simon, Griffiths had made connections with student activists. Among other things, he developed a Selective Service seminar, possibly the first such course to be taught in any American law school,[403] that helped create a new field of law.[404] Griffiths also wrote a widely distributed 1968 pamphlet on the draft law.[405] He and a student made a foray into Law and Society, which Griffiths considered the only "source of intellectual excitement" at Yale when he taught there,[406] empirically demonstrating that the draft protesters they had urged to keep their mouths shut when the FBI interrogated them routinely waived their right to counsel and spilled their guts.[407] Griffiths believed that his colleagues, many of whom shared his opposition to the war, did not mind his work with students and may even have appreciated it.[408] But with Abel, Griffiths had supported the moratorium, [409] and he also recalled making it clear that he considered Eugene Rostow a war criminal.[410] The remainder of the voluminous Griffiths corpus included two essays,[411] one quite critical,[412] condemning contemporary American liberal ideology and the work of Stanford's Herbert Packer in particular — a person to whom some of "Gene's boys" were close and to whom the faculty had extended a tenured offer some years earlier.[413] To make matters worse for Griffiths, Packer had recently suffered a massive stroke, which he blamed on the demands of student radicals when he was vice provost of Stanford.[414] Packer had made Bickel, Abe Goldstein, and others among his Yale friends aware that he found Griffiths' tone "belligerently bludgeoning and personal."[415] Though some remembered him as experiencing problems with his teaching, it stretches credibility to think that Griffiths was having so much trouble as to warrant denial of an associate professorship, especially because, as Rostow had said, teaching was secondary, and the record indicates that some students found Griffiths excellent in the classroom.[416] Did the faculty's action reflect its dislike for Griffiths, rather than its opinion of his scholarship?

The cases point up the difficulty of determining exactly what the faculty's "standards" for promotion were at the time. Why did the faculty consider Abel's case so hopeless that a vote seemed fruitless? Why did Griffiths fail to receive a routine advancement? Why did Simon come the closest to receiving tenure? Did "Gene's boys" perceive him and his work as being most like them and theirs? Or did they believe they had made an implicit promise to him? Simon thought they had. "I felt they broke the deal," he recalled. As he saw it, everyone knew his *Journal* article was very good, and "I was doing all this stuff" at his colleagues' urging. Surely they understood that he had less time to publish.[417] Here, too, it seems, the 1960s may have cast a long shadow. Guido

Calabresi thought so. As he saw it, the times "scarred" some "extraordinarily promising" young academics and prevented them from teaching or writing to their fullest potential. "The fact was that it was an extremely hard time for anyone to accomplish anything."[418]

Whatever the reason for the decisions, they created a hole. In letting go Griffiths, Trubek, and Abel, representatives of the Law and Society movement, itself an outgrowth of the 1960s, the faculty indicated that it would not proceed in one direction as it regrouped. By the 1980s, Stanton Wheeler was the chief remaining professor identified with Law and Society. Yale's tenured faculty had turned its back on sociology.

The story proved similar with Critical Legal Studies. With Law and Economics, Critical Legal Studies proved one of the two most significant jurisprudential developments of the second half of the seventies through the mid-1980s.[419] But Yale showed little enthusiasm for CLS. In addition to viewing Critical Legal Studies as warmed-over legal realism, Yale professors probably viewed CLS as an outgrowth of the "Dark Ages."

And why not? To be sure, Critical Legal Studies could not have happened without Harvard. Duncan Kennedy, Morton Horwitz, and Roberto Unger were professors there by 1977; their students, foot soldiers in the movement. Still, the sixties and New Haven had provided the deeper seed ground for Critical Legal Studies. Duncan Kennedy characterized critical legal scholars as "a rag-tag band of leftover '60s people and young people with nostalgia for the great events [of the 1960s]."[420] Many had met at Yale. Consider the composition of the first CLS organizing committee in 1976. Of the nine members—Abel, Trubek, Duncan Kennedy, Rand Rosenblatt, Mark Tushnet, Roberto Unger, Thomas Heller, Morton Horwitz, and Stewart Macaulay—seven possessed strong ties to the Yale of the sixties. Kennedy, Rosenblatt, and Tushnet were members of the class of 1970 or 1971; Abel and Trubek had taught at Yale, and Trubek had directed the Program in Law and Modernization; Unger had a connection with the Law and Modernization Program and was offered a visit at Yale while Trubek was still there;[421] and after graduating from Yale in 1968, Heller had been a fellow in the program.[422]

Yale figured in the movement's genesis in another way. Even more ostentatiously than Law and Society, Critical Legal Studies deliberately rooted itself in what law professors considered the most important jurisprudential movement in recent history, the legal realism that had briefly held sway in the late 1920s and 1930s. CLS was "best understood as an extension and development of American legal realism," Duncan Kennedy contended.[423]

Yale, which celebrated its association with realism, became well known for its alleged intolerance to Critical Legal Studies. Most thought Yale had no use for the very movement to which both its realists and its "Dark Ages" had given birth. Yale was not alone, of course: Stanford was the only elite law school other than Harvard at which Critical Legal Scholars established a significant presence. Given its history, though, the perception Yale was antagonistic to CLS still caused talk.[424]

Yet Duncan Kennedy, who was to become the star of CLS, was offered an assistant professorship at Yale after his graduation. That might suggest that Yale wanted a radical presence. But faculty members had to invite Kennedy to join them. He had compiled an extraordinary record, and to have refused him an offer would have proven Yale cared about politics, in addition to quality of mind.[425] So Kennedy was courted—though, unusually, one quarter of the faculty voted against his appointment.[426] As Kennedy remembers it, he turned Yale down because he felt that the influence flowed from Harvard and that if he could create a haven for left legal scholarship in Cambridge, the center of "standpattism" and legal process thought, one could exist anywhere.[427]

Other Critical Legal Scholars or allies also received offers from Yale in the late 1970s and early 1980s. Yale Law School graduate Martha Minow was offered an assistant professorship in 1978.[428] Like Kennedy, she turned down the offer to go to Harvard, where she became a "CLS fellow-traveler."[429] But at the time of her Yale offer, she would have seemed a conventional liberal,[430] and as one of her teachers said in promoting her as a "superb" potential dean of another law school, she always occupied a special place in Critical Legal Studies: "Though associated with the 'left' at Harvard (everybody there has to be associated with one side or the other), [she] has always tried to pull the place together and is very well respected by young people who are associated with the opposite side."[431] William Fisher, a Harvard J.D./Ph.D. and another CLS ally, opted to stay where he was.[432] So did another CLS fellow-traveler, Paul Brest, who turned down Yale's offer of a full professorship in 1982 to remain at Stanford.[433] Brest's colleague, Robert Gordon, whom Yale began pursuing in the early 1980s at a time when he was still relatively foul-tempered about persecution of critical legal scholars, decided to stay put for the moment too.[434] Is it fair to blame Yale for hostility to CLS when so many individuals sympathetic to the movement proved immune to the school's blandishments?[435]

Taken together, the offers do suggest that Yale may have proven somewhat more hospitable to Critical Legal Studies than it has received credit for being. But that is not saying much. One story that circulated had Dean Harry Wellington protesting that none of his faculty had been invited to the first Conference on Critical Legal Studies, then retreating in satisfaction when the reply came that his professors had not been excluded because they were not smart enough, but because they were insufficiently progressive.[436]

How do we explain the unfriendliness of Yale to the very movement for which it is partially responsible? Begin with the message of Critical Legal Studies. It was at once too familiar and too threatening.

At the time Critical Legal Studies made its appearance in the late 1970s, Harvard was vulnerable. Its great legal scholars of the 1950s and 1960s were retiring. And in Harvard, critical legal scholars found the ideal foil. Their rebellion against its elitism and allegiance to process theory provided the movement both power and publicity. The CLS themes also proved arresting in Cambridge because Harvard had rejected legal realism during the 1930s and remained relatively untouched by it afterward.[437]

In contrast, when CLS scholars talked about indeterminacy, and declared that "[b]y its own criteria, legal reasoning cannot resolve questions in an 'objective' manner; nor can it explain how the legal system works or how judges decide cases,"[438] old Yale realists asked "so what?" Guido Calabresi overstated the case when he said of Arthur Corbin that "CLS would not have surprised or troubled *him* one bit (though he was politically quite conservative)."[439] In fact, Corbin deplored those realists he considered dangerous reformers.[440] But Calabresi was on the mark when he told Paul Carrington that there was no way Critical Legal Scholars could prove more nihilistic (if nihilistic they were, which I doubt),[441] than Grant Gilmore or Arthur Leff.[442] Some Critical Legal scholarship would have reminded Yale law professors of the work of, say, their own Wesley Sturges or Walter Wheeler Cook. The idea that CLS scholars asked new questions about the legal system, Calabresi contended to one of them, was "both wrong and ahistorical." He maintained that "those who disagree with CLS at the Harvard Law School have rather foolishly let CLS dominate the field of 'questioning fundamental assumptions' and that leads graduates of that marvelous school to believe that the egg Duncan [Kennedy] and others claim to have discovered had not been discovered many, many times before."[443]

On another occasion, Calabresi was more specific: "I have always thought that the reason CLS took hold at Harvard and not at Yale was the fact that, unlike Harvard, we all were/are so tied to the Realist tradition in New Haven. And unfortunate, because pejorative metaphor should be that those with Cow Pox don't get Small Pox."[444] Calabresi's tone, though more good-natured, resembled that of Dean Roscoe Pound of Harvard toward the realists in the 1930s. Why credit the youngsters with originality, rather than their parents?

Why fuss? Thus Calabresi and other prominent Yale law professors defended critical legal scholars against those who claimed they were nihilists who should depart the legal academy[445] — but did not hire them.

For the CLS message was also threatening. It was threatening because of its insistence that law is politics. It was threatening because by going beyond the realists, as CLS scholars most assuredly did, and focusing on the relative autonomy of law, CLS demonstrated that law obscured the value systems of all decision makers, rather than of individual judges, the realists' point of focus.[446] It was threatening because the CLS critique of rights underscored the peril of the rights-consciousness that the liberals' Warren Court made possible. It was threatening because CLS thrived on "trashing" legal texts.[447] The authorial voice of many CLS scholars during the movement's early years had to have reminded the Yale faculty of the very students who had made their lives difficult during the 1960s, such as Duncan Kennedy in "How the Yale Law School Fails."

And CLS was threatening because of the sense that it meant conflict: The Yale faculty steered clear of CLS, some have stressed,[448] out of fear CLS might turn Yale into the same battleground Harvard became. Other schools with CLS enclaves were not war zones, but as always, it was Harvard that mattered. Though she herself was not affiliated with the movement, the ghost of CLS loomed large during the controversy over Catharine MacKinnon's appointment at Yale. Professors told the press that its "political overtones" reminded them "of the very public war . . . over Critical Legal Studies at Harvard Law School."[449] Once again, we see the specter of the sixties. Having lived through one civil war, the Yale Law School faculty did not want another. For Yale, CLS represented the road not taken.

Coda: Triumph?

That was significant because Yale needed to rebuild. The gap left by the departures of the six untenured professors was made larger by a number of retirements.[450] There were other departures too. Bickel died prematurely; Pollak, Summers, Reich, and Ronald Dworkin left. When Harry Wellington took over the deanship from Abe Goldstein in 1975, he headed a depleted group. Wellington hired some thirty professors during the next ten years,[451] beginning the process of creating the contemporary school.

Under Wellington, Yale turned to tenured appointments, sometimes preceded by a visit, as the faculty became more cautious. Why would a junior person take a chance on Yale when he or she could go to Harvard or elsewhere and almost certainly be promoted?[452] Thus, with a few exceptions — Paul Gewirtz, for example, who told the press he had considered the "bloodbath stories" of the early 1970s very carefully before coming and that untenured candidates routinely asked about them[453] — the trend moved toward lateral hires.

And those brought in often had doctorates, as well as law degrees. With his enthusiasm for interdisciplinarity, Goldstein had brought in three individuals with Ph.D.s in their scholarly fields.[454] Under Wellington, this trend accelerated. Six lawyers with Ph.D.s in economics, history, or philosophy, or who were working toward Ph.D.s, joined the faculty.[455] The school now possessed a critical mass of J.D./Ph.D.s.

Yale could successfully woo those with doctorates because job prospects in humanities and social sciences were so grim, and those in law teaching so bright. Many who might have once opted to become humanists or social scientists chose to go where the positions were.[456] In the 1970s, business was booming for Yale, as it was for other law schools; 3,682 students applied to become members of Yale's class of 1981, of whom only 329 were accepted. Of the 175 registered in the first year class, thirty-eight held an M.A., and almost 10 percent held a Ph.D.[457]

And Yale wanted to hire those with doctorates because increasingly, as Wellington understood, law professors of the 1970s spoke in terms of what Arthur Leff called "law and."[458] Law and Economics had made interdisciplinary work respectable and fashionable. And so, of course, Yale wanted to lead the bandwagon. From the perspective of a law school determined to avoid conflict and be cutting edge, such developments may have made matters simple. Why hire CLS scholars when you could hire humanists and social scientists grateful just to have a job?

As professors reached out to other disciplines, they paid special attention to economics. The trend toward Law and Economics had been apparent since 1974, when Goldstein pointed to the "remarkable group of faculty interested in the area": Bruce Ackerman, Robert Bork, Ward Bowman, Guido Calabresi, Marvin Chirelstein, Alvin Klevorick, and Ralph Winter.[459] "There is no law school in the world which is doing more systematic work in law and economics than Yale," Wellington claimed.[460] That was an overstatement. Chicago did more, though Yale's approach to Law and Economics was more varied and often proved more progressive.

The Law School that was emerging, then, possessed a certain aura. The tenure denials had not just scared Yale off rookies. Nor had they simply soured it on sociology. They had also pushed it toward a politically liberal brand of Law and Economics that placed it in the center-liberal mainstream of the legal academy. And unlike Chicago, Yale did not put all its eggs in the basket of Law and Economics. To a lesser extent, it demonstrated interest in history and philosophy as well. This Yale was decidedly academic, training Ph.D.s and others to become law professors and policy wonks, and carrying the inter-disciplinarity of the 1930s to a new level. In the academic world, in fact, Yale was the interdisciplinarians' beachhead. "What we teach," Wellington proudly said, "is dictated primarily by the scholarly interests of the faculty. This approach to the curriculum is why Yale is what it is: the most theoretical and academically oriented law school in America."[461] Sometimes it made Wellington uneasy. As dean, he worried about "two culture" phenomenon, the growing divide between the trendy young interdisciplinarians and the bar. [462]

That was the least of the school's problems, if problem it was. Despite the fifteen appointments during Wellington's first term alone,[463] despite his insistence that this was the best group of young academics in teaching today *and* was as good as Rostow's group,[464] times were tough. Since the 1930s, Yale had played a proud number two to Harvard, always glorying in its past and its reputation as realist, small and the quirky alternative to Harvard — even when students wondered whether Yale merited it. By the time Guido Calabresi had replaced Wellington as dean in 1985, Bruce Ackerman, Robin Bork, and Marvin Chirelstein had left. Art Leff had died. Median salaries for full professors were lower than those for their counterparts at Harvard, Stanford, Columbia, NYU, and Penn.[465] The building was a disaster. The homeless slept underneath the stairs to the dorm basement and in the utility tunnels in the building's basement.[466] Yale had none of the loan forgiveness programs for public interest lawyers its competitors did. As it had since the 1930s, Woodbridge Hall treated the Law School as its cash cow, which gave alumni little incentive to make large contributions. And though Wellington proved an excellent fundraiser under the circumstances,[467] the 1970s was no time to solicit money. The *National Law Journal* sparked a flood of letters from concerned alumni when it published a front-page article in 1981 asking, "Has the Yale Law School Lost Its Fizz?" Rumors abounded of rejected offers, impending departures, and student dissatisfaction. "The place is falling apart," one departing graduate told a reporter.[468]

Yet Calabresi, who combined the charm of Hutchins with the doggedness of Clark and the ego of Rostow, was undaunted. On becoming dean he was quoted as claiming that "Yale is the only school going where someone has the chance to be serious about legal thought, but in a way that can still influence the world."[469] What was he saying about Harvard, a friend in Cambridge asked? Unembarrassed Calabresi insisted, "individuals aren't enough — size and faculty-student ratios matter, too — and I do think we have an advantage."[470] He was talking through his hat. As Stephen Yandle, his associate dean, said, Calabresi mounted a smoke and mirrors game to pretend there was no problem until there was no longer a problem.[471] In fact, the emperor's clothes had gotten ratty.

What was needed was money. Once Calabresi and Yandle had negotiated the school's financial independence from the university over the next three years, donations skyrocketed. Now anything — from improved loan forgiveness programs, to higher salaries, to Ackerman's return, to renovated buildings — was possible. Now Yale could embrace the culture of "yes."

The yes extended to the students. Calabresi domesticated the spirit of the sixties. As he took the helm, student activism was again sweeping universities, and a debate about diversity in the legal academy was underway at Harvard that made that law school still more contentious.[472] But unlike their predecessors and Harvard Law School administrators, the Calabresi administration *seemed* to revel in the demands for diversity. "I can't imagine anyone not being influenced by today," said Yandle of the law students' one-day 1989 strike to protest the scarcity of women and minorities on the faculty, which he characterized as a "smashing success."[473] Calabresi applauded "the reawakening of student activism" and "the rebirth of the teach-in" in his letter to the school's friends and alumni, while using the occasion to reinforce the image of the Law School as a community. "Passions ran high," he wrote of the strike, "but when, at the senior dinner, the graduating class gave awards to those who had done most for the School, lo and behold, one of the most dedicated and fire-eating strike leaders, and one of the strongest and most thoughtful opponents of the strike, were among those chosen by their classmates (and both got universal standing applause)."[474]

Encouraging "love for the school on the part of the students"[475] and using every instance that occurred to teach the need for amiable argument and small-l liberalism always seemed the dean's mission. When Yale's *Journal of Law and Liberation* invited Abdul Alim Muhammed, the national spokesman for the Nation of Islam, to speak on the drug war in the black community, Calabresi joined a picket line of two hundred to protest Muhammed's anti-Semitism and carried a placard reading, "Racism is garbage no matter who speaks it."[476] Characteristically, he made the speech an occasion for education. He issued one letter to the Law School community, "speaking as Dean . . . remind[ing] all of you of the rules of this School and this University that guarantee complete freedom of speech to all visitors invited by appropriate groups."[477] He distributed another "as a *member*" of the Law School community arguing that the invitation was "a terrible wrong," but concluding:

> And yet what can I say of those who would invite such a . . . [person] while decrying that person's bigotry? Can I say that they cannot be members of a community with me, that they cannot be my friends? No, I would denounce

what for me is their error — their lack of feeling and of sensitivity, their, admittedly unintended, support of bigotry — but still embrace them. And what can I say of those who would no longer deal with those who made such an invitation? Would I exclude them? No. Again I would attack what I view as their error — their concentration on their own justifiable pain, their lack of understanding of the terrible needs of others — and then embrace them. . . . I pray that all in this fragile but worthy place will try to understand what motivates those who hold, so deeply, views, so different, on this issue, in the hope that in time, the wounds that this event is causing on all sides may heal, and that even from these wounds we may all have learned something of value about the needs, weaknesses, and fundamental humanity of all our sisters and brothers in this School.[478]

And after Muhammed's visit had ended, the dean was on the scene to promote healing. "Consider whether clever questions or piercing rhetoric, now, do more good, than quiet talk with those who before they hurt you or were hurt by you were friends, or even just pleasant-seeming acquaintances," he advised the Law School community. "Ponder whether silence, a smile, and even a hug may not be more eloquent than the analytical and forensic skills you all have in such great abundance."[479] Among elite law school administrators who followed, only the "hyperbolic enthusiasm and salesmanship" of John Sexton, "the hugging dean," matched Calabresi's.[480]

Calabresi's focus on speakers' rights, his appearance of welcoming dissent, his lack of defensiveness, and his apparent delight in hearing criticism from students (whose notes to him, which he always answered, frequently closed by thanking him for being the sort of dean to whom they could vent), alumni, and outsiders — whether they be complaints that Yale had betrayed its past by turning its back on law and social science,[481] or by surrendering to the forces of political correctness[482] — fostered tranquility. ("When I get letters of complaint," Calabresi confided to one Yale Administration official, "I always telephone. I find that it takes little time and it almost always bowls them over to be called. They expect a 'form' letter and while they are only sometimes convinced of the rightness of my position, they always go away feeling flattered and happy.")[483] Calabresi also took on disappointments. Wellington had instituted "a formal preference" for all alumni children when he became dean because "[w]e are indeed dependent on our alumni for our continued financial health,"[484] but it was his successor who spent hours talking with disappointed alumni of Yale Law School *and* their children about other options and reminding the latter of the possibility of transferring to Yale if they did well elsewhere.[485] Just as important were the telephone calls to individuals to rejoice with them.[486] He was ubiquitous.

Calabresi liked to think of Yale Law School as a "village,"[487] "a place where singers can sing and dancers can dance, a place that stands for excellence with decency and humanity, an exciting and loving place."[488] As part of his drive to spread "warmth and affection" through the Sterling Law Buildings, he reinstituted the tradition of the Children's Holiday Party that Pollak had inaugurated for offspring of faculty, students, and staff. Different professors played Santa; Calabresi, clad in green tights and pointed shoes, was always Santa's elf.[489] One student bluntly characterized Calabresi's decanal style as "somewhat touchy-feely — the 'let's hug-one-another approach' to law school,"[490] an affect the dean attributed to his politics: "Like most — though not all — liberals I tend to try to see the best (to be a lover) and not see the worst (to be a hater) in people," he said.[491] And as the student acknowledged, it worked.[492]

With Calabresi at the helm and overflowing coffers, it seemed as if the millennium was arriving early. Then came the *U.S. News & World Report* rankings. When first they were published in 1987, Harvard and Yale tied for first place.[493] But when next they appeared in 1990, Yale was ranked number one, and Harvard number five.[494] The *Harvard Law Record* reserved editorial space in 1991 to proclaim that "Yale Law School *is* Number One. . . . While Harvard continues to rely, almost categorically, on the reputation established by Holmes, Langdell, and other admittedly awesome figures in the nascent development and structuring of American law, Yale moves in modern times with unrivaled stature."[495] And beginning in the early 1990s, about four out of every five admittees enrolled at Yale.[496]

But the school still needed a presence outside the legal academy. During the Bork hearings, the media mentioned that the candidate had been a Yale Law School professor largely as a shorthand way of showing he was smart.[497] In the Thomas confirmation hearings, as Anita Hill confronted fellow graduate Clarence Thomas, Yale Law School itself became news. It was not just because Calabresi, in one of his moments of excess, had said he believed both candidates, either.[498] Rather, the images of two Yale Law graduates facing off against each other in a confirmation process that involved alumni as senators (Thomas's mentor John Danforth, and Arlen Spector), Senate staffers (James Brudney); key witnesses (Calabresi, for Thomas; Drew Days, against; and John Doggett against Anita Hill); scholars (Catharine MacKinnon); and observers (the media took care to capture Yale Law students, many interviewed multiple times, watching the televised hearings, and the large banner in the school's foyer, "Congratulations, Justice Thomas," with a second message appended in print nearly as large: "Tough Luck, Women!"); created fascination with Yale.[499] Now reporters fell over themselves to report that just as the Bork battle had featured Yale law alumni on every side, so, once again, was New Haven the point of convergence, spawning "a family tragedy" — and also "considerable institutional pride." That pride seemed peculiar, the *New York Times* observed, "given the pathos and tawdriness of the Thomas story, until one realizes how chauvinistic this community can be." [500]

Add Dark Ages alumna Hillary Clinton and her husband, Bill, to the mix, and is it any wonder Yale Law School became a celebrity in its own right? Now, "suddenly," the school "occupied a prominent place on America's cultural map." [501] Now, alumni could claim Yale was the best *and* most recognized law school. "Almost every event on which national attention focused this year seems to have had a Yale Law School label," Calabresi said in 1992. "The Clarence Thomas–Anita Hill hearings, the rebirth of Democratic party hopes after Harris Wofford's Senate victory in Pennsylvania, the Presidential primaries among Jerry Brown, Bill Clinton, and Paul Tsongas, Jack Danforth's role in passing the Civil Rights Act of 1992, the brave fight by Fay Vincent over the future of baseball, Pat Robertson's speech at the Republican Convention, Hillary Rodham Clinton's role in the Presidential campaign, the achievement of the North American Free Trade Agreement by Carla Hills, and the election of Bill Clinton as President of the United States, all had as key participants — good, bad or indifferent — graduates of this small school." [502] (Note that Republicans received their due, too, and in the same missive, Calabresi welcomed back the two professors, hired during his deanship, who had just returned to school after service in the Bush administration. [503]) As a *Boston Globe* reporter, himself a Yale Law School graduate, said, if so many prominent political figures "came from the same town of 1,600 people, or the same high school, reporters would be hiding in lockers trying to figure out why the place had assumed such an influence in the life of the nation." [504]

This, too, was sweet. When Hillary Clinton returned to Yale in 2001, this time as a U.S. senator from New York, she told a story about how she had chosen its law school. A friend at Harvard had invited her to a cocktail party to meet some of the faculty. Introducing her to "a professor who looked as though he had stepped out of the set of the *Paper Chase*," her companion announced that Rodham was "trying to make up her mind between us and our nearest competitor. And he looked down at me and he said, first of all we don't have a nearest competitor, and secondly, we don't need more women." [505] The story might have seemed contrived to please her audience, had not it rung so true. And the implication was obvious. However arrogant Harvard had once been, Yale had, for the time being, won.

Yale had not become Harvard. Its small size prevented that. But beginning in the late 1980s, though the Dark Ages still cast a shadow, the school had escaped another shadow.

This was good news for an institution of legendary self-absorption. But complacency was not supposed to be the Yale way. Historically, it was its sense of insecurity, indeed its existence in Harvard's shadow, that had shaped the school's identity. Calabresi liked to quote Grant Gilmore: " 'The Golden Age of the Yale Law School is never *now*. It was always in the past . . . and can be *again* in the future if only we do a few things right.' Always close, always striving, never quite there yet except in memory and hope."[506]

I wonder what Charles E. Clark would say. At one level, I can imagine him smiling proudly. But he was a fearful soul, where the school he loved was concerned, and I can also imagine him worrying. I can hear him asking whether students now choose Yale because of the shape he gave it, as so many of their predecessors in the sixties did, or because of *U.S. News & World Report*. If Yale is number one, can Yale still be Yale?

Notes

This essay draws on my forthcoming book about Yale Law School, where I explore the themes and events discussed here in greater depth. I am very grateful for the outstanding research assistance of Melissa Murray, Derek Dorn, Lucas Cupps, Dixie Rodgers, and Matt Sneddon; the invaluable help provided by Nancy Lyon and Manuscripts and Archives, as well as by Karen Alderman, Marge Camera, Nancy Moore, Georganne Rogers, and Elizabeth Stauderman; the interviews Bonnie Collier has done for the school's oral history project; the indefatigability of Gene Coakley; and the numerous individuals who took the time to talk with me about their Yale Law School. I thank Richard Abel, Bruce Ackerman, Christine Adams, Lee Albert, Jack Balkin, John Blum, Guido Calabresi, Paul Carrington, Otis Cochran, Daniel Ernst, William L. F. Felstiner, Owen Fiss, Justin Florence, Robert Gordon, Sarah Barringer Gordon, Thomas Green, John Griffiths, John Harrison, Hendrik Hartog, Tom Hilbink, Ann Hill, N. E. H. Hull, Geoffrey Kabaservice, Pnina Lahav, Sandy Levinson, William E. Nelson, Louis Pollak, Ed Purcell, David Rabban, Charles Reich, John Henry Schlegel, Eran Shalev, Larry Simon, Avi Soifer, Elizabeth Stauderman, Robert Stevens, Eleanor Swift, David Trubek, Mark Tushnet, Walt Wagoner, Harry Wellington, and G. Edward White for reading versions of the manuscript, sometimes more than once. I am indebted to Rutgers-Camden and Harvard Law Schools for giving me the opportunity to present it and for the many helpful comments I received when I did so. I am most grateful for the many forms of encouragement provided by Anthony Kronman and, above all, W. Randall Garr.

1. Laura Kalman, *Legal Realism at Yale, 1927–1960* (1986).

2. Robert Stevens, "History of the Yale Law School: Provenance and Perspective."

3. Thurman Arnold, *Fair Fights and Foul* 35 (1965).

4. Kalman, supra note 1, at 105.

5. Charles E. Clark, "Admission and Exclusion of Law Students," in Steve Sheppard, ed., *The History of Legal Education in the United States: Commentaries and Primary Sources* 903, 905 (1999).

6. Robert W. Gordon, "Professors and Policymakers: Yale Law School Faculty in the

New Deal and After"; Gaddis Smith, "Politics and the Law School: The View from Woodbridge Hall, 1921–1963."

7. This theme recurred frequently in Clark's deanship reports. Kalman, supra note 1, at 263 n. 36.

8. Grant Gilmore, *The Ages of American Law* 87 (1977).

9. Stevens, "History," supra note 2.

10. Eugene Rostow, "The Great Talent Hunt — 1955–1959: Renewing the Yale Law Faculty," *Yale L Report* 7 (Winter 1961).

11. Pollak was hired during Harry Shulman's deanship and promoted during Rostow's.

12. Gerald Rosenberg, *The Hollow Hope: Can Courts Bring About Social Change?* 4 (1991).

13. Mel Eflin, "The Case for Yale Law School: Students, Faculty, Ideals Take It to the Top," *Newsweek,* 100, 104 (June 10, 1963); 347 U.S. 483 (1954).

14. See, e.g., Louis Pollak, "Racial Discrimination and Judicial Integrity: A Reply to Professor Wechsler," 108 *U. Pa. L. Rev.* 1 (1959); Charles Black, "The Lawfulness of the Segregation Decisions," 69 *Yale L. J.* 421 (1960).

15. "I don't want to get crabbing just because things are drifting away from me, since the oldster is almost always wrong, but it is, well, strange to see the Yale Law School overrun with FF's Happy Hot Dogs!" Clark said privately a year after Rostow had become dean. Quoted in Kalman, supra note 1, at 206. In 1959, Clark told his former colleague Thurman Arnold that Yale "seems to be now becoming a Harvard adjunct." Id.

16. Louis Pollak, "Ralph Brown: Farewell to a Friend," 108 *Yale L. J.* 1473, 1477 (1999).

17. A Vigorous and Fruitful Tree: The First Annual Report of the Academic Committee to the Yale Law School Student Association, May 1967, Box 55, Student Association — Academic Committee First Annual Report Folder, Dean's Files, Yale University Archives (hereafter Dean's Files). The report drew on a student questionnaire, which listed the top three reasons first-year students listed for choosing Yale Law School over another law school: They believed it the "best law school in the country" (51 percent listed this as one of their top three reasons); liked its reputation for teaching "the social approach to law" (24 percent); and believed they would have small classes there (18 percent). The Yale Law Survey of Student Opinion, n.d. (administered March 1967), Box 54, Student Associations Folder, Dean's Files.

18. Eugene Rostow to Deans Tate and Runyon, November 13, 1957, Box 46, Chron File, October, Dean's Files.

19. A 1962 memorandum by the Admissions Committee lamented "Harvard's ability to attract more students of ability," reporting that "one of Harvard Law School's greatest advantages over us is its apparent ability to keep nearly all the best graduates of Harvard College and lure away a fair proportion of the best from Yale College. Out of some 1,595 students Harvard claims, 317 hold Harvard degrees and 158 Yale; we have (out of 591) some 137 Yale men, but only 26 from Harvard." Yale University Law School, A Memorandum on Admissions and Scholarships, 1962, Yale Law Library.

20. Louis Pollak to Kingman Brewster, November 2, 1965, Box 36, Memoranda Folder, Dean's Files.

21. As the *Student Guide to Yale Law School, 2001–02,* issued by the Yale Law

Women Association, put it: "Yale basically doesn't have grades. In your first semester, all of your classes are credit/fail, and there is no known instance of actual failure. (Although there are rumors that certain professors have, on *rare* occasion, asked students to retake unsatisfactory examinations). After the first semester, courses are graded on a scale of honors-pass-low pass-fail. Low passes and fails are rare. Honors are unpredictable — some professors give *very* few, while others give honors at a rate that makes them roughly analogous to As or B pluses. The upshot of not having grades is that students are generally willing to share notes, form large outline groups, and help each other. (There is still competition for things like recommendations from certain professors, spots on the *Yale Law Journal,* and certain clerkships — just not for grades). The downside is that employers don't know how to interpret Yale transcripts, and you will spend a lot of time explaining what grades mean and looking for other ways to make yourself appealing to employers."

22. Jeff Greenfield, "The Yale Plot to Take Over America," *M,* at 76 (May 1992).

23. Guido Calabresi to Friends and Graduates of Yale Law School, September 27, 1985 (Letters from the dean to friends and graduates of the law school are hereafter cited as Dean's Letters. I am grateful to Georganne Rogers for making her folder of Dean's Letters available to me.)

24. Yale Law School: Rules of the Wall, n.d. (c. 1995) ("The Wall" Folder, in possession of Georganne Rogers); conversation with Mike Thompson, June 2001.

25. See, e.g., "Yale U. Spreads Its Vision of the Law by Educating Professors," *The Yale Herald,* March 4, 1999, via U-Wire: "According to Yale Law School figures, alumni constitute only one percent of all law degree holders in this country. But at the same time, 11 percent of legal educators in the approximately 180 American Bar Association-approved law schools attend Yale Law."

26. "At the Bar: The Lawyer Who Helped Set the Flag Debate Aflame Calmly Prepares to Go On," *New York Times,* June 22, 1990, at B5.

27. "[S]trange as it may seem when virtually every volume [tracing the history of a particular law school] marks the beginning and endings of eras with changes in the deanship, there is almost no evidence that who the dean was made any difference. A larger collection of noisy barrels it would be hard to find. Few after Langdell seem to have had any coherent, much less original, thoughts on legal education and those who did, for example, Harlan F. Stone, had little impact beyond their office door." Alfred Konefsky and John Schlegel, "Mirror, Mirror on the Wall: Histories of American Law Schools," 95 *Harv. L. Rev.* 833, 39–40 (1982).

28. There are many ways to conceive of "the sixties." One might argue, for example, that as a political era in American history, "the sixties" began with Kennedy's assassination in 1963 and ended when the last American helicopter left Vietnam in 1975. Or one might say it began with the lunch-counter sit-ins in 1960 and ended with Kent State in 1970. One might maintain that, culturally, the "sixties" began with "the British invasion" in 1964 and ended with the release of the Beatles' last album, *Abbey Road,* in the United States in 1969. Or one might contend that the overlap between politics and culture made "the sixties" unique. In that case, the "sixties" might begin with the song and image of "Camelot" and end with the occupation of Columbia in 1968 or with the release in 1970 of "Ohio," the lament by Crosby, Stills, Nash, and Young for the four students killed at

Kent State. The possibilities are endless. The period remains highly contested. Few American historians agree on its definition.

29. Class Notes, *Yale L. Report* 42 (Spring 1993): "There was a major gathering of the clan for the inauguration. After all, even if Bill wasn't at Yale during the Dark Ages, Hillary [Rodham] was." Bill Clinton entered in the fall of 1970. The class of 1970 was the first to identify with the "Dark Ages," the class of 1972 the last. Yet reverberations of the Dark Ages continued to sound while Bill Clinton was a student.

30. That is, they were part of: "(1) informal networks, based (2) on shared beliefs and solidarity, which mobilize about (3) conflictual issues, through (4) the frequent uses of various forms of protest." Donatella Della Porta and Mario Diani, *Social Movements: An Introduction* 16 (1999).

31. Robert Borosage, "Can the Law School Succeed? A Proposal," 1 *Yale Rev. of Law and Social Action* 92, 94 (1970).

32. See, e.g., Paul Savoy, "Towards A New Politics of Legal Education," 79 *Yale L. J.* 444, 450 (1970).

33. Laura Kalman, *The Strange Career of Legal Liberalism* 52 (1996).

34. Dedication, 84 *Yale L. J.* 405 (1975). The occasion of the dedication was Earl Warren's death, by which time the high tide of sixties "radicalism" had passed. But many Yale Law students of the sixties felt a similar pull to Warren and his Court.

35. Lucas Powe, *The Warren Court and American Politics* (2000).

36. Paul Campos, "Advocacy and Scholarship," 81 *Cal. L. Rev.* 817, 819, n.4 (1993).

37. "Huge Demand For Law Grads Seen for 1969–70," *The Commentator*, October 28, 1969, at 6.

38. Jerold Auerbach, *Unequal Justice: Lawyers and Social Change in Modern America* 278–79 (1976). When Cravath, Swaine, and Moore began offering associates a starting salary of $15,000 in 1968, the associate dean of NYU Law School commented that this was "the most dramatic raise I've been witness to in my career." "Major Wall Street Law Firm Greatly Increases Salaries," *The Commentator,* February 14, 1968, at 1.

39. "Law Firm Offers $15,000," *Harvard Law Record,* February 15, 1968, at 1, 4.

40. "$15,000 Beginning Salary Evokes Reaction: Fears Loss to Service Jobs," *Columbia Law School News,* February 19, 1968.

41. Michael Garret and Jean Pennington, "Will They Enter Private Practice?" 57 *A.B.A. J.* 663 (July 1971); John Robson, "Private Lawyers and Public Interest," 56 *A.B.A. J.* 332 (April 1970); John McGonagle, "New Lawyers and New Law Firms," id. at 1139 (December 1970).

42. Philip Kazanjian, "Trouble in the Law: A Student's View," 58 *A.B.A. J.* 701 (July 1970).

43. Albert Conard, "Remarks on Induction to the Presidency of the Association of American Law Schools, December 30, 1970," 23 *J. Legal Ed.* 366, 366 (1970).

44. "Campus Events Close Law School; 'Pass-Incomplete' Grading Adopted," *Columbia Law School News,* May 13, 1968, at 1, 3. Pass-incomplete grading was adopted for that semester only.

45. "Siegel Trial Begins, Federal Suit Dismissed," *The Writ,* November 5, 1969, at 1. He was acquitted. "Law and Order Wins—People Free Siegel," id., November 26, 1969, at 1.

46. "BALSA Stages Study-In; Black Admissions Key Issue," *Columbia Law School News*, May 13, 1969, at 1; "BALSA's Formal Proposal," id., April, 24, 1969, at 5; "Faculty Resolution of May 9, 1969," id., May 13, 1969, at 7.

47. "The Rutgers Report: The White Law School and the Black Liberation Struggle," *Law Against the People: Essays to Demystify Law, Order and the Courts*, ed. Robert Lefcourt 232, 233, 240 (1971); and see Arthur Kinoy, "The Present Crisis in American Legal Education," 24 *Rutgers L. Rev.* 1 (1970).

48. "Howard Students Seize Law School," *New York Times*, February 19, 1969, at A34.

49. "Law Students Take Case to Court: Medical Protesters Return to Class," *Hilltop*, February 28, 1969, at 1; "Washington replaces Harris as Dean of the Law School," id. at 3.

50. "Firebomb Hits Library Amid Wave of Blasts; No Clues Yet," *Columbia Law School News*, March 2, 1970, at 1.

51. "Sound and Fury," *Harvard Law Record*, April 24, 1969, at 8.

52. See, e.g., "Yale Law School Studies Revised Grading System," *The Commentator*, February 14, 1968, at 3; "Public Interest Law Firms," *Stanford Law School Journal*, November 19, 1970, at 4 (recommending a *Yale Law Journal* student note on public interest law firms in the May 1970 issue as "essential reading for anyone currently interested in the current status of public interest law in America"); "Journals Veering from Grades-Only: National Trend to New Criteria," *Georgetown Law Weekly*, November 12, 1969, at 1 (an article including a subsection, "Yale Moves Away from Grades Only" in selection of *Law Journal* members).

53. See, e.g., "Apathy Marks Student Views," *Columbia Law School News*, October 7, 1968, at 1; "Small Step Forward," id., October 28, 1968, at 4 (discussing "tremendous apathy of the majority of the student body").

54. By one set of calculations, 15 percent of Yale Law School graduates in 1969, 9 percent in 1970, and 11 percent in 1971 took "public service" jobs (jobs such as legal aid, public-interest law firms, VISTA, the Peace Corps, the NAACP, and the ACLU) on graduation. At Pennsylvania, the figure was 0 percent (1969), 8 percent (1970), and 10 percent (1970); at Harvard, 6 percent (1969), 6 percent (1970), and 7 percent (1970); at Columbia, 0 percent (1969), 5 percent (1970), and 5 percent (1971). Mark Green, "The Young Lawyers, 1972: Goodbye to Pro Bono," *New York*, February 21, 1972, 29, 33.

55. Compare any article in *The Yale Advocate* with "Total Student Control," *Harvard Law Record*, November 21, 1968, at 8 (branding one student proposal with respect to participation on faculty committees as something "worthy of a Columbia undergraduate radical" and suggesting that radical students wanted "to take over the Law School lock, stock and barrel"); "The Front Page," *Stanford Law School Journal*, December 10, 1970), at 2 (discussing "irresponsible journalism" of *Stanford Daily* and alleging it ignored the violence perpetrated on campus by "radicals and high school students" that "grievously" hurt the university); or "SBA Blunder No. 671," *Georgetown Law Weekly*, April 19, 1972, at 2 (characterizing Student Bar Association members' disruption of a faculty meeting on grading when they entered the faculty lounge and demanded to remain for the discussion of grading as "second-rate petty demagoguery and springtime radicalism"). *The Columbia Law School News* took positions to the left of the *Record* and *Weekly*, but

I would not characterize it as a "radical" paper until about 1969–70, when, according to its editor, the administration became so upset that it allegedly tried to censor the *News*. Barry Morris, "Letter to the Students, Faculty and Alumni," *Columbia Law School News*, November 11, 1969, at 8. Faculty also complained when Boalt's *Writ* evinced greater radicalism beginning in 1968–69. "Constructive Criticism Please," *The Writ*, November 6, 1968, at 2.

56. "Worst Piece of Shit I Ever Saw," *Yale Advocate*, October 2, 1969, at 2.

57. For a study of Walter Pollak's professional career, see Louis Pollak, "Advocating Civil Liberties: A Young Lawyer Before the Old Court," 17 *Harvard C.R.-C.L. L. Rev.* 1 (1982).

58. 358 U.S. 1 (1958).

59. Bickel interview with Maggie Scarf, October 28, 1974, Box 13, Folder 8, M. Scarf tapes, Box 13, Folder 8, Alexander Bickel Papers, Yale University Archives (hereafter Bickel Papers).

60. Dedication, 84 *Yale L. J.* (December 1974).

61. Anne Standley, "Alexander Bickel, Charles Black, and the Ambiguous Legacy of Brown v. Board of Education," Ph.D. diss. 168 (1993).

62. Interview with Charles Reich, 2002. Unless otherwise indicated, I conducted the interviews. See also Standley, supra note 61, at 168, 79.

63. Alexander Bickel to J. Kirkpatrick Sale, May 18, 1967, Box 9, Folder 186, Bickel Papers.

64. Alexander Bickel to Harold Leventhal, January 10, 1968, Box 10, Folder 148, id.

65. Statement, May 17, 1968, Box 35, Folder 4, id.

66. See, e.g., Alexander Bickel to William Hackett, June 18, 1968, Box 10, Folder 191, Bickel Papers.

67. Alexander Bickel to Anthony Lewis, July 16, 1968, id.

68. Edward Purcell, "Alexander Bickel and the Post-Realist Constitution," 11 *Harv. C.R.-C.L. L. Rev.* 521, 548 (1976).

69. Boris Bittker, "Eugene V. Rostow," in *Collected Legal Essays* 148, 150 (1989).

70. See, e.g., "Law School Statement Blasts Vietnam Policy," *Yale Daily News*, February 15, 1968, at 1. (indicating that 157 Yale law students and half the faculty had signed a statement denouncing U.S. Vietnam policy; claiming that its war aims could not be achieved; and calling for political and military de-escalation. Faculty signatories were Alexander Bickel, Boris Bittker, Ralph Brown, Guido Calabresi, Arthur Charpentier, Marvin Chirelstein, Jan Deutsch, Thomas Emerson, Abraham Goldstein, Joseph Goldstein, John Griffiths, Robert Hudec, Jay Katz, Friedrich Kessler, Ellen Peters, Louis Pollak, Charles Reich, Egon Schwelb, John Simon, Edward Sparer, Clyde Summers, David Trubek, and Harry Wellington.)

71. In the spring of 1968, the Johnson administration announced an end to automatic deferments for graduate students who were not in medical, dental, or divinity school and who had not completed two years of coursework. James Patterson, *Grand Expectations* 632 (1996). Three members of Kennedy's class, represented by Professors John Griffiths and Steven Duke, filed a class action suit against Selective Service Administrator General Lewis Hershey, charging that he had acted improperly when he instructed local draft boards to deny I-S deferments, which allowed students who had begun the school year to

complete it without being inducted, to those who had possessed graduate II-S deferments since amendment of the Selective Service Act in 1967. They were unsuccessful. "Students Here Sue Hershey," *Yale Advocate,* November 22, 1968, at 1; "Law Students Win, Draw In Draft Cases," id., February 20, 1969, at 1.

72. Kingman Brewster was the brother of Kennedy's stepmother, and Kennedy presented his pamphlet to Yale's president and his step-uncle at a family gathering as a "taunting joke." Interview with Duncan Kennedy, 2001. It is in Kingman Brewster Papers, Box 130, Folder 8, 1 of 2, Yale University Archives (hereafter Brewster Papers). For the published version, from which I have taken citations, see Kennedy, "How the Law School Fails," 1 *Yale Rev. of Law and Social Action* 71 (1970).

73. Kennedy, supra note 72, at 77, 84.

74. Id. at 84.

75. Robert Stevens, "Law School and Law Students," 59 *Va L. Rev.* 551, 638, 641 (1973).

76. Kennedy, supra note 72, at 72.

77. Id. at 76.

78. Id. at 85.

79. "No Consensus On Grades Among First-Year Students," *Yale Advocate,* September 26, 1968, at 1.

80. Id., Photo, at 3. The 1967–68 academic year was the waiters' final one.

81. Results of First Year Grade Referendum, December 1967, Box 38, Grading Folder 1967–70, Dean's Files.

82. Report on the Meeting of the First Year Class, March 13, 1968, Box 38, Grading Folder, Dean's Files.

83. "A Too Modest Proposal," *Yale Advocate,* October 24, 1968, at 2.

84. "Yale Law School Studying Grading," *New York Times,* January 28, 1968, at 4; "Law Students Vote for Reform," *Yale Daily News,* December 12, 1968, at 1.

85. Results of First Year Grade Referendum, supra note 81.

86. "Law Students Vote for Reform," supra note 84.

87. Yale Law School Faculty Minutes (hereafter YLS Faculty Minutes), December 18, 1968; Further Report of the Curriculum Committee on the Grading System, December 16, 1968, Box 38, Grading Folder 1967–70, Dean's Files; Additional Statement of Thomas Emerson, n.d., id.

88. YLS Faculty Minutes, December 18, 1968.

89. Id.

90. Louis Pollak to Class of 1972, Box 36, Memoranda Folder, Dean's Files; YLS Faculty Minutes, December 18, 1968.

91. "Revolution at Yale: Credit/No Credit Replaces Traditional Grades," *Harvard Law Record,* January 30, 1969, at 5. The article was reprinted in the University of Michigan Law School's *Res Gestae,* "Yale Adopts Pass-Fail Grading System," February 28, 1969, at 5.

92. As one student at Boalt concluded after reading law school newspapers sent there, "it appears that all law schools are in some manner considering grading revisions." "Grading Reform," *The Writ,* March 18, 1970, at 1. A Davis law student who reviewed the materials from the different schools labeled the complaints about grades "fairly

obvious, fairly uniform, and fairly widespread: grades tend to accentuate competition, they are not an accurate [indicator of success at] legal thoughts, they are not valuable feedback for the students." So too, were faculty responses: "first, grades are needed to provide incentive, and second, they help employers to make accurate hiring decisions." "New Grading Policy Urged," *The Barrister,* May 11, 1970, at 2, 8. Law schools such as Stanford or Harvard, which adopted pass-fail grades during this period, often allowed students to opt for them or letter or number grades. That created the impression that pass-fail grades were the refuge of weaker students. All students at Yale, on the other hand, were graded on the same scale.

93. *Yale Law Reporter,* 1970, at 40.

94. YLS Faculty Minutes, December 18, 1968.

95. Louis Pollak to Macklin Fleming, June 23, 1969, Box 7, Judge Macklin Fleming Folder, Dean's Files; see also "Affirmative Action at Yale Law School," *Yale L. Report* 5 (Fall 1991).

96. Yale Law School Admissions Committee, A Memorandum on Admissions and Scholarships, supra note 19.

97. "Affirmative Action at YLS," supra note 95.

98. YLS Faculty Minutes, May 2, 1968.

99. "Active BLSU Prepares for New Courses," *Yale Advocate,* March 12, 1969, at 1.

100. Presentments to the Administration of Yale University Law School, n.d. Box 131, Folder 9, Brewster Papers; Yale University Council Report of the Committee on the Law School, April 18, 1969, id., Folder 3.

101. Louis Pollak to J. Otis Cochran, December 16, 1968, Box 131, Folder 9, id.

102. Black Law Students Union, Memorandum, December 16, 1968, id.

103. YLS Faculty Minutes, December 19, 1968.

104. Standley, supra note 61, at 49.

105. Id. at 143–44.

106. Id. at 138.

107. Charles Black, "Some Notes on Law Schools in the Present Day," 79 *Yale L. J.* 505, 506 (1970).

108. Louis Pollak to Kingman Brewster and Charles Taylor, December 18, 1968, Box 131, Folder 9, Brewster Papers.

109. YLS Faculty Minutes, December 19, 1968.

110. "Active BLSU Prepares Outlines for New Courses," *Yale Advocate,* March 12, 1969, at 1, 3.

111. YLS Faculty Minutes, December 19, 1968.

112. Id., December 31, 1968.

113. Id., December 24, 1968.

114. Id.

115. Louis Pollak to the Black Law Students Union, December 31, 1968, Box 131, Folder 3, Brewster Papers.

116. Louis Pollak to Macklin Fleming, June 23, 1969, Box 7, Judge Macklin Fleming Folder, Dean's Files. The exchange between Pollak and Fleming was reprinted in 19 *Public Interest* 44 (September 1970).

117. A Statement to the Members of the Law School Community by Dean Francis A. Allen, October 8, 1969, included in University of Michigan Collection of *Res Gestae.*

118. "And a Stillness Descended Upon Them," *Res Gestae,* October 17, 1969, at 10 ("After all the hoot and holler, there remains only 38 black law students at Michigan and the response that 'we haven't got the cash, brother' is not good enough. Yale had the cash, Rutgers had the cash. Yes, even the University of Mississippi had the cash.").

119. "Support the BLSA Demands," *Res Gestae,* October 31, 1969, at 1, 2.

120. Black Law Students Union to Yale Law School Faculty and Student Body, February 13, 1969, Box 56, BLSU Folder, Dean's Files.

121. Ralph Brown to Richard Cahn, Box 56, BLSU Folder, Dean's Files; Yale University Council, Report of the Committee on the Law School, December 3, 1970, Box 43, University Council Folder, Dean's Files.

122. Jerome Frank, "Why Not a Clinical Lawyer-School?" 81 *U. Pa. L. Rev.* 907 (1933).

123. "Legal Aid Program Plans Expansion; Stress On Urban Law," *Yale Advocate,* October 10, 1968, at 1.

124. Laura Holland, "Invading the Ivory Tower: The History of Clinical Education at Yale Law School," 49 *J. Legal Ed.* 504, 512, 514 (1999).

125. Id. at 512–21.

126. Borosage, supra note 31, at 95.

127. Pollak to Black Law Students Union, December 31, 1968, supra note 115.

128. "Doing Their Clinical Thing: The Legal Services Program at Yale," *Yale L. Report* at 9, 11 (Fall 1970) (quoting Leon Lipson).

129. Holland, supra note 124, at 523–24.

130. Abraham Goldstein, "Educational Planning at Yale," 20 *J. Legal Ed.* 402, 406 (1968).

131. "Negotiating Committee Asks Joint Student-Faculty Rule," *Yale Advocate,* February 6, 1969, at 1.

132. Id. at 1, 4.

133. "Groping for Community," id., May 1, 1969, at 2; "Bridging the Chasm," id., February 6, 1969, at 2.

134. "Law, Grad Schools Face Changes; Tension High in Law School; 'Peaceful Revolution' at Hand," *Yale Daily News,* February 14, 1969, at 1.

135. The faculty group included Thomas Emerson, Pollak, Marvin Chirelstein, Abe Goldstein, and Rostow.

136. The First Meeting of the Committee, n.d., Richard Hughes File (hereafter Hughes File). I am grateful to Richard Hughes for providing me with his file of notes on the committee. The text of the provisions of the Yale By-Laws on faculty was reprinted in *The Yale Advocate,* April 3, 1969, at 4.

137. "Faculty Rejects Proposals: Resolution Bars Voting, Any Regular Representation in Faculty Meetings; Committee Members Walk Out," *Yale Advocate,* April 3, 1969, at 1, 4; "Negotiating Committee Message," id at 2, 4.

138. The First Meeting of the Committee, Hughes File.

139. Id.

140. "'The Great Debate,' Being a more or less exact transcription from notes of the exchange between the STUDENT NEGOTIATORS and the assembled FACULTY at a meeting BEHIND CLOSED DOORS, the thirteenth day of March, in 1969." The sub-heading of the memorandum read "Confidential: For Eyes of Student Negotiators Only, Top Secret: Don't Let Eugene Rostow See This," n.d., Hughes File.

141. Michael Egger to Louis Pollak, March 5, 1969, id.

142. "Text of Summers Memorandum on Student Proposal," *Yale Advocate*, April 3, 1969, at 3.

143. YLS Faculty Minutes, March 28, 1969. Goldstein would have limited student participation to a nonvoting role on committees (id.), an issue Pollak wanted, and succeeded in leaving, fuzzed. (Pollak to Brewster, February 27, 1969, Box 37, President's Office Folder, Dean's Files: "At least as to a few committees, I would expect that voting participation would be regarded as a permissible arrangement [as it has been, on an interim basis, in one or two committees, this fall and winter], but only on the understanding that the Faculty retains full decisional authority to adopt, modify or reject committee proposals.") Emerson would have regularly permitted 6–10 students to attend (but not vote) at faculty meetings, regardless of whether they were on faculty committees. YLS Faculty Minutes, March 28, 1969.

144. The 3rd Meeting, April 1, 1969, Hughes File.

145. Faculty Resolution, March 28, 1969, YLS Faculty Minutes.

146. SNC to Dear Faculty Member, April 2, 1969, id. (*The Yale Advocate* reprinted the letter in the April 3, 1969 issue, at 2).

147. Id.

148. Id.

149. Id.

150. Jim Laney, Jim Phelan, Robert Borosage, Robert Vizas, Patricia Wynn, "Negotiations Lead to 'Weak Compromise,'" *Yale Advocate*, March 12, 1969, at 2.

151. "It is with some regret that we yield to those who predicted doom for our efforts from the beginning, and ourselves move to the time-consuming disruptive arena." SNC to Dear Faculty Member, April 2, 1969, supra note 146.

152. "An End to Peace," *Yale Advocate*, April 3, 1969, at 2.

153. Peter Yaeger, "Heroic Struggle," *The New Journal*, April 27, 1969, Hughes File; "To Boycott or Not or What?" *Yale Advocate*, April 17, 1969, at 1 (estimating the crowd at 300–400 students and faculty members).

154. "Negotiations to Reopen," *Yale Daily News*, April 14, 1969.

155. The Open Meeting, n.d., Hughes File; see also "Heroic Struggle," supra note 153.

156. Negotiations Reopened, April 16, 1969, Hughes File.

157. Pollak to Class of 1972, supra note 90.

158. The Admissions Committee would include student representatives, but they would not participate in the disposition of individual cases.

159. Supplement to Resolution on Student Participation, YLS Faculty Minutes, May 5, 1969.

160. Faculty Minute on Principles Regarding Student Participation, April 28, 1969, id. Negotiations Reopened, April 16, 1969, Hughes File (appointed representatives would take part only in those meetings addressing an issue their committees had considered).

161. Memorandum from McL to KB, April 11, 1969, Box 131, Folder 3, Brewster Papers.

162. McL to Brewster, April 10, 1969, id.

163. Statement of Messrs. Hughes, Lewis, Spearman, Speth, Taylor, and Chairman Egger, Hughes File.

164. Pollak to Class of 1972, supra note 90.

165. "Negotiations Lead to 'Weak Compromise,' " supra note 150.

166. Borosage, supra note 31, at 96.

167. Jonathan Krown emails to Laura Kalman, March 24, 2001, April 10, 2001; "Merry Pranksters at Yale," *Yale Advocate,* February 20, 1969, at 1; "Blow Your Mind," id., February 6, 1969, at 1.

168. "The Last Day Down," *Yale Advocate,* May 1, 1969, at 2.

169. "Another group which has demanded space is the 'legal hippies' (or yippies, since law students all tend to be somewhat political.)" Borosage, supra note 31, at 95.

170. See the various memoranda from Security Director John Powell to Jack Tate in Box 43, Yale University-Police Folder, Dean's Files.

171. "It's Official Now — Girls Are Planning All-Year Live-In at the Law School," *Yale Advocate,* March 3, 1968, at 2.

172. Jack Tate to John Embersits, February 14, 1968, Box 36, Memoranda Folder, Dean's Files; "Legalized Coed Living Only Needs Approval by University Officials," *Yale Advocate,* February 22, 1968, at 1.

173. Vicky Jackson, Louise Nemschoff, and Anne Simon, *The Women's Law School Companion* 12 (June 1973; revised August 1974).

174. Id. at 12.

175. "Mixer!" *Yale Advocate,* September 26, 1968, at 3.

176. The course was taught by Barbara Babcock.

177. Barbara Brown, Thomas Emerson, Gail Falk, and Ann Freedman, "The Equal Rights Amendment: A Constitutional Basis for Equal Rights for Women," 80 *Yale L. J.* 871 (1971). The note identifying the authors described Brown, Falk, and Freedman as "members of the Class of 1971 of the Yale Law School," who were "active in the women's movement." Id. at 872.

178. Ann Freedman email to Laura Kalman, October 26, 2002; Jane Lazarre, *The Mother Knot* 32–44 (1997); Ann Hill, "If Men Were Taught Cooking," *The Advocate* (formerly *The Yale Advocate),* February 26, 1970, at 1.

179. *Abele v. Markle,* 342 F. Supp. 800 (1972).

180. Jackson, Nemschoff, and Simon, supra note 173, at 13; Hill, "If Men Were Taught Cooking," supra note 178, at 2.

181. "Women Say Law Firms Discriminate," *Yale Advocate,* November 7, 1968, at 1.

182. See, e.g., future California Supreme Court Chief Justice Rose Bird's comment on the situation of third-year women law students at Boalt in 1965, "3d Year Girls Lament (Fondly Dedicated to Dean Hill)," *The Writ,* May 1965, at 2.

183. W. Haywood Burns, Betsy Levin, Peter Zimroth to Eugene Rostow, October 20, 1964, Box 2, Unmarked Folder, Dean's Files.

184. Recommendations of the Yale Law School Placement Committee, February 18, 1971, Box 131, Folder 3, Brewster Papers.

185. Joanne Stern email to Laura Kalman, March 12, 2002.

186. "Women Say Law Firms Discriminate," supra note 181, at 1.

187. "Women Need Not Apply," *Yale Advocate,* April 13, 1970, at 12.

188. Panel: Concerns of the Yale Law Student Today, *Yale L. Report,* Special Report, September, 1969, at 4, 6 (hereafter 1969 Special Report).

189. Judith Areen, Oral History (interview by Mary Clark); Stein, "Crazy Days," *The Washingtonian,* September 1996, at 50, 52.

190. Jill Abramson and Barbara Franklin, *Where They Are Now: The Story of the Women of Harvard Law 1974* 11 (1986).

191. 1969 Special Report, supra note 188, at 8.

192. Id. at 15, 21.

193. "Students Provide Welcome for Alumni," *Yale Advocate,* May 1, 1969, at 1; Dennis Black email to Laura Kalman, March 28, 2001.

194. Hughes File, n.d.

195. "When Generations Collide," *Yale Advocate,* May 1, 1969, at 6.

196. Id.

197. Macklin Fleming to Louis Pollak, June 9, 1969, Box 7, Judge Macklin Fleming Folder, Dean's Files.

198. Interview with Louis Pollak, 2001.

199. Myres McDougal to Maxwell Cohen, July 3, 1969, Box 31, Dean's Files.

200. Interview with Pollak; "Two Yale Law Deans to Relinquish Posts," *New York Times,* September 13, at A55.

201. "Students Camp at Law School," *Yale Daily News,* September 22, 1969, 1.

202. Borosage, supra note 31, at 95. I am unsure how long the tent city remained in existence. At the time, Borosage said students maintained it for "most of the fall," id., but according to an article in the *Harvard Law Record,* the students remained in the Yale Law School courtyard for two weeks. "Yale Bubbles Up to Harvard's Hark," *Harvard Law Record,* October 23, 1969, at 1, 15.

203. See, e.g., "Criminals Approach Boalt Hall Takeover," *The Writ,* October 15, 1969, at 1 ("Eighty-eight percent of last year's students at Boalt Hall committed a marijuana crime; 72 percent were potential felons"); "Law School News: Pot Survey, 491 Respond: 339 (69%) Say They Smoke Marihuana," *Columbia Law School News,* November 11, 1969, at 1; "Two-Thirds in *Commentator* Poll Smoke Pot; Three-Fifths of Non-Users for Legalization," *The Commentator,* November 20, 1968, at 2; "Responses to Commentator Survey Indicate Users [of Marijuana] More Socially Aware, Liberal, Bold," id., December 4, 1968, at 2; "Marijuana Use High," *Stanford Law School Journal,* November 2, 1972, at 1.

204. Krown email to Kalman, March 24, 2001.

205. Charles Reich to Alexander Bickel, July 20, 1967, Box 7, Folder 125, Bickel Papers.

206. Interview with Reich.

207. Charles Reich, *The Greening of America* 394 (1970).

208. Krown email to Kalman, March 24, 2001.

209. Interview with Abe Goldstein, 2001.

210. Interview with Pollak.

211. Patterson, supra note 71, at 751.

212. Pollak to the Faculty, October 1, 1969; YLS Faculty Minutes, October 2, 1969.

213. Statement of October 2, 1969, YLS Faculty Minutes.

214. YLS Faculty Minutes, October 2, 1969.

215. Id.

216. "Reviewer's Corner: One Principle Under God," *Yale Advocate*, October 23, 1969, at 3.

217. Anthony Kronman, "My Senior Partner," 104 *Yale L. J.* 2129, 2131 (1995).

218. Immanuel Wallerstein and Paul Starr, eds., *The University Crisis Reader: The Liberal University Under Attack* 69–70 (1971).

219. Joseph Fashing and Steven Deutsch, *Academics in Retreat: The Politics of Educational Innovation* 281 (1971).

220. Id. at 282.

221. "50,000 Mass at Convocation on Green: Brewster, Lee, Udall, Denounce Viet War," *Yale Daily News*, October 16, 1969, at 1.

222. "Brewster Responds to Harassment of Blacks," *Yale Daily News*, October 17, 1969, at 1.

223. Yale Law School Student Association to Kingman Brewster, Statement, October 15, 1969, reprinted in *Yale Advocate*, October 15, 1969, at 1.

224. "City Police Charge Seale in Murder," *Yale Daily News*, September 18, 1969, at 1; see generally, Yohuru Williams, *Black Politics/White Power: Civil Rights, Black Power, and the Black Panthers in New Haven* 136–158 (2000).

225. John Taft, *May Day at Yale: A Case Study in Student Radicalism* 8–9 (1976).

226. Standley, supra note 61, at 145.

227. "Blacks at Yale Ask Changes in Police," *New York Times*, October 21, 1969, at A32.

228. Report of the Disciplinary Committee to the Dean and Teaching Faculty concerning Mr. Eric L. Clay '72, Box 63, Folder 22, Bickel Papers.

229. George Lefcoe email to Laura Kalman, September 1, 2002.

230. Confidential interview.

231. Testimony of Otis Cochran, reported in Report of the Disciplinary Committee, supra note 228.

232. Lefcoe email to Kalman, September 1, 2002.

233. "Blacks Disrupt Classes in Law School," *Yale Daily News*, October 21, 1969, at 1. The *New York Times* put the number of demonstrators closer to sixty. "Blacks at Yale Ask Changes in Police," supra note 227.

234. "Blacks Disrupt Classes," supra note 233.

235. Pollak to All Members of the Yale Law School, October 20, 1969, Box 131, Folder 2, Brewster Papers.

236. Report of the Disciplinary Committee, supra note 228.

237. I have been unable to determine who requested the meeting in executive session. Pollak thought it might have been Bickel, Kessler, and perhaps Goldstein, but was uncertain. Interview with Pollak.

238. Louis Pollak to Walt Wagoner, October 27, 1969, Box 54, Student Associations Folder, Dean's Files.

239. The Board of the Yale Law School Student Association, "Factual Statement Regarding Events of October 26," Box 131, Folder 8, Brewster Papers.

240. YLS Faculty Minutes, October 26, 1969.

241. Interview with Reich. Boris Bittker reported that while faculty members were not made to feel as if they were hostages, they were given the sense that they were in prison. Interview, 2001.

242. "BLSU Hits Disciplinary Proceedings," *Yale Daily News*, October 28, 1969, at 1.

243. "Boycott Affects Yale Law School," *New York Times*, October 29, 1969, at A52; "Law Students to Strike if Demands Not Met," *Yale Daily News*, October 27, 1969, at 1; "Law School Strike Depends Upon Radical Leaders' Appeal," id., October 28, 1969, at 1.

244. Louis Pollak, Statement, October 29, 1969, Box 131, Folder 4, Brewster Papers.

245. Standley, supra note 61, at 147.

246. "Faculty Tribunal to Hear Student's Case," *Yale Daily News*, November 3, 1969, at 1.

247. Standley, supra note 61, at 151.

248. "Faculty Tribunal," supra note 246, at 1.

249. Standley, supra note 61, at 147.

250. Id. at 146.

251. That was the reason remembered by Sam Chauncey, then the Secretary of the University. Conversation with Chauncey, 2001.

252. Interview with George Lefcoe, 2002.

253. *Watts v. United States*, 394 U.S. 705 (1969).

254. Standley, supra note 61, at 146.

255. Report of the Disciplinary Committee, supra note 228.

256. Interview with Lefoce; "Eric Lee Clay," www.jtbf.org/article_iii_judges/clay_e.htm.

257. George Lefcoe email to Laura Kalman, September 2, 2002. I have been unable to locate a transcript of the trial or to speak with Watt, Clay, or the late Joe Goldstein about it.

258. Kristine Olson, Kingsley Buh, Bob Herbat, Kirk McKenzie, Jeff Melnick, Raphael Podolsky, Barbara Rosenberg, Russell Zuckerman to Louis Pollak, December 4, 1969, Box 33, Discipline Committee *1963–69* Folder, Dean's Files.

259. Lefcoe email to Kalman, September 1, 2002; interview with Lefcoe.

260. Id.

261. Report of the Disciplinary Committee, supra note 228.

262. Standley, supra note 61, at 148; David Trubek email to Laura Kalman, January 4, 2002.

263. Report of the Disciplinary Committee, supra note 228.

264. Harold McDougall email to Laura Kalman, May 29, 2002.

265. Id., May 31, 2002.

266. Interview with Reich.

267. I do not know whether Clay had apprised Watt of how he intended to answer such a question.

268. Report of the Disciplinary Committee, supra note 228. Joseph Goldstein and Ward Bowman were in the minority.

269. Id. Robert Bork, Jay Katz, and Robert Hudec made up the majority.

270. Interview with Pollak.

271. Id.

272. Memorandum of L.H. Pollak on the Report of the Disciplinary Panel of November 25, 1969, relating to Eric L. Clay, '72, Box 131, Folder 2, Brewster Papers.

273. Supra, text accompanying note 152.

274. "Committee Readmits Suspended Students," *Yale Daily News*, November 11, 1969, at 1; "Executive Committee Decision on Wright Hall Occupation," id., November 12, 1969, at 2; "Suspended Yale Students Reinstated on Probation," *New York Times*, November 12, 1969, at A96. In the aftermath of the Clay incident, the faculty did decide — over the objection of a significant minority — to allow for student representation on law school disciplinary panels. YLS Faculty Minutes, May 6 and 11, 1970.

275. "Who We Are: Lewis and Munday, A Professional Corporation," www.lewismunday .com/who1.htm.

276. "Clay Sworn in as 6th Circuit Judge," *Michigan Lawyers Weekly*, November 10, 1997.

277. *Simmons-Harris v. Zelman*, 234 F.3d 945 (2000), reversed, 536 U.S. 639 (2002); *Grutter v. Bollinger*, 288 F.3d 732, 758 (2002).

278. Interview with Lefcoe.

279. Standley, supra note 61, at 150.

280. Louis Pollak to Joseph Goldstein, December 2, 1969, Box 132, Law School Discipline Folder, Brewster Papers.

281. Id.

282. Richard Abel email to Laura Kalman, April 30, 2002; Standley, supra note 61, at 156.

283. Friedrich Kessler, Alexander Bickel, Guido Calabresi, and Ralph Winter to the Faculty, November–December, 1969, Box 60, Folder 10, Bickel Papers.

284. Kronman, "My Senior Partner," supra note 217, at 2131.

285. Standley, supra note 61, at 171.

286. "Campus Unrest," Notes for Remarks, Peninsula Harvard Club, California 1970, November 4, Box 28, Folder 37, Bickel Papers.

287. Standley, supra note 61, at 151.

288. May Day Chronology, Box 8, Folder 81, Brewster Papers.

289. Taft, supra note 225, at 79–80; and see Geoffrey Kabaservice, *The Guardians: Kingman Brewster, His Circle, and the Rise of the Liberal Establishment* (2004).

290. Taft, supra note 225, at 96.

291. Id. at 86.

292. May Day Chronology, supra note 288; Taft, supra note 225, at 84–97.

293. May Day Chronology, supra note 288.

294. Robert Brustein, *Making Scenes: A Personal History of Turbulent Years at Yale, 1966–1979* 105 (1981).

295. "Hopes and Fears at Yale," *Washington Post*, May 1, 1970, Box 37, President's Office Folder, Dean's Files; May Day Chronology, supra note 288.

296. Taft, supra note 225, at 22.

297. Id.

298. Undated, untitled BLSU brochure, Box 56, BLSU Folder, Dean's Files.

299. Conversation with Ann Freedman and Harriet Katz, 2001.

300. To Members of the Yale Community, From Trial Report Committee, Re: The Proceedings in the Black Panther Case, April 29, 1970, Box 60, Folder 11, Bickel Papers. The memo was signed by Stuart Beck, Alexander Bickel, Fleming James, Daniel Freed, Mary Gallagher, Joseph Goldstein, David Kendall, John Kuhns, Kristine Olson, John Rupp, Irving Schloss, and Clyde Summers.

301. May Day Chronology, supra note 288. Pollak's statement to the Yale News Bureau maintained that the "polemics of the Vice President of the United States dramatically illustrate the concern voiced by President Kingman Brewster last week over 'the ability of black revolutionaries to achieve a fair trial anywhere in the United States.'" Statement, April 29, 1970, Box 37, President's Office Folder, Dean's Files.

302. Alexander Bickel, "The Tolerance of Violence on Campus," *The New Republic,* June 13, 1970, at 15.

303. Alexander Bickel, Joseph Bishop, Charles Black, J. H. Hexter, Martin Shubik, and C. Vann Woodward to Kingman Brewster, Box 10, Folder 206, Bickel Papers.

304. Taft, supra note 225, at 30.

305. May Day Chronology, supra note 288.

306. James McNulty to Louis Pollak, April 27, 1970, Box 43, Yale University-Police Folder, Dean's Files.

307. Id. See also May Day Chronology, supra note 288. Pollak put the number of students who helped at more than a hundred. Louis Pollak to Joseph McCrindle, May 12, 1970, Box 32, Mac/Mc Folder, Dean's Files.

308. Class Notes, *Yale L. Report 48* (Spring 1974), at 47–48.

309. Id. at 48.

310. Interview with Pollak.

311. Pollak to McCrindle, May 12, 1970, supra note 307.

312. Pollak to S. Burns Weston, June 24, 1970, Box 32, Letter from Dean Pollak to Alumni and Friends of the Law School Folder, June 1, 1970, Dean's Files.

313. Collier interview with Goldstein.

314. Abe Goldstein, "A Law School Memoir," *Yale Alumni Magazine* 38 (February 1977).

315. Collier interview with Goldstein.

316. *Durham v. U.S.,* 214 F. 2d 862 (1954).

317. Abraham Goldstein to Erwin Griswold, February 24, 1964, Box 129, Folder 14, Brewster Papers.

318. Collier interview with Goldstein. For Goldstein's work on law and social science, see, e.g., Abraham Goldstein, *The Insanity Defense* (1967).

319. "Immigrant's Son to Head Yale Law," *New York Times,* March 10, 1970, at A1; "Action-Oriented Dean," id. at A49.

320. It was moved to the fall and has remained there.

321. Robert Bork, *Slouching Towards Gomorrah: Modern Liberalism and American Decline* 42 (1996).

322. Harry Wellington to Carl Dreyfus, April 11, 1968, Box 1, Folder D, Dean's Files; "Riot Insurance," 77 *Yale L. J.* 541 (1968).

323. Bork, supra note 321, at 42.

324. Standley, supra note 61, at 156.

325. Interview with Lefcoe.

326. Pollak to McCrindle, May 12, 1970, supra note 307.

327. "Students Reject Yale Law Strike," *New York Times,* April 28, 1970, at 1, 44; Law School Vote Rejects Showdown," *Yale Daily News,* April 28, 1970, at 1.

328. McNulty to Pollak, April 27, 1970, supra note 306.

329. Pollak to Weston, June 24, 1970, supra note 312.

330. Interview with Pollak; Pollak, supra note 16, at 1476.

331. Remarks of Senator Hillary Rodham Clinton, Class Day, Yale University, May 20, 2001, http://clinton.senate.gov~/clinton/speeches/010520.html.

332. Bork, supra note 321, at 1, 37.

333. Bickel, supra note 302, at 17.

334. Brustein, supra note 294, at 115.

335. May Day Chronology, supra note 288.

336. Taft, supra note 225, at 168. .

337. "Endorse Strike: Law Students Hit War," *Yale Daily News*, May 5, 1970, at 1.

338. Louis Pollak to Alumni and Other Friends of the Law School, June 1, 1970, Box 32, Letter from Dean Pollak to Alumni and Friends of the Law School Folder, Dean's Files.

339. Bill Brocket, Statement, n.d., Box 34, Alumni Weekend October 1970 Folder, Dean's Files.

340. Walt Wagoner, Commentary, WYNBC News, May 6, 1970, 12 noon, id.

341. Taft, supra note 225, at 168–69. Brewster later vetoed the plan.

342. "Endorse Strike: Law Students Hit War," supra note 337.

343. Richard Hughes email to Laura Kalman, August 25, 2001.

344. Brocket, Statement, supra note 339.

345. YLS Faculty Minutes, May 5, 1970.

346. Id.

347. "All that the Faculty resolution authorized an instructor to do was to grade a student on the work done up to that point in classes small enough so that an instructor could reasonably determine whether by that time a student had satisfactorily completed work which substantially fulfilled the requirements of the course. In any course in which an instructor could not adequately evaluate a student on the basis of work done up to that point (and this was in the majority of our courses), then the ordinary examination or paper obligation had to be fulfilled (subject to flexibility as to the timing of the completion of these obligations). In short, the Faculty resolution of May 5 reflected insistence that academic credit could be awarded only for satisfactory academic work actually completed." Pollak to C. Dickerman Williams, June 26, 1970, Box 32, Letter from Dean Pollak to Alumni and Friends of the Law School Folder, June 1, 1970, Dean's Files.

348. Robert Schaus and James Arnone, *University at Buffalo Law School: 100 Years 1887–1987* 87 (1992).

349. Interview with Abe Goldstein by Bonnie Collier, October 16, 1996.

350. WYNBC News Commentary, supra note 340.

351. Id.

352. See generally Stevens, supra note 75.

353. Pollak, to the Alumni and Friends of the Law School, supra note 338.

354. Alexander Bickel to Phil Neal, October 5, 1971, Box 10, Folder 219, Box 10, Folder 219, Bickel Papers.

355. Mary McGrory, "Law Students' Peace Lobby: Senate Doors Open for Yale," May 18, 1970, Box 2, Folder 125, Bickel Papers.

356. Pollak, Letter to Alumni and Friends of the Law School, supra note 338.

357. Report of the Dean of the Law School, 1965–1970, Record Unit 12, Box 19, Brewster Papers.

358. "Lexcetera" (quoting Brewster), *Yale L. Report* 1 (Summer 1971).

359. Yale University Council, Report of the Committee on the Law School, December 30, 1970, Box 43, University Council Folder, Deans Files.

360. Dean's Report, 1970–71. All deans' reports since 1970 are housed in the Yale Law School Library and Yale University Archives.

361. "I suppose it is well known by now that the dean of a small but eminent eastern law school has publicly referred to the years 1967 through 1970 as 'the dark years of the Yale Law School,' or words to that effect, and I take it to be no coincidence that that period, more or less, defines the tenure of our class at Yale," the secretary of the class of 1970 wrote in his class notes. *Yale L Report* 39 (Spring 1973). I have not been able to locate reference in print by Goldstein to "the dark years." Goldstein most likely would have done so at an alumni weekend. Email, Abraham Goldstein to Laura Kalman, April 24, 2003, see, e.g., "The Changing Mood: A Report From the Dream," *Yale L. Report* 19, Fall–Winter 1971–72. Some reports have Goldstein alluding to "the dark ages."

362. "Lexcetera," supra note 358, at 1.

363. Wini Breines, *The Great Refusal: Community and Organization in the New Left, 1962–1968* 18 (1989) (quoting Todd Gitlin).

364. See, e.g., Class Notes, *Yale L. Report* 84 (Winter 1981–82).

365. Arthur Charpentier to Richard N. Cooper, November 1, 1972, Box 53, Budget-Related Correspondence Folder, Dean's Files.

366. Unmarked, undated statement, Box 53, '72–73 Budget Folder, Dean's Files. Goldstein's successor, Harry Wellington, felt similarly. Wellington to Howard Friedman, October 13, 1977, Box 16, Wellington Chron File: "The Law School, like most institutions of higher education, is having financial problems. Ours are much less than many and certainly less than most of Yale."

367. Interview with Goldstein.

368. Collier interview with Goldstein.

369. Id.

370. Kalman, supra note 1, at 195–99.

371. Yale Law School Governing Board Minutes, March 7, 1959 (hereafter YLS Governing Board Minutes). Announcement of the promotions was staggered.

372. Goldstein interview with Collier.

373. Eugene Rostow to Tonia Ouellette, December 3, 1992, Box 25, Folder O, Dean's Files.

374. Rostow to Ouellette, February 11, 1993, id.

375. Interview with Guido Calabresi, 2001.

376. The faculty also denied a promotion to John Frank during the 1950s, but its decision was based on some members' evaluation of his work as superficial. Kalman, *Legal Realism,* supra note 1, at 195–99.

377. Louis Pollak to Victor Stone, March 13, 1968, Box 32, Folder R, Dean's Files.

378. Rostow to Ouelette, February 11, 1993, supra note 374.

379. Louis Pollak to Truman Hobbs, July 12, 1966, Box 31, Folder H, Dean's Files.

380. Douglas Lavine, "Has the Faculty Lost Its 'Fizz?' Yale Law: Fork in the Road," *The National Law Journal,* June 29, 1981, at 1, 26; John Henry Schlegel, "Critical Legal Studies: Notes Toward an Intimate, Opinionated, and Affectionate History of the Conference on Critical Legal Studies," 36 *Stanford L. Rev.* 391, 392 (1984).

381. John Griffiths to Tonia Ouellette, February 11, 1993 (I am grateful to John Griffiths for giving me a copy of this letter).

382. Tonia Ouellette, "The History of Academic Freedom and Tenure: A Study of the Departures from Yale Law School in the Late 1960s and Early 1970s," quoting Trubek (hereafter "Study of the Departures"). I am grateful to Ouellette for sharing her paper with me.

383. Interview with Reich.

384. Ouelette, supra note 382.

385. Lavine, supra note 380, at 27.

386. Abraham Goldstein to Governing Board, November 30, 1974, Box 291, Folder 5, Brewster Papers.

387. Louis Pollak to Kingman Brewster and Charles Taylor, August 14, 1967, Box 130, Folder 7, Brewster Papers.

388. Supra, text accompanying notes 214 and 215.

389. Confidential interviews.

390. Abel email to Kalman, April 30, 2003.

391. Guido Calabresi to Michael Reisman, September 12, 1989, Box 27, Chron File, Dean's Files.

392. John Simon to Earl Warren, October 24, 1966, letter given to me by Larry Simon. (Larry Simon and John Simon were not related to each other.)

393. Interview with Larry Simon, 2002.

394. "Law in High School Is Course Objective," *Yale Advocate,* April 3, 1969, at 1.

395. Larry Simon, "The School Finance Decisions: Collective Bargaining and Future Finance Systems," 82 *Yale L. J.* 409 (1973). Another article, "Serrano Symposium: The Death Knell to Ad Valorem School Financing: Part III," appeared in 5 *Urban Lawyer* 104 (1973).

396. See, e.g., interviews with Steven Duke, 2001 and Calabresi.

397. Interviews with Lee Albert, 2001, and Simon.

398. Larry Simon to Art Leff, October 22, 1973, Box 34, Appointments Committee 1970–73 Folder, Dean's Files.

399. Addenda, November 20, 1973, Minutes of the Governing Board (hereafter YLS Governing Board Minutes).

400. YLS Governing Board Minutes, December 26, 1974.

401. Interview with Larry Simon.

402. YLS Governing Board Minutes, June 8, 1965.

403. John Griffiths and William Heckman, *The Draft Law: A "College Outline" for the Selective Service Act and Regulations* vii (1970).

404. Almost nothing was available to inform those with draft problems about their legal rights. Students in the seminar set out to fill the vacuum by producing articles and creating the body of material that would form the basis for the *Selective Service Law Reporter*.

405. John Griffiths, *The Draft Law: A "College Outline" for the Selective Service Act and Regulations* (1968). One journal described it as "[o]ne of the best sources . . . on the present perplexing draft law regulations." "The Draft," *Student Lawyer Journal*, March 1969, at 24.

406. John Griffiths email to Laura Kalman, February 5, 2002.

407. John Griffiths and Richard Ayres, "A Postscript to the Miranda Project: Interrogation of Draft Protestors," 77 *Yale L. J.* 300 (1967).

408. John Griffiths email to Laura Kalman, June 1, 2003.

409. Supra, text accompanying notes 214 and 215.

410. Ouelette, "Study of the Departures," supra note 382; Griffiths email to Kalman, February 7, 2002.

411. Griffiths had published two pieces of his own in the *Yale Law Journal* as a student, and one of his final examination essays had been extracted in the Journal by an admiring professor. John Griffiths, "Charity versus Social Insurance in Unemployment Compensation Laws," 73 *Yale L. J.* 357 (1963); "Extradition Habeas Corpus," 74 *Yale L. J.* 78 (1964); Charles Reich, "The Law of the Planned Society," 75 *Yale L. J.* 1227, 1235 (1966). The two essays related to ideology were John Griffiths, "Ideology in Criminal Procedure, or a Third 'Model' of the Criminal Process," 79 *Yale L. J.* 359 (1970), and "The Limits of Criminal Law Scholarship," 79 *Yale L. J.* 1388 (1970) (reviewing Herbert Packer, *The Limits of the Criminal Sanction* [1968]).

412. Griffiths, "The Limits of Criminal Law Scholarship," supra note 411.

413. YLS Governing Board Minutes, November 5, 1965.

414. George Packer, *Blood of the Liberals* 246–51, 268–69, 270–71 (2000).

415. Herbert Packer to Leon Lipson, March 17, 1970, Box 6, Folder 16, Bickel Papers. Packer sent copies of the letters to Bickel, Goldstein, and Wellington.

416. Alex Capron to Louis Pollak, April 20, 1970, Box 131, Folder 4, Brewster Papers; Malcolm Pfunder to Louis Pollak, April 19, 1970, id.

417. Interview with Simon.

418. Interview with Guido Calabresi, 2003.

419. I discuss Critical Legal Studies at greater length in Kalman, supra note 33, at 82–87.

420. "A Discussion on Critical Legal Studies at the Harvard Law School," presented by The Harvard Society and The Federalist Society, The Harvard Club, New York City, May 13, 1985, 8–9.

421. See David Trubek to Professors, Associate Professors, Assistant Professors, October 29, 1970, Box 34, Appointments Committee 1970–74 Folder, Dean's Files.

422. By 1976, Heller, like Tushnet and Trubek, was teaching at Wisconsin.

423. "A Discussion on Critical Legal Studies," supra note 420, at 9.

424. See, e.g., Mark Tushnet, "Critical Legal Studies: A Political History," 100 *Yale L. J.* 1515, 1544, n. 107 (1991): "[T]he reception of cls at Yale Law School rather strongly suggests that it is not among the law schools responding sensibly to the threat they perceive from critical legal studies."

425. Wellington was a very strong supporter of Kennedy's, whom he compared to the later Perry Miller (Harry Wellington to Albert Sacks, December 2, 1975, Box 16, Chron File, Dean's Files; Wellington to Kennedy, January 9, 1976, id.), though interestingly, Wellington did apparently send Kennedy's polemic to a psychologist for evaluation. William Kessen to Wellington, October 22, 1969, Box 1, Folder K, Dean's Files.

426. Memorandum of Poll, Governing Board, YLS Governing Board Minutes, December 15, 1970 (reporting vote of 21–7).

427. Interview with Kennedy. One of the projects on which Kennedy had already embarked was his famous — and for years, unpublished — critique of the Hart and Sacks legal process materials. Calabresi to the Governing Board, November 30, 1970). Perhaps that was another reason to place his head in the lion's den.

428. Harry Wellington to Governing Board, November 9, 1979, Box 12, HHW Masters 1975–76, Dean's Files.

429. Gary Minda, *Postmodern Legal Movements* 108 (1995).

430. Martha Minow email to Laura Kalman, August 12, 2001.

431. Guido Calabresi to Dan Tarlock, August 3, 1990, Box 58, Chron File, Dean's Files.

432. YLS Governing Board Minutes, December 21, 1982.

433. Id., February 10, 1982. The characterization of Brest as a CLS fellow-traveler is open to question. Brest's colleague, Mark Kelman, who was more obviously a Critical Legal Scholar, was turned down in the 1970s. YLS Governing Board Minutes, March 30, 1977; Harry Wellington to Ellen Peters, April 1, 1977, Box 16, Chron File (asking her to call or write Kelman: "[I]t may turn out that we will want to invite him sometime down the line, and I would rather not have a conversation with him at this point.")

434. YLS Governing Board Minutes, November 11, 1981.

435. The person most sympathetic to Critical Legal Studies who actually accepted an offer during the 1970s and 1980s was Lucinda Finley, who later left Yale without tenure for reasons I believe were unassociated with the movement.

436. Schlegel, supra note 380, at 400–401.

437. Even if one advocates a broad enough definition of realism so that it encompasses the jurisprudence of Holmes, Pound, and Frankfurter (see William Fisher, Morton Horwitz, and Thomas Reed, *American Legal Realism* xiiii [1993]; Kalman, supra note 33, at 250, n. 1), it still seems clear legal realism did not affect most legal education at Harvard during the 1930s. Kalman, supra note 1, at 45–66.

438. Joseph Singer, "The Player and the Cards: Nihilism and Legal Theory," 94 *Yale L. J.* 1, 6 (1984).

439. Guido Calabresi to David Trubek, November 24, 1986, Box 57, Chron File, Dean's Files.

440. Kalman, *Legal Realism,* supra note 1, at 139.

441. Richard Fischl rebuts the charge in "The Question That Killed Critical Legal Studies," 17 *Law & Soc. Inq'y.* 779 (1992).

442. Guido Calabresi to Paul Carrington, 35 *J. Legal Ed.* 1, 23, 24 (1985). Calabresi also included Arthur Leff in the group of nihilists. As Calabresi reminds me, his comments to Carrington about the similarity between Critical Legal Scholars and the realists were made in answer to Carrington's suggestion that critical legal scholars should depart

the law schools (Paul Carrington, "Of Law and the River," 34 *J. Legal Ed.* 222 [1984]), and not in reply to the argument that Yale should hire some critical legal scholars. "That is, my statement that none were more nihilistic than (the universally respected and loved) Grant Gilmore . . . [was] not Yale-defensive but [was] . . . a way of saying how misguided the attacks on the Crits seemed to me to be. As such, the letter . . . is more worthy of credence because deans can say almost anything when they are defending their schools, but will only say things they clearly believe when they go out of their way to defend" scholars at other institutions. Guido Calabresi email to Laura Kalman, August 21, 2001. There speaks a true dean.

443. Guido Calabresi to Richard Fischl, September 4, 1987, Box 27, Chron File, Dean's Files.

444. Id., September 28, 1987.

445. Calabresi to Carrington, supra note 442, at 23–24; Owen Fiss to Paul Carrington, " 'Of Law and the River,' and of Nihilism and Academic Freedom," 35 *J. Legal Educ.* 1,24, 26 (1985); Kalman, supra note 33, at 83.

446. Robert Gordon, "New Developments in Legal Theory," in David Kairys, ed., *The Politics of Law* 413, 417 (1990).

447. Mark Kelman, "Trashing," 36 *Stanford L. Rev.* 292 (1984).

448. Interviews with Bittker and Paul Gewirtz, 2001.

449. Edward Adams, "A Battle for Yale Law School's Soul? Offer to a Feminist Draws Fury," *National Law Journal,* February 15, 1988, at 3.

450. In 1970–76: Kessler, Harold Lasswell, Fleming James, James William Moore, Fred Rodell, Myres McDougal, and Emerson.

451. The group included Barbara Black, Robert Burt, Morris Cohen, Harlon Dalton, Mirjan Damaska, Drew Days, Donald Elliot, Jack Getman, Paul Gewirtz, Reinier Kraakman, Anthony Kronman, Jerry Mashaw, George Priest, Jay Pottenger, Peter Schuck, John Pottenger, Lea Brilmayer, Stephen Carter, Henry Hansmann, Perry Dane, Lucinda Finley, Michael Graetz, Oliver Williamson, and Roberta Romano.

452. Interview with Calabresi, 2001.

453. Lavine, supra note 380, at 27.

454. Alvin Klevorick, Robert Clark, and William Nelson. I do not include Grant Gilmore, who rejoined the faculty during Goldstein's deanship and whose doctorate was in French literature, in this group.

455. Jerry Mashaw, Anthony Kronman, Barbara Black, Reinier Kraakman, Henry Hansmann, and Oliver Williamson.

456. Martha Minow, "Law Turning Outward," 73 *Telos* 79, 91 (1987).

457. YLS Faculty Minutes, October 24, 1978.

458. Arthur Leff, "Law And," 87 *Yale L. J.* 989 (1978).

459. Dean's Report, 1973–74.

460. Harry Wellington to Michael Horowitz, June 16, 1976, Box 16, Chron File, Dean's Files.

461. Harry Wellington to A. Bartlett Giamatti, April 17, 1984, Box 17, Chron File, id.

462. Harry Wellington, "Challenges to Legal Education: The 'Two Cultures' Phenomenon," 37 *J. Legal Ed.* 327, 329 (1987).

463. Barbara Black, Robert Burt, Morris Cohen, Harlon Dalton, Mirjan Damaska, Drew Days, Donald Elliot, Jack Getman, Paul Gewirtz, Reinier Kraakman, Anthony Kronman, Jerry Mashaw, George Priest, Jay Pottenger, and Peter Schuck.

464. Dean's Report, 1980–81; Harry Wellington to Jasper Cummings, August 6, 1981, Box 4, Yale University Council Committee on Yale Law School Folder, Dean's Files.

465. Harry Wellington, Letter to Partners of Major Law Firms, January 1981, Box 17 Chron File, Dean's Files; Wellington to John Subak, November 14, 1980, id.

466. Interview with Stephen Yandle, 2001.

467. Abraham Goldstein, "On Harry Wellington at Yale," 45 N.Y. *Law Sch. Rev.* 13, 14 (2001).

468. Lavine, supra note 380, at 26.

469. David Shapiro to Guido Calabresi, February 4, 1984, Box 23, Folder S, Dean's Files (repeating quotation).

470. Guido Calabresi to David Shapiro, February 7, 1985, id.

471. Interview with Yandle.

472. Paul Loeb, *Generation at the Crossroads: Apathy and Action on the American Campus* 264 (1994); Elaine Kerlow, *Poisoned Ivy: How Egos, Ideology and Power Politics Almost Ruined Harvard Law School* 49 (1994); Derrick Bell, *Confronting Authority: Reflections of an Ardent Protester* 44–46 (1995).

473. "Law Students Stage Boycott," *Yale Daily News*, April 7, 1989, at 1, 7.

474. Guido Calabresi to Friends and Graduates of the Yale Law School, October 20, 1989, Dean's Letters.

475. Guido Calabresi to Marnia Robinson, May 5, 1993, Box 21, Chron File, Dean's Files. Calabresi continued: "If there is anything I am proud of in my Deanship, it is my emphasis on that. I think it has happened and the current students really love this place." Id.

476. "200 Protest Speech by Nation of Islam Leader," *Yale Daily News Review*, March 2, 1990, at 6. Feb, at 1.

477. Guido Calabresi to the Law School Community, February 8, 1990, Box 58, Chron File, Dean's Files. That reminder may not have been necessary. "Both sides have been quick to point out that they do not see this as a free speech issue. He has a right to speak here," stressed one student active in the Committee Against Bigotry, an organization formed by members of the Jewish Law Students Association after Muhammed's visit was announced, which staged a peaceful protest against it. "We don't want to prevent him, but we are hurt by the invitation to him to speak here." "Nation of Islam Spokesman Brings Controversy to Yale," *Yale Daily News*, February 9, 1990, at 1.

478. Calabresi to the Law School Community, February 8, 1990, supra note 477.

479. Guido Calabresi to Faculty, Staff, and Students, February 16, 1990, Box 58, Chron File, Dean's Files.

480. "John Sexton Pleads (and Pleads and Pleads) His Case," *New York Times Magazine*, May 25, 1997 ("hyperbolic"); "Ivy Envy," id., June 8, 2003 ("hugging dean").

481. Calabresi recalled receiving an eloquent and bitter complaint from William Felstiner to this effect, which he passed along to the Appointments Committee. He said he wished he had received more such complaints. He seemed sincere. Interview with Calabresi, 2001.

482. This was a frequent theme of letters from alumni whenever a negative article about the school appeared in the *Wall Street Journal*.

483. Guido Calabresi to Dorothy Robinson, September 22, 1992, Box 21, Chron File, Dean's Files.

484. Harry Wellington to Mark Zimmerman, November 10, 1981, Box 17, Chron File, id. He continued: "That preference is helpful in some situations but it operates only at the margins." As Calabresi explained it, "The Law School's policy on children of graduates is a very simple one. After each file is read separately by three different members of the faculty as part of a file of 100 (every faculty member in the School reads admissions files), and is rated 4–3–2–1, with 4 being the top, to the cumulative score a point is added if the applicant is the child of a graduate. This is a limited, but not insignificant, advantage that is given. It means essentially that children of graduates who had been rated equivalent to children of non-graduates get taken first. Yale College and most other Law Schools have no such 'formal' program. But informally they often do far more in particular cases. This, I think is worse." Guido Calabresi to Louis Mangone, November 1, 1991, Box 60, Chron File, id.

485. See, e.g., Guido Calabresi to Leonard Marks, April 19, 1988, Box 62, Folder M, id.: "I looked at his file and, as you said, he looked terrific to me. Could you urge him to give me a call? I'd love to talk to him during the summer about the possibilities of transferring after a year at another school." The files are full of such letters.

486. See, e.g., Catherine Weiss to Guido Calabresi, May 3, 1993, Box 25, Folder W, Dean's Files: "I was stunned when you called me at home the other evening to tell me that [an individual she had recommended] had been admitted to the law school. My reaction was not to [his] admission — as you know, I think Yale will benefit greatly by its decision — but to your calling me personally with the good news. You are a busy man. I cannot imagine how you find time for the personal contacts you maintain, but I am touched and grateful that you manage somehow." Having reviewed much of Calabresi's correspondence, I share Weiss's wonder. Indeed, I defy anyone to read it without exclaiming of Calabresi at some point, even if in exasperation: "Damn, he's good!"

487. Norman Boucher, "Yale Law Review: Is the Law School of Bill Clinton, Jerry Brown, Clarence Thomas, and Anita Hill Still Producing Public Servants, or Has the Ivy League's Conscience Gone Corporate?" *Boston Globe Magazine*, April 26, 1992, at 14, 39.

488. Alan Hirsch, "Yale Law," *Connecticut*, at 103 (November 1994); see also "Yale Law: Inside the School That Cast the Thomas/Hill Drama," *Chicago Tribune,* October 28, 1991, at 1, 4.

489. Guido Calabresi to Friends and Graduates of Yale Law School, November 2, 1987, Dean's Letters; interview with Calabresi, 2001.

490. Owen Jones to Guido Calabresi, February 15, 1988, January 30, 1988, Box 61, Folder J, Dean's Files.

491. Guido Calabresi to Louise Frankel, November 1, 1991, Box 60, Chron File, id.

492. Jones to Calabresi, February 15, 1988, supra note 490.

493. "Brains for the Bar," *U.S. News & World Report,* November 2, 1987, at 72, 73.

494. "Law," *U.S. News & World Report,* March 19, 1990, at 59; "America's Top-Ranked Law School," id., at 61.

495. "Yale Law School *is* Number One," *Harvard Law Record,* November 1, 1991, at 4; see also "Yale #1 Again!!," *Harvard Law Record,* March 20, 1992, at 1.

496. Henry Hansman, "Higher Education as an Associative Good," www.educause .edu/ir/library.

497. See, e.g., "Robert Bork Is More Than Just A Resume," *Business Week,* July 20, 1987, at 190: "Bork's impressive legal credentials—he is a former Yale Law School professor now serving on the nation's most important appeals court—weigh heavily in his favor."

498. "At the Bar: In a Confirmation Hearing Filled with Yalies, the Law School's Dean Is Caught in the Crossfire," *New York Times,* October 11, 1991, at B7.

499. See, e.g., "Yale Law: Inside the School That Cast the Thomas/Hill Drama," supra note 484, at 1, 4.

500. "Yale Law School Focuses on Reunion," *New York Times,* October 31, 1991.

501. Hirsch, "Yale Law," supra note 488, at 104.

502. Guido Calabresi to Friends and Graduates of the Yale Law School, November 19, 1992, Dean's Letters.

503. Id. They were Donald Elliott and Michael Graetz.

504. Steve Stark, "The Yale Connection," *Boston Globe,* March 22, 1992.

505. Remarks of Senator Clinton, supra note 331.

506. Guido Calabresi to Friends and Graduates of Yale Law School, November 19, 1992, supra note 501.

Contributors

Robert W. Gordon is Chancellor Kent Professor of Law and Legal History, Yale Law School.

Laura Kalman is Professor of History, University of California at Santa Barbara.

Anthony T. Kronman is Dean and Edward J. Phelps Professor of Law, Yale Law School.

John H. Langbein is Sterling Professor of Law and Legal History, Yale Law School.

Gaddis Smith is Larned Professor of History, Emeritus, Yale University.

Robert Stevens is the former Master of Pembroke College, Oxford. He is of Counsel, Covington & Burling, Washington, D.C., and London and a Bencher of Gray's Inn. From 1959 to 1976 he was a professor at the Yale Law School, and was Georges Lurcy Visiting Professor in 1999.

Index

Abel, Richard, 179, 193, 197, 199, 200, 202, 203
Abolitionism, 10
Acheson, Dean, 134*n*128, 137*n*166, 144, 148, 149–50
Ackerman, Bruce, 207, 208, 209
Act of Settlement (1701), 5
Adair, Douglass, 91–92
Affirmative action: debate over, ix; and blacks, 166–69, 177; and women's movement, 176
African Americans. *See* Black Law Students Union; Blacks
Agnew, Spiro, 189, 190, 228*n*301
Agricultural Adjustment Administration (AAA), 85, 104, 107, 108
Ahern, James, 180–81
Albany Law School, 58
Albert, Lee, 197, 199
Aldrich, Malcolm, 146–47
Amalgamated Clothing Workers, 84
American Bar Association: and legal education, 20, 39*n*25; and Baldwin, 59; and Yale Law School faculty, 97
American Civil Liberties Union, 84
American Historical Association, 59
American Law Institute, 97, 98, 100
American Revolution, 8, 22
American Social Science Association, 59
Ames, James Barr, 78, 130*n*64
Amistad case, 33
Angell, James R.: and interdisciplinary studies, 84; and New Deal, 104, 105, 138, 141–42; and Frank, 126*n*21; and anti-Semitism, 138, 139, 143; and Yale University–Yale Law School relationship, 139, 151; and Sterling estate, 140–41; Griswold compared to, 149
Antitrust Division, and Arnold, 87, 108, 109–10
Areen, Judith, 177
Arnold, Fortas and Porter (law firm), 87, 89–90, 121